time for cow trivia!
Real cows don't have any front teeth in their upper jaw.

ue story – when I went to get a shiatsu massage after making my last deadline, the masseuse said to me, "Your right shoulder is really tense." I almost replied to him, "That's because it's auto-mail!" because I was sleepy and my head was in a daze as I was thinking about some ideas for the next chapter.

—Hiromu Arakawa, 2005

Born in Hokkaido (northern Japan), Hiromu Arakawa first attracted national attention in 1999 with her award-winning manga *Stray Dog*. Her series *Fullmetal Alchemist* debuted in 2001 in Square Enix's monthly manga anthology *Shonen Gangan*.

FULLMETAL ALCHEMIST
VOL. 11

Story and Art by Hiromu Arakawa

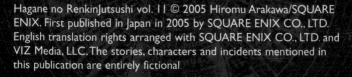

Translation/Akira Watanabe
English Adaptation/Jake Forbes
Touch-up Art & Lettering/Wayne Truman
Design/Amy Martin
Editor/Andy Nakatani

Managing Editor/Annette Roman
Editorial Director/Elizabeth Kawasaki
Editor in Chief/Alvin Lu
Sr. Director of Acquisitions/Rika Inouye
Sr. VP of Marketing/Liza Coppola
Exec. VP of Sales & Marketing/John Easum
Publisher/Hyoe Narita

Hagane no RenkinJutsushi vol. 11 © 2005 Hiromu Arakawa/SQUARE
ENIX. First published in Japan in 2005 by SQUARE ENIX CO., LTD.
English translation rights arranged with SQUARE ENIX CO., LTD. and
VIZ Media, LLC. The stories, characters and incidents mentioned in
this publication are entirely fictional.

Printed in the U.S.A.

Published by VIZ Media, LLC
P.O. Box 77010
San Francisco, CA 94107

10 9 8 7 6 5 4 3 2 1
First printing, January 2007

鋼の錬金術師
FULLMETAL ALCHEMIST

HIROMU ARAKAWA
荒川弘

11

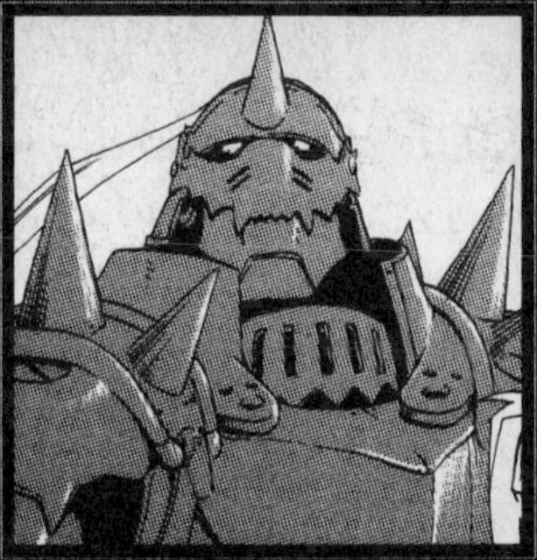

アルフォンス・エルリック

Alphonse Elric

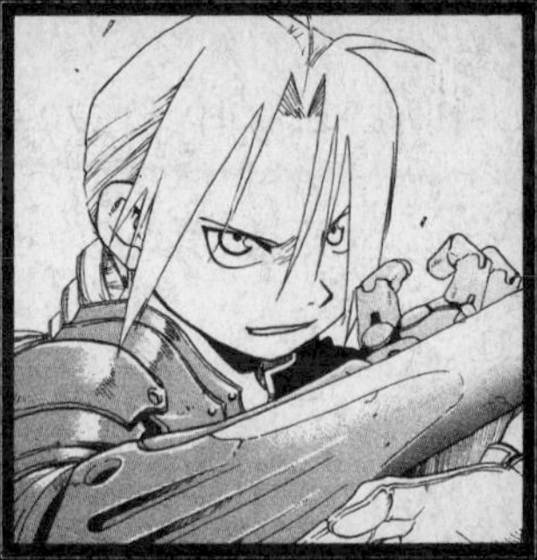

エドワード・エルリック

Edward Elric

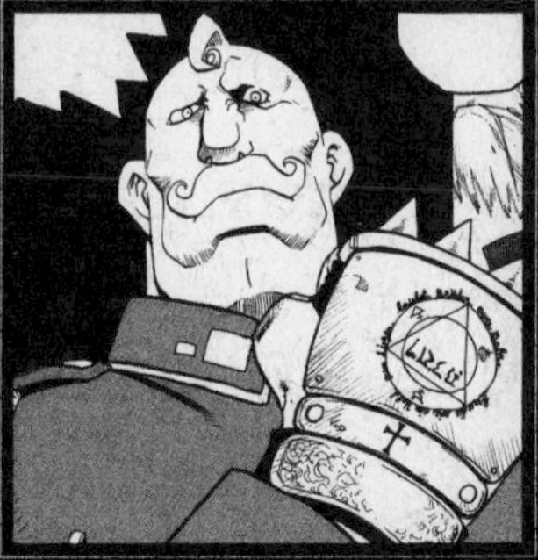

アレックス・ルイ・アームストロング

Alex Louis Armstrong

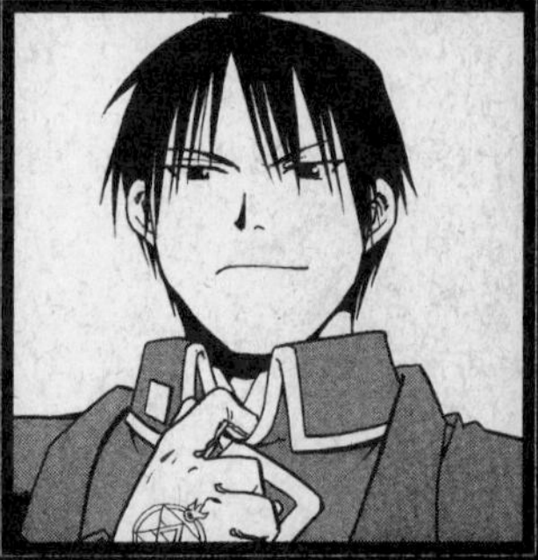

ロイ・マスタング

Roy Mustang

OUTLINE
FULLMETAL ALCHEMIST

Using a forbidden alchemical ritual, the Elric Brothers attempted to bring their dead mother back to life. But the ritual went wrong, consuming Edward Elric's leg and Alphonse Elric's entire body. At the cost of his arm, Edward was able to graft his brother's soul into a suit of armor. Equipped with mechanical "auto-mail" to replace his missing limbs, Edward becomes a state alchemist, serving the military on deadly missions. Now, the two brothers roam the world in search of the Philosopher's Stone, the legendary substance with the power to restore what they have lost...

The Elric Brothers aren't the only state alchemists on a mission. Colonel Roy Mustang and his team have been following many of the same leads as young Edward in an attempt to uncover a conspiracy within the military that could go all the way to the top. Using Barry the Chopper and the wrongfully accused Maria Ross as bait, Roy manages to track the Homunculi to their underground base. In a harrowing battle, Roy destroys the beautiful and cunning Lust once and for all, but at a great cost--Jean Havoc is left paralyzed and Maria Ross must remain in exile. Meanwhile, Ed returns home to Resembool where he sees the most shocking sight imaginable--**his father**.

鋼の錬金術師

FULLMETAL ALCHEMIST

CHARACTERS

FULLMETAL ALCHEMIST

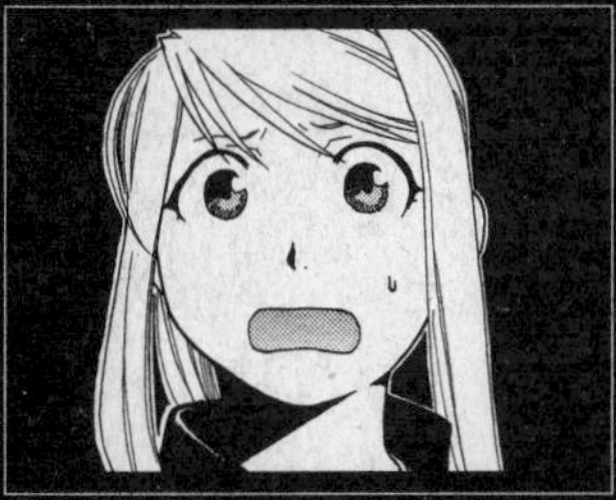

ウィンリィ・ロックベル

Winry Rockbell

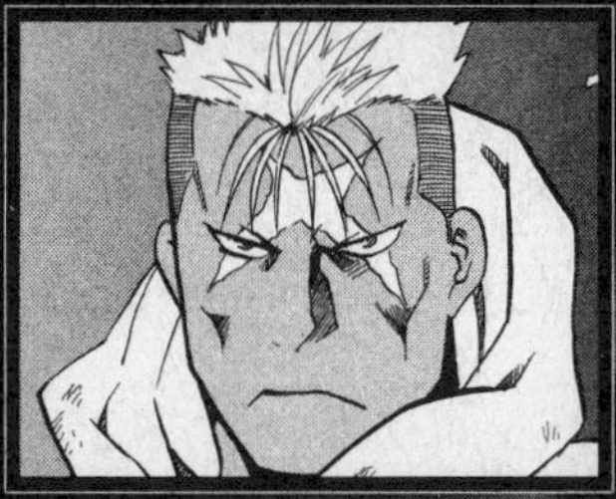

スカー

Scar

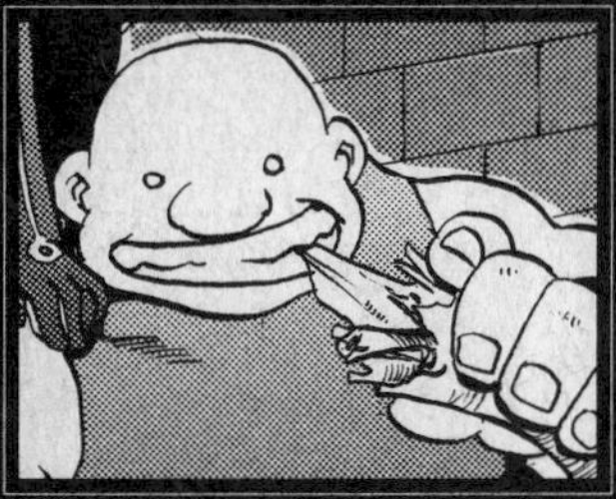

グラトニー

Gluttony

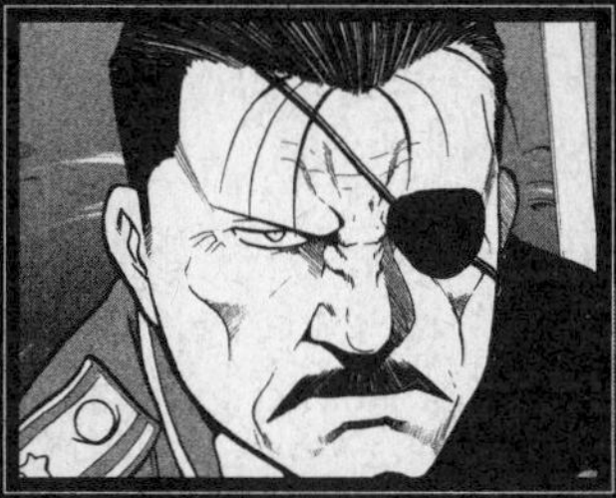

キング・ブラッドレイ

King Bradley

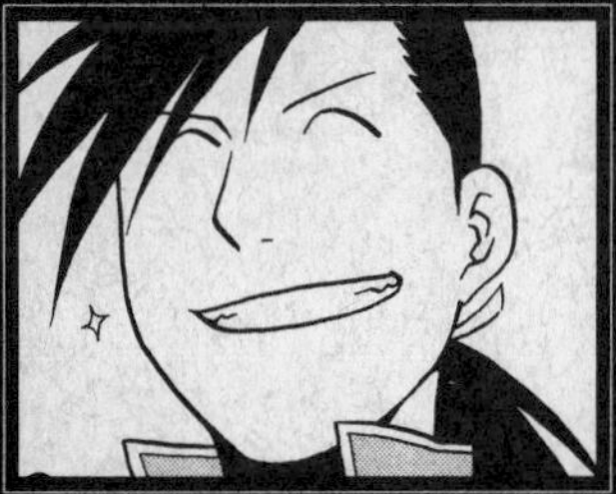

リン・ヤオ

Lin Yao

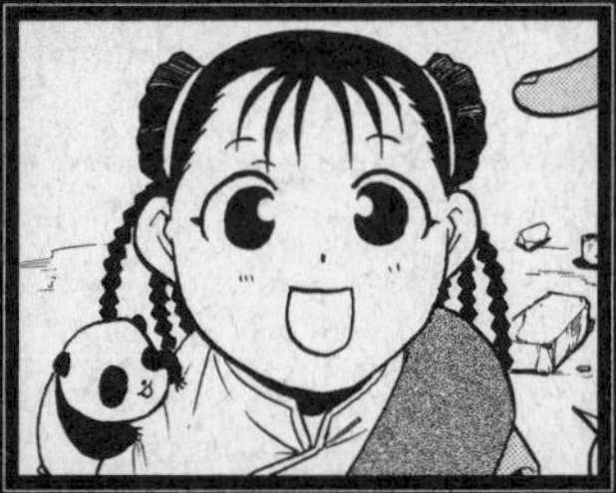

メイ・チャン

May Chang

CONTENTS

Chapter 42 The Father Standing Before a Grave   7

Chapter 43 River of Mud   51

Chapter 44 The Unnamed Grave   91

Chapter 45 Scar's Return   139

Extra   185

Preview   186

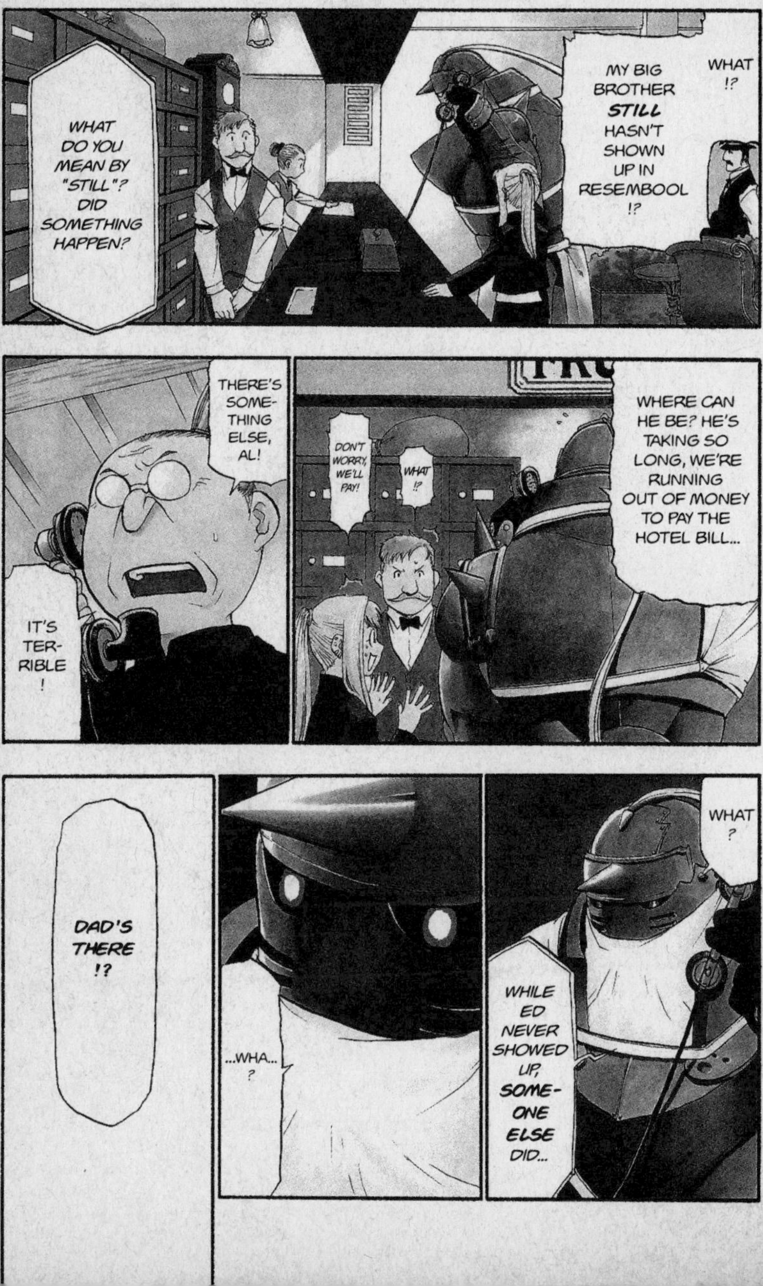
WHAT !?
MY BIG BROTHER **STILL** HASN'T SHOWN UP IN RESEMBOOL !?
WHAT DO YOU MEAN BY "STILL"? DID SOMETHING HAPPEN?
WHERE CAN HE BE? HE'S TAKING SO LONG, WE'RE RUNNING OUT OF MONEY TO PAY THE HOTEL BILL...
WHAT !?
DON'T WORRY, WE'LL PAY!
THERE'S SOME-THING ELSE, AL!
IT'S TER-RIBLE!
WHAT ?
WHILE ED NEVER SHOWED UP, **SOME-ONE ELSE** DID...
...WHA... ?
DAD'S THERE !?

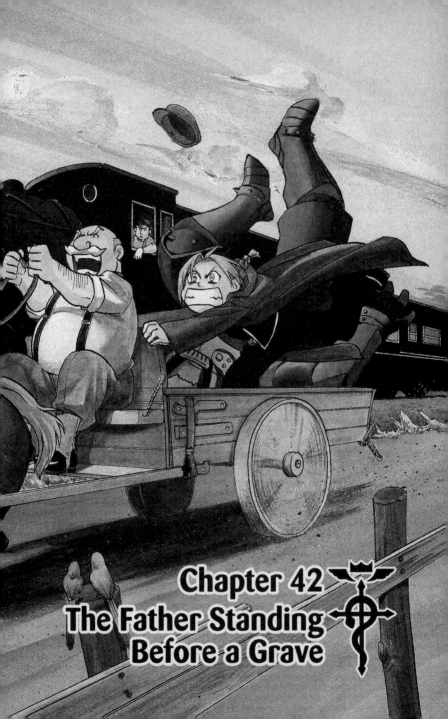

Chapter 42
The Father Standing Before a Grave

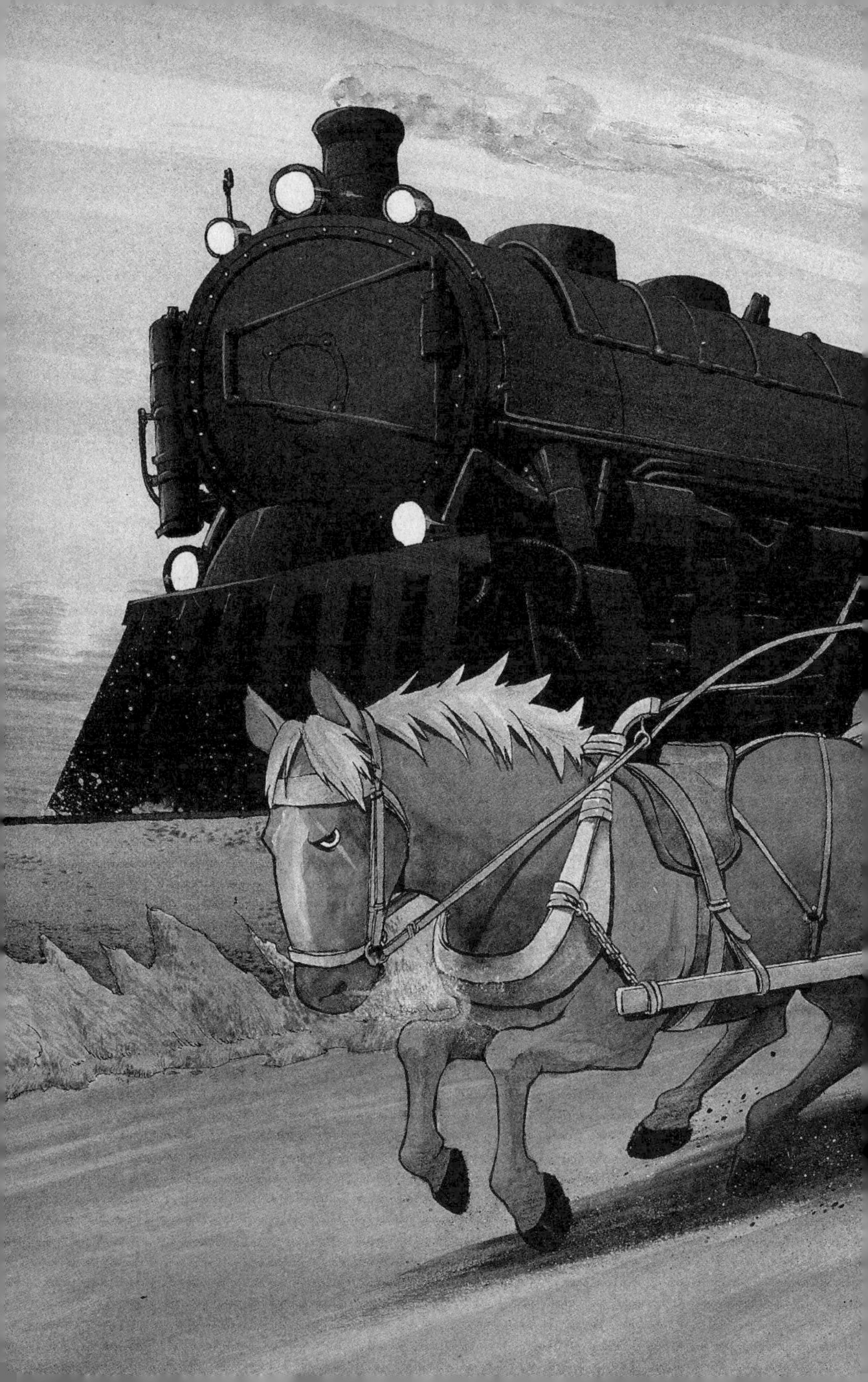

FULLMETAL
ALCHEMIST

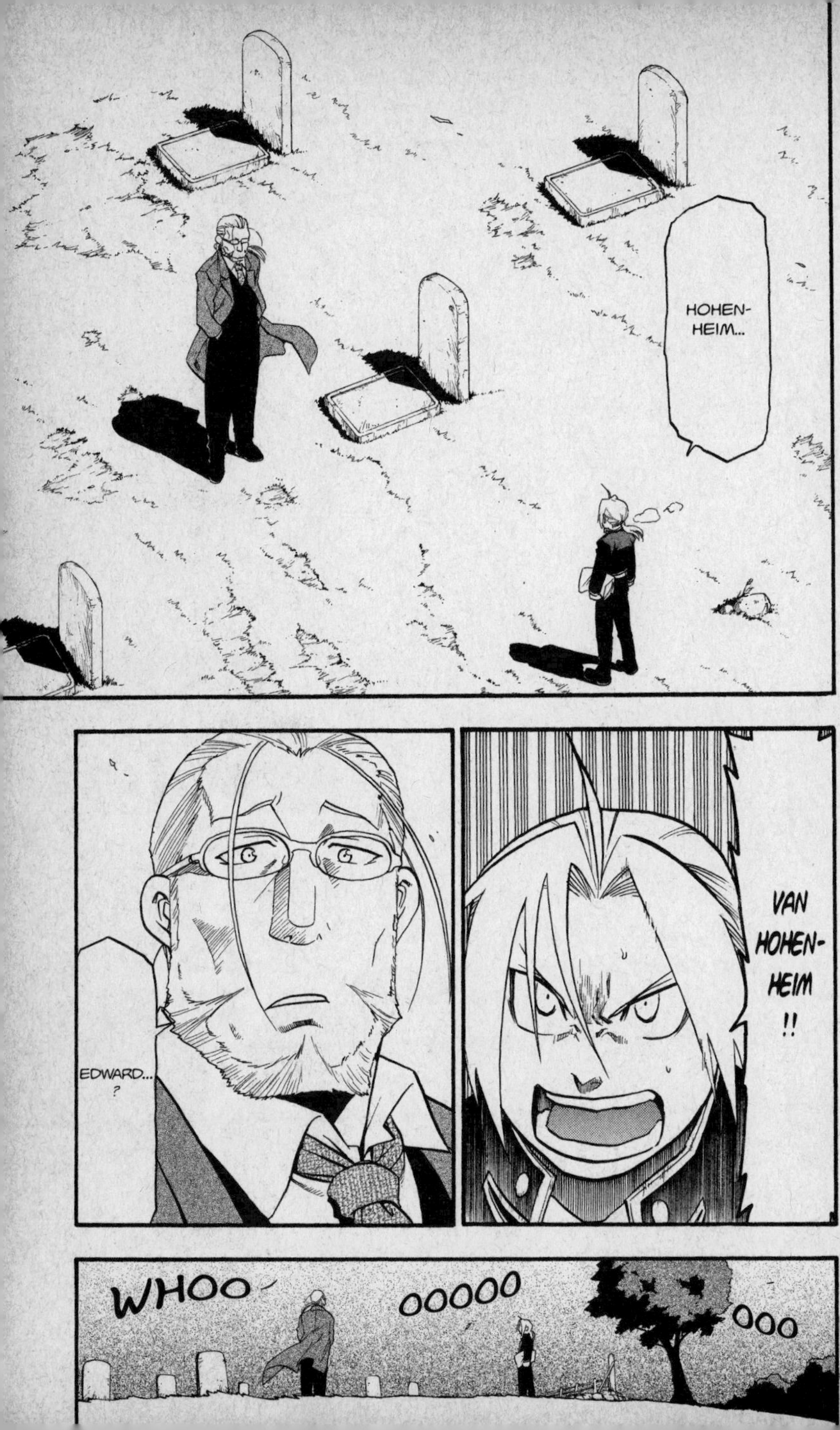
HOHEN-HEIM...
VAN HOHEN-HEIM !!
EDWARD... ?
WHOO OOOOO OOO

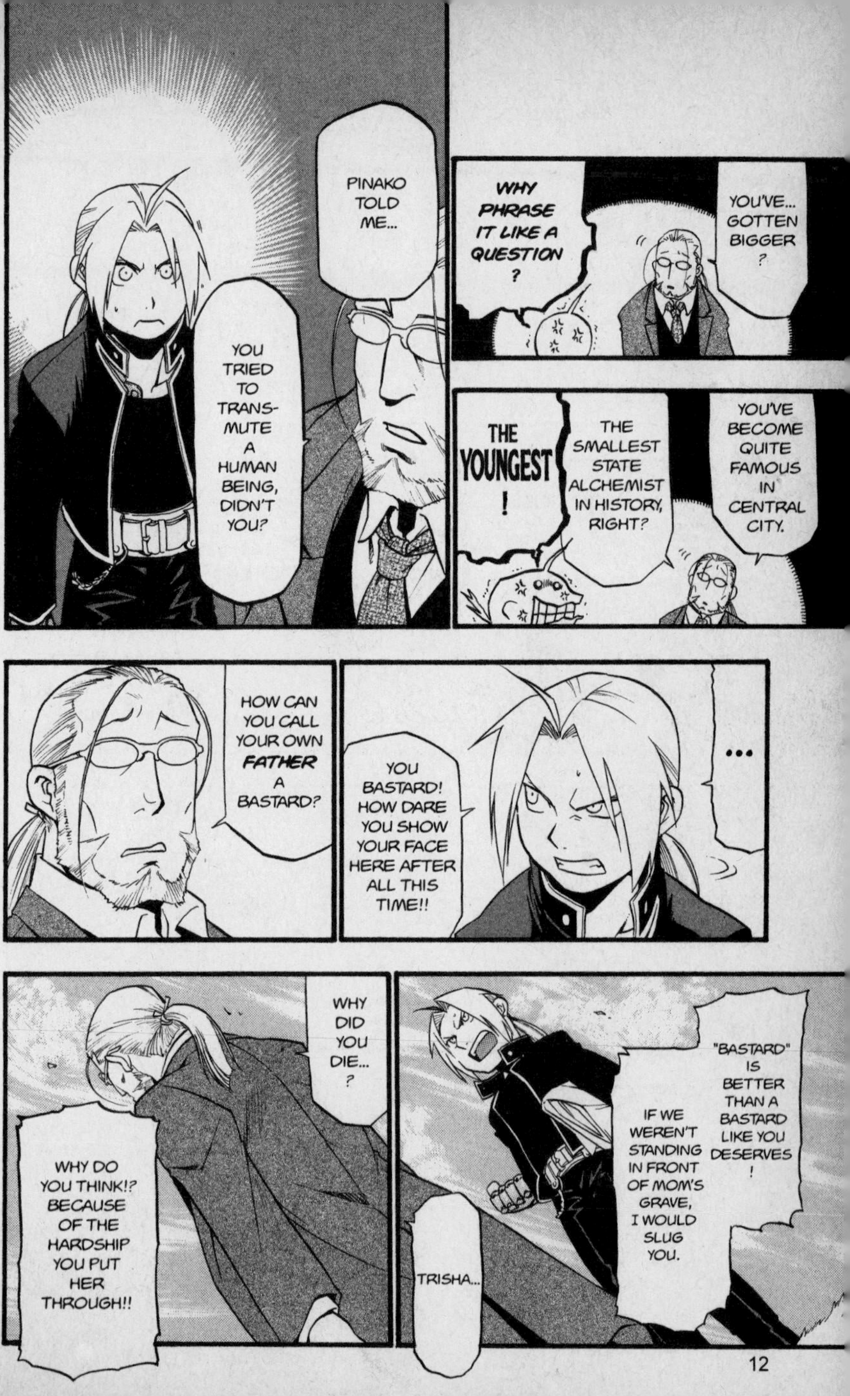
YOU'VE... GOTTEN BIGGER ?
WHY PHRASE IT LIKE A QUESTION ?
YOU'VE BECOME QUITE FAMOUS IN CENTRAL CITY.
THE SMALLEST STATE ALCHEMIST IN HISTORY, RIGHT?
THE YOUNGEST !
PINAKO TOLD ME...
YOU TRIED TO TRANS-MUTE A HUMAN BEING, DIDN'T YOU?
...
YOU BASTARD! HOW DARE YOU SHOW YOUR FACE HERE AFTER ALL THIS TIME!!
HOW CAN YOU CALL YOUR OWN FATHER A BASTARD?
"BASTARD" IS BETTER THAN A BASTARD LIKE YOU DESERVES !
IF WE WEREN'T STANDING IN FRONT OF MOM'S GRAVE, I WOULD SLUG YOU.
TRISHA...
WHY DID YOU DIE... ?
WHY DO YOU THINK!? BECAUSE OF THE HARDSHIP YOU PUT HER THROUGH!!

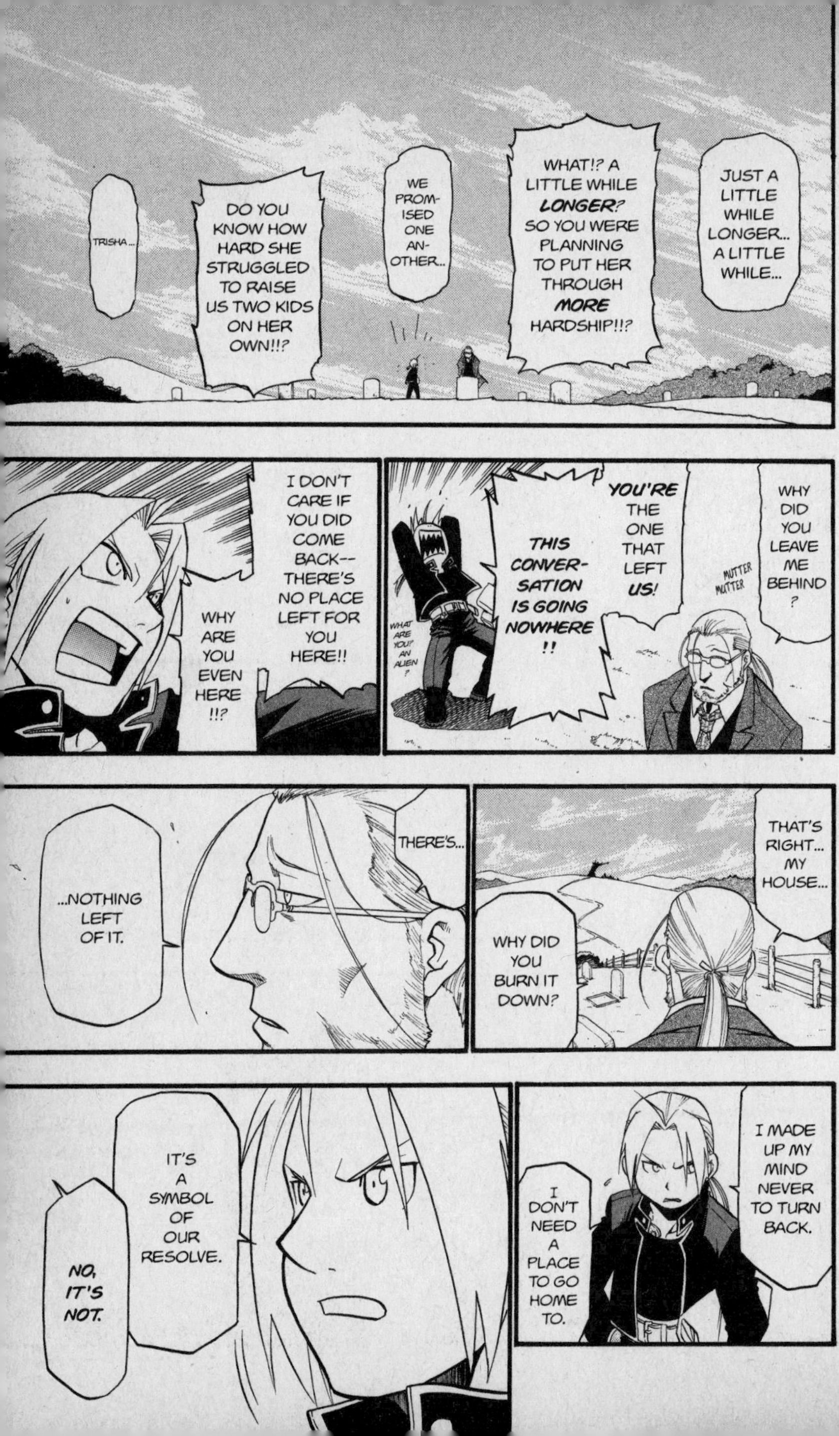
JUST A LITTLE WHILE LONGER... A LITTLE WHILE...
WHAT!? A LITTLE WHILE LONGER? SO YOU WERE PLANNING TO PUT HER THROUGH MORE HARDSHIP!!?
WE PROMISED ONE ANOTHER...
DO YOU KNOW HOW HARD SHE STRUGGLED TO RAISE US TWO KIDS ON HER OWN!!?
TRISHA...
WHY DID YOU LEAVE ME BEHIND?
MUTTER MUTTER
YOU'RE THE ONE THAT LEFT US!
THIS CONVERSATION IS GOING NOWHERE!!
WHAT ARE YOU? AN ALIEN?
I DON'T CARE IF YOU DID COME BACK-- THERE'S NO PLACE LEFT FOR YOU HERE!!
WHY ARE YOU EVEN HERE!!?
THAT'S RIGHT... MY HOUSE...
WHY DID YOU BURN IT DOWN?
THERE'S...
...NOTHING LEFT OF IT.
I MADE UP MY MIND NEVER TO TURN BACK.
I DON'T NEED A PLACE TO GO HOME TO.
IT'S A SYMBOL OF OUR RESOLVE.
NO, IT'S NOT.

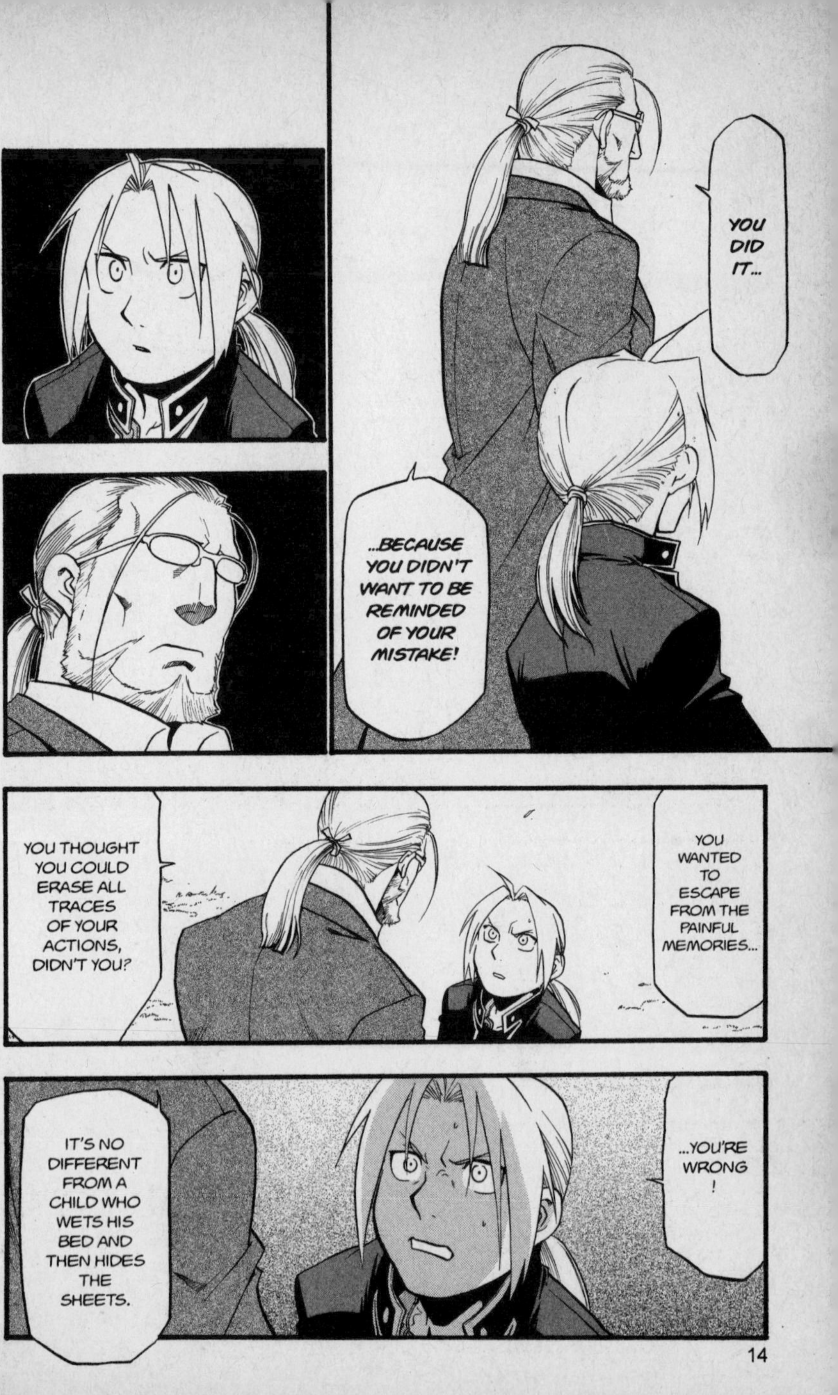
YOU DID IT...
...BECAUSE YOU DIDN'T WANT TO BE REMINDED OF YOUR MISTAKE!
YOU WANTED TO ESCAPE FROM THE PAINFUL MEMORIES...
YOU THOUGHT YOU COULD ERASE ALL TRACES OF YOUR ACTIONS, DIDN'T YOU?
...YOU'RE WRONG!
IT'S NO DIFFERENT FROM A CHILD WHO WETS HIS BED AND THEN HIDES THE SHEETS.

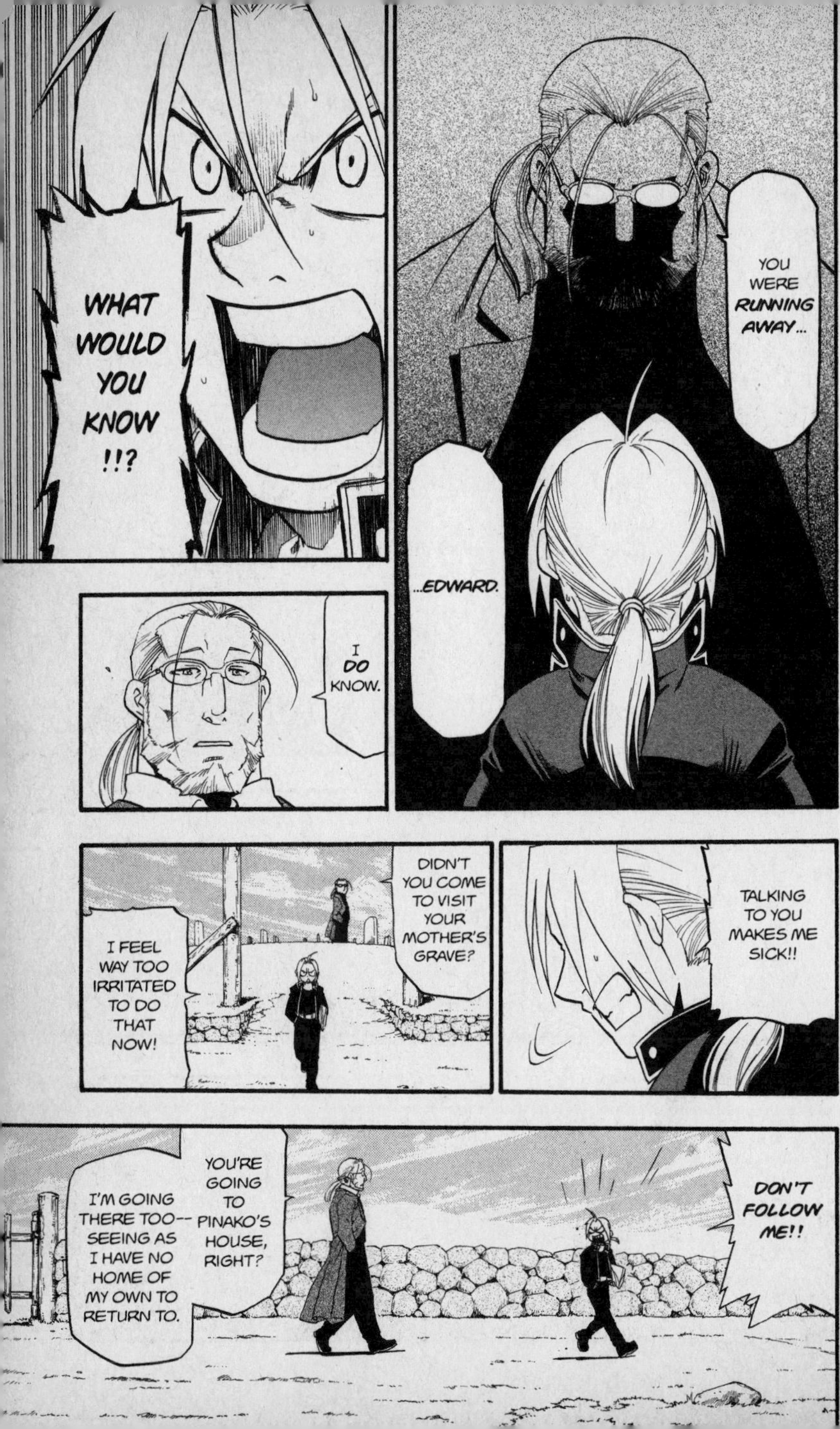
YOU WERE RUNNING AWAY...
...EDWARD.
WHAT WOULD YOU KNOW!!?
I DO KNOW.
TALKING TO YOU MAKES ME SICK!!
DIDN'T YOU COME TO VISIT YOUR MOTHER'S GRAVE?
I FEEL WAY TOO IRRITATED TO DO THAT NOW!
DON'T FOLLOW ME!!
YOU'RE GOING TO PINAKO'S HOUSE, RIGHT?
I'M GOING THERE TOO-- SEEING AS I HAVE NO HOME OF MY OWN TO RETURN TO.

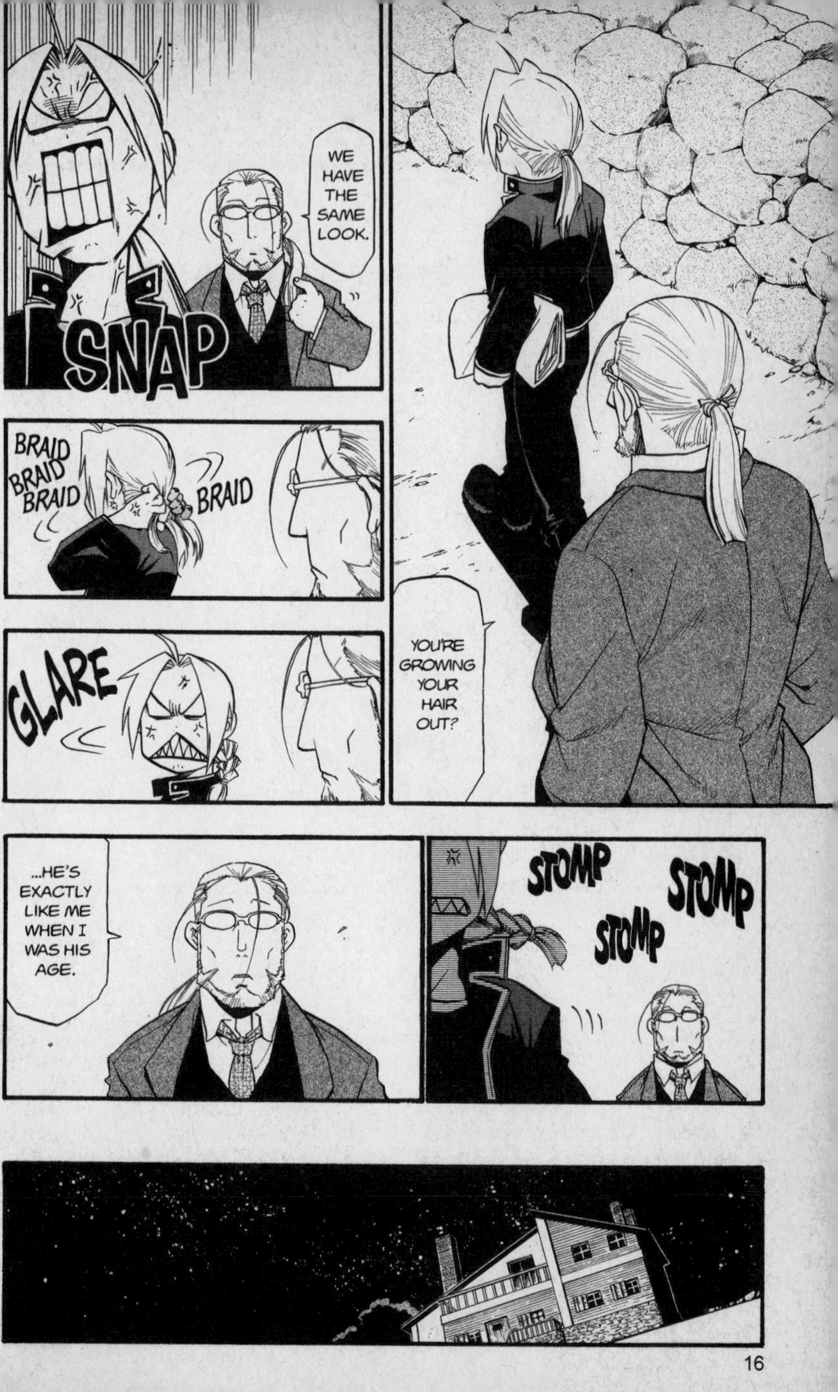
YOU'RE GROWING YOUR HAIR OUT?
WE HAVE THE SAME LOOK.
SNAP
BRAID
BRAID BRAID BRAID
GLARE
STOMP
STOMP
STOMP
...HE'S EXACTLY LIKE ME WHEN I WAS HIS AGE.

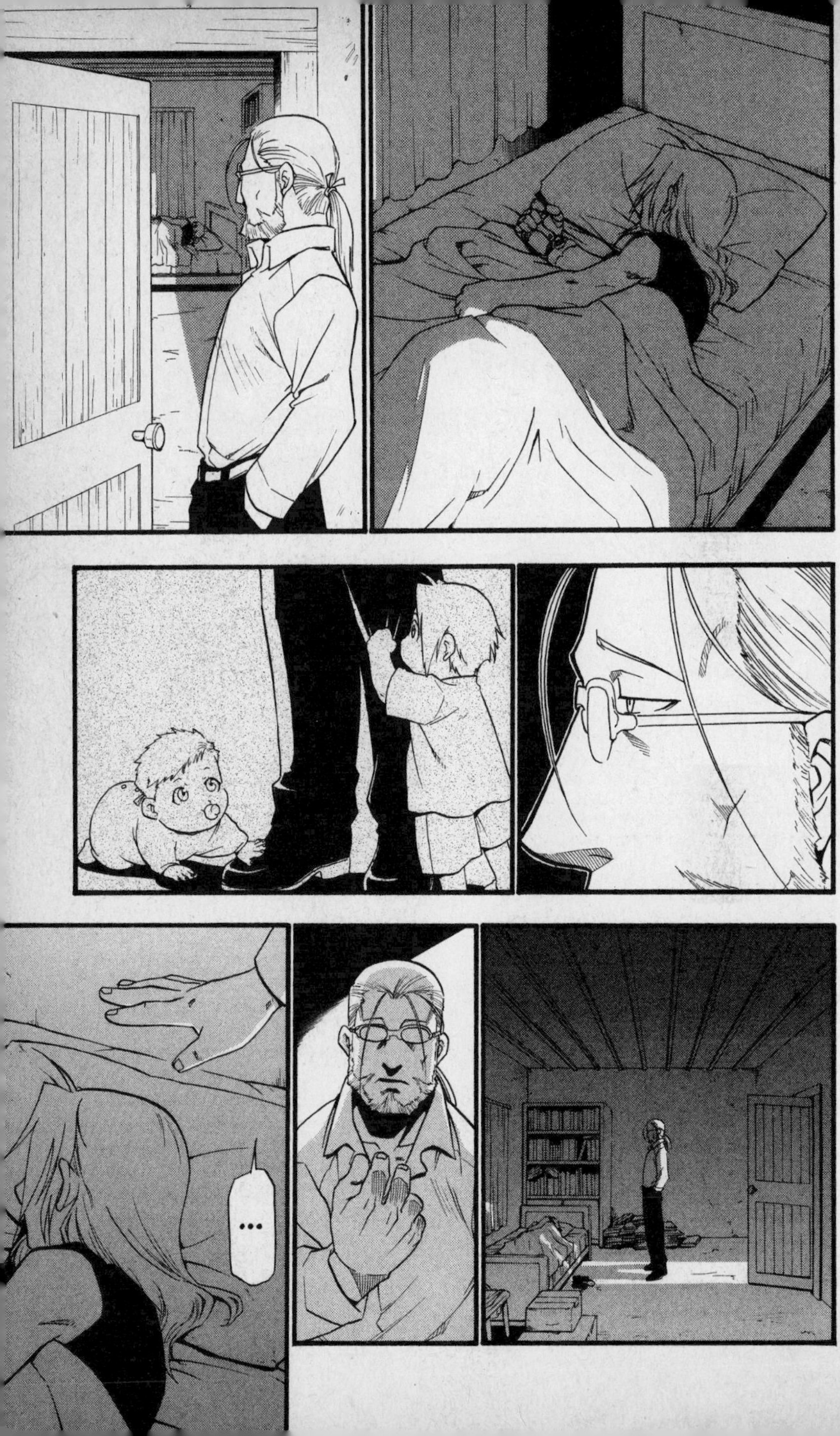
...

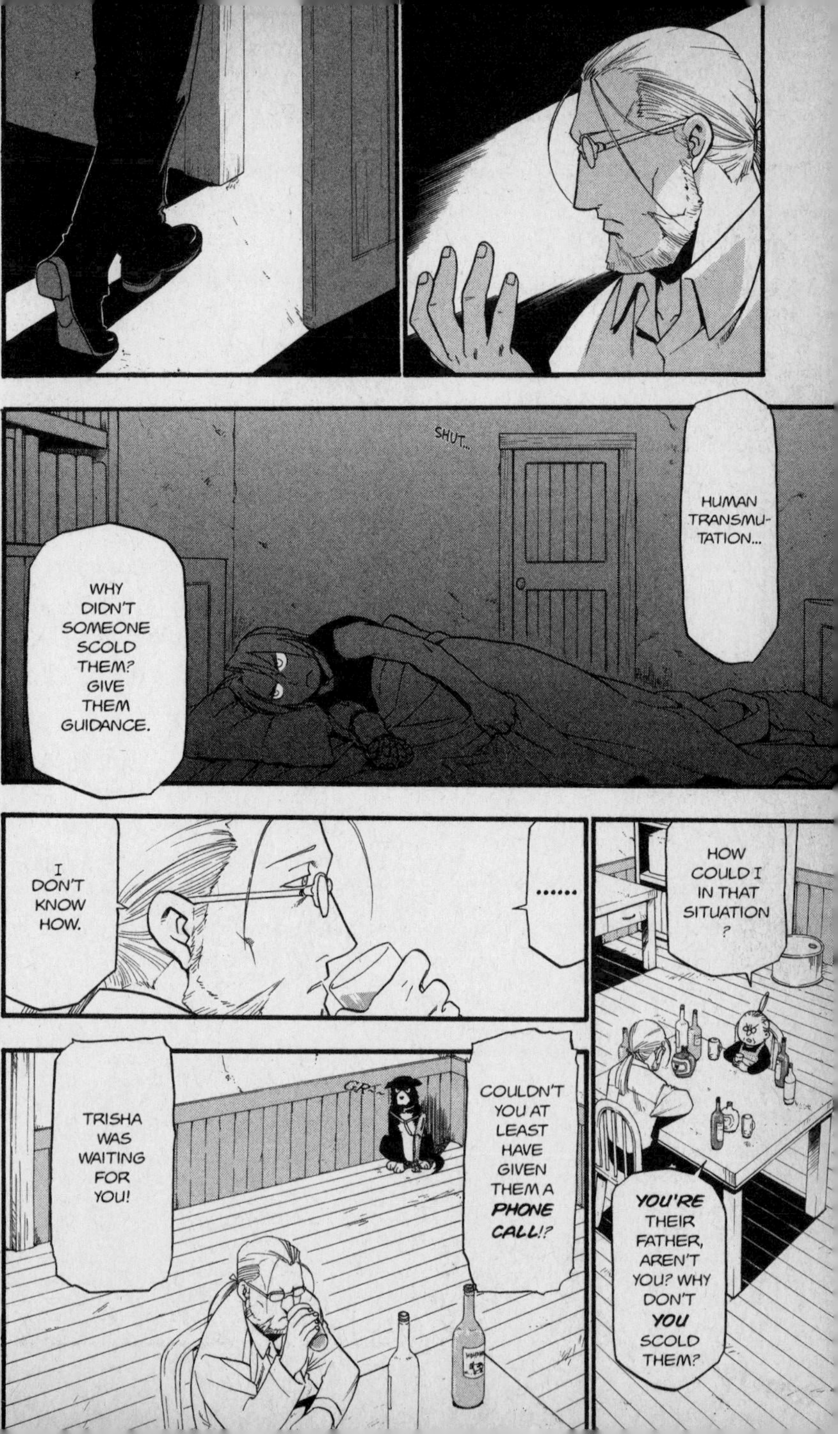
HUMAN TRANSMUTATION...
SHUT...
WHY DIDN'T SOMEONE SCOLD THEM? GIVE THEM GUIDANCE.
HOW COULD I IN THAT SITUATION?
YOU'RE THEIR FATHER, AREN'T YOU? WHY DON'T YOU SCOLD THEM?
......
I DON'T KNOW HOW.
COULDN'T YOU AT LEAST HAVE GIVEN THEM A PHONE CALL!?
TRISHA WAS WAITING FOR YOU!

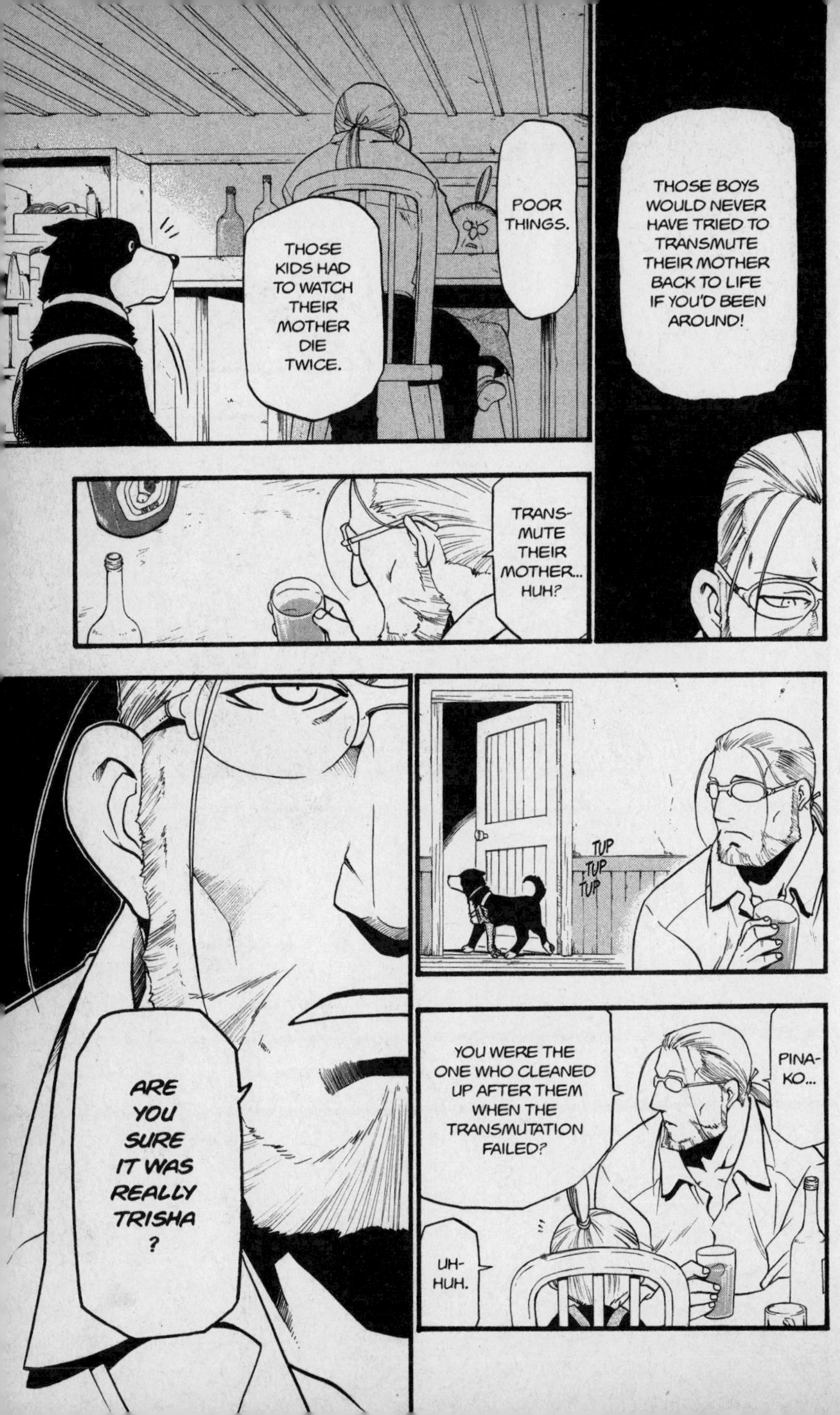
THOSE BOYS WOULD NEVER HAVE TRIED TO TRANSMUTE THEIR MOTHER BACK TO LIFE IF YOU'D BEEN AROUND!
POOR THINGS.
THOSE KIDS HAD TO WATCH THEIR MOTHER DIE TWICE.
TRANS-MUTE THEIR MOTHER... HUH?
TUP TUP TUP
PINA-KO...
YOU WERE THE ONE WHO CLEANED UP AFTER THEM WHEN THE TRANSMUTATION FAILED?
UH-HUH.
ARE YOU SURE IT WAS REALLY TRISHA?

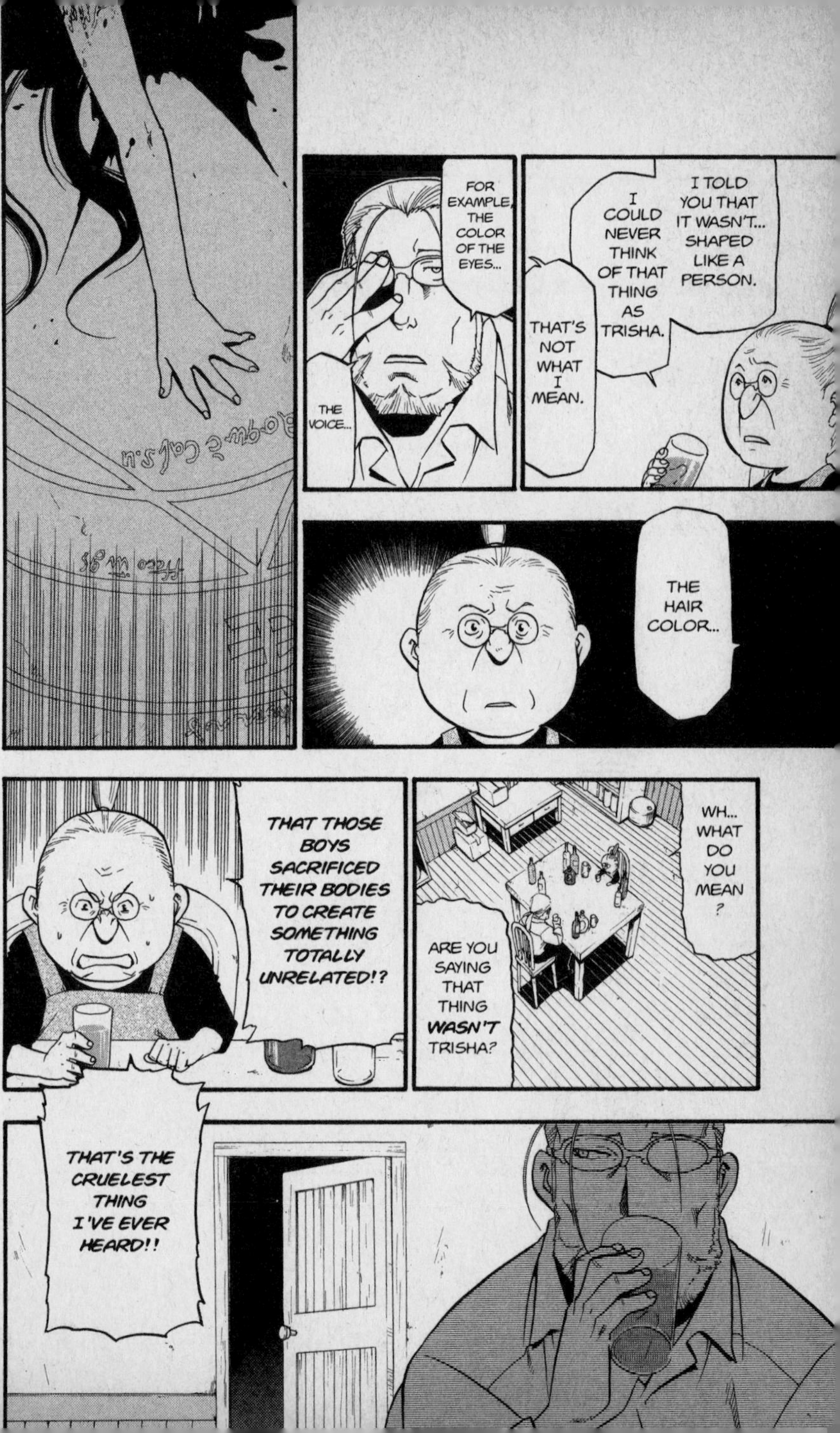
I TOLD YOU THAT IT WASN'T... SHAPED LIKE A PERSON.
I COULD NEVER THINK OF THAT THING AS TRISHA.
THAT'S NOT WHAT I MEAN.
FOR EXAMPLE, THE COLOR OF THE EYES...
THE VOICE...
THE HAIR COLOR...
WH... WHAT DO YOU MEAN?
ARE YOU SAYING THAT THING WASN'T TRISHA?
THAT THOSE BOYS SACRIFICED THEIR BODIES TO CREATE SOMETHING TOTALLY UNRELATED!?
THAT'S THE CRUELEST THING I'VE EVER HEARD!!

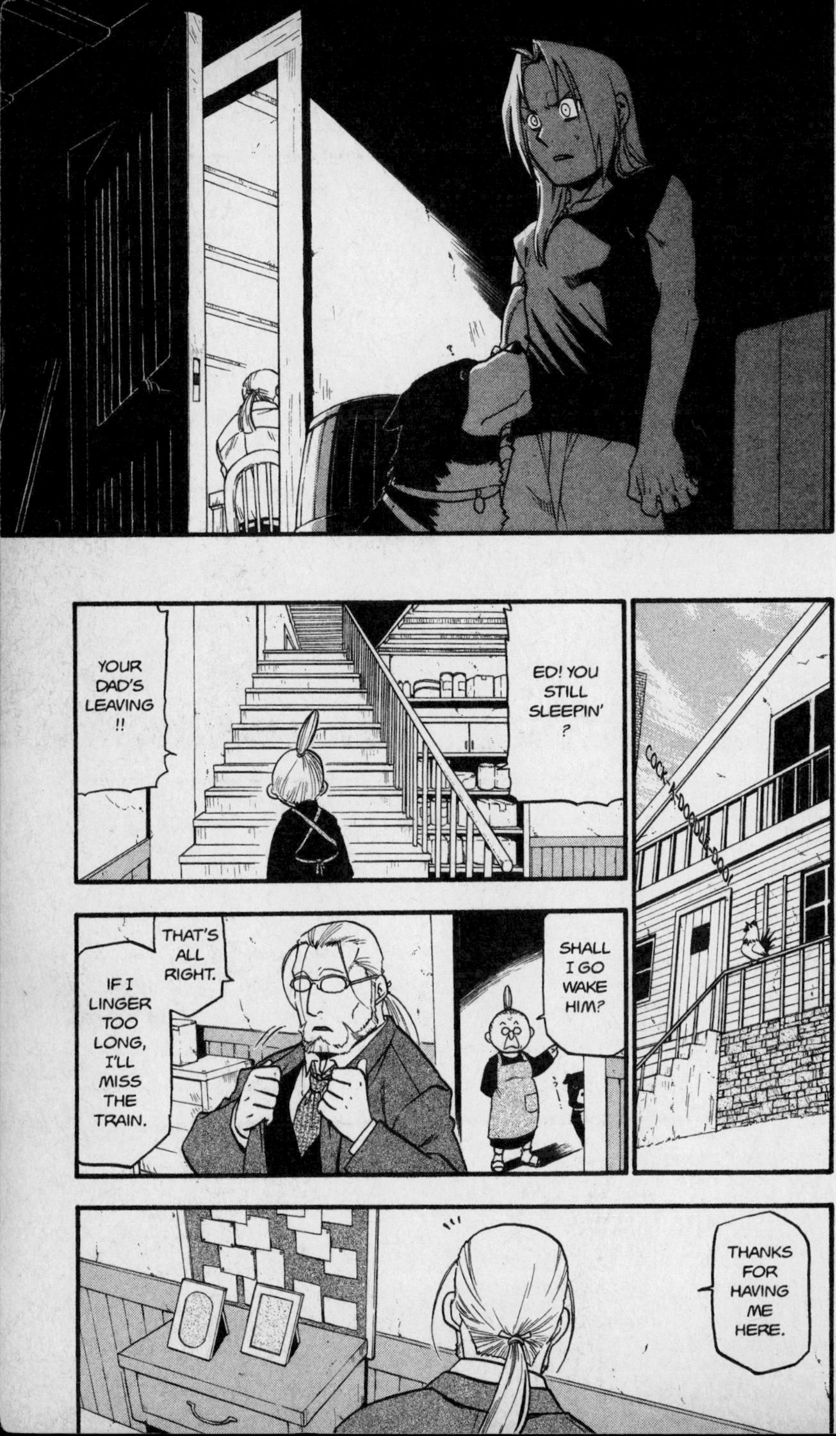
COCK-A-DOODLE-DOO!
ED! YOU STILL SLEEPIN'?
YOUR DAD'S LEAVING!!
SHALL I GO WAKE HIM?
THAT'S ALL RIGHT.
IF I LINGER TOO LONG, I'LL MISS THE TRAIN.
THANKS FOR HAVING ME HERE.

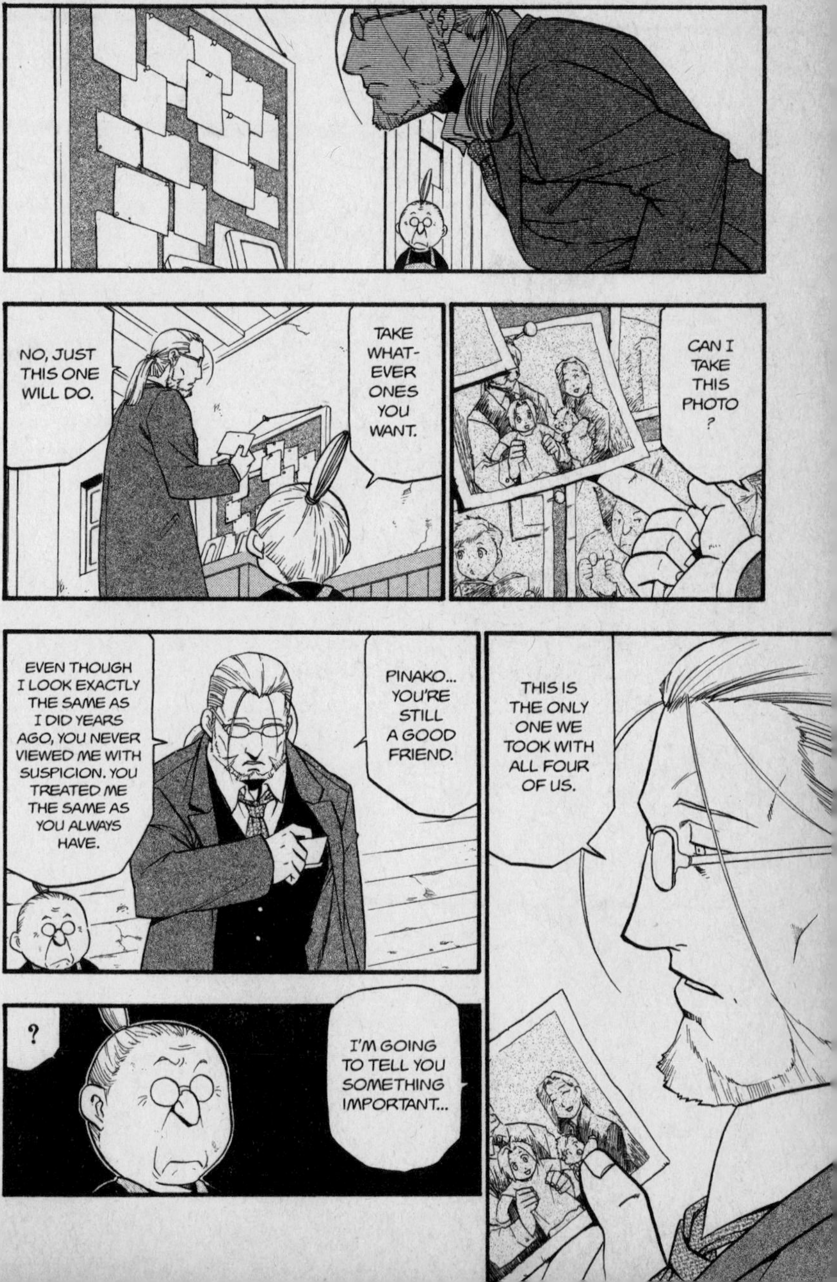
CAN I TAKE THIS PHOTO ?
TAKE WHATEVER ONES YOU WANT.
NO, JUST THIS ONE WILL DO.
THIS IS THE ONLY ONE WE TOOK WITH ALL FOUR OF US.
PINAKO... YOU'RE STILL A GOOD FRIEND.
EVEN THOUGH I LOOK EXACTLY THE SAME AS I DID YEARS AGO, YOU NEVER VIEWED ME WITH SUSPICION. YOU TREATED ME THE SAME AS YOU ALWAYS HAVE.
I'M GOING TO TELL YOU SOMETHING IMPORTANT...
?

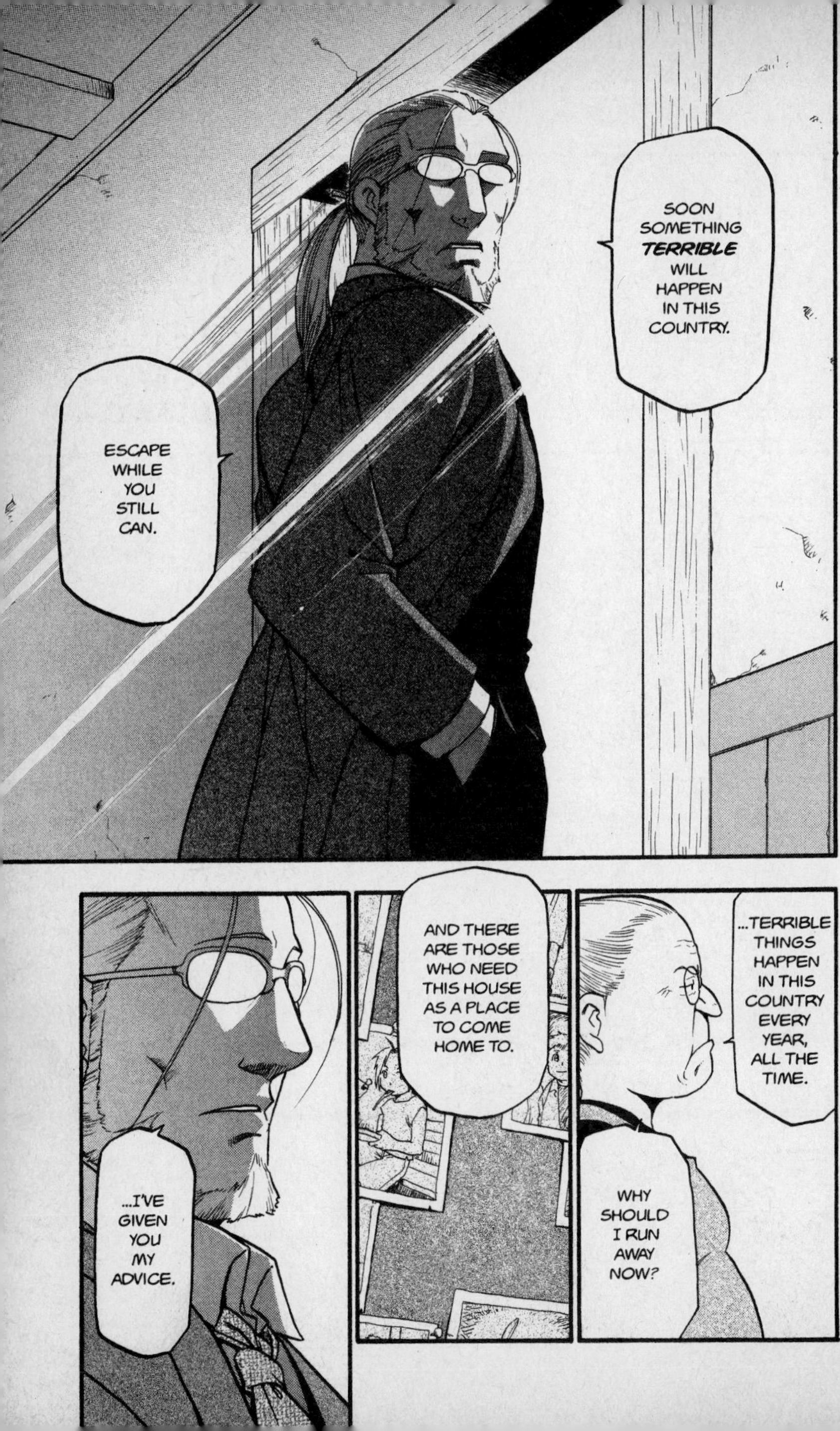
SOON SOMETHING TERRIBLE WILL HAPPEN IN THIS COUNTRY.
ESCAPE WHILE YOU STILL CAN.
...TERRIBLE THINGS HAPPEN IN THIS COUNTRY EVERY YEAR, ALL THE TIME.
WHY SHOULD I RUN AWAY NOW?
AND THERE ARE THOSE WHO NEED THIS HOUSE AS A PLACE TO COME HOME TO.
...I'VE GIVEN YOU MY ADVICE.

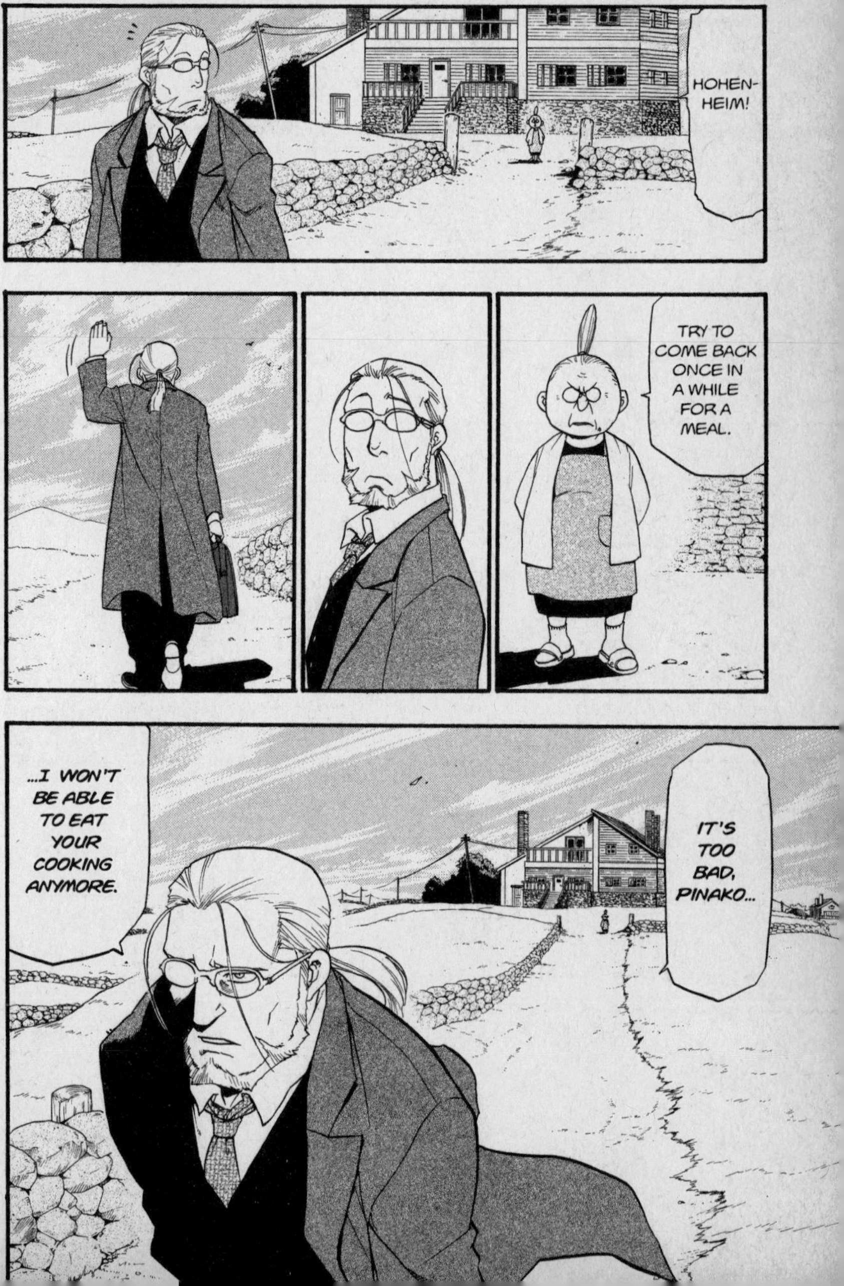
HOHEN-HEIM!
TRY TO COME BACK ONCE IN A WHILE FOR A MEAL.
IT'S TOO BAD, PINAKO...
...I WON'T BE ABLE TO EAT YOUR COOKING ANYMORE.

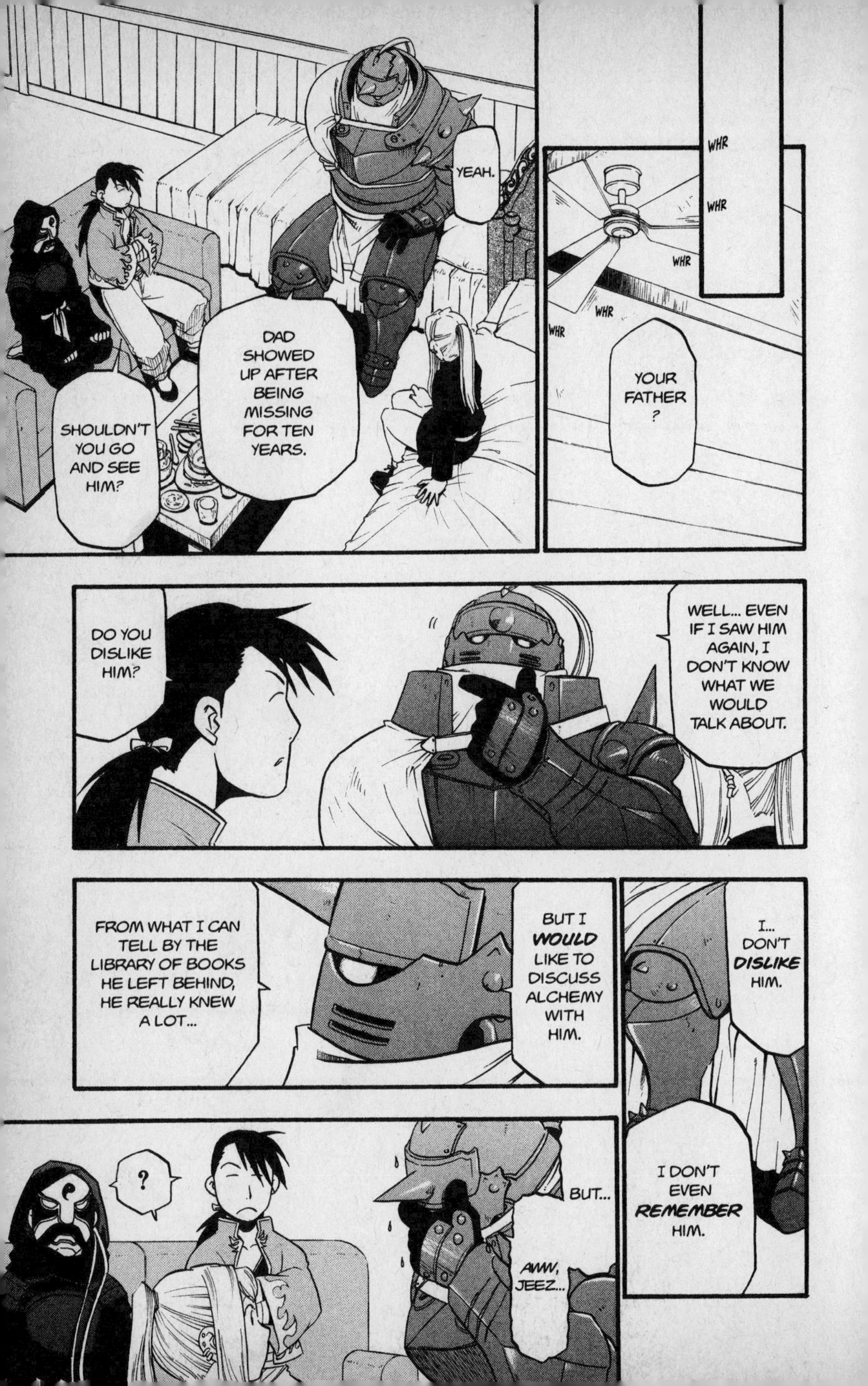
WHR
WHR
WHR
WHR
WHR
YOUR FATHER ?
YEAH.
DAD SHOWED UP AFTER BEING MISSING FOR TEN YEARS.
SHOULDN'T YOU GO AND SEE HIM?
WELL... EVEN IF I SAW HIM AGAIN, I DON'T KNOW WHAT WE WOULD TALK ABOUT.
DO YOU DISLIKE HIM?
I... DON'T DISLIKE HIM.
I DON'T EVEN REMEMBER HIM.
BUT I WOULD LIKE TO DISCUSS ALCHEMY WITH HIM.
FROM WHAT I CAN TELL BY THE LIBRARY OF BOOKS HE LEFT BEHIND, HE REALLY KNEW A LOT...
BUT...
AWW, JEEZ...
?

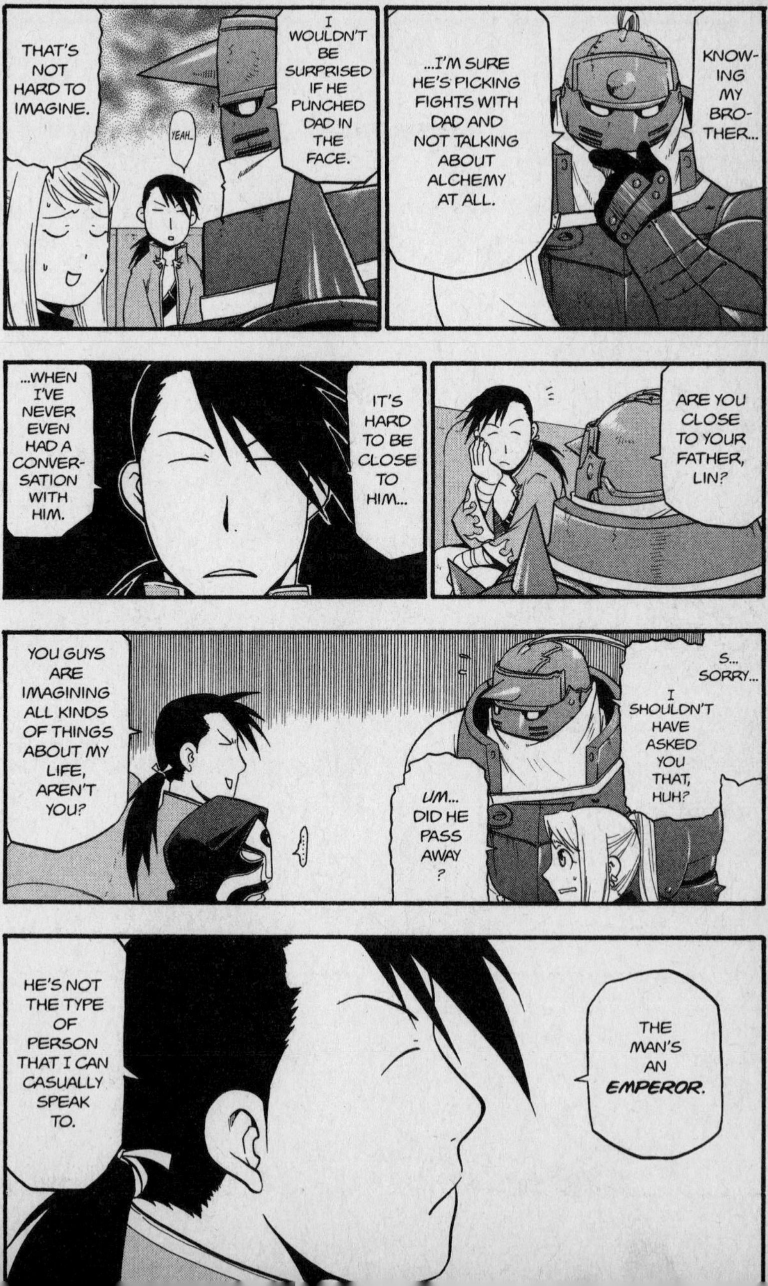
KNOWING MY BROTHER...
...I'M SURE HE'S PICKING FIGHTS WITH DAD AND NOT TALKING ABOUT ALCHEMY AT ALL.
I WOULDN'T BE SURPRISED IF HE PUNCHED DAD IN THE FACE.
YEAH...
THAT'S NOT HARD TO IMAGINE.
ARE YOU CLOSE TO YOUR FATHER, LIN?
IT'S HARD TO BE CLOSE TO HIM...
...WHEN I'VE NEVER EVEN HAD A CONVERSATION WITH HIM.
S... SORRY...
I SHOULDN'T HAVE ASKED YOU THAT, HUH?
UM... DID HE PASS AWAY?
...
YOU GUYS ARE IMAGINING ALL KINDS OF THINGS ABOUT MY LIFE, AREN'T YOU?
THE MAN'S AN *EMPEROR*.
HE'S NOT THE TYPE OF PERSON THAT I CAN CASUALLY SPEAK TO.

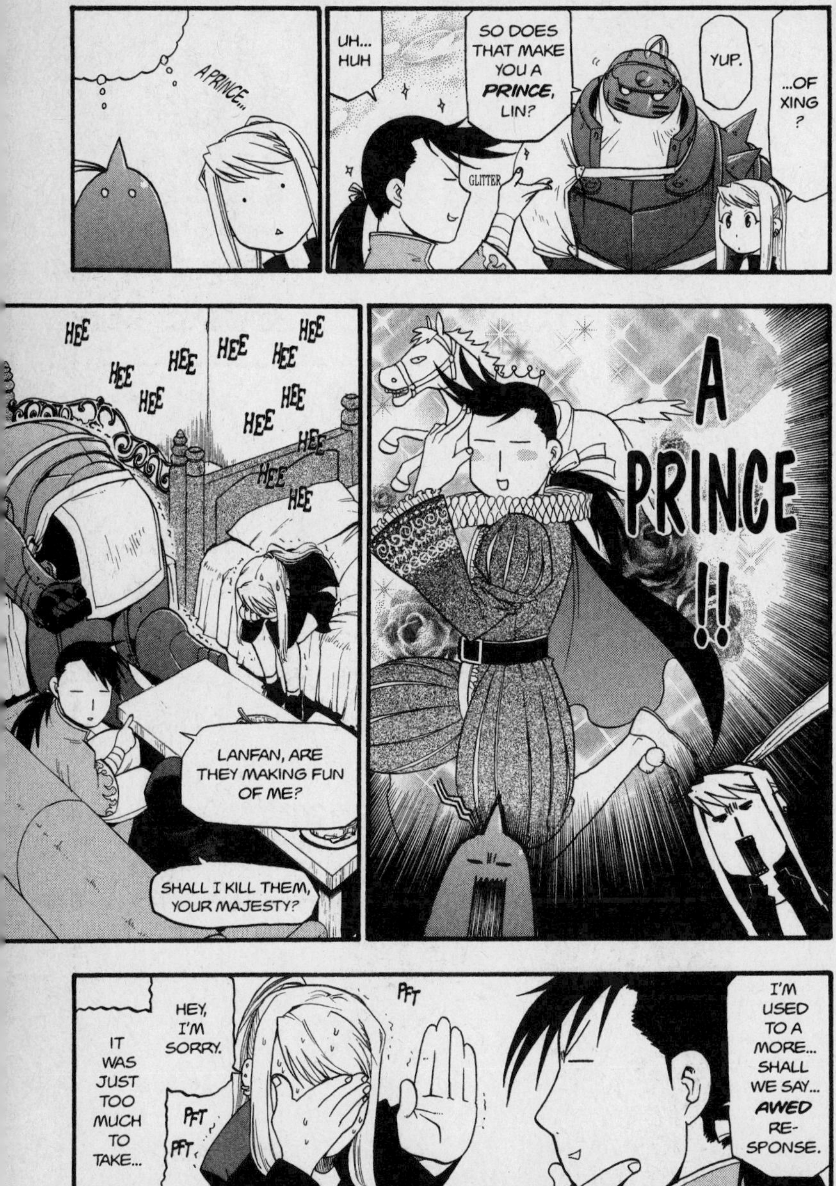

...OF XING?
YUP.
SO DOES THAT MAKE YOU A PRINCE, LIN?
UH... HUH
GLITTER
A PRINCE...
A PRINCE!!
HEE HEE HEE HEE HEE HEE HEE HEE HEE HEE HEE HEE
LANFAN, ARE THEY MAKING FUN OF ME?
SHALL I KILL THEM, YOUR MAJESTY?
I'M USED TO A MORE... SHALL WE SAY... AWED RESPONSE.
PFT
HEY, I'M SORRY.
PFT PFT
IT WAS JUST TOO MUCH TO TAKE...

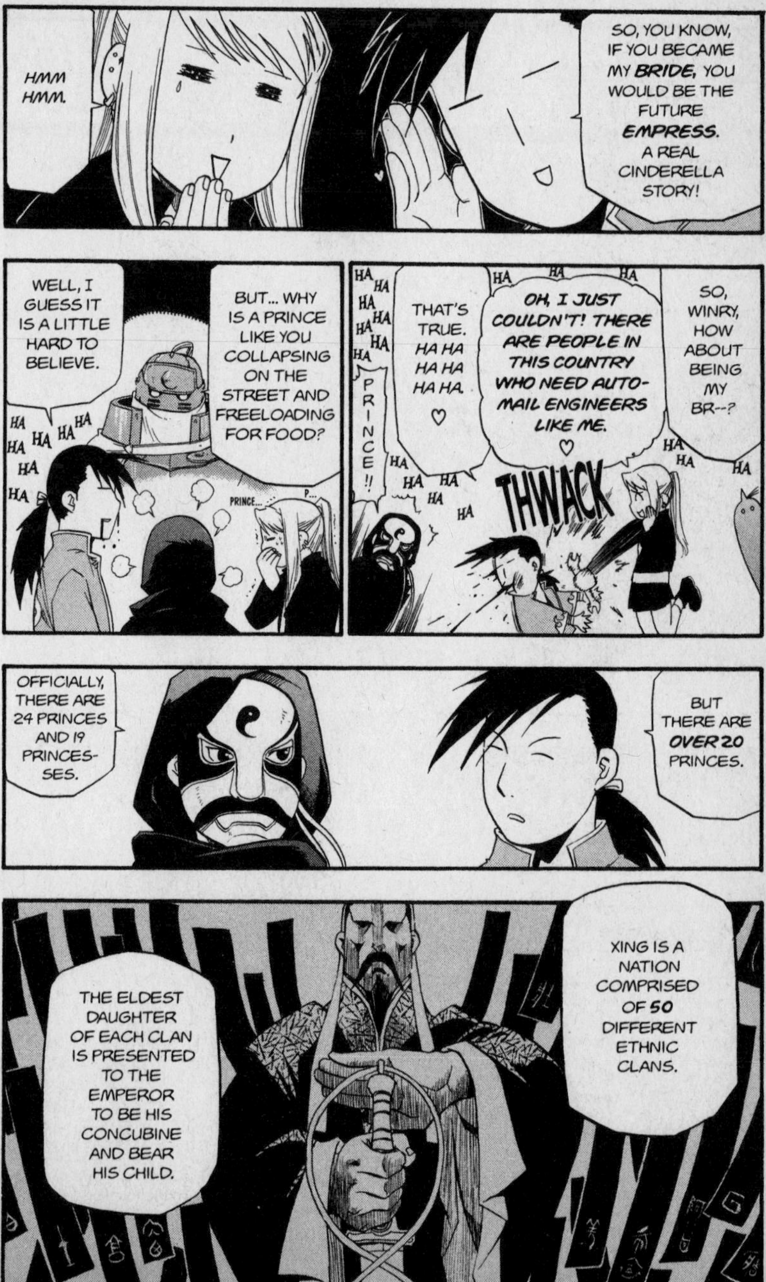
SO, YOU KNOW, IF YOU BECAME MY BRIDE, YOU WOULD BE THE FUTURE EMPRESS. A REAL CINDERELLA STORY!
HMM HMM.
SO, WINRY, HOW ABOUT BEING MY BR--?
OH, I JUST COULDN'T! THERE ARE PEOPLE IN THIS COUNTRY WHO NEED AUTO-MAIL ENGINEERS LIKE ME. ♡
THWACK
THAT'S TRUE. HA HA HA HA HA HA. ♡
PRINCE!!
BUT... WHY IS A PRINCE LIKE YOU COLLAPSING ON THE STREET AND FREELOADING FOR FOOD?
P...
PRINCE...
WELL, I GUESS IT IS A LITTLE HARD TO BELIEVE.
BUT THERE ARE OVER 20 PRINCES.
OFFICIALLY, THERE ARE 24 PRINCES AND 19 PRINCESSES.
XING IS A NATION COMPRISED OF 50 DIFFERENT ETHNIC CLANS.
THE ELDEST DAUGHTER OF EACH CLAN IS PRESENTED TO THE EMPEROR TO BE HIS CONCUBINE AND BEAR HIS CHILD.

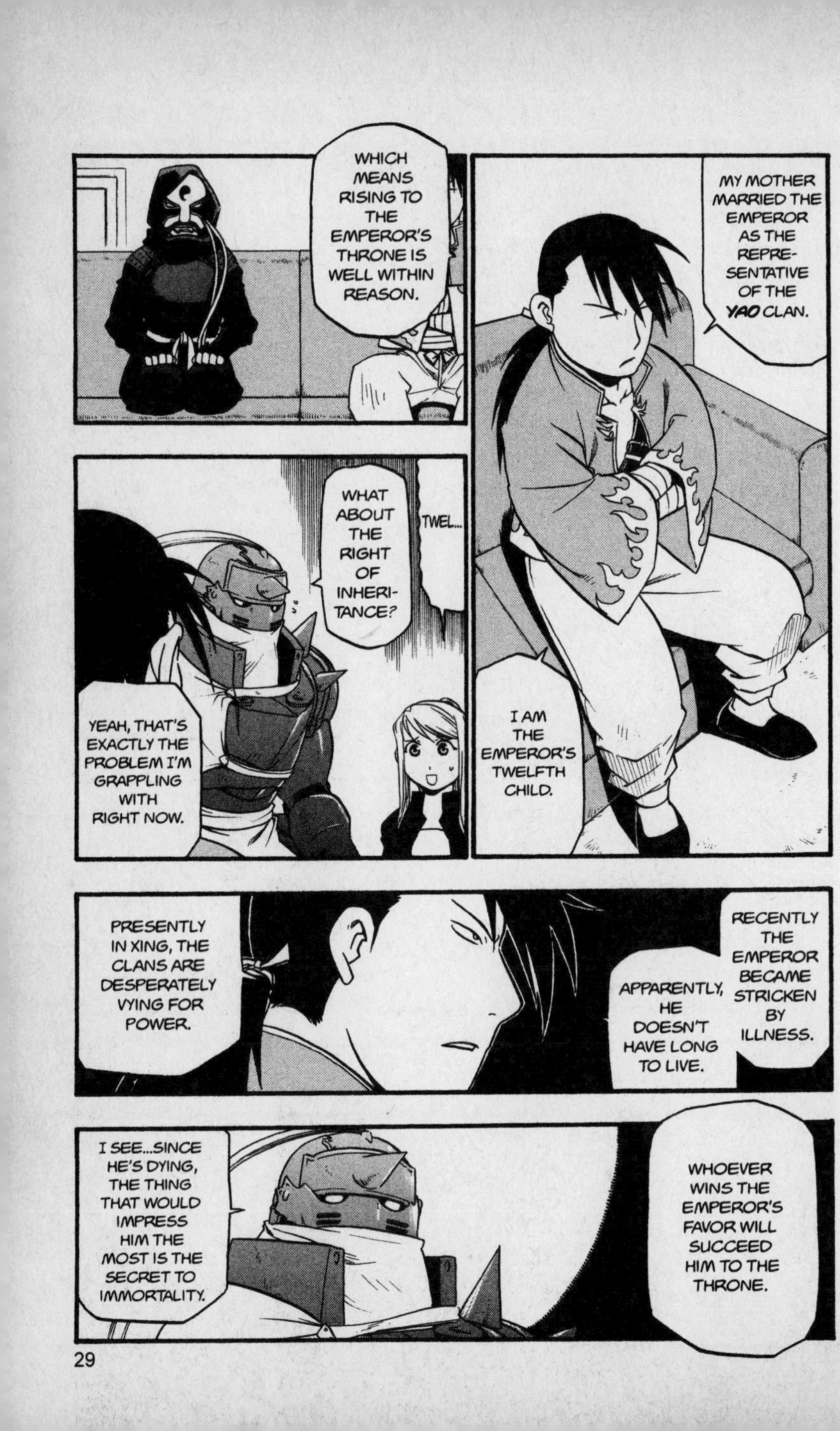
MY MOTHER MARRIED THE EMPEROR AS THE REPRE-SENTATIVE OF THE YAO CLAN.
I AM THE EMPEROR'S TWELFTH CHILD.
WHICH MEANS RISING TO THE EMPEROR'S THRONE IS WELL WITHIN REASON.
WHAT ABOUT THE RIGHT OF INHERI-TANCE?
TWEL...
YEAH, THAT'S EXACTLY THE PROBLEM I'M GRAPPLING WITH RIGHT NOW.
RECENTLY THE EMPEROR BECAME STRICKEN BY ILLNESS.
APPARENTLY, HE DOESN'T HAVE LONG TO LIVE.
PRESENTLY IN XING, THE CLANS ARE DESPERATELY VYING FOR POWER.
WHOEVER WINS THE EMPEROR'S FAVOR WILL SUCCEED HIM TO THE THRONE.
I SEE...SINCE HE'S DYING, THE THING THAT WOULD IMPRESS HIM THE MOST IS THE SECRET TO IMMORTALITY.

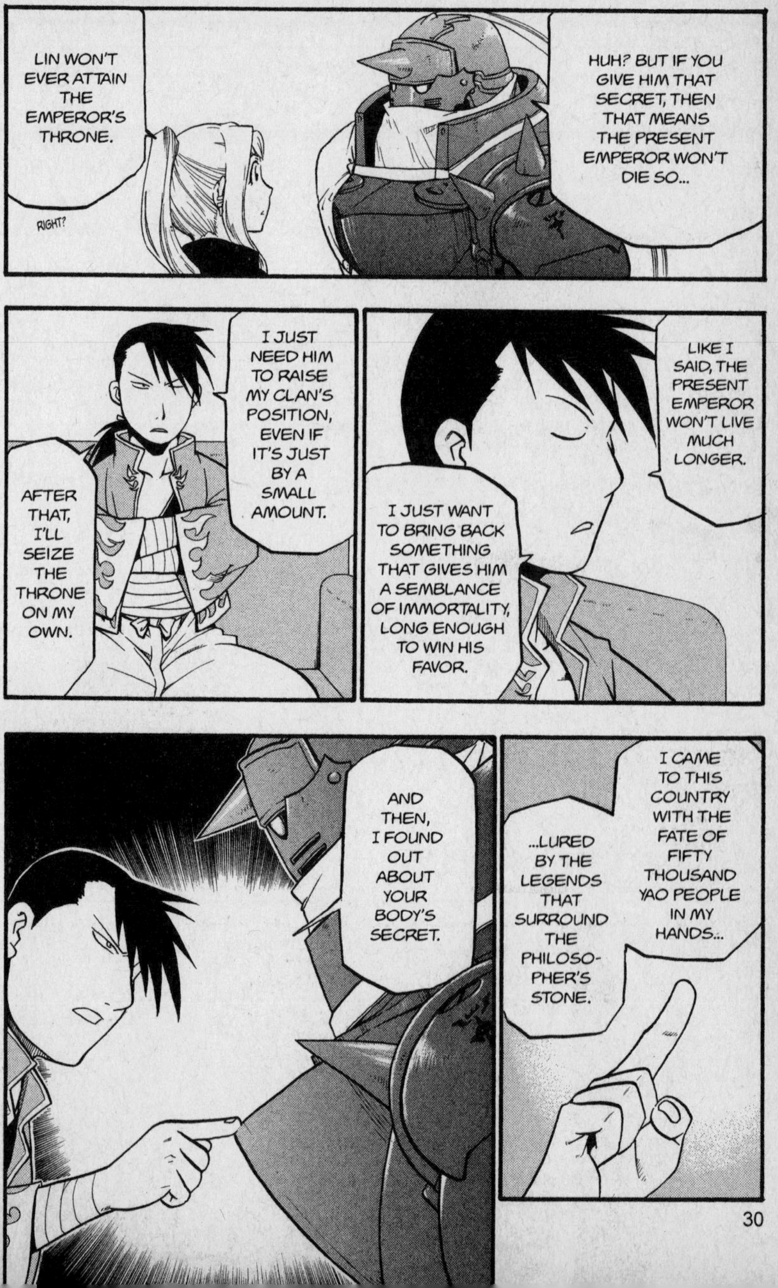
HUH? BUT IF YOU GIVE HIM THAT SECRET, THEN THAT MEANS THE PRESENT EMPEROR WON'T DIE SO...
LIN WON'T EVER ATTAIN THE EMPEROR'S THRONE.
RIGHT?
LIKE I SAID, THE PRESENT EMPEROR WON'T LIVE MUCH LONGER.
I JUST WANT TO BRING BACK SOMETHING THAT GIVES HIM A SEMBLANCE OF IMMORTALITY, LONG ENOUGH TO WIN HIS FAVOR.
I JUST NEED HIM TO RAISE MY CLAN'S POSITION, EVEN IF IT'S JUST BY A SMALL AMOUNT.
AFTER THAT, I'LL SEIZE THE THRONE ON MY OWN.
I CAME TO THIS COUNTRY WITH THE FATE OF FIFTY THOUSAND YAO PEOPLE IN MY HANDS...
...LURED BY THE LEGENDS THAT SURROUND THE PHILOSO-PHER'S STONE.
AND THEN, I FOUND OUT ABOUT YOUR BODY'S SECRET.

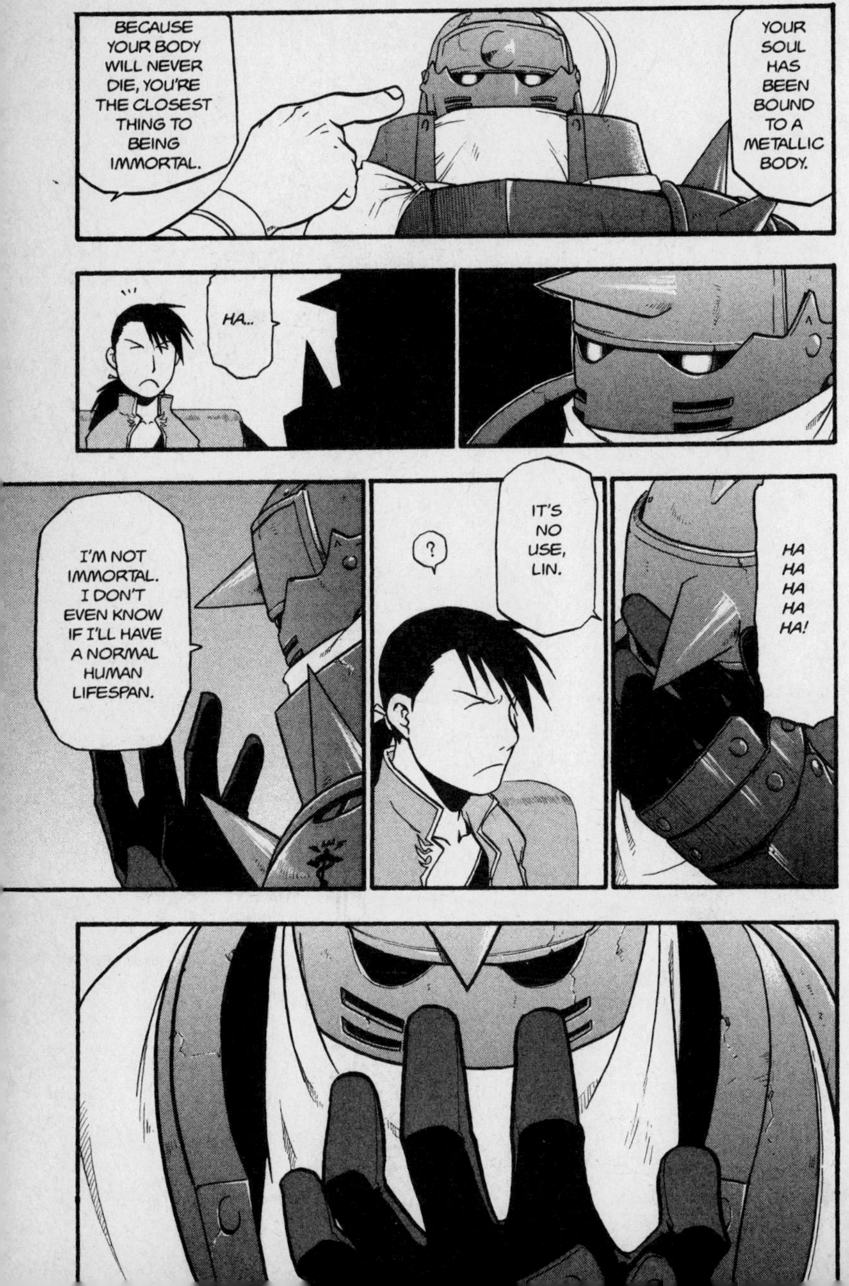
YOUR SOUL HAS BEEN BOUND TO A METALLIC BODY.
BECAUSE YOUR BODY WILL NEVER DIE, YOU'RE THE CLOSEST THING TO BEING IMMORTAL.
HA...
HA HA HA HA HA!
IT'S NO USE, LIN.
?
I'M NOT IMMORTAL. I DON'T EVEN KNOW IF I'LL HAVE A NORMAL HUMAN LIFESPAN.

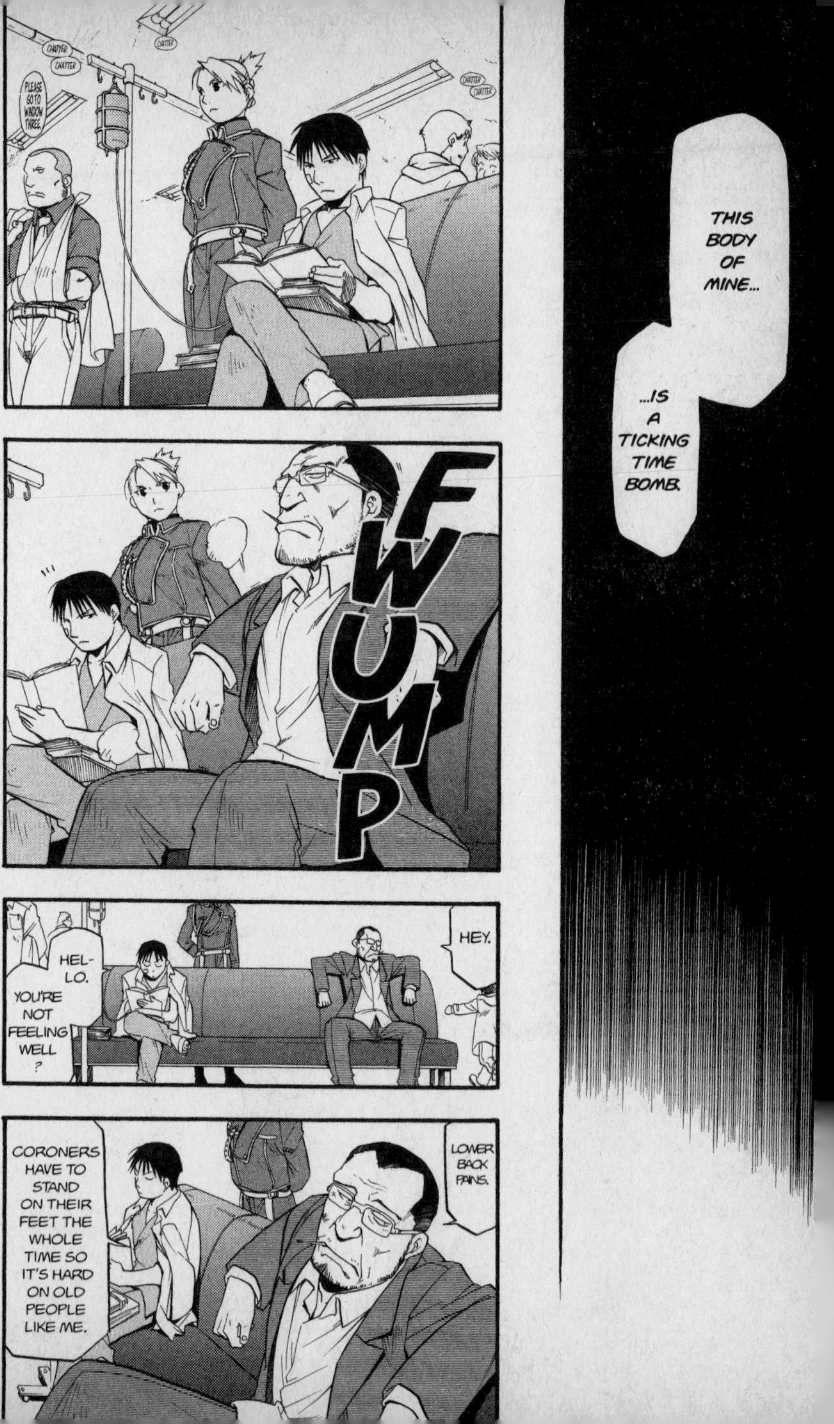
THIS BODY OF MINE...
...IS A TICKING TIME BOMB.
CHATTER CHATTER
CHATTER
CHATTER CHATTER
PLEASE GO TO WINDOW THREE.
FWUMP
HEY.
HEL-LO. YOU'RE NOT FEELING WELL?
LOWER BACK PAINS.
CORONERS HAVE TO STAND ON THEIR FEET THE WHOLE TIME SO IT'S HARD ON OLD PEOPLE LIKE ME.

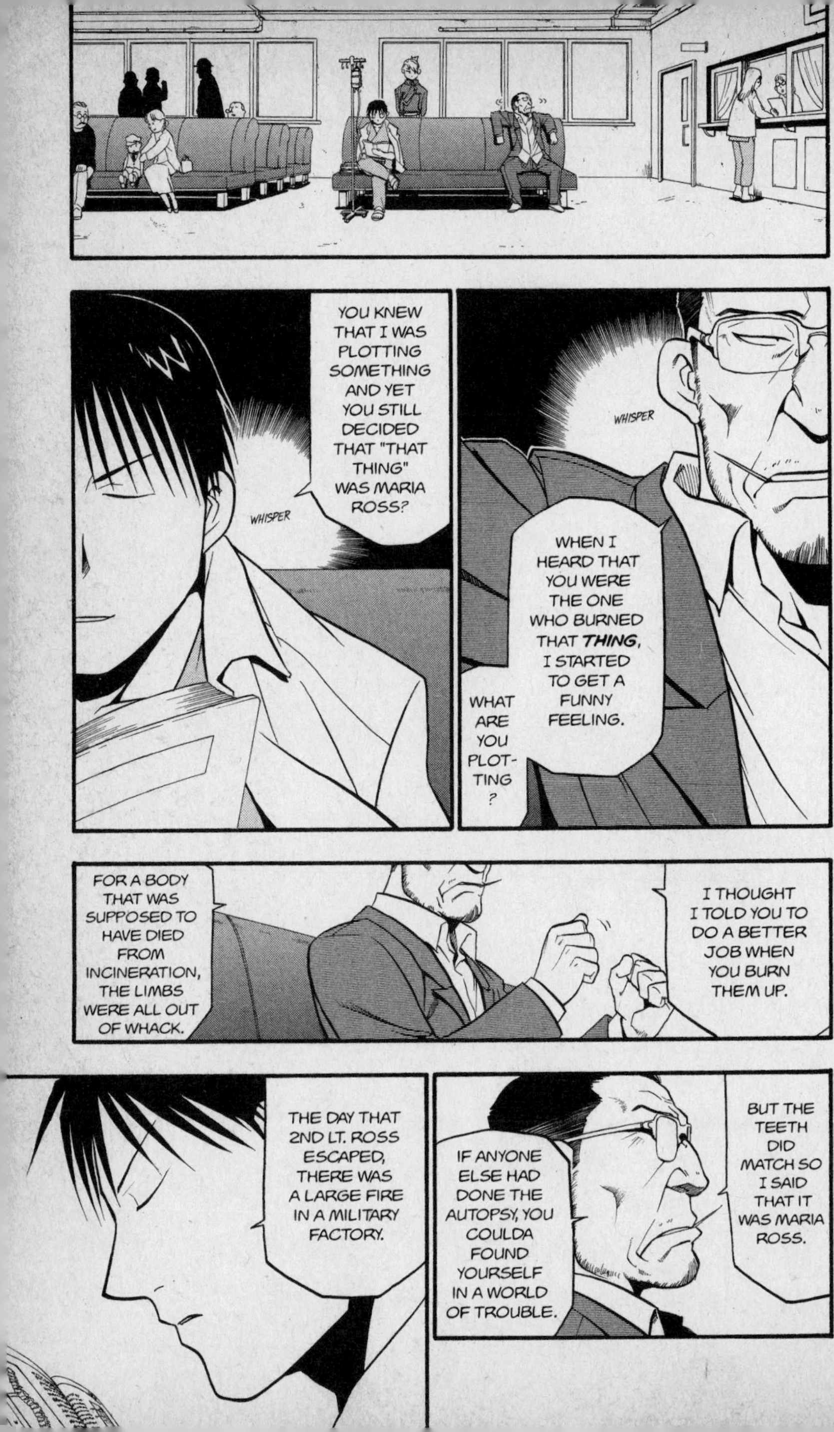
WHISPER
WHEN I HEARD THAT YOU WERE THE ONE WHO BURNED THAT ***THING***, I STARTED TO GET A FUNNY FEELING.
WHAT ARE YOU PLOTTING?
YOU KNEW THAT I WAS PLOTTING SOMETHING AND YET YOU STILL DECIDED THAT "THAT THING" WAS MARIA ROSS?
WHISPER
I THOUGHT I TOLD YOU TO DO A BETTER JOB WHEN YOU BURN THEM UP.
FOR A BODY THAT WAS SUPPOSED TO HAVE DIED FROM INCINERATION, THE LIMBS WERE ALL OUT OF WHACK.
BUT THE TEETH DID MATCH SO I SAID THAT IT WAS MARIA ROSS.
IF ANYONE ELSE HAD DONE THE AUTOPSY, YOU COULDA FOUND YOURSELF IN A WORLD OF TROUBLE.
THE DAY THAT 2ND LT. ROSS ESCAPED, THERE WAS A LARGE FIRE IN A MILITARY FACTORY.

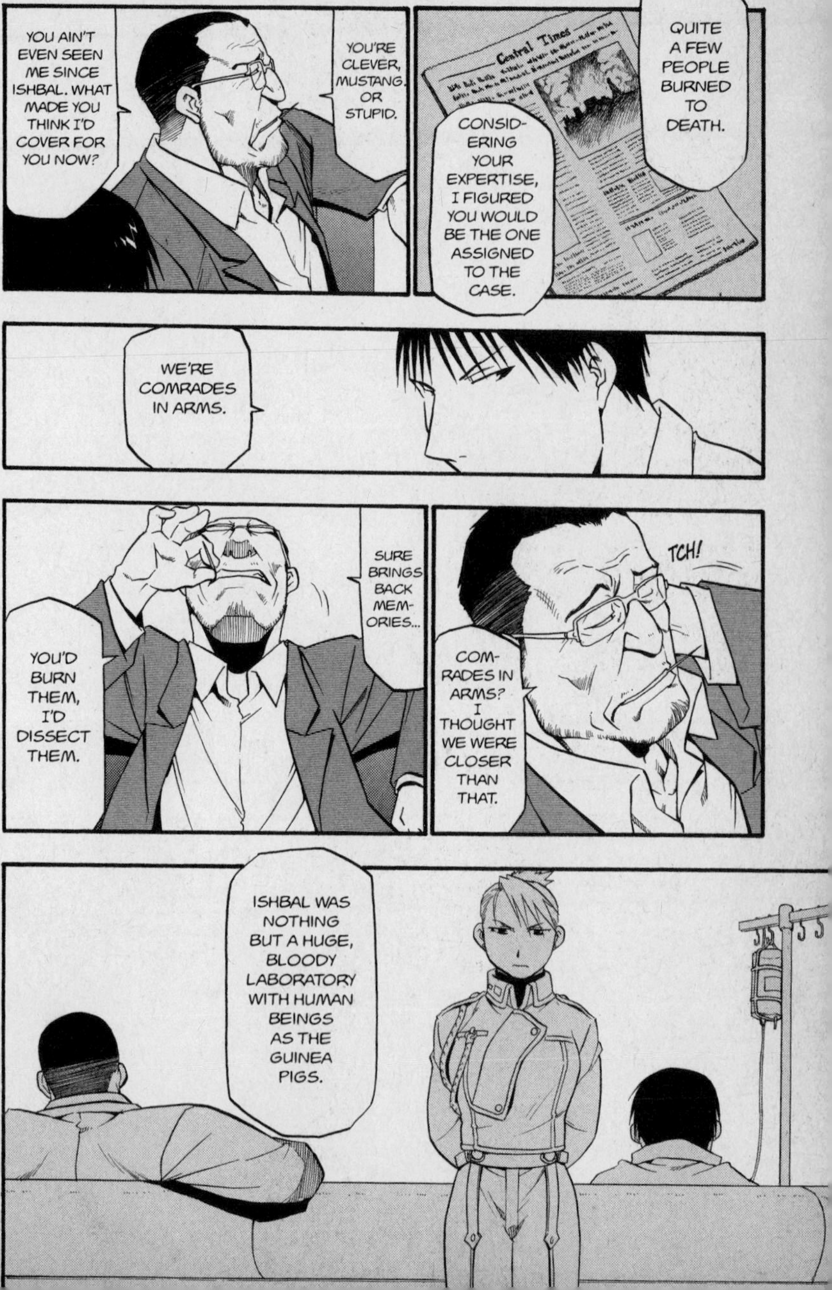
QUITE A FEW PEOPLE BURNED TO DEATH.
Central Times
CONSID-ERING YOUR EXPERTISE, I FIGURED YOU WOULD BE THE ONE ASSIGNED TO THE CASE.
YOU'RE CLEVER, MUSTANG. OR STUPID.
YOU AIN'T EVEN SEEN ME SINCE ISHBAL. WHAT MADE YOU THINK I'D COVER FOR YOU NOW?
WE'RE COMRADES IN ARMS.
TCH!
COM-RADES IN ARMS? I THOUGHT WE WERE CLOSER THAN THAT.
SURE BRINGS BACK MEM-ORIES...
YOU'D BURN THEM, I'D DISSECT THEM.
ISHBAL WAS NOTHING BUT A HUGE, BLOODY LABORATORY WITH HUMAN BEINGS AS THE GUINEA PIGS.

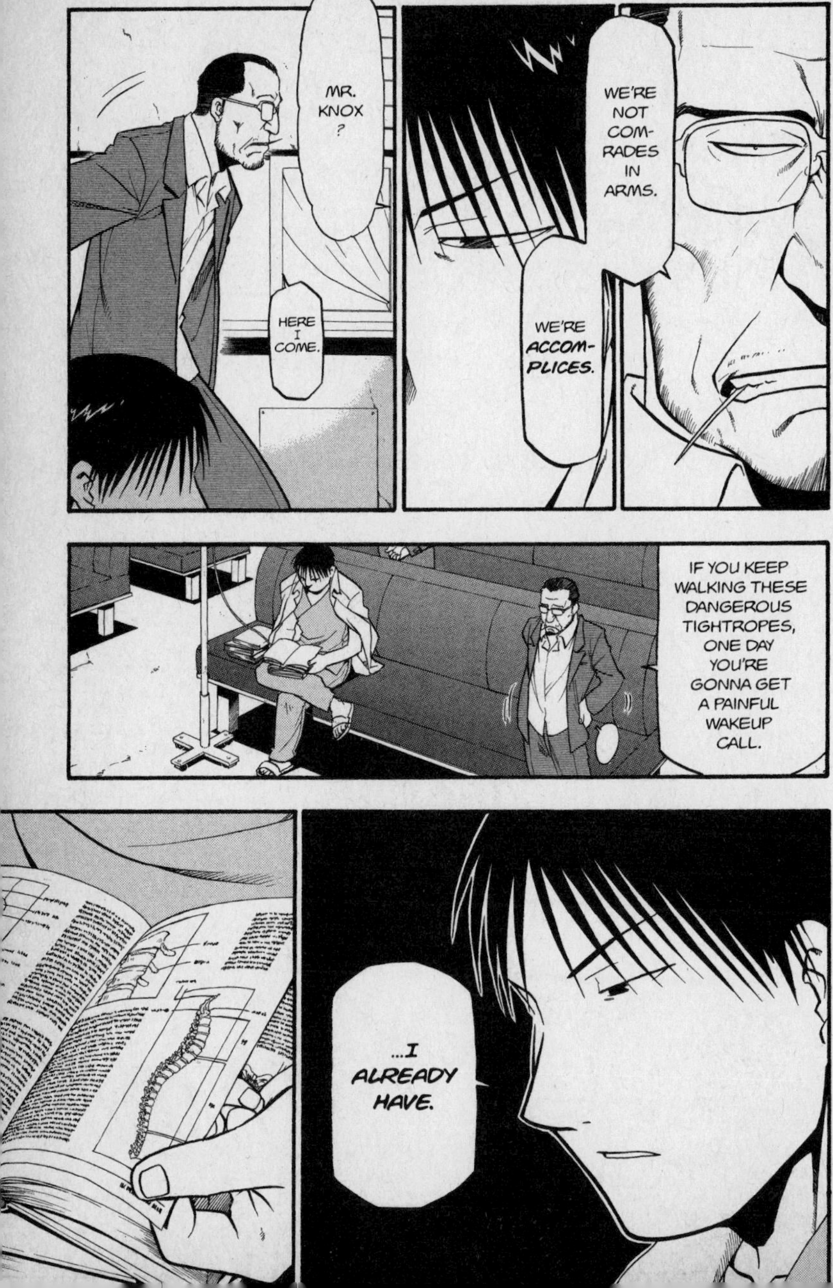
WE'RE NOT COM-RADES IN ARMS.
WE'RE ACCOMPLICES.
MR. KNOX?
HERE I COME.
IF YOU KEEP WALKING THESE DANGEROUS TIGHTROPES, ONE DAY YOU'RE GONNA GET A PAINFUL WAKEUP CALL.
...I ALREADY HAVE.

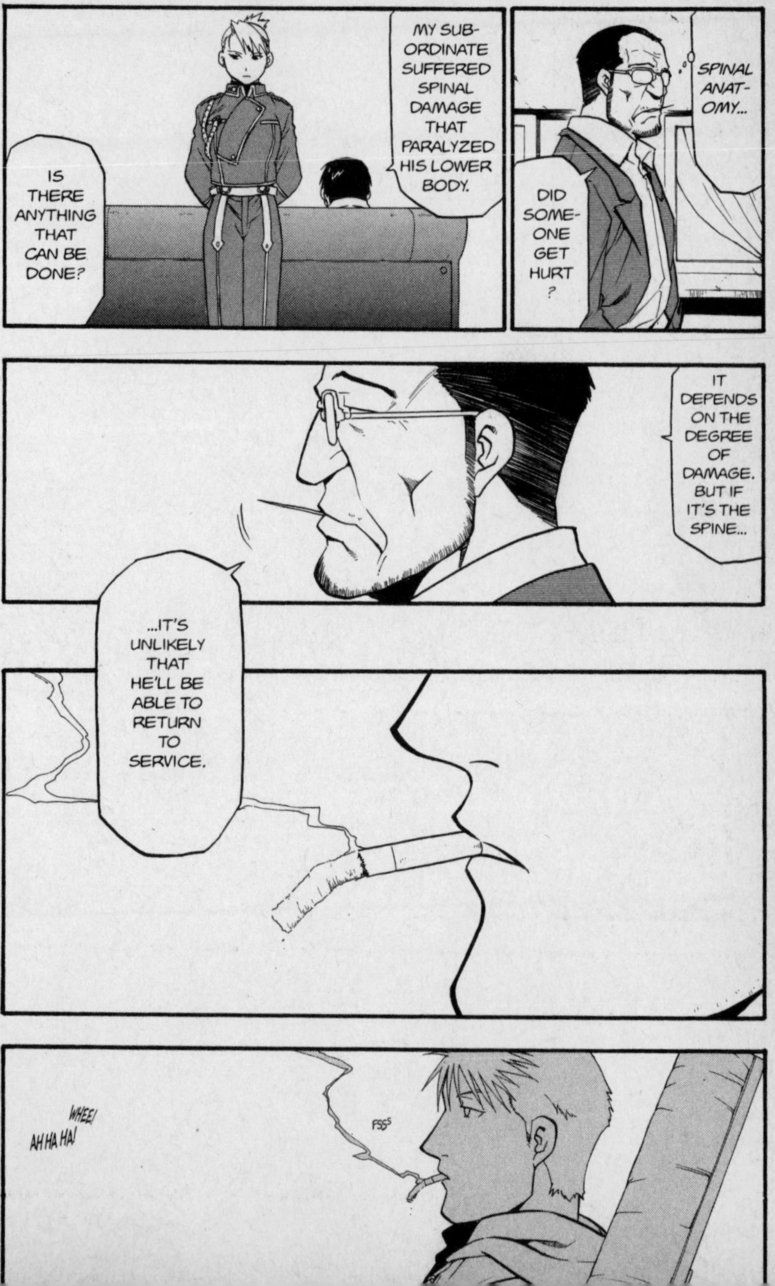
SPINAL ANATOMY...
DID SOMEONE GET HURT?
MY SUBORDINATE SUFFERED SPINAL DAMAGE THAT PARALYZED HIS LOWER BODY.
IS THERE ANYTHING THAT CAN BE DONE?
IT DEPENDS ON THE DEGREE OF DAMAGE. BUT IF IT'S THE SPINE...
...IT'S UNLIKELY THAT HE'LL BE ABLE TO RETURN TO SERVICE.
FSSS
WHEE!
AH HA HA!

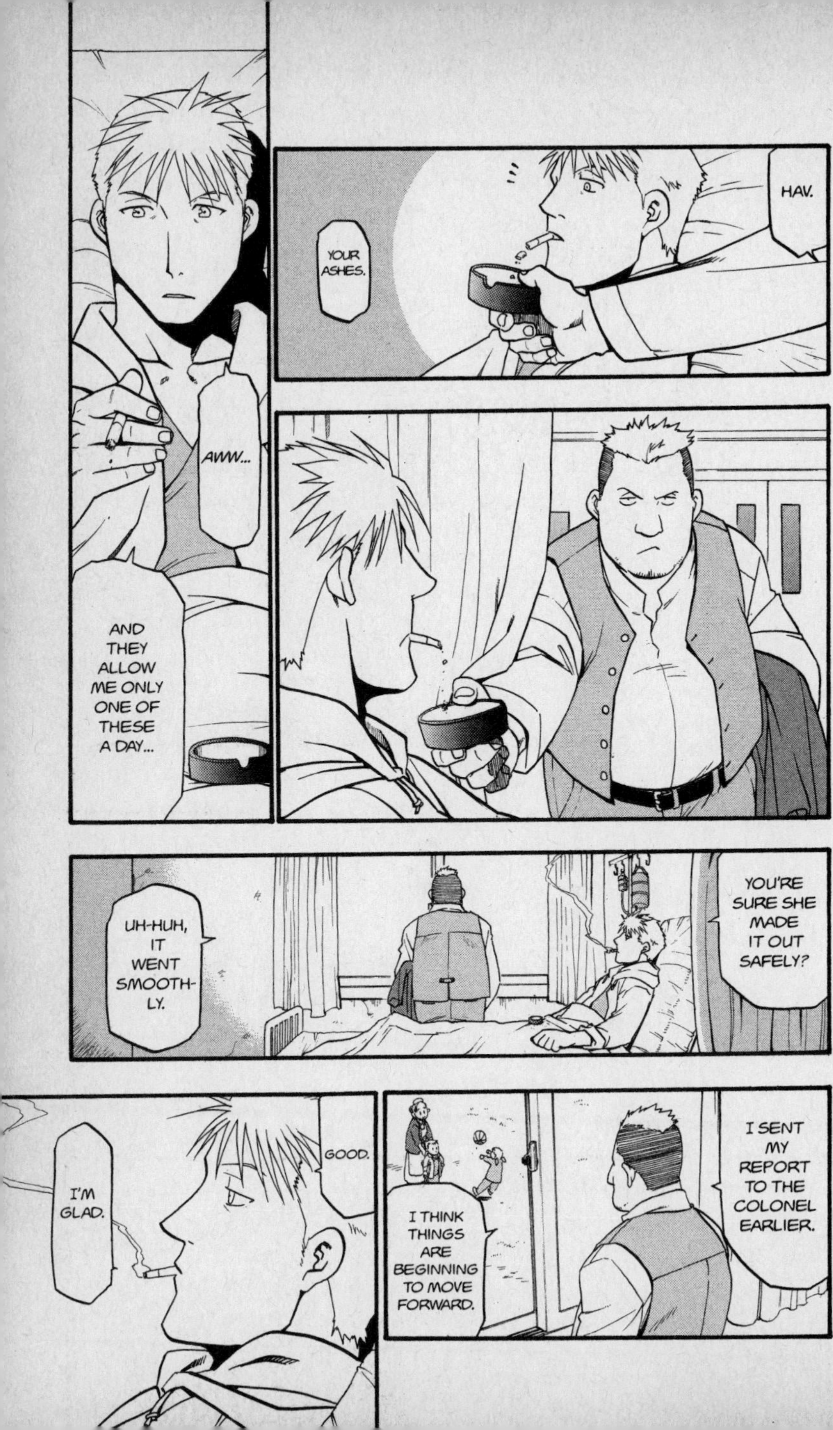
HAV.
YOUR ASHES.
AWW...
AND THEY ALLOW ME ONLY ONE OF THESE A DAY...
YOU'RE SURE SHE MADE IT OUT SAFELY?
UH-HUH, IT WENT SMOOTH-LY.
I SENT MY REPORT TO THE COLONEL EARLIER.
I THINK THINGS ARE BEGINNING TO MOVE FORWARD.
GOOD.
I'M GLAD.

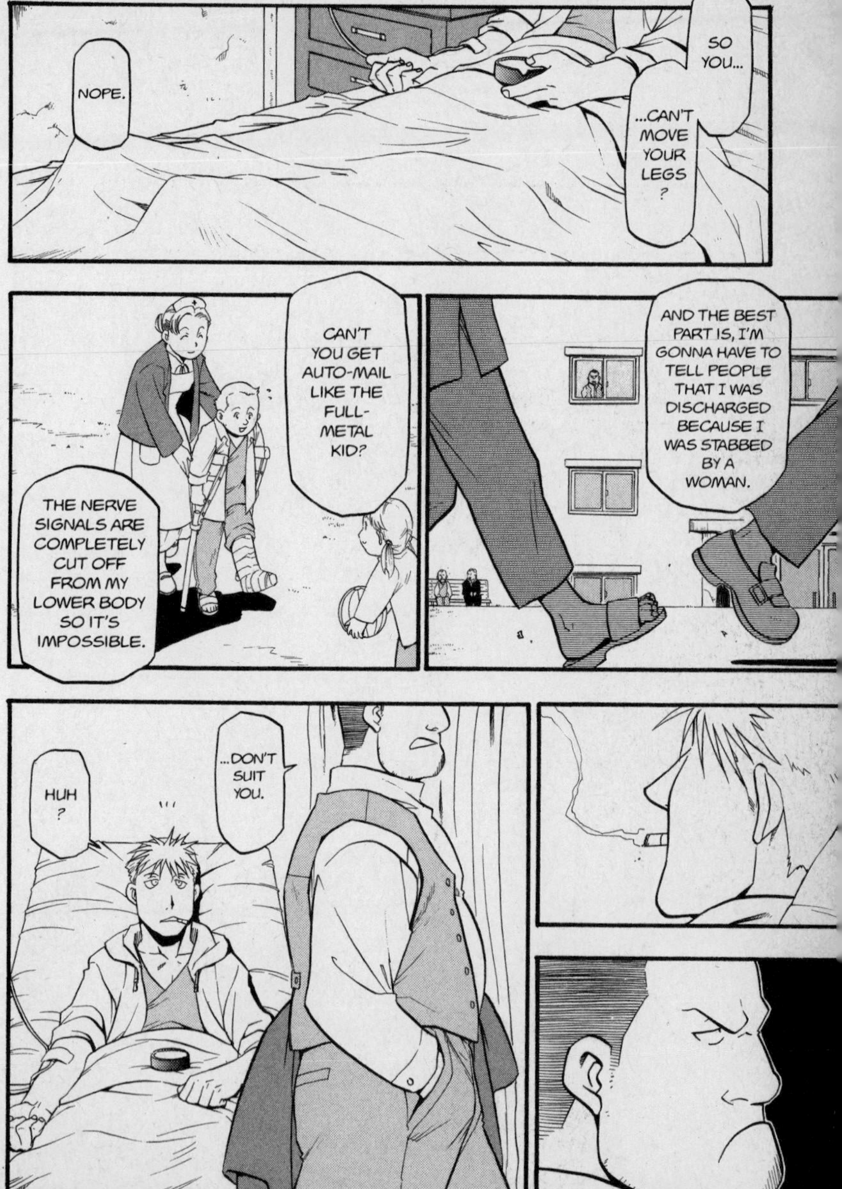
SO YOU...
...CAN'T MOVE YOUR LEGS?
NOPE.
AND THE BEST PART IS, I'M GONNA HAVE TO TELL PEOPLE THAT I WAS DISCHARGED BECAUSE I WAS STABBED BY A WOMAN.
CAN'T YOU GET AUTO-MAIL LIKE THE FULL-METAL KID?
THE NERVE SIGNALS ARE COMPLETELY CUT OFF FROM MY LOWER BODY SO IT'S IMPOSSIBLE.
...DON'T SUIT YOU.
HUH?

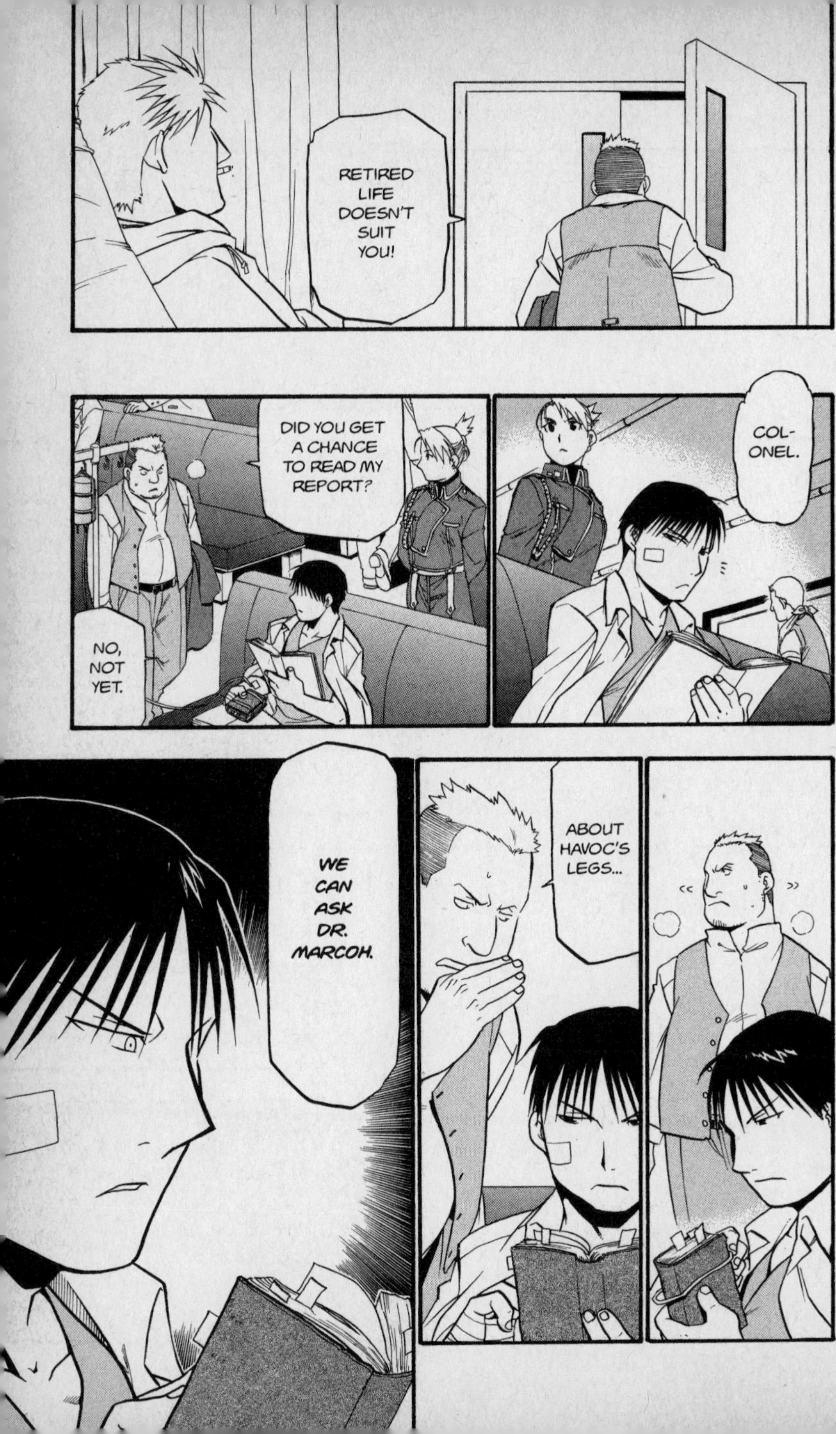
RETIRED LIFE DOESN'T SUIT YOU!
COL-ONEL.
DID YOU GET A CHANCE TO READ MY REPORT?
NO, NOT YET.
ABOUT HAVOC'S LEGS...
WE CAN ASK DR. MARCOH.

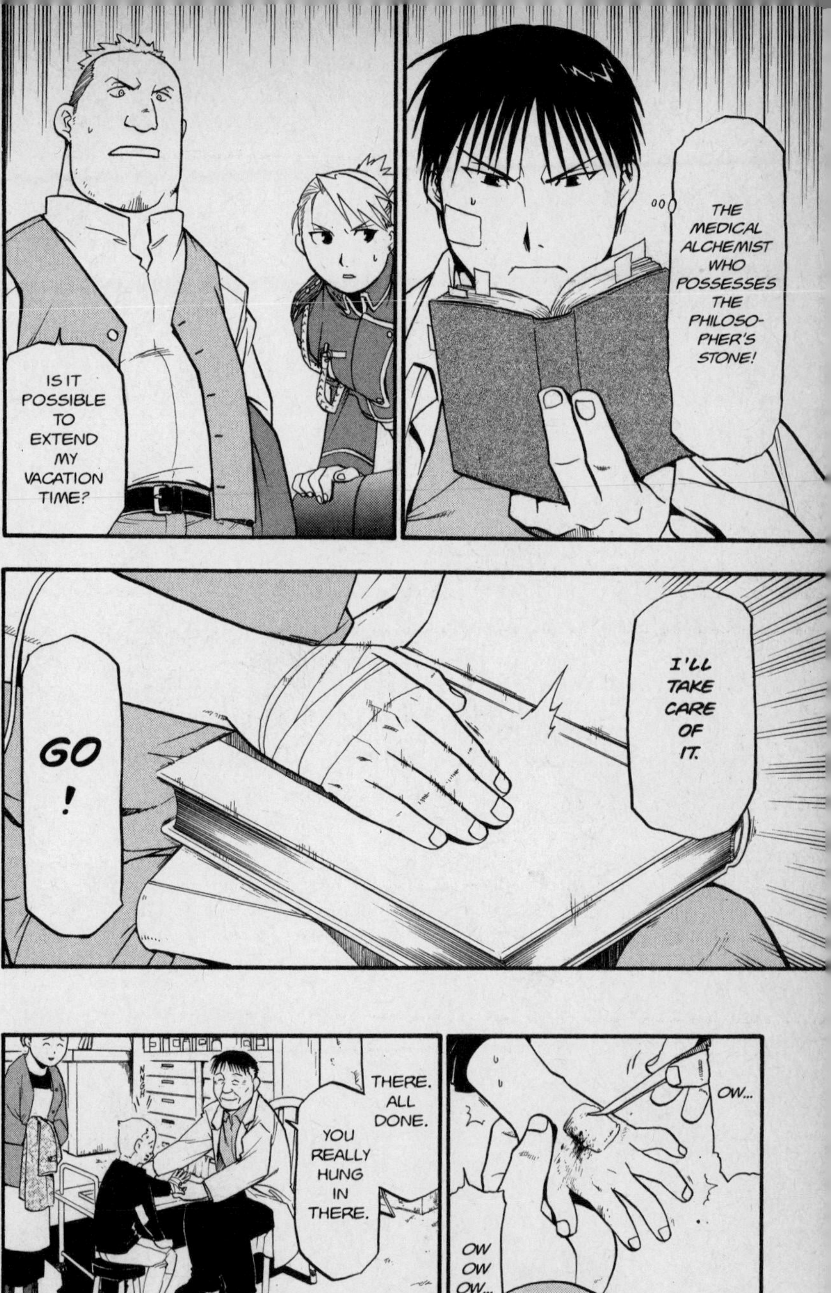
THE MEDICAL ALCHEMIST WHO POSSESSES THE PHILOSO-PHER'S STONE!
IS IT POSSIBLE TO EXTEND MY VACATION TIME?
I'LL TAKE CARE OF IT.
GO!
OW...
OW OW OW...
THERE. ALL DONE.
YOU REALLY HUNG IN THERE.

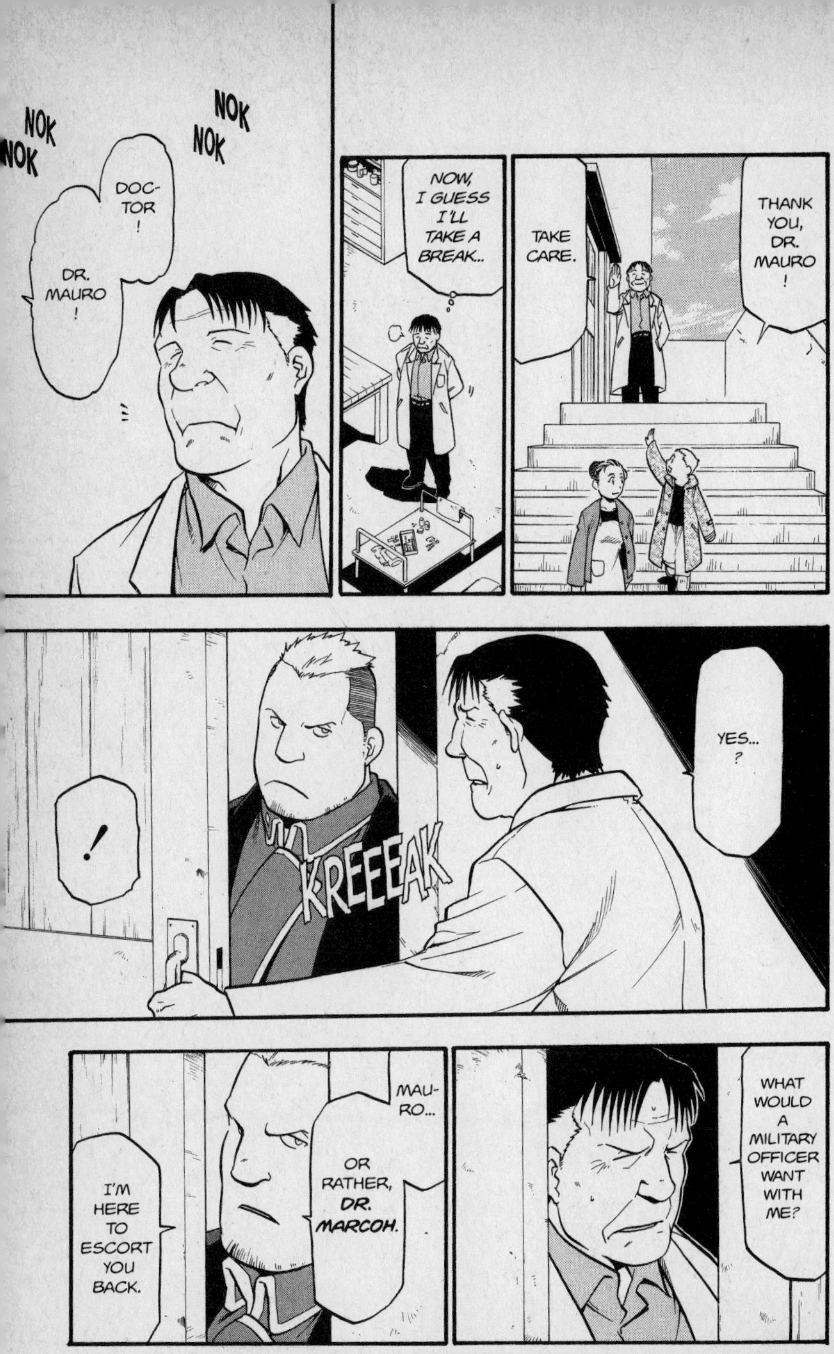
THANK YOU, DR. MAURO!
TAKE CARE.
NOW, I GUESS I'LL TAKE A BREAK...
NOK NOK
NOK NOK
DOC-TOR!
DR. MAURO!
YES...?
KREEEAK
!
WHAT WOULD A MILITARY OFFICER WANT WITH ME?
MAU-RO...
OR RATHER, **DR. MARCOH.**
I'M HERE TO ESCORT YOU BACK.

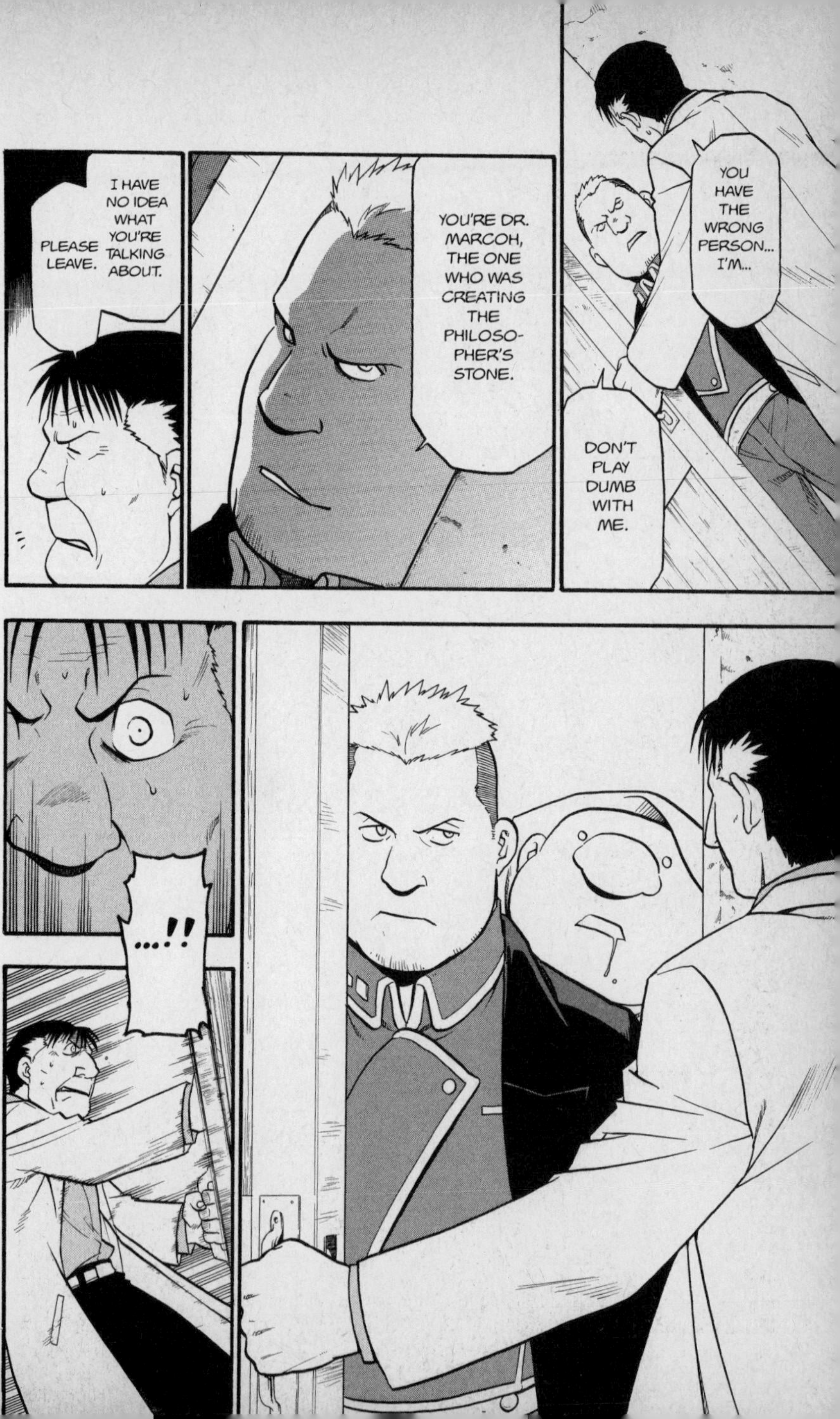
YOU HAVE THE WRONG PERSON... I'M...
DON'T PLAY DUMB WITH ME.
YOU'RE DR. MARCOH, THE ONE WHO WAS CREATING THE PHILOSOPHER'S STONE.
I HAVE NO IDEA WHAT YOU'RE TALKING ABOUT.
PLEASE LEAVE.
...!!

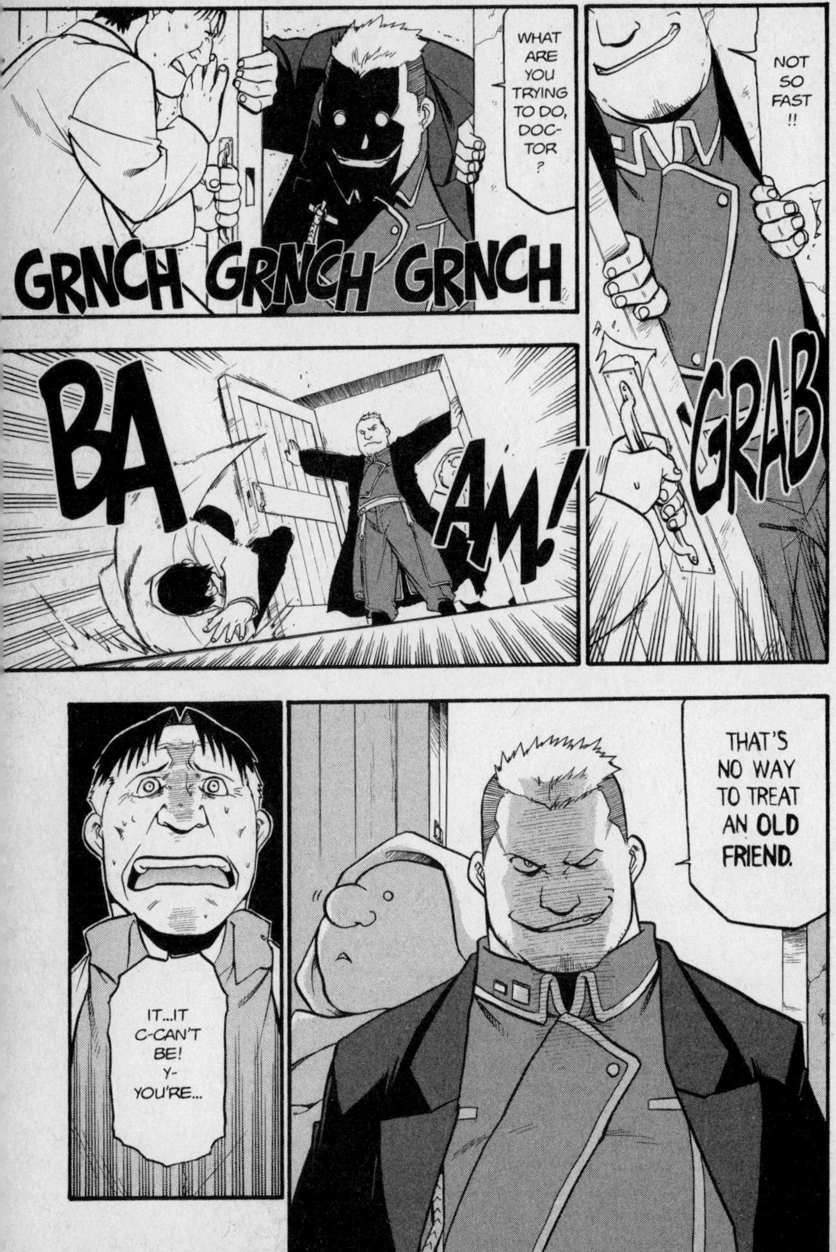
NOT SO FAST !!
GRAB
WHAT ARE YOU TRYING TO DO, DOCTOR ?
GRNCH GRNCH GRNCH
BA
AM!
THAT'S NO WAY TO TREAT AN OLD FRIEND.
IT...IT C-CAN'T BE! Y- YOU'RE...

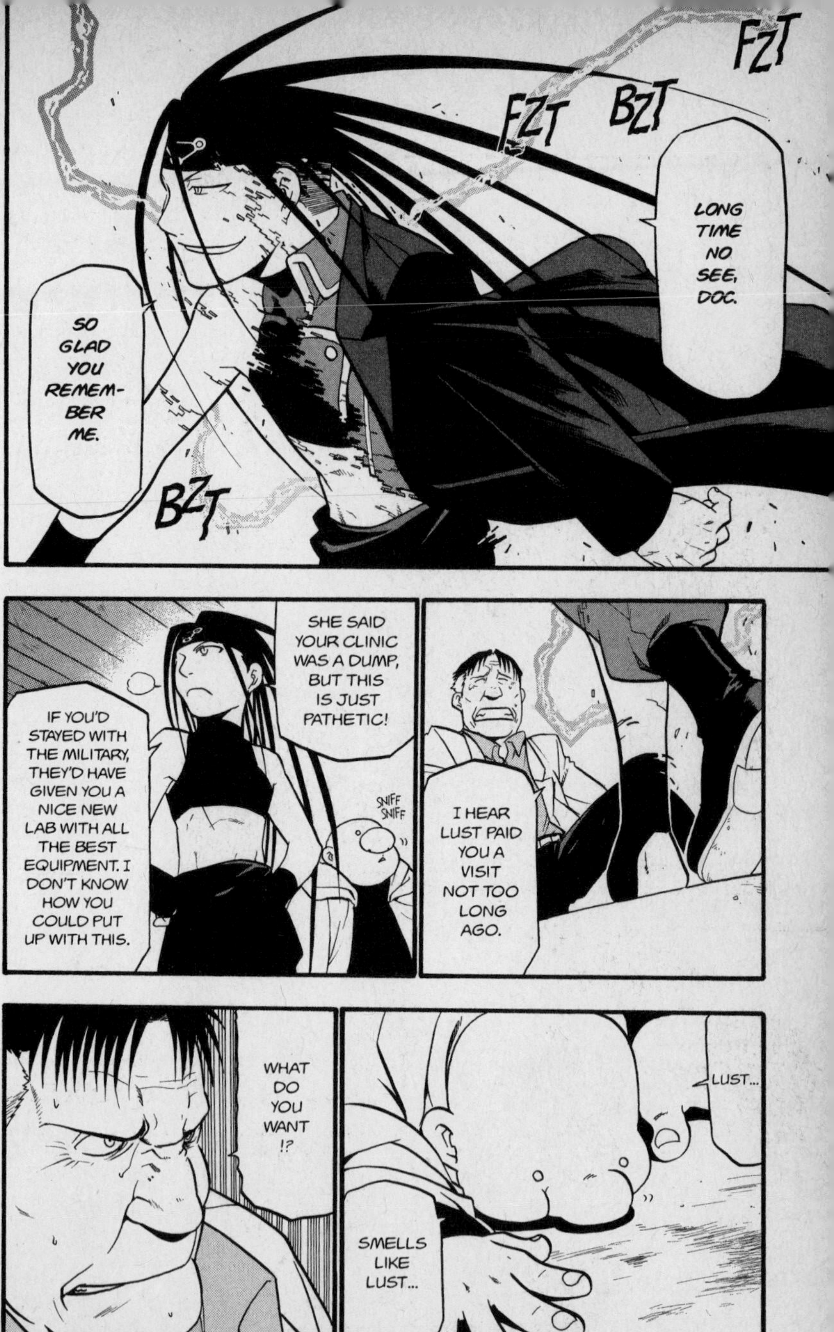
FZT
BZT
FZT
LONG TIME NO SEE, DOC.
SO GLAD YOU REMEMBER ME.
BZT
I HEAR LUST PAID YOU A VISIT NOT TOO LONG AGO.
SHE SAID YOUR CLINIC WAS A DUMP, BUT THIS IS JUST PATHETIC!
IF YOU'D STAYED WITH THE MILITARY, THEY'D HAVE GIVEN YOU A NICE NEW LAB WITH ALL THE BEST EQUIPMENT. I DON'T KNOW HOW YOU COULD PUT UP WITH THIS.
SNIFF SNIFF
LUST...
SMELLS LIKE LUST...
WHAT DO YOU WANT!?

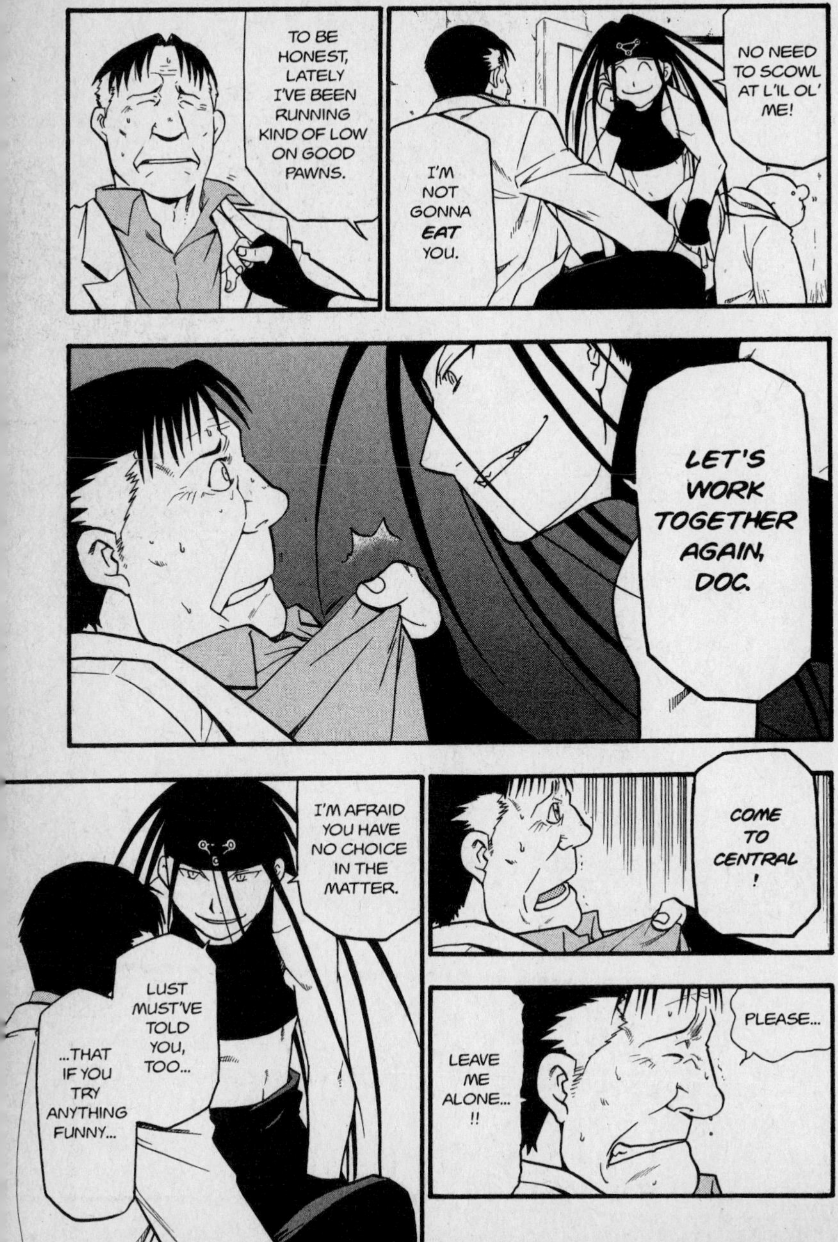
NO NEED TO SCOWL AT L'IL OL' ME!
I'M NOT GONNA *EAT* YOU.
TO BE HONEST, LATELY I'VE BEEN RUNNING KIND OF LOW ON GOOD PAWNS.
LET'S WORK TOGETHER AGAIN, DOC.
COME TO CENTRAL!
PLEASE...
LEAVE ME ALONE...!!
I'M AFRAID YOU HAVE NO CHOICE IN THE MATTER.
LUST MUST'VE TOLD YOU, TOO...
...THAT IF YOU TRY ANYTHING FUNNY...

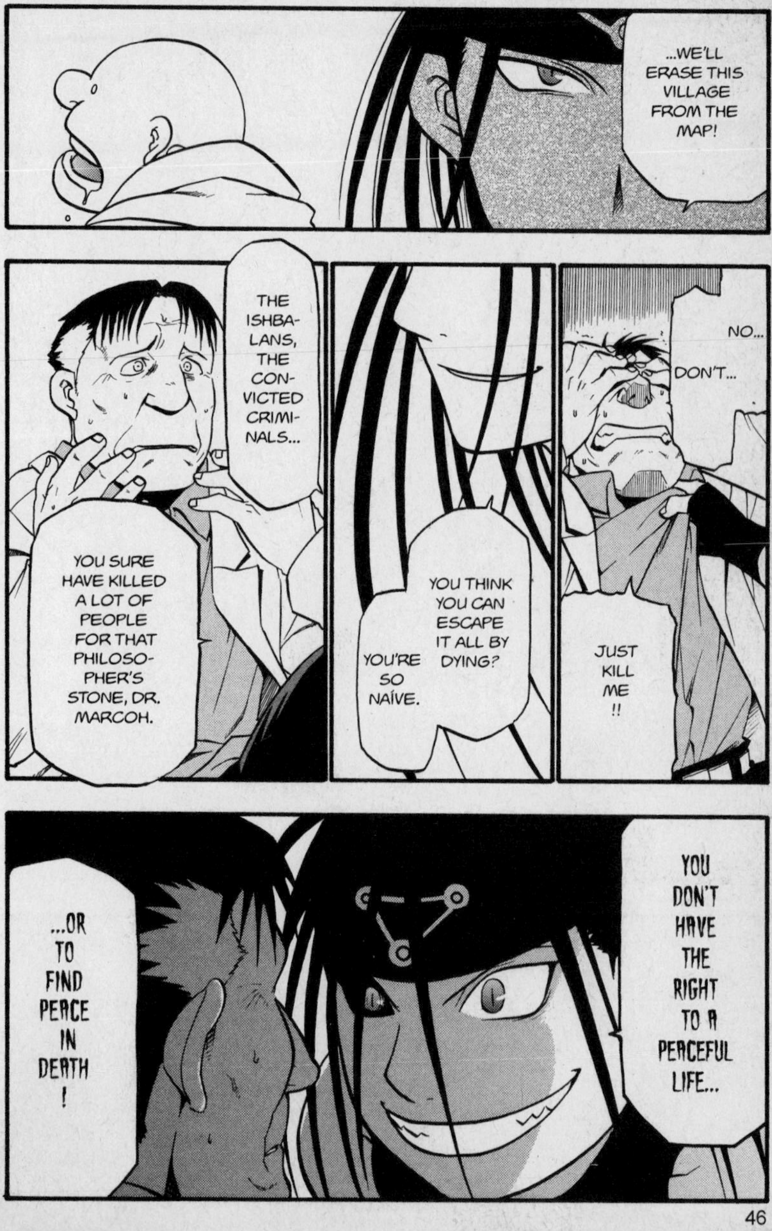
...WE'LL ERASE THIS VILLAGE FROM THE MAP!
NO... DON'T...
JUST KILL ME !!
YOU THINK YOU CAN ESCAPE IT ALL BY DYING?
YOU'RE SO NAÏVE.
THE ISHBALANS, THE CONVICTED CRIMINALS...
YOU SURE HAVE KILLED A LOT OF PEOPLE FOR THAT PHILOSOPHER'S STONE, DR. MARCOH.
YOU DON'T HAVE THE RIGHT TO A PEACEFUL LIFE...
...OR TO FIND PEACE IN DEATH !

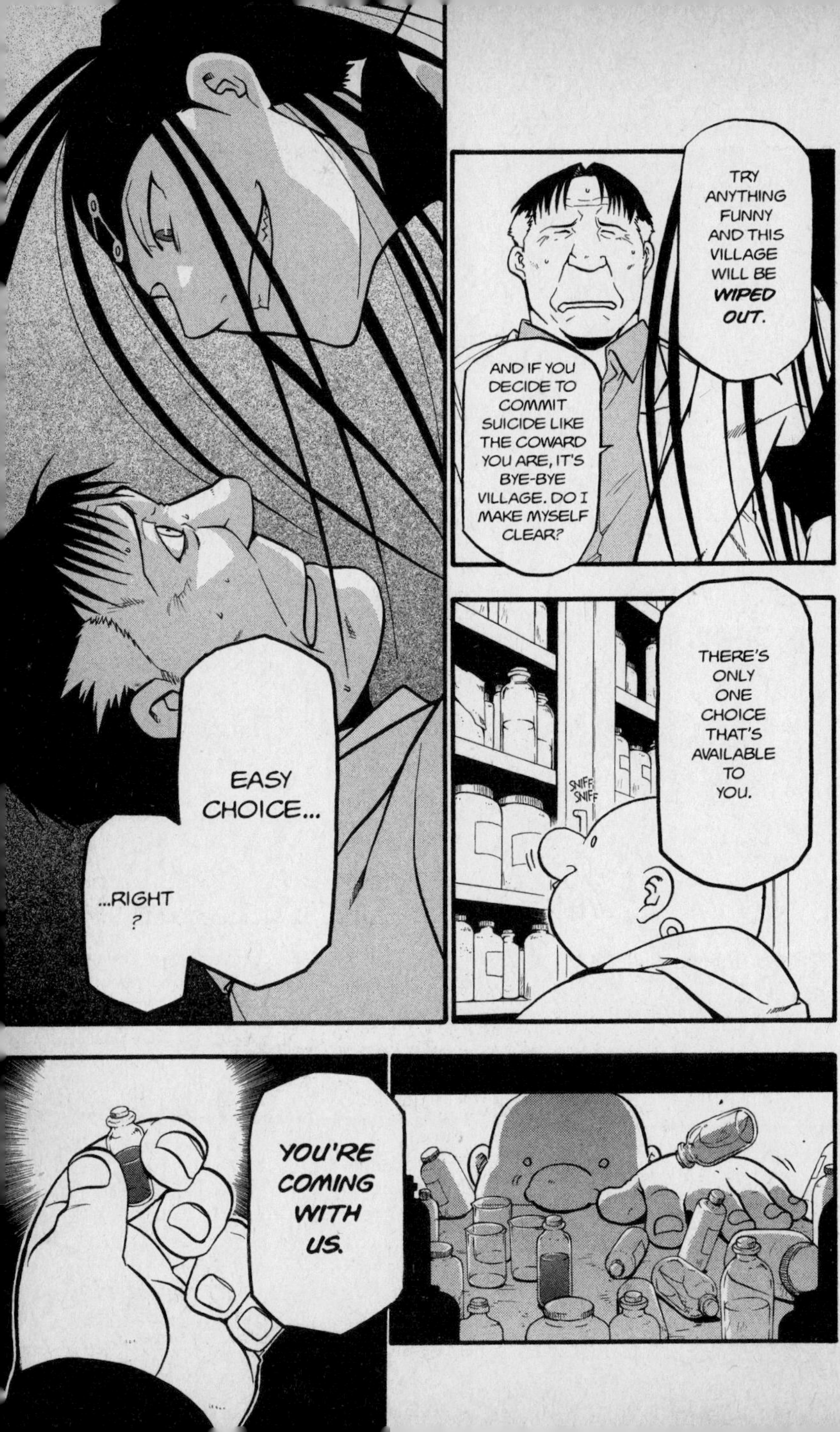

TRY ANYTHING FUNNY AND THIS VILLAGE WILL BE ***WIPED OUT***.
AND IF YOU DECIDE TO COMMIT SUICIDE LIKE THE COWARD YOU ARE, IT'S BYE-BYE VILLAGE. DO I MAKE MYSELF CLEAR?
THERE'S ONLY ONE CHOICE THAT'S AVAILABLE TO YOU.
SNIFF SNIFF
EASY CHOICE...
...RIGHT?
YOU'RE COMING WITH US.

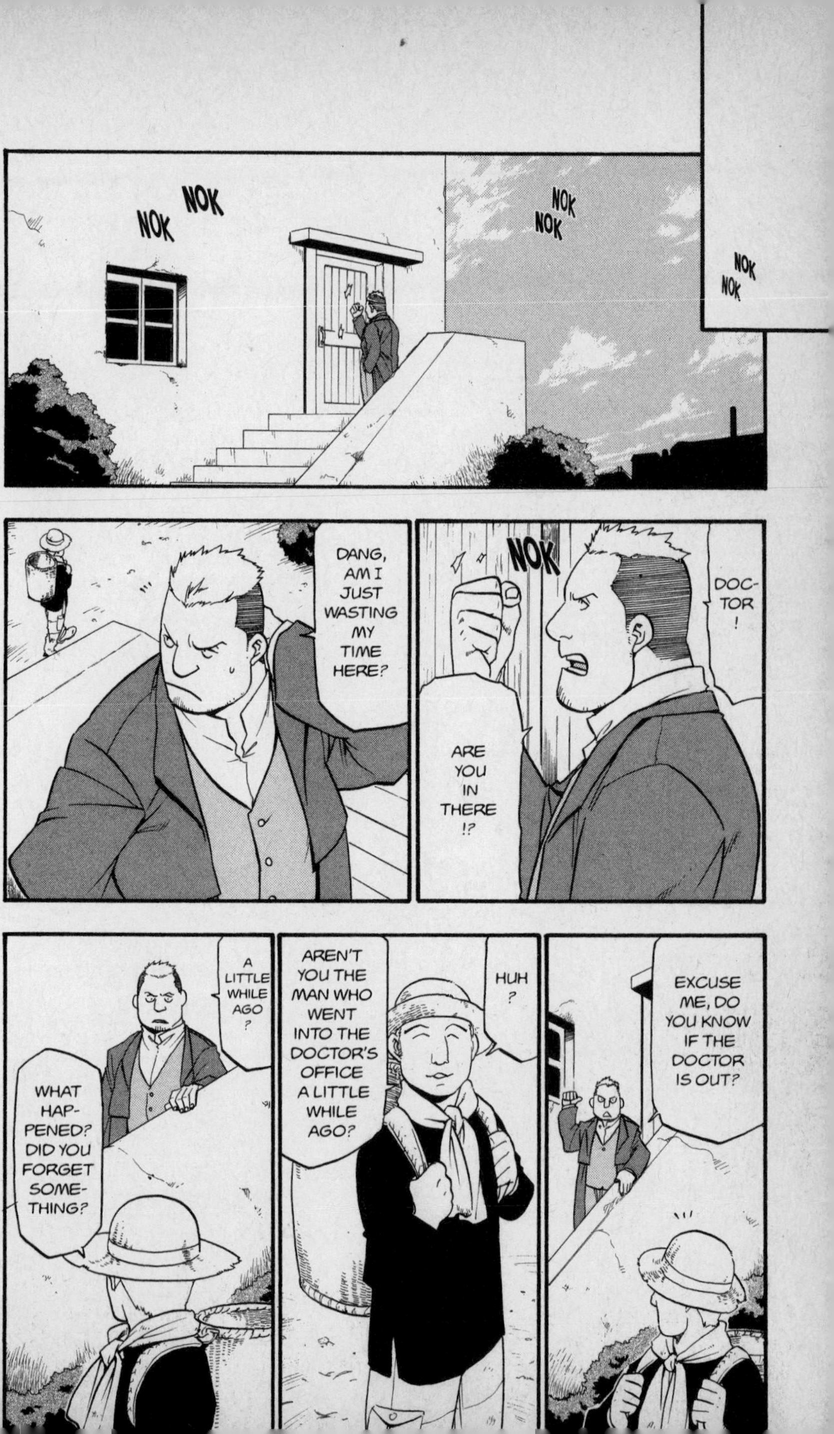
NOK
NOK
NOK
NOK
NOK
NOK
NOK
DOC-TOR!
ARE YOU IN THERE!?
DANG, AM I JUST WASTING MY TIME HERE?
EXCUSE ME, DO YOU KNOW IF THE DOCTOR IS OUT?
HUH?
AREN'T YOU THE MAN WHO WENT INTO THE DOCTOR'S OFFICE A LITTLE WHILE AGO?
A LITTLE WHILE AGO?
WHAT HAP-PENED? DID YOU FORGET SOME-THING?

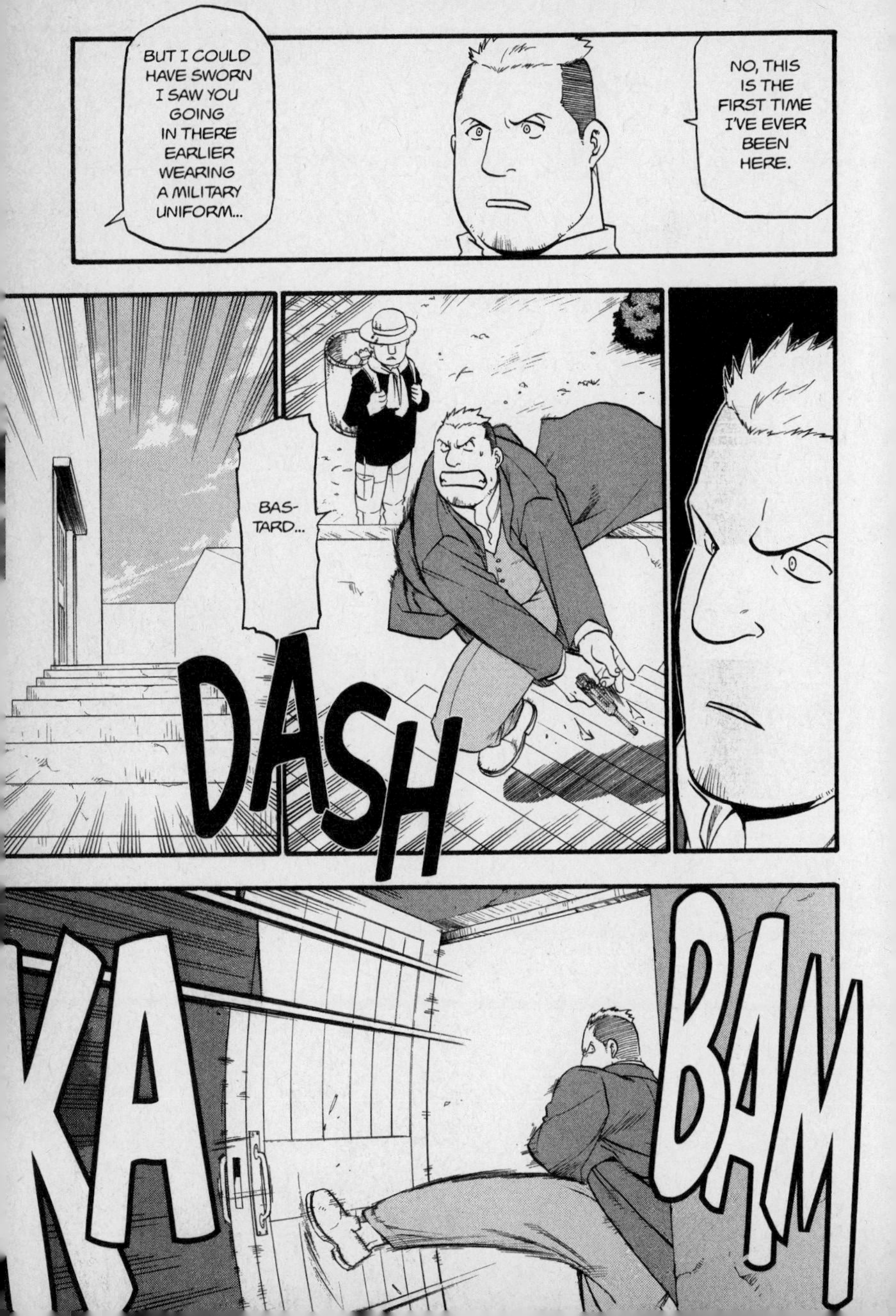
NO, THIS IS THE FIRST TIME I'VE EVER BEEN HERE.
BUT I COULD HAVE SWORN I SAW YOU GOING IN THERE EARLIER WEARING A MILITARY UNIFORM...
BAS-TARD...
DASH
KA
BAM

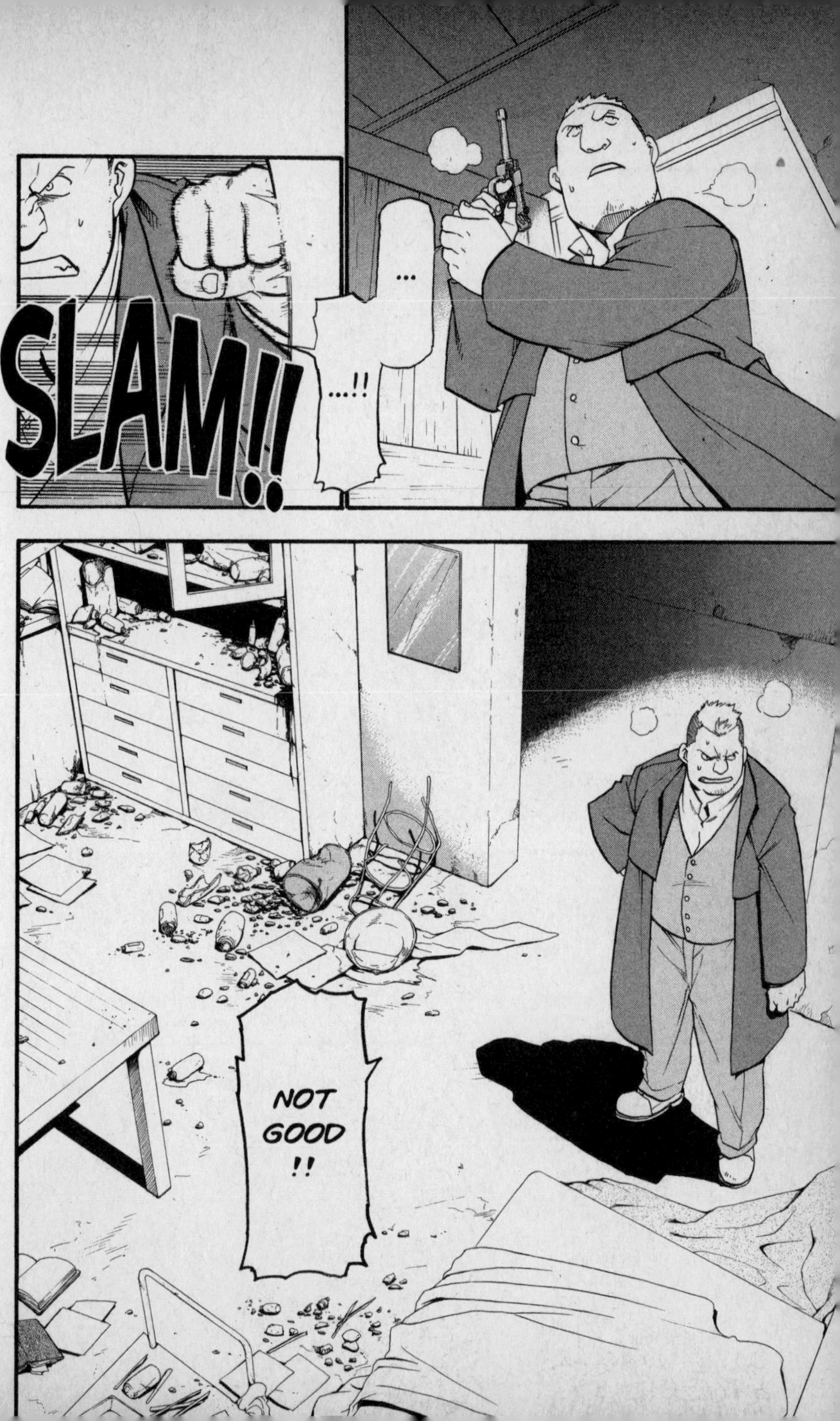
...
...!!
SLAM!!
NOT GOOD !!

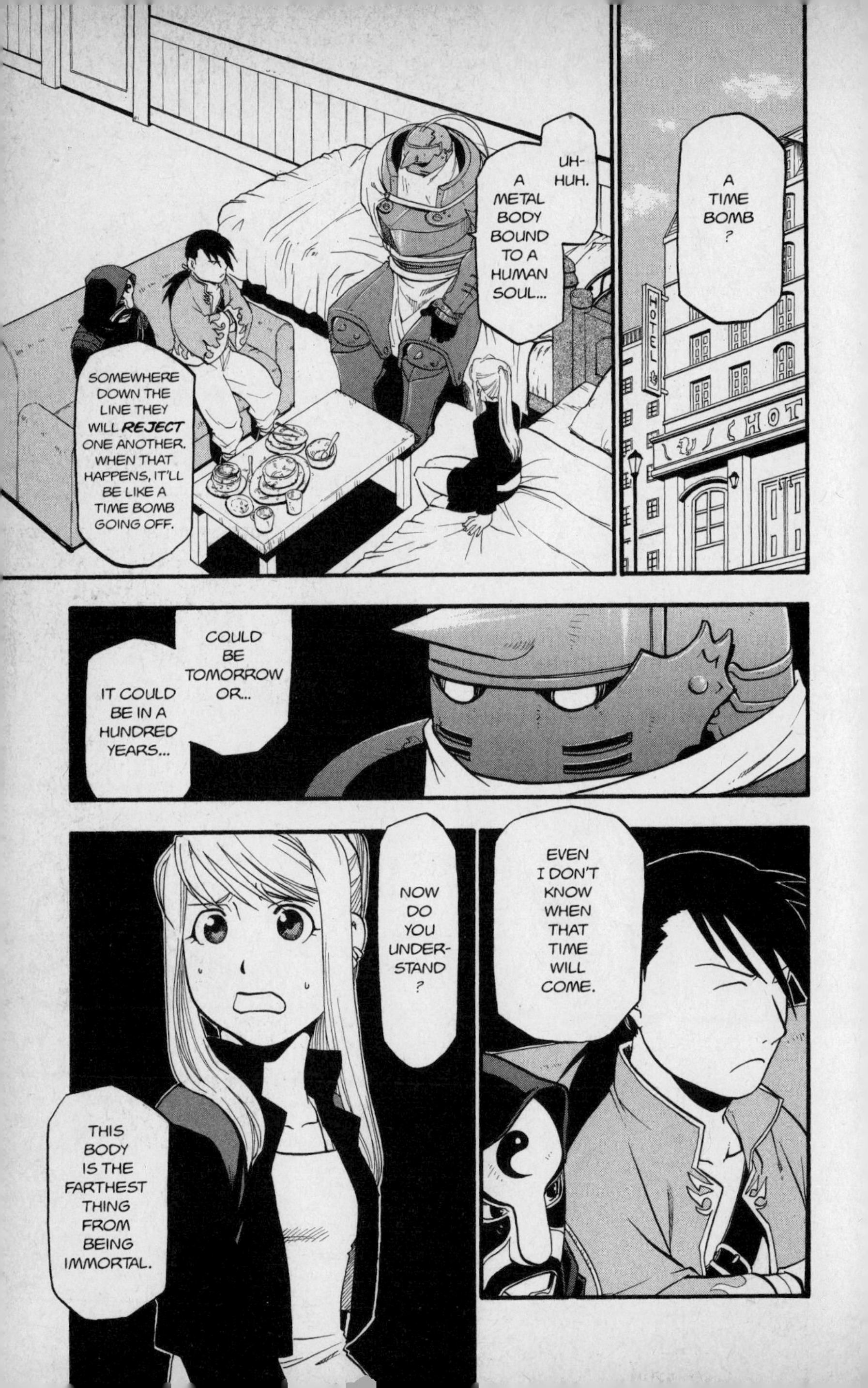
A TIME BOMB?
UH-HUH.
A METAL BODY BOUND TO A HUMAN SOUL...
SOMEWHERE DOWN THE LINE THEY WILL *REJECT* ONE ANOTHER. WHEN THAT HAPPENS, IT'LL BE LIKE A TIME BOMB GOING OFF.
COULD BE TOMORROW OR...
IT COULD BE IN A HUNDRED YEARS...
EVEN I DON'T KNOW WHEN THAT TIME WILL COME.
NOW DO YOU UNDERSTAND?
THIS BODY IS THE FARTHEST THING FROM BEING IMMORTAL.

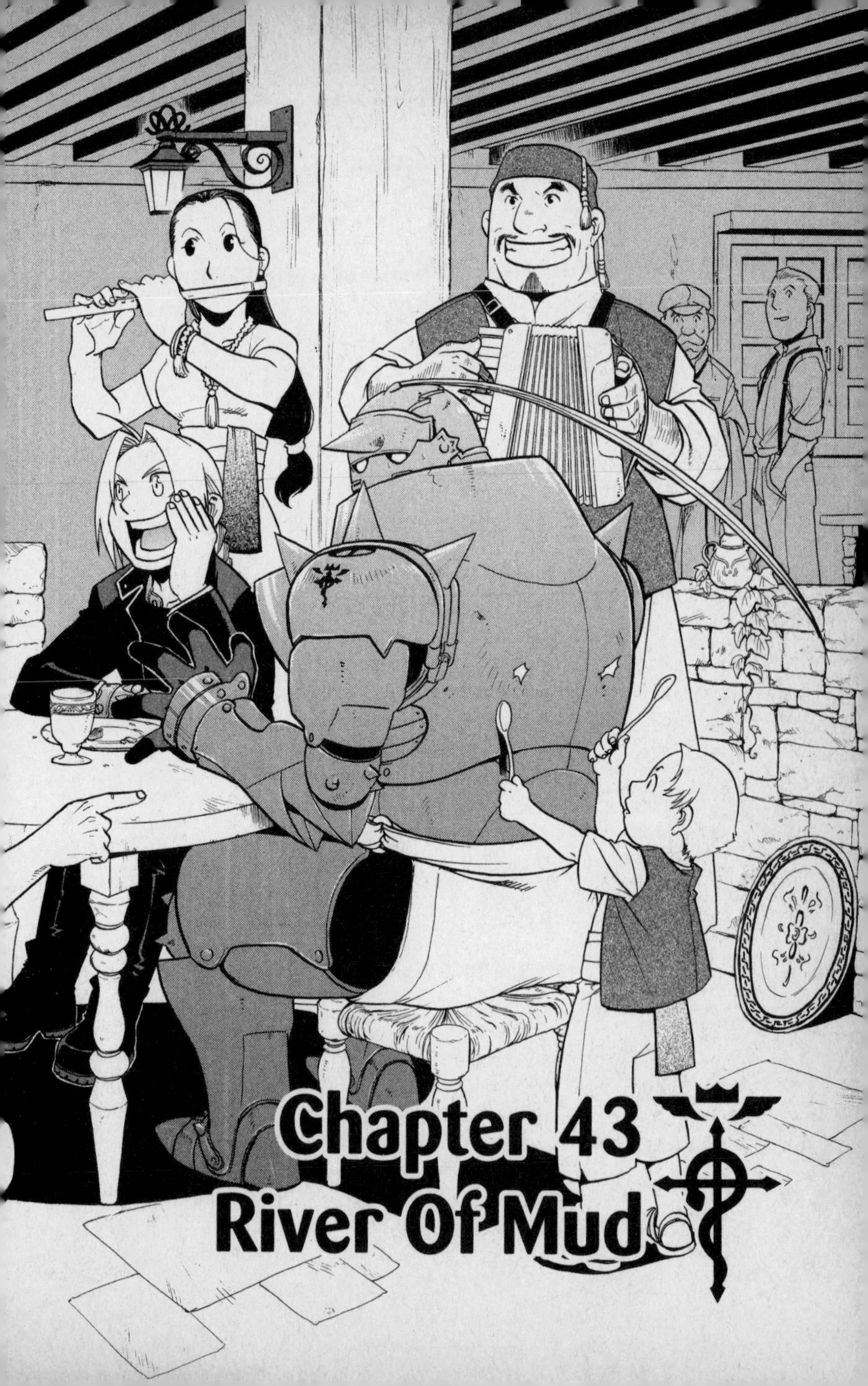
Chapter 43
River Of Mud

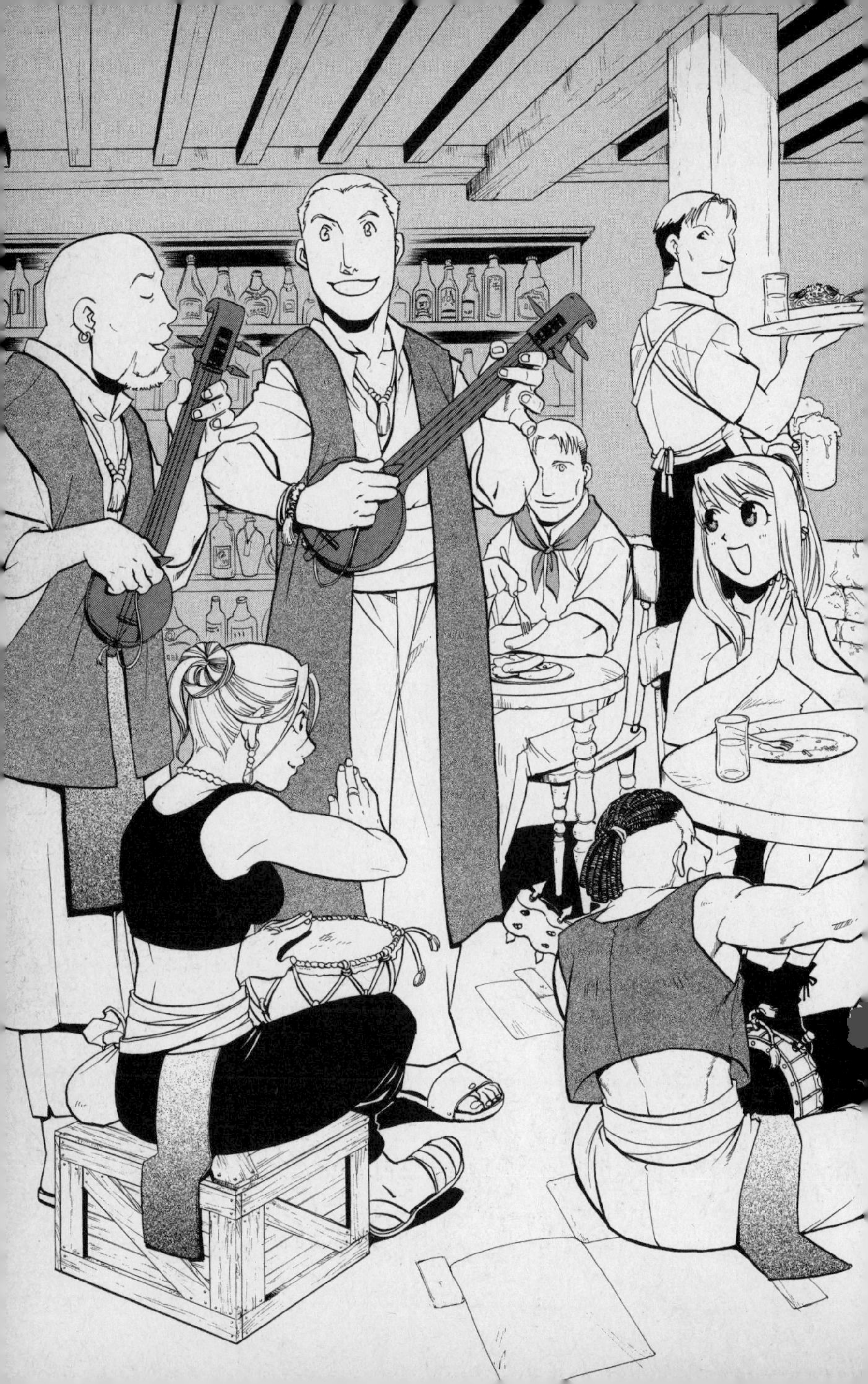

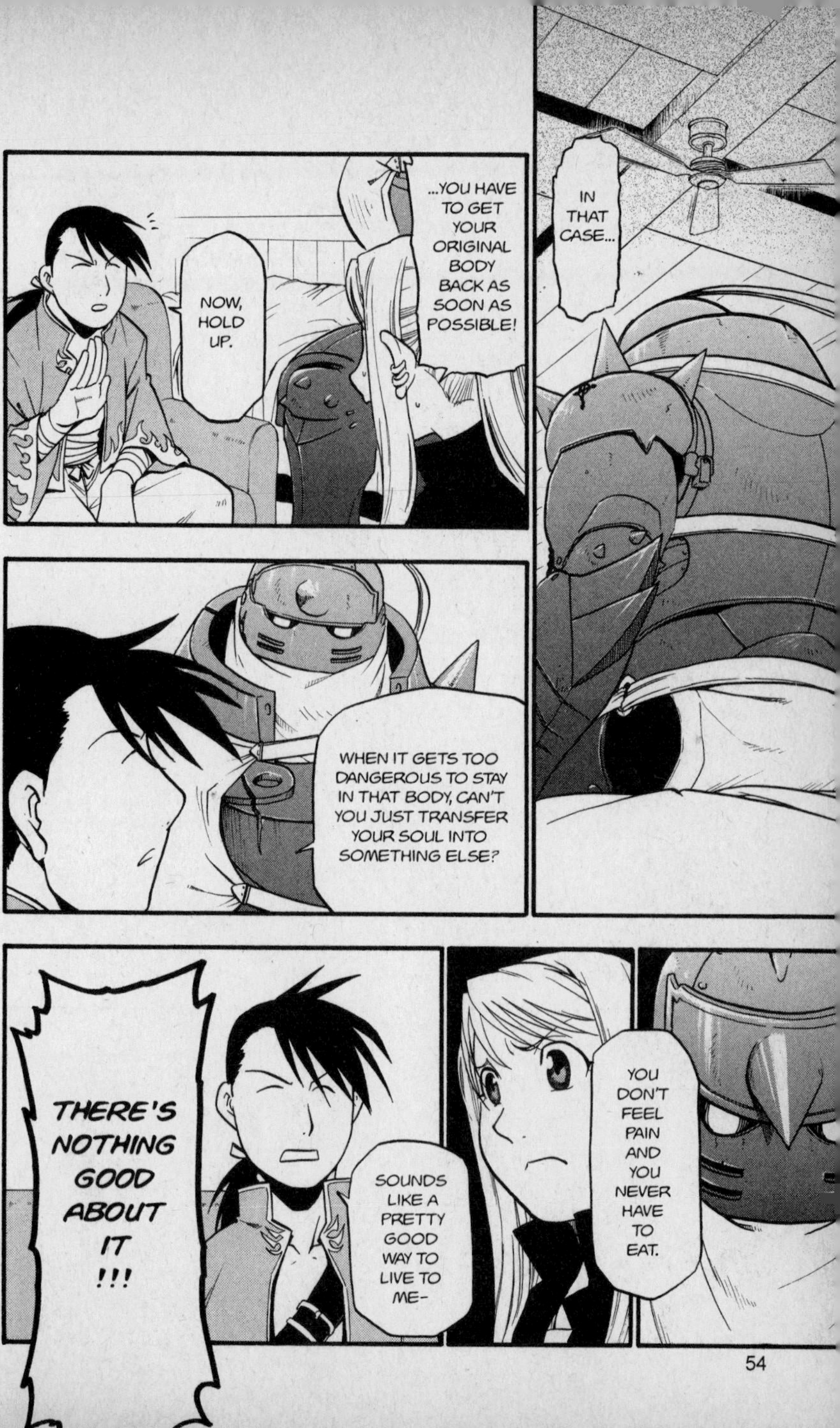
IN THAT CASE...
...YOU HAVE TO GET YOUR ORIGINAL BODY BACK AS SOON AS POSSIBLE!
NOW, HOLD UP.
WHEN IT GETS TOO DANGEROUS TO STAY IN THAT BODY, CAN'T YOU JUST TRANSFER YOUR SOUL INTO SOMETHING ELSE?
YOU DON'T FEEL PAIN AND YOU NEVER HAVE TO EAT.
SOUNDS LIKE A PRETTY GOOD WAY TO LIVE TO ME-
THERE'S NOTHING GOOD ABOUT IT!!!

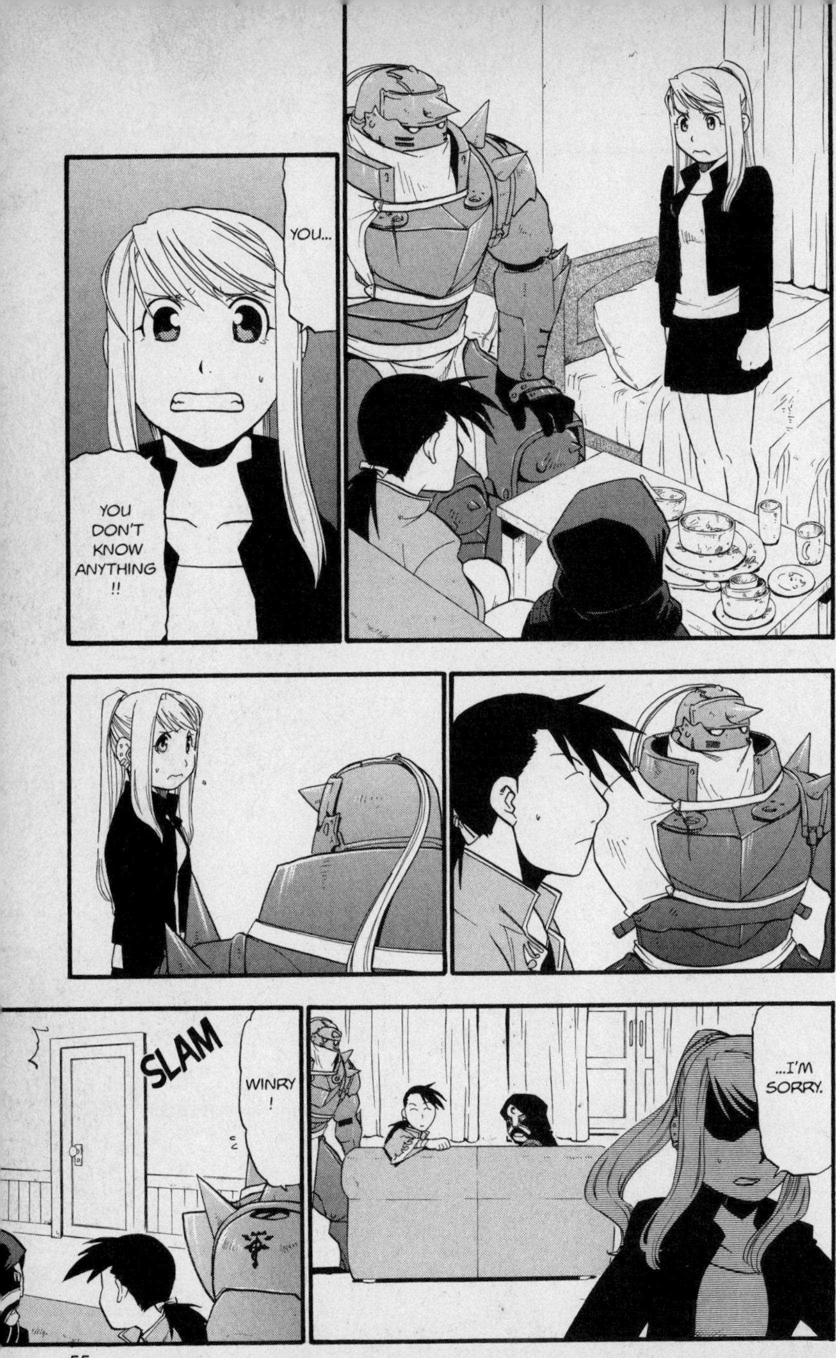
YOU...
YOU DON'T KNOW ANYTHING !!
...I'M SORRY.
SLAM
WINRY !

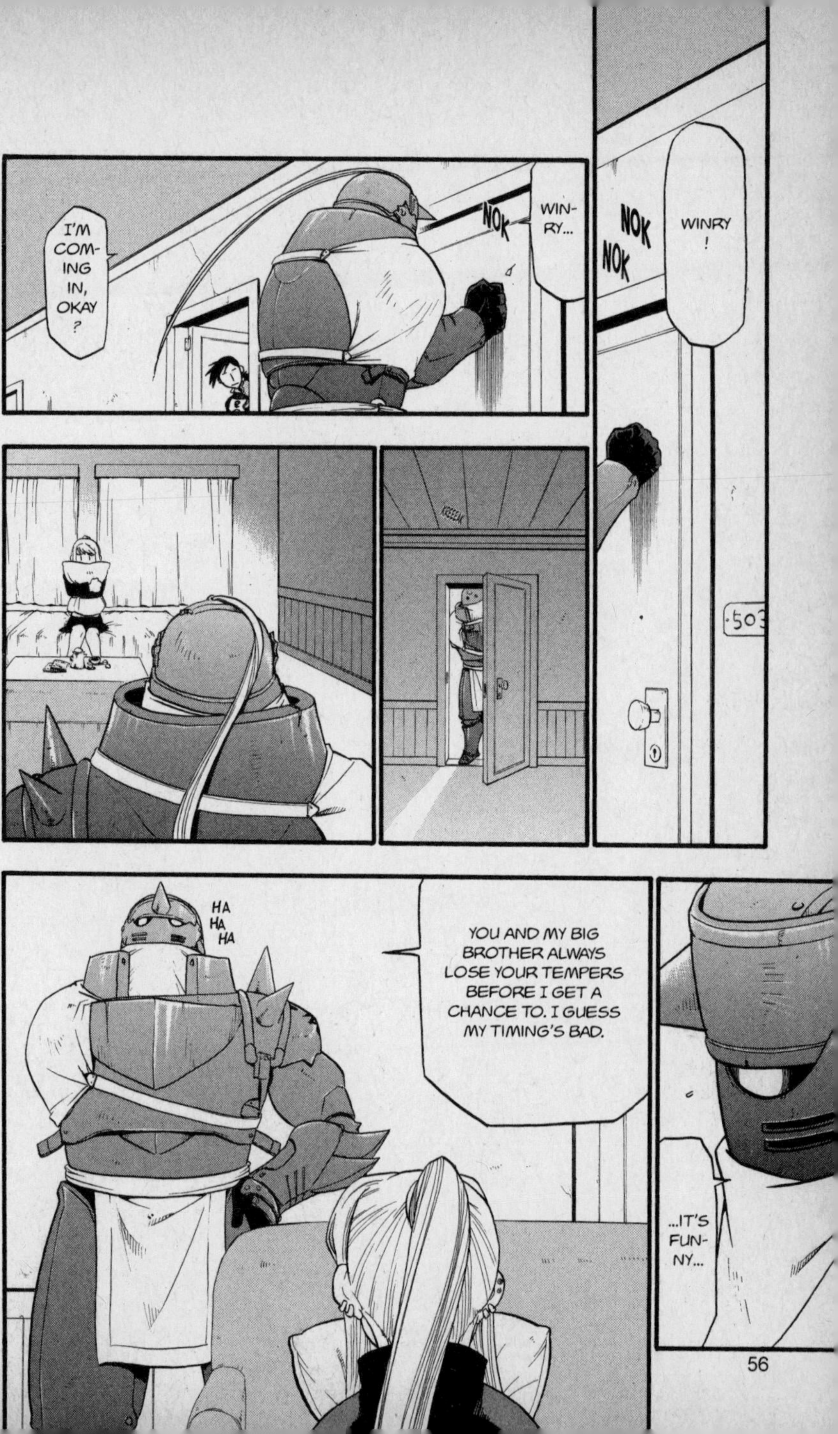
NOK
NOK
WINRY!
NOK
WINRY...
I'M COMING IN, OKAY?
...IT'S FUNNY...
YOU AND MY BIG BROTHER ALWAYS LOSE YOUR TEMPERS BEFORE I GET A CHANCE TO. I GUESS MY TIMING'S BAD.
HA HA HA

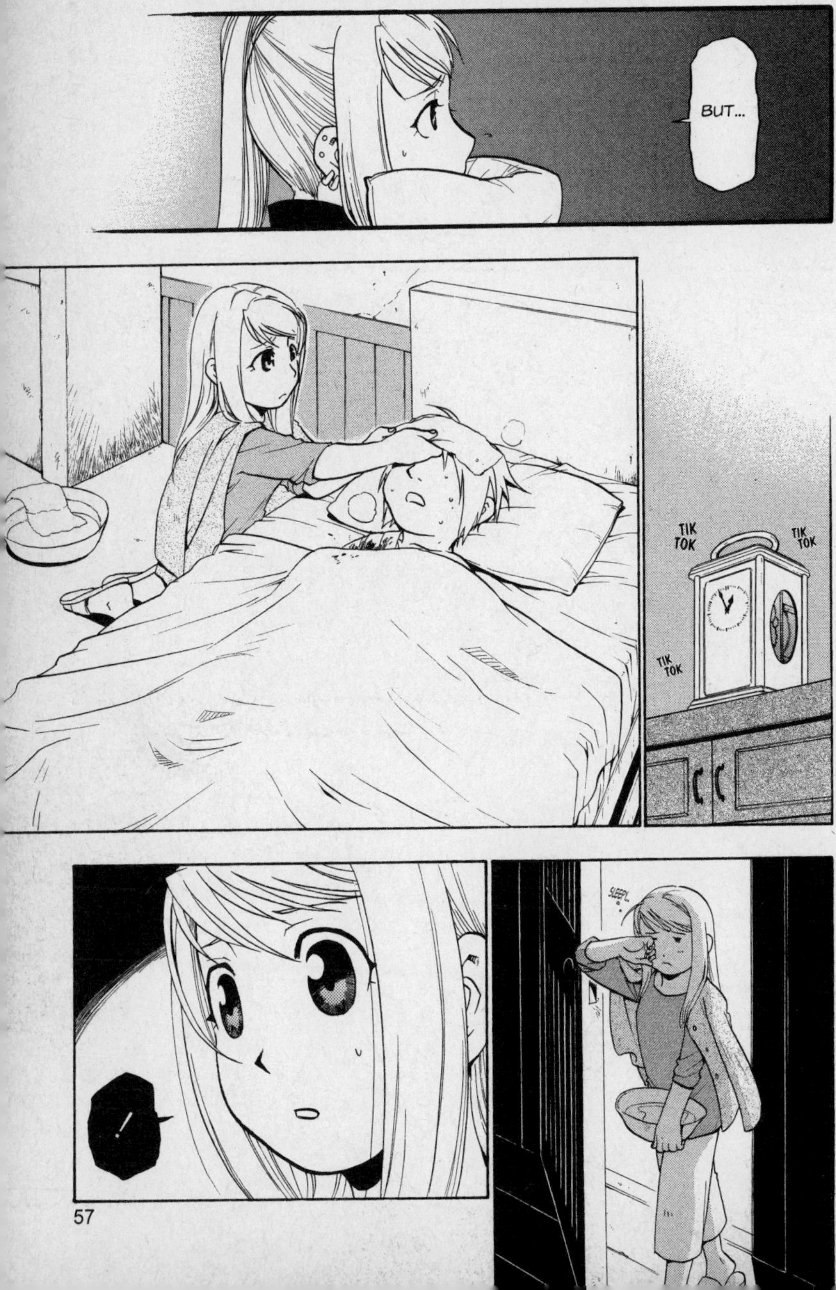
BUT...
TIK TOK
TIK TOK
TIK TOK
SLEEPL...
!

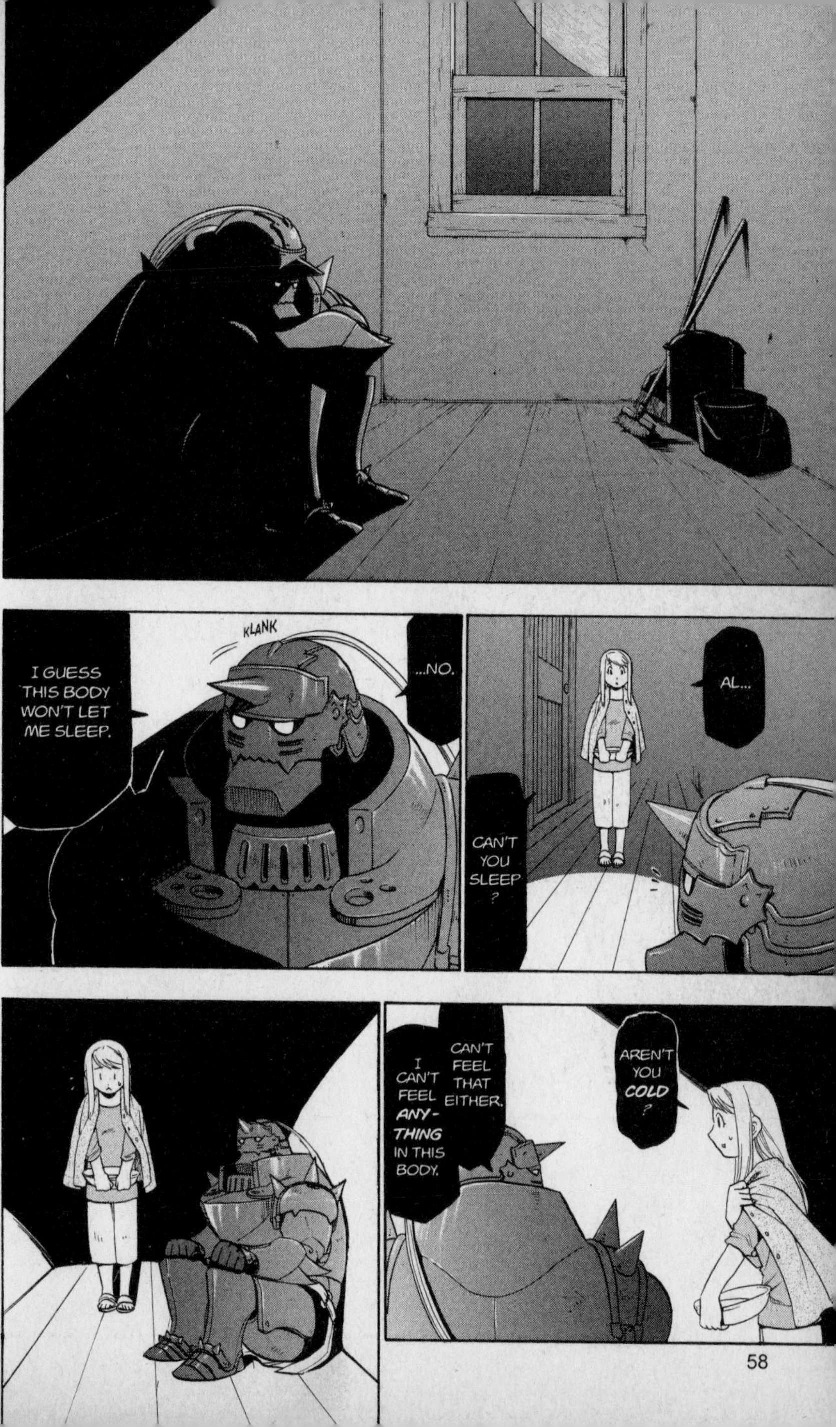
AL...
CAN'T YOU SLEEP?
...NO.
KLANK
I GUESS THIS BODY WON'T LET ME SLEEP.
AREN'T YOU COLD?
CAN'T FEEL THAT EITHER.
I CAN'T FEEL ANYTHING IN THIS BODY.

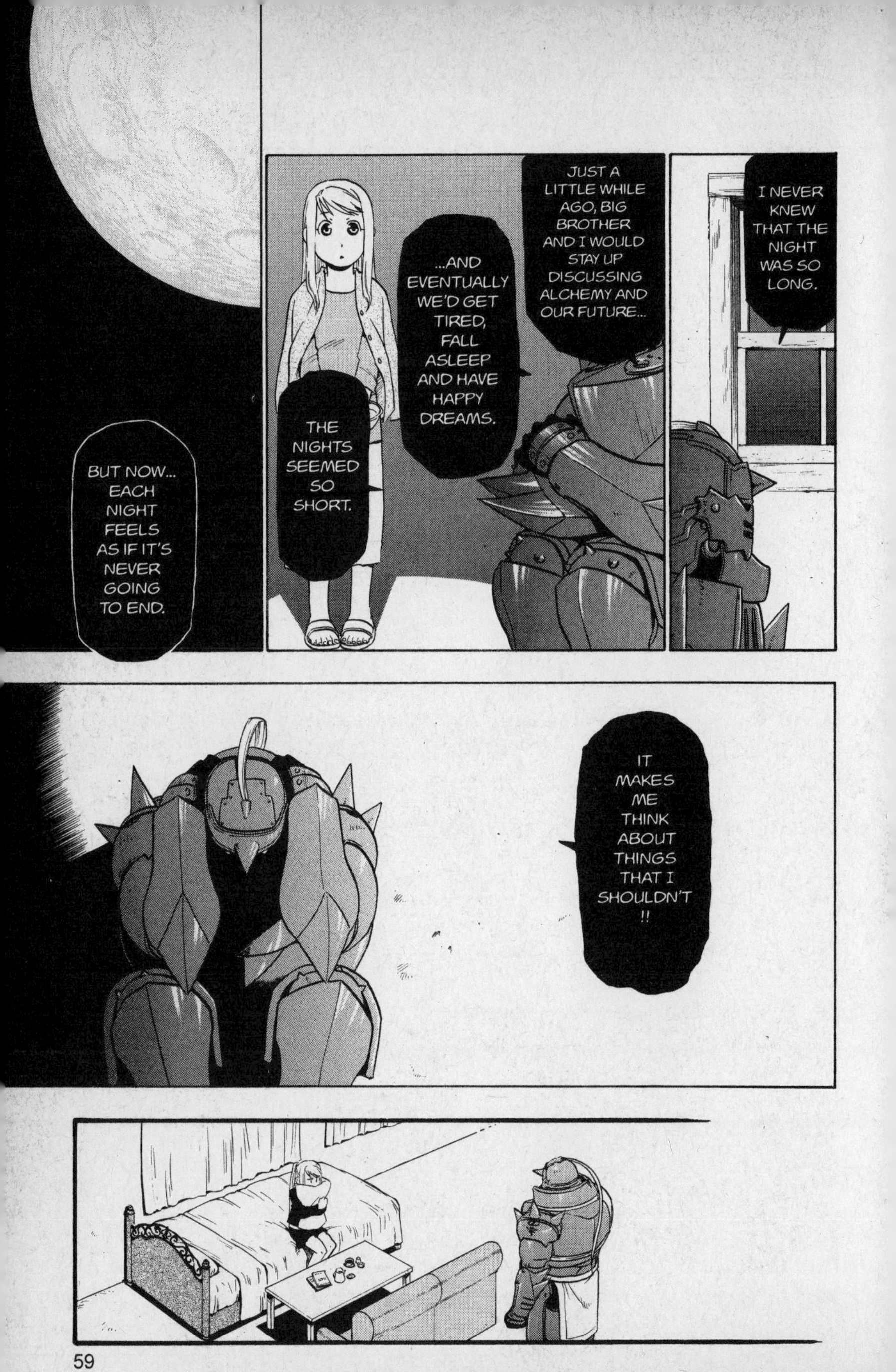
I NEVER KNEW THAT THE NIGHT WAS SO LONG.
JUST A LITTLE WHILE AGO, BIG BROTHER AND I WOULD STAY UP DISCUSSING ALCHEMY AND OUR FUTURE...
...AND EVENTUALLY WE'D GET TIRED, FALL ASLEEP AND HAVE HAPPY DREAMS.
THE NIGHTS SEEMED SO SHORT.
BUT NOW... EACH NIGHT FEELS AS IF IT'S NEVER GOING TO END.
IT MAKES ME THINK ABOUT THINGS THAT I SHOULDN'T !!

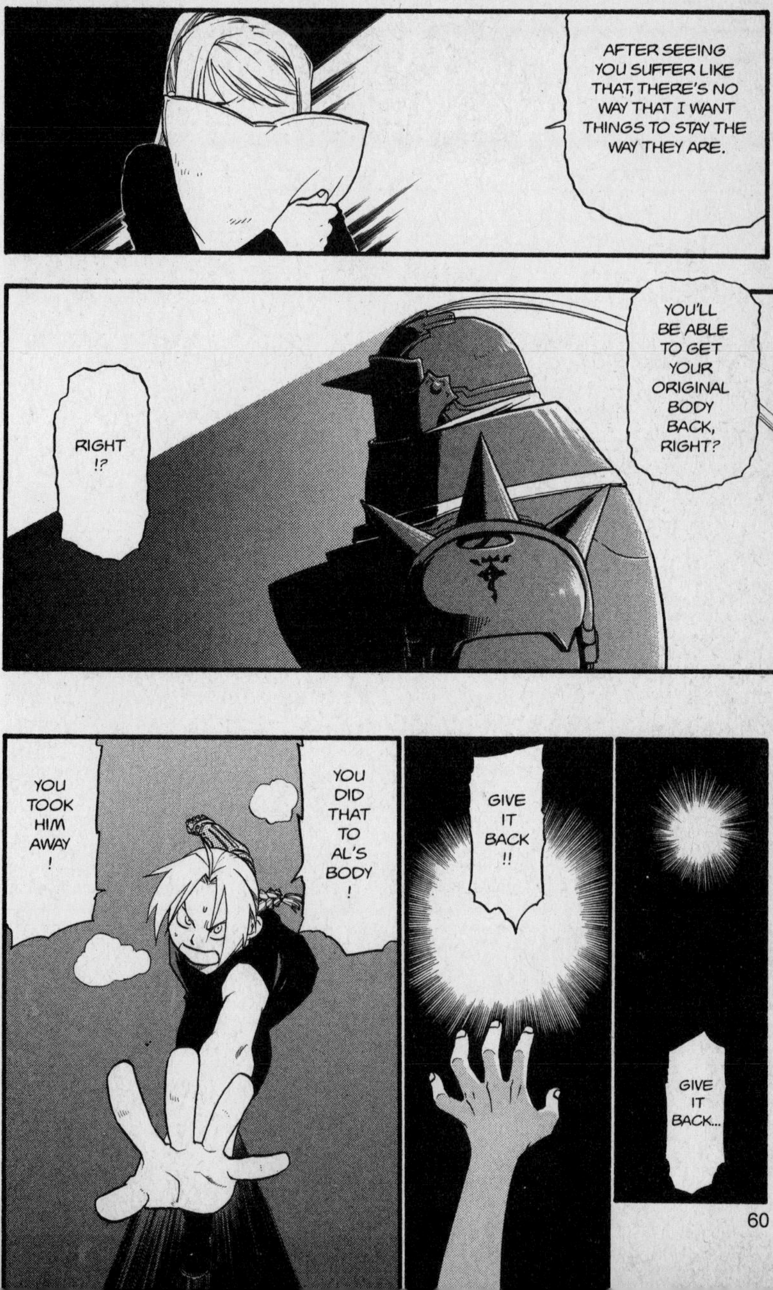
AFTER SEEING YOU SUFFER LIKE THAT, THERE'S NO WAY THAT I WANT THINGS TO STAY THE WAY THEY ARE.
YOU'LL BE ABLE TO GET YOUR ORIGINAL BODY BACK, RIGHT?
RIGHT !?
GIVE IT BACK...
GIVE IT BACK !!
YOU DID THAT TO AL'S BODY !
YOU TOOK HIM AWAY !

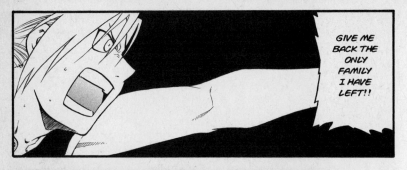

GIVE ME BACK THE ONLY FAMILY I HAVE LEFT!!
GIVE HIM BACK?
WHAT-EVER DO YOU MEAN?
THE PERSON WHO PULLED BACK YOUR BROTHER'S SOUL...
...AND GAVE HIM A BODY THAT CAN'T SLEEP...
...THAT CAN'T FEEL PAIN...
...THAT CAN'T FEEL WARMTH...
...A BODY THAT CAN'T EVEN CRY...

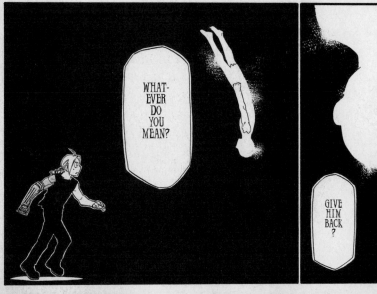

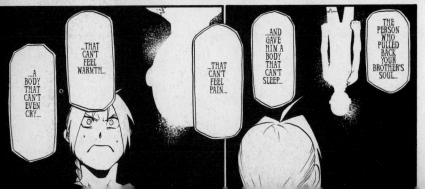

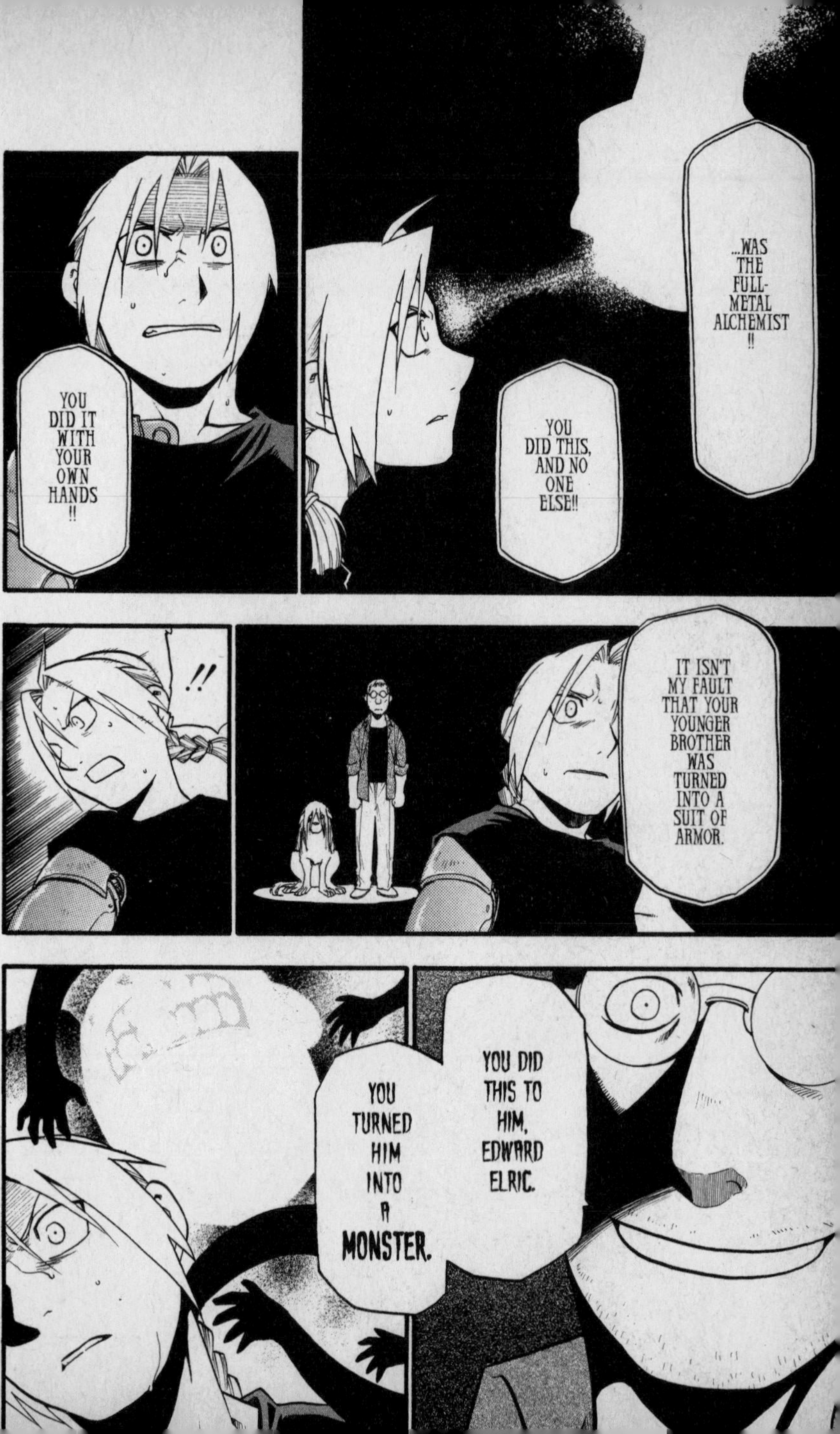
...WAS THE FULL-METAL ALCHEMIST!!
YOU DID THIS, AND NO ONE ELSE!!
YOU DID IT WITH YOUR OWN HANDS!!
IT ISN'T MY FAULT THAT YOUR YOUNGER BROTHER WAS TURNED INTO A SUIT OF ARMOR.
!!
YOU DID THIS TO HIM, EDWARD ELRIC.
YOU TURNED HIM INTO A MONSTER.

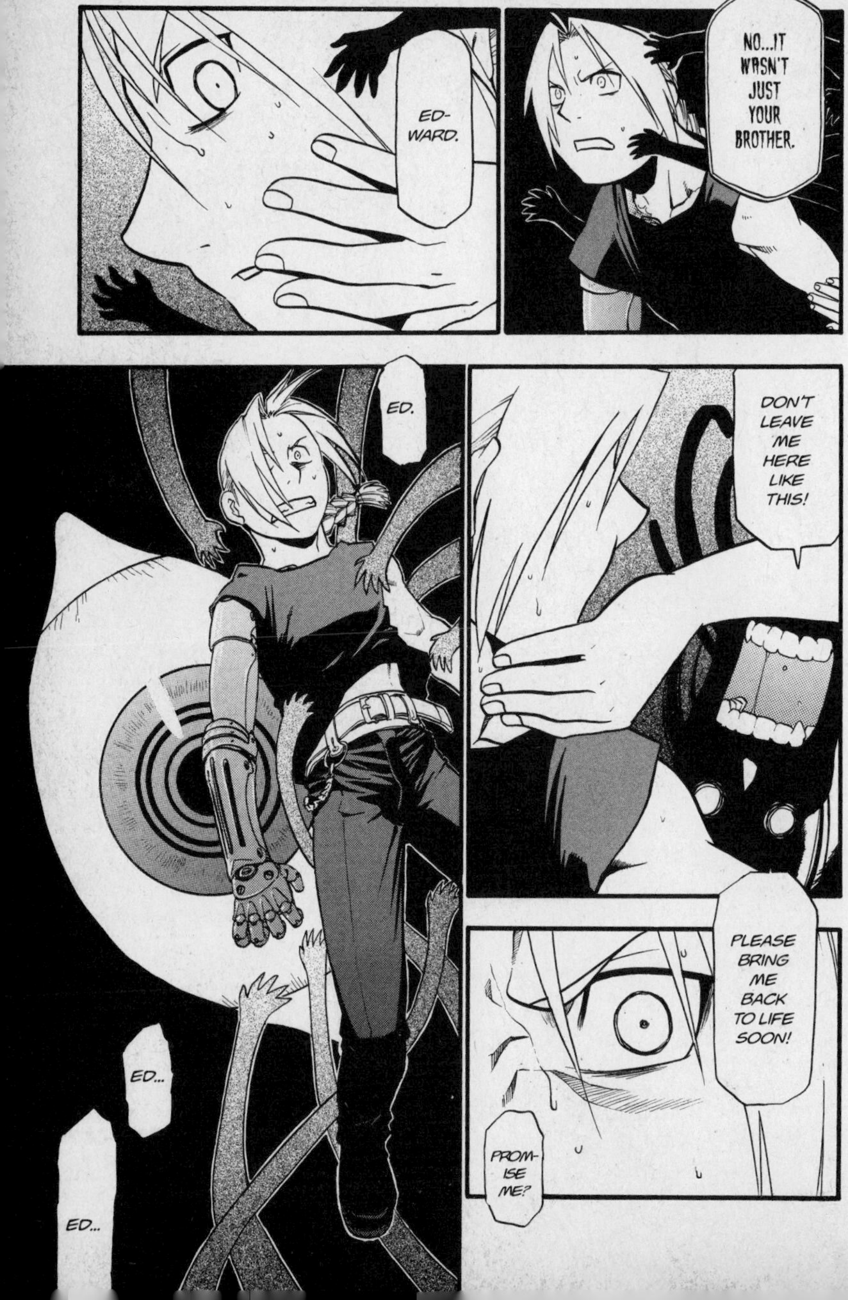
NO...IT WASN'T JUST YOUR BROTHER.
ED-WARD.
DON'T LEAVE ME HERE LIKE THIS!
PLEASE BRING ME BACK TO LIFE SOON!
PROMISE ME?
ED.
ED...
ED...

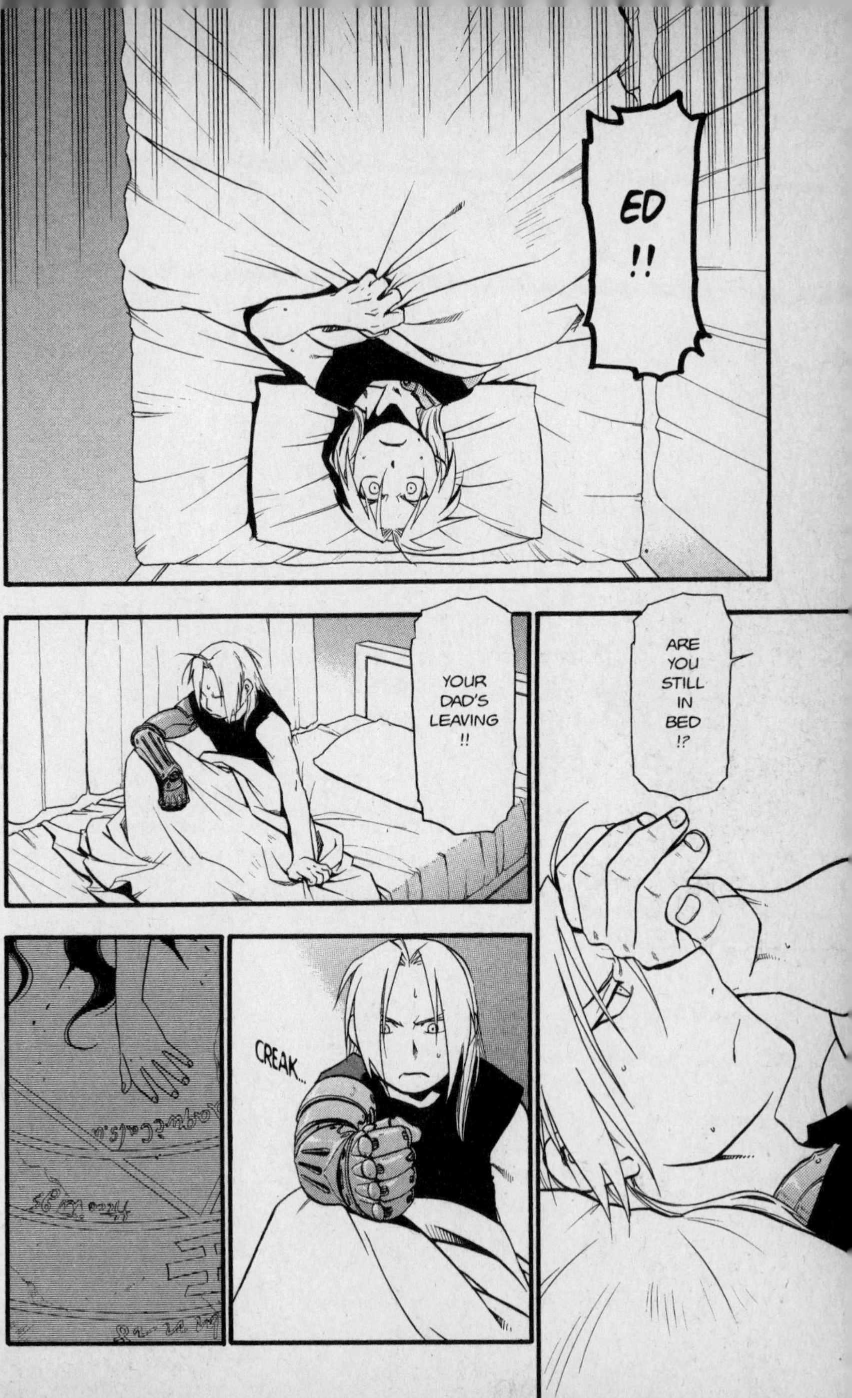
ED !!
ARE YOU STILL IN BED !?
YOUR DAD'S LEAVING !!
CREAK...

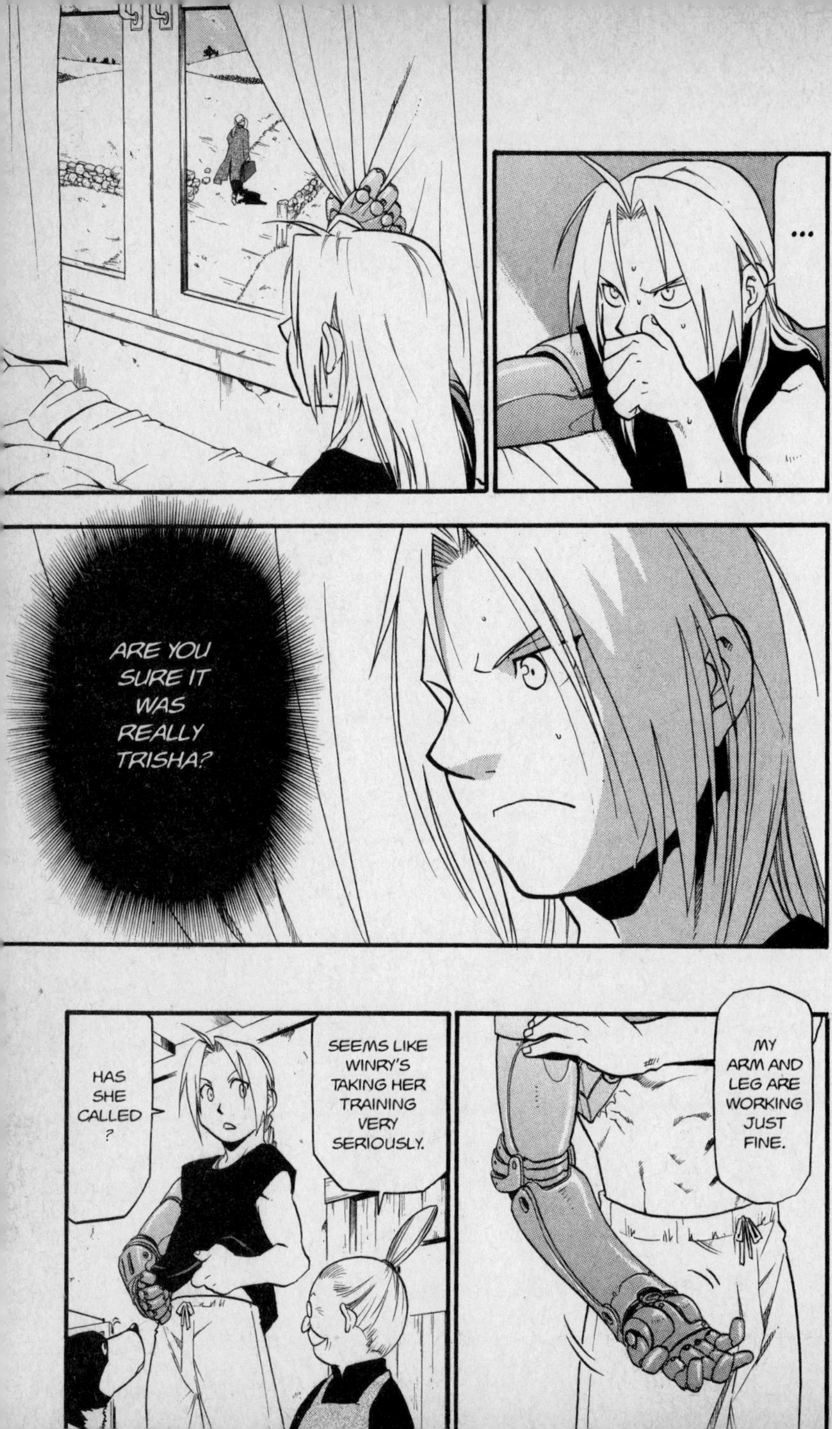
...
ARE YOU SURE IT WAS REALLY TRISHA?
MY ARM AND LEG ARE WORKING JUST FINE.
SEEMS LIKE WINRY'S TAKING HER TRAINING VERY SERIOUSLY.
HAS SHE CALLED?

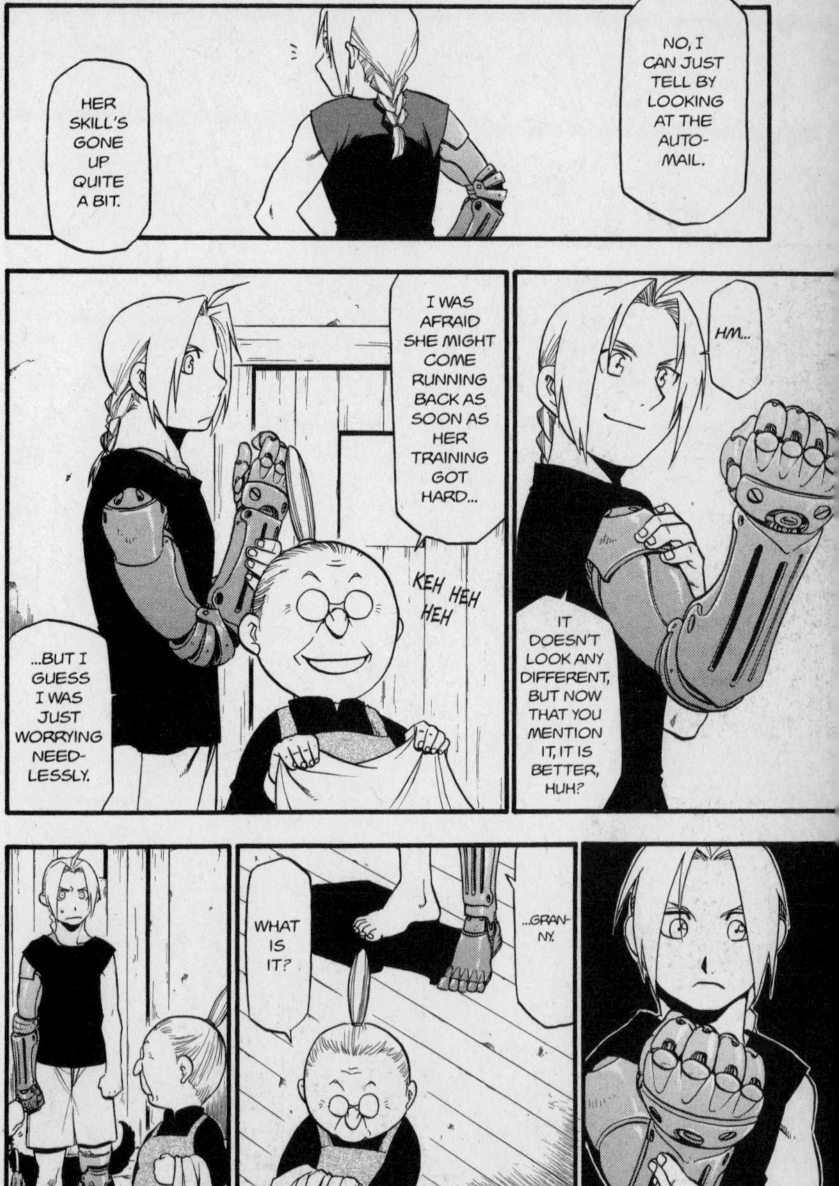
NO, I CAN JUST TELL BY LOOKING AT THE AUTO-MAIL.
HER SKILL'S GONE UP QUITE A BIT.
HM...
IT DOESN'T LOOK ANY DIFFERENT, BUT NOW THAT YOU MENTION IT, IT IS BETTER, HUH?
I WAS AFRAID SHE MIGHT COME RUNNING BACK AS SOON AS HER TRAINING GOT HARD...
KEH HEH HEH
...BUT I GUESS I WAS JUST WORRYING NEED-LESSLY.
...GRAN-NY.
WHAT IS IT?

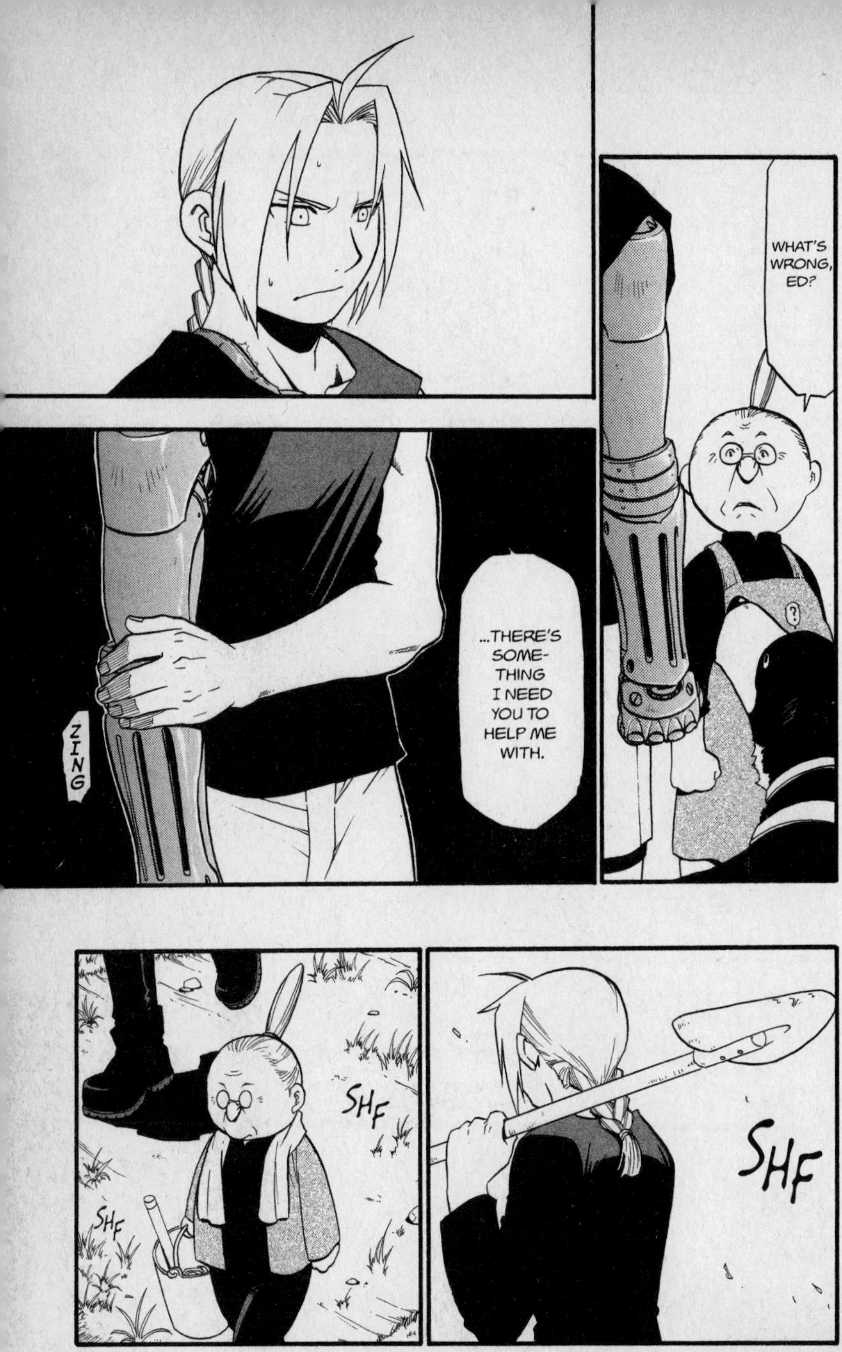
WHAT'S WRONG, ED?
...THERE'S SOME-THING I NEED YOU TO HELP ME WITH.
ZING
SHF
SHF
SHF

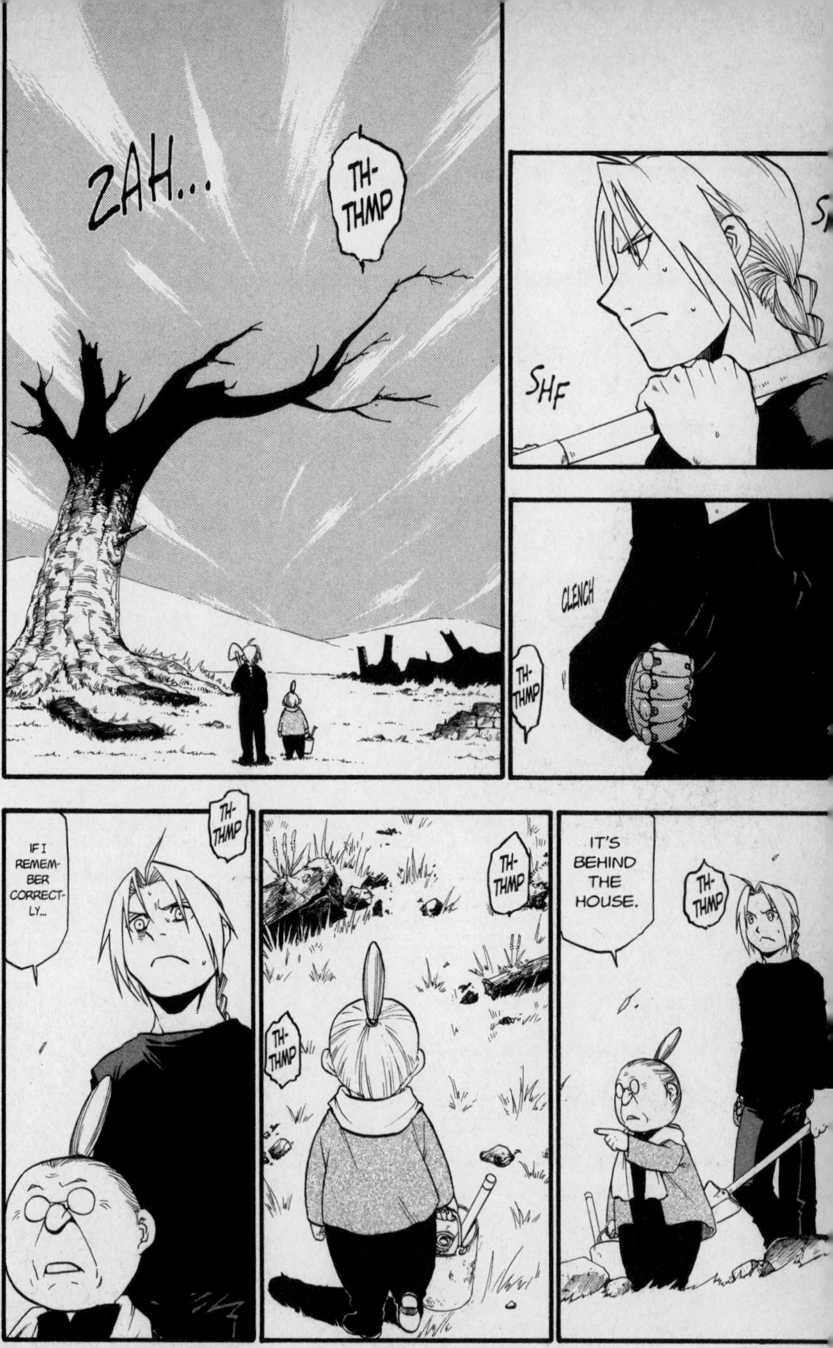
SHF
CLENCH
TH-THMP
TH-THMP
ZAH...
IT'S BEHIND THE HOUSE.
TH-THMP
TH-THMP
TH-THMP
TH-THMP
IF I REMEMBER CORRECTLY...

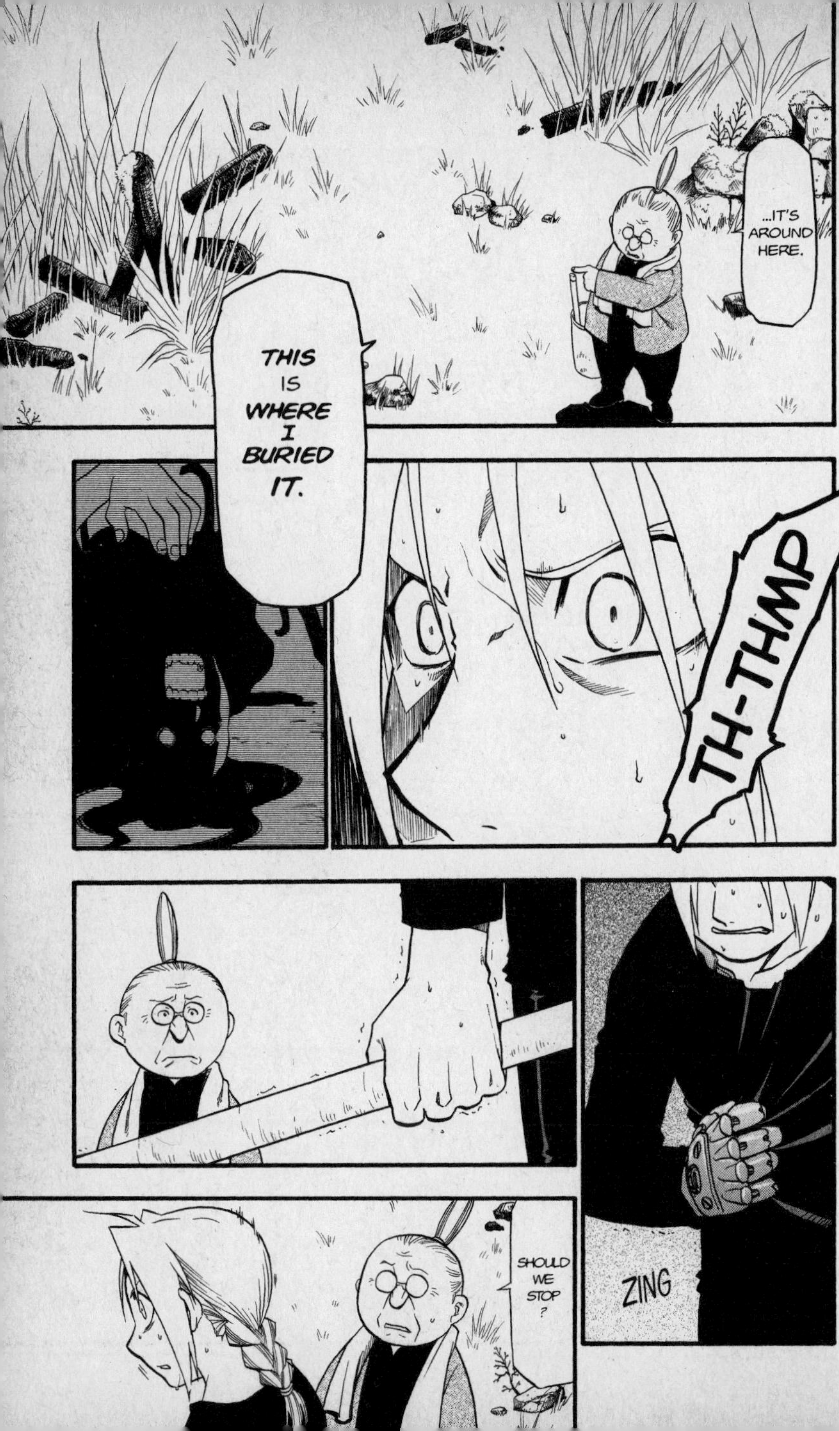
...IT'S AROUND HERE.
THIS IS WHERE I BURIED IT.
TH-THMP
ZING
SHOULD WE STOP?

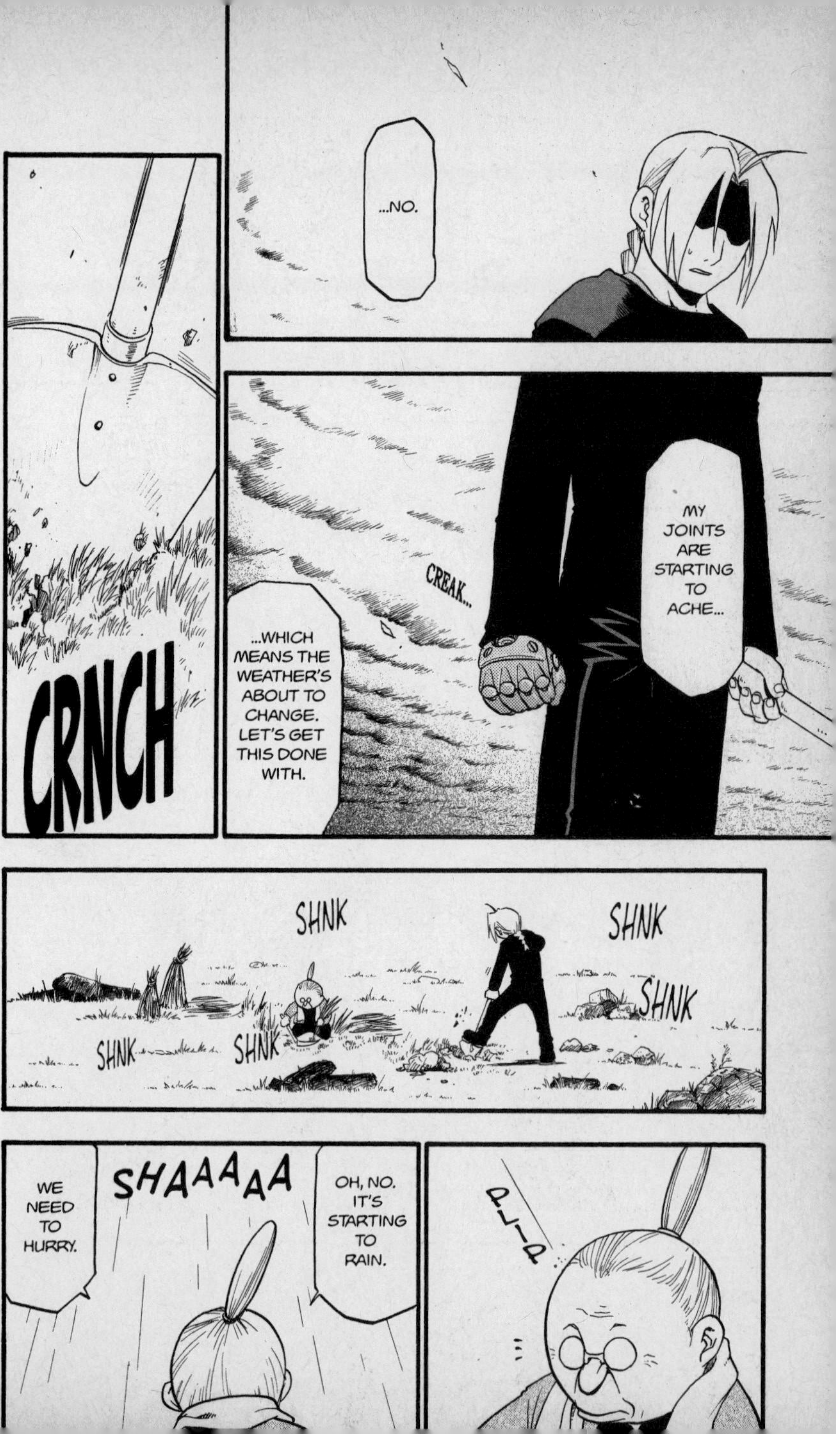
...NO.
MY JOINTS ARE STARTING TO ACHE...
CREAK...
...WHICH MEANS THE WEATHER'S ABOUT TO CHANGE. LET'S GET THIS DONE WITH.
CRNCH
SHNK
SHNK
SHNK
SHNK
SHNK
PLIP
OH, NO. IT'S STARTING TO RAIN.
SHAAAAA
WE NEED TO HURRY.

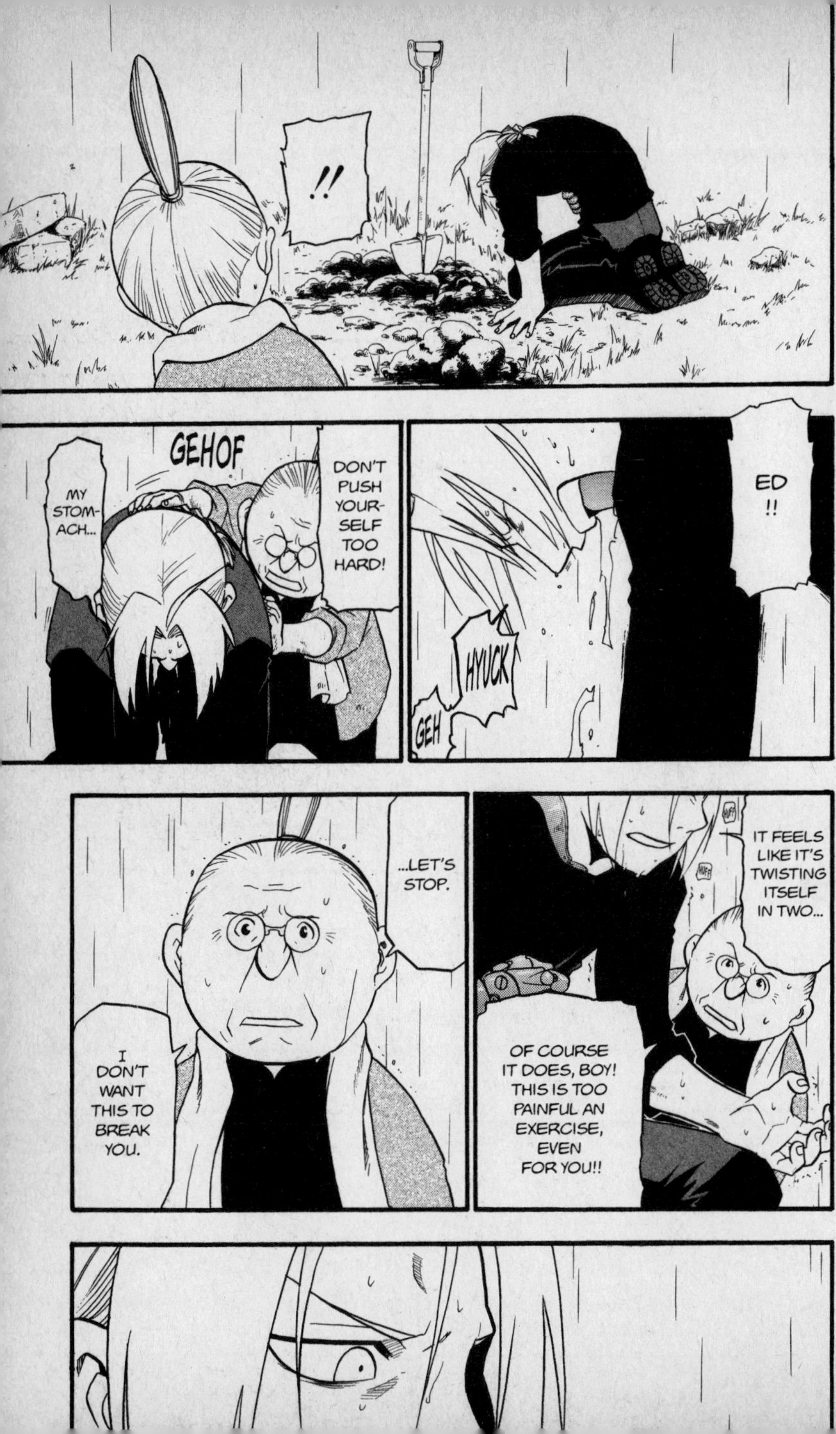
!!
ED !!
HYUCK
GEH
DON'T PUSH YOURSELF TOO HARD!
GEHOF
MY STOMACH...
HUFF
IT FEELS LIKE IT'S TWISTING ITSELF IN TWO...
HUFF
OF COURSE IT DOES, BOY! THIS IS TOO PAINFUL AN EXERCISE, EVEN FOR YOU!!
...LET'S STOP.
I DON'T WANT THIS TO BREAK YOU.

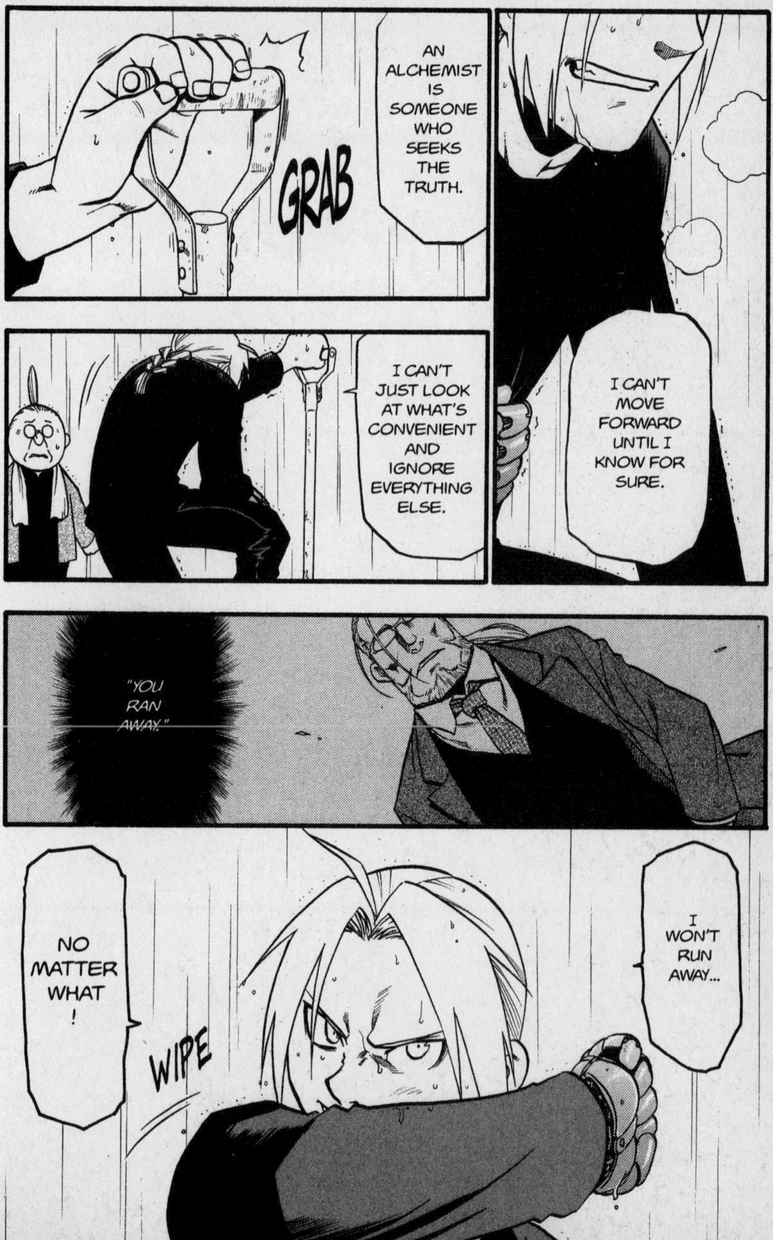
I CAN'T MOVE FORWARD UNTIL I KNOW FOR SURE.
AN ALCHEMIST IS SOMEONE WHO SEEKS THE TRUTH.
GRAB
I CAN'T JUST LOOK AT WHAT'S CONVENIENT AND IGNORE EVERYTHING ELSE.
"YOU RAN AWAY."
I WON'T RUN AWAY...
NO MATTER WHAT!
WIPE

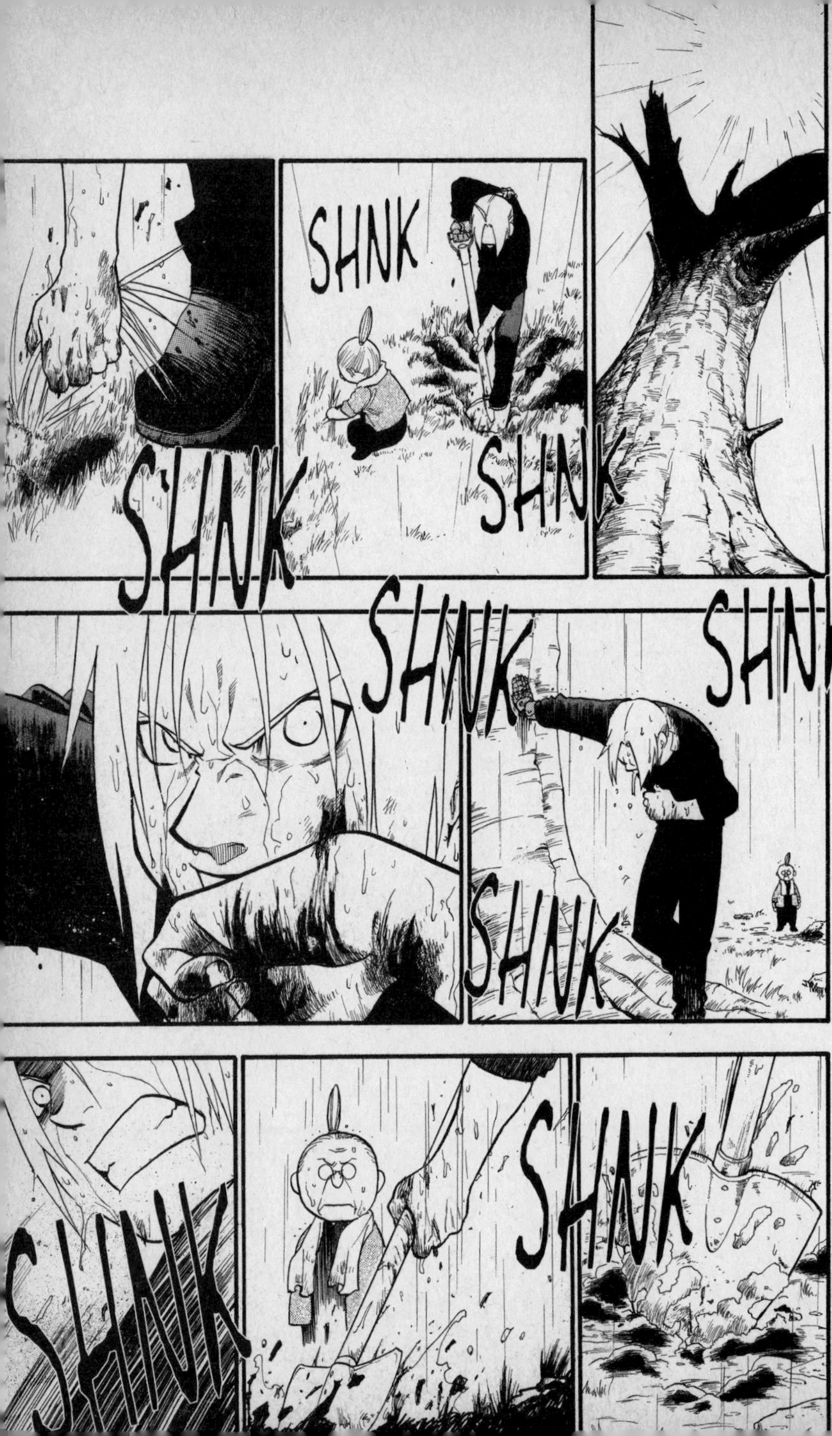
SHNK
SHNK
SHNK
SHNK
SHNK
SHNK
SHNK
SHNK
SHNK

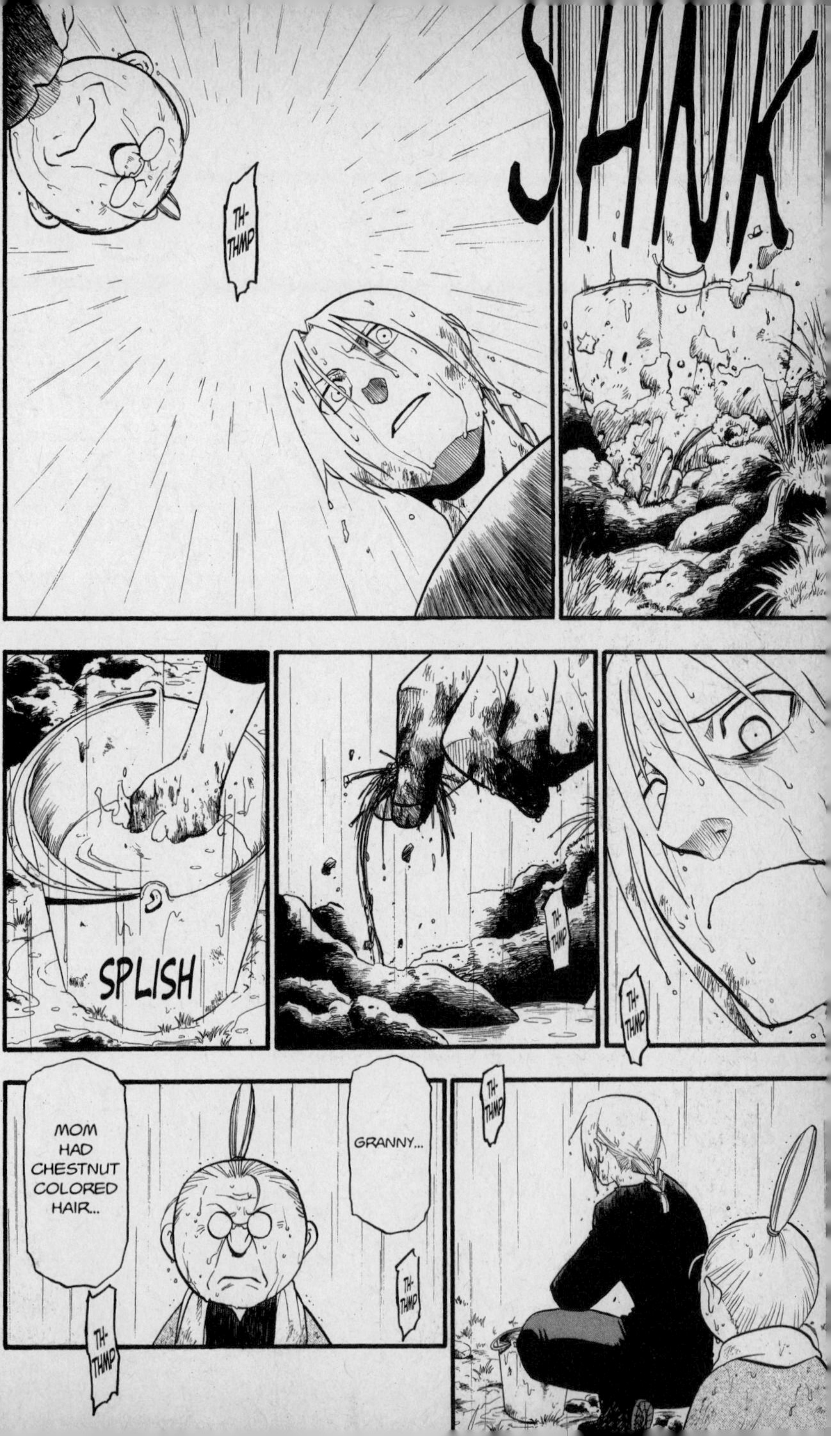
SHNK
TH-THMP
TH-THMP
TH-THMP
SPLISH
TH-THMP
GRANNY...
MOM HAD CHESTNUT COLORED HAIR...
TH-THMP
TH-THMP

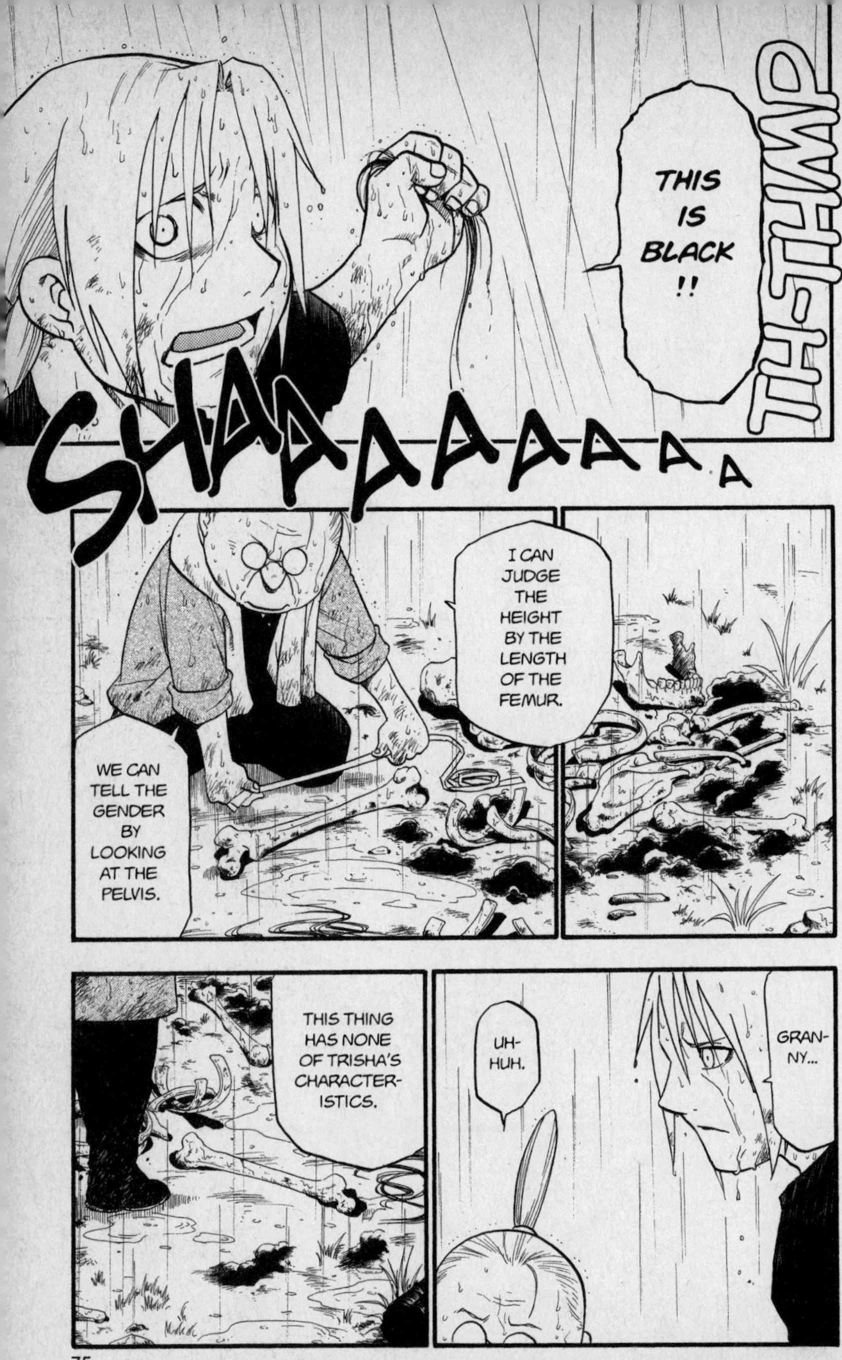
TH-THMP
THIS IS BLACK!!
SHAAAAAAAAA
I CAN JUDGE THE HEIGHT BY THE LENGTH OF THE FEMUR.
WE CAN TELL THE GENDER BY LOOKING AT THE PELVIS.
GRAN-NY...
UH-HUH.
THIS THING HAS NONE OF TRISHA'S CHARACTER-ISTICS.

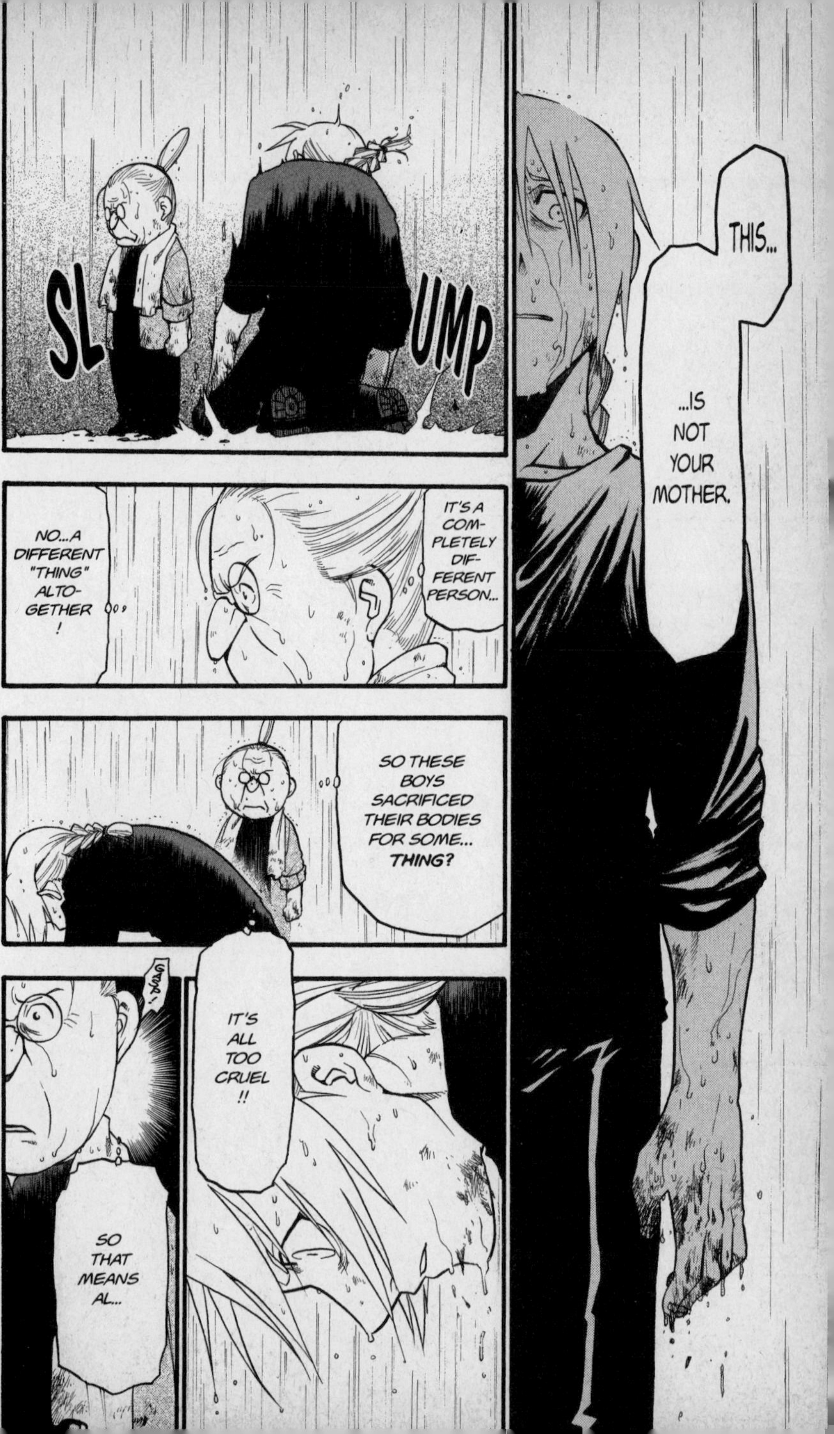

THIS...
...IS NOT YOUR MOTHER.
SL
UMP
IT'S A COMPLETELY DIFFERENT PERSON...
NO...A DIFFERENT "THING" ALTOGETHER!
SO THESE BOYS SACRIFICED THEIR BODIES FOR SOME... THING?
IT'S ALL TOO CRUEL!!
GASP!
SO THAT MEANS AL...

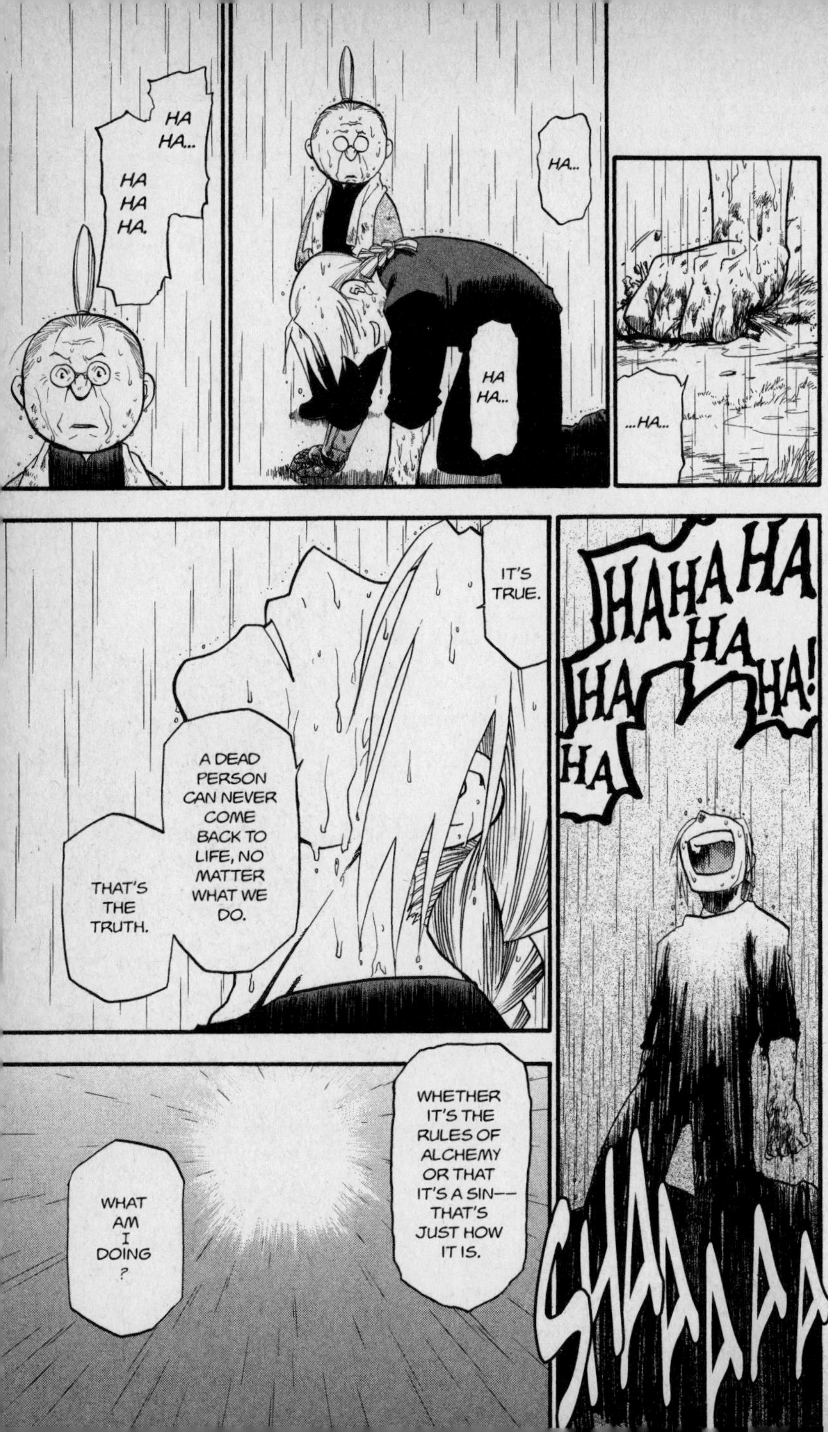
...HA...
HA...
HA HA...
HA HA...
HA HA HA.
HA HA HA HA HA HA HA HA!
SHAAAAA
IT'S TRUE.
A DEAD PERSON CAN NEVER COME BACK TO LIFE, NO MATTER WHAT WE DO.
THAT'S THE TRUTH.
WHETHER IT'S THE RULES OF ALCHEMY OR THAT IT'S A SIN-- THAT'S JUST HOW IT IS.
WHAT AM I DOING?

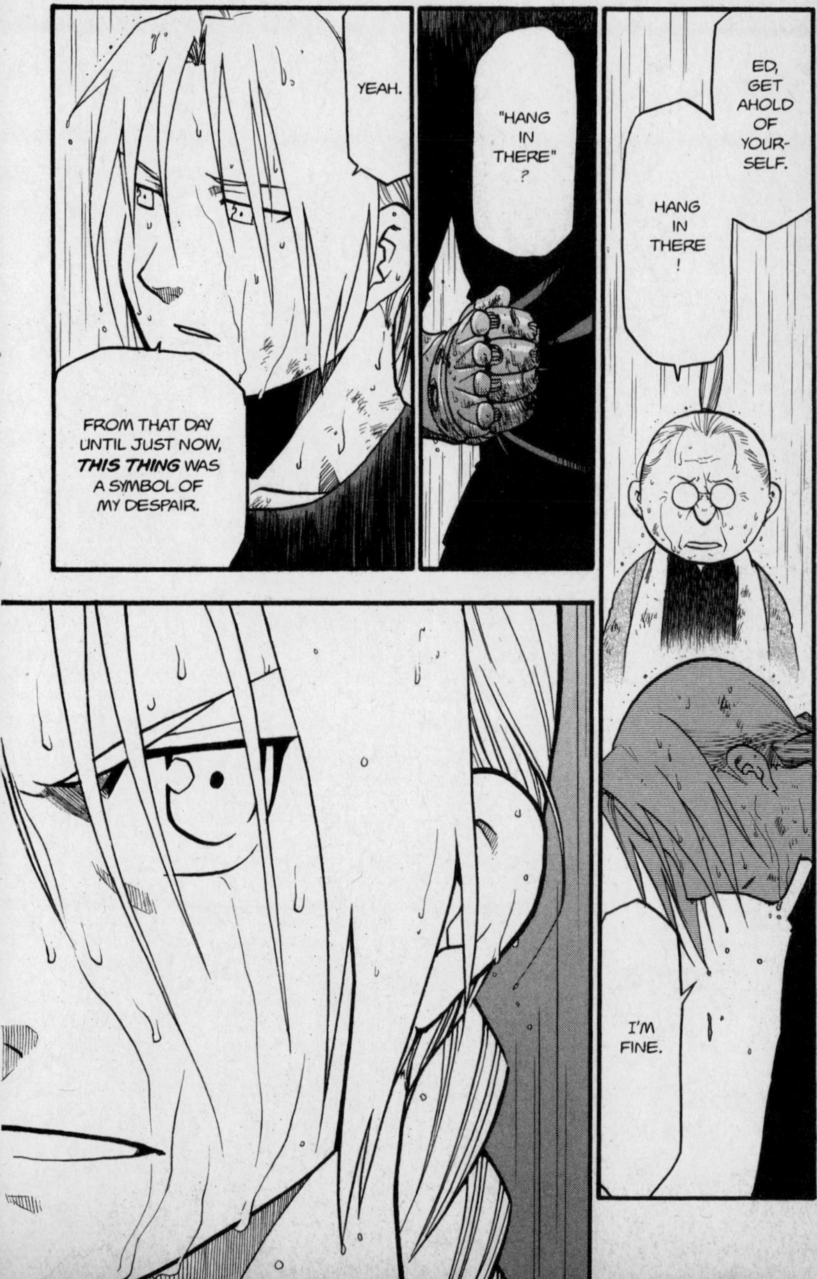

ED, GET AHOLD OF YOURSELF.
HANG IN THERE!
I'M FINE.
"HANG IN THERE"?
YEAH.
FROM THAT DAY UNTIL JUST NOW, THIS THING WAS A SYMBOL OF MY DESPAIR.

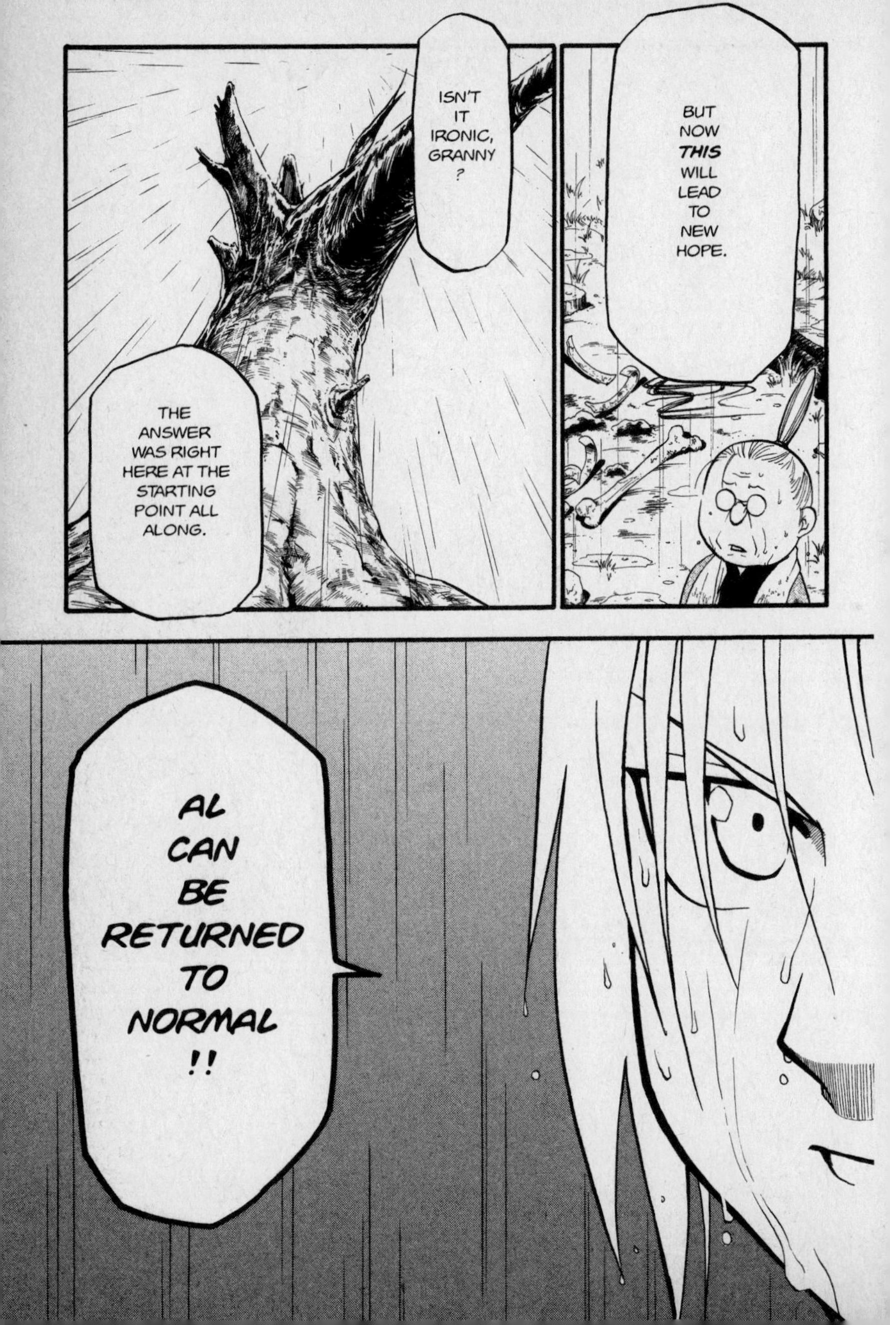
BUT NOW **THIS** WILL LEAD TO NEW HOPE.
ISN'T IT IRONIC, GRANNY?
THE ANSWER WAS RIGHT HERE AT THE STARTING POINT ALL ALONG.
AL CAN BE RETURNED TO NORMAL!!

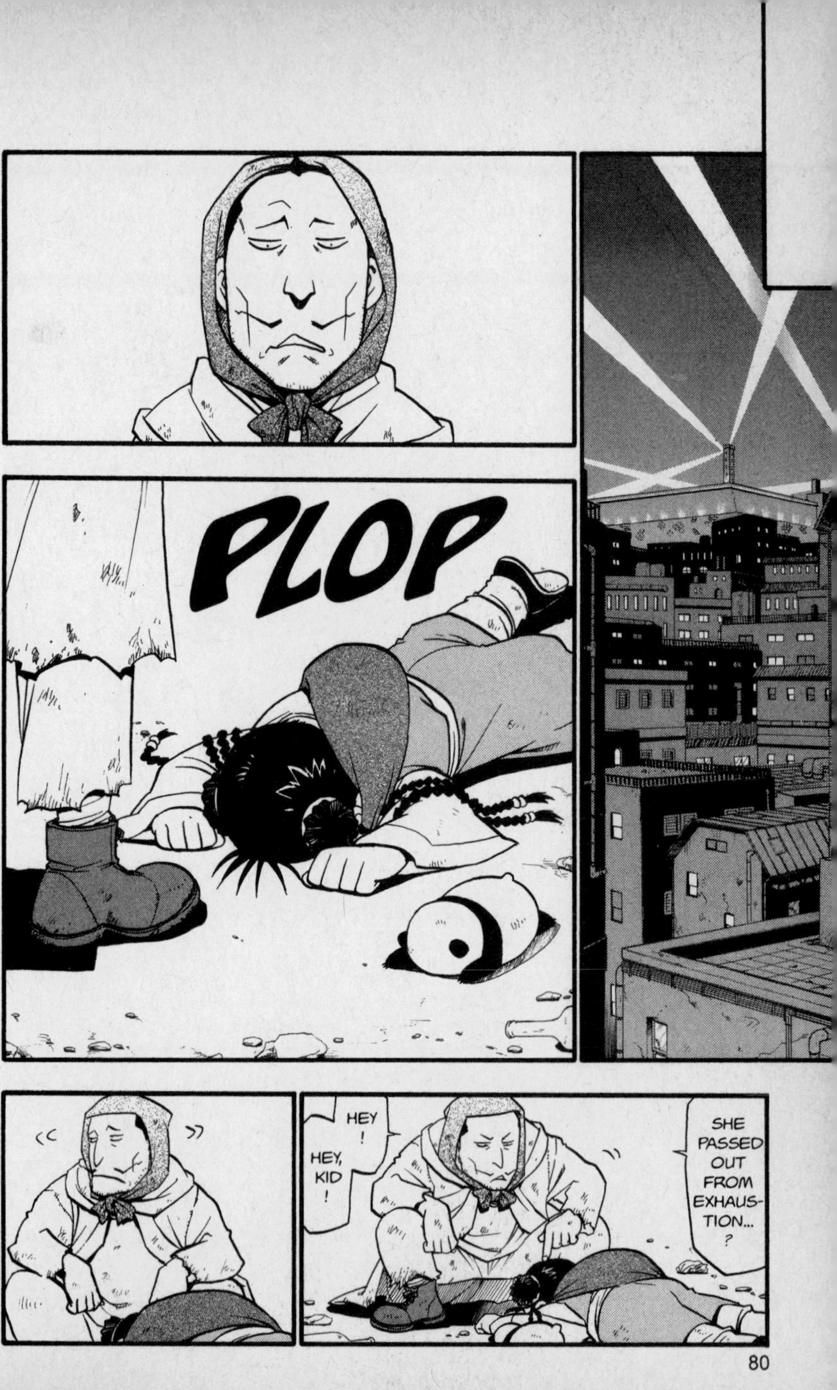
PLOP
HEY!
HEY, KID!
SHE PASSED OUT FROM EXHAUSTION...?

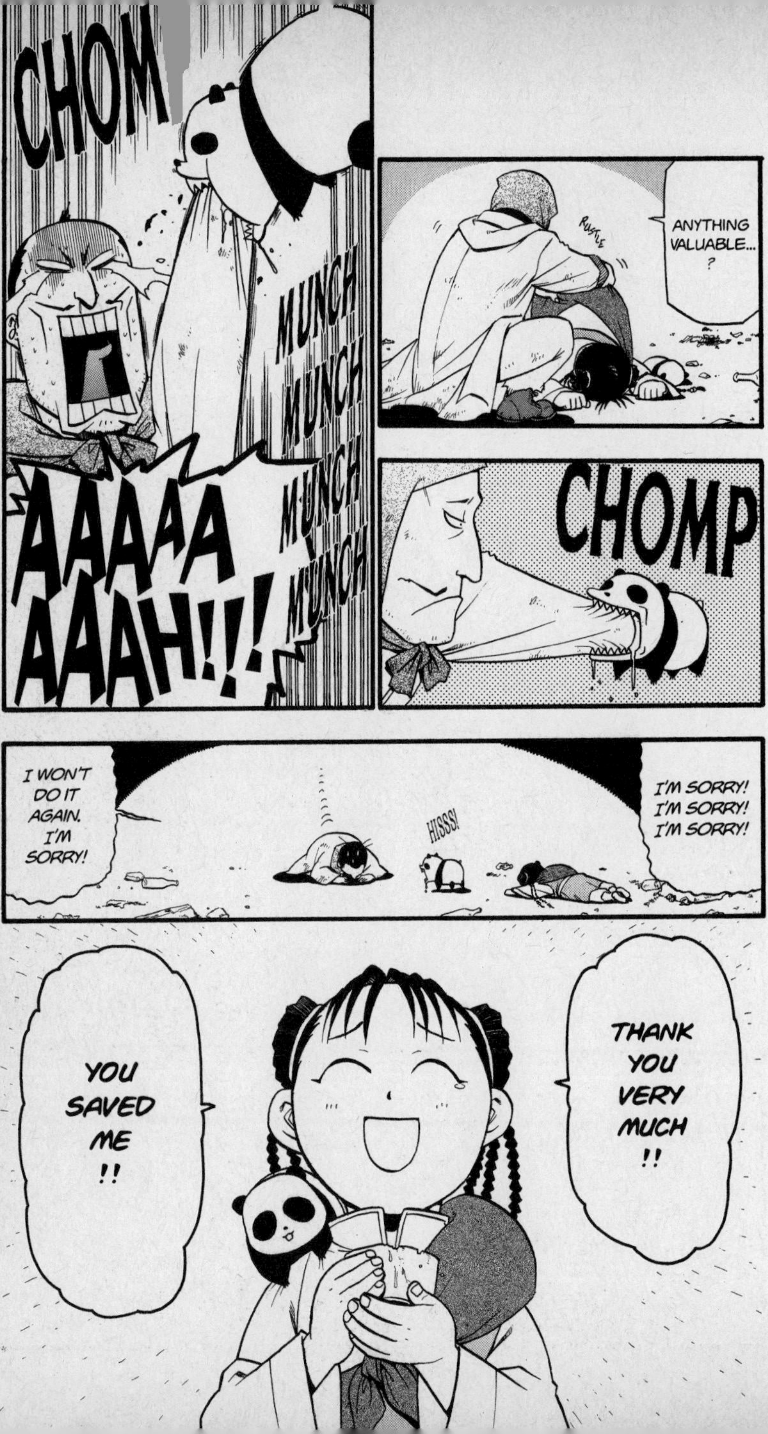

RUSTLE
ANYTHING VALUABLE... ?
CHOMP
CHOM
MUNCH MUNCH MUNCH MUNCH
AAAAAAAH!!!
I'M SORRY! I'M SORRY! I'M SORRY!
HISSS!
I WON'T DO IT AGAIN. I'M SORRY!
THANK YOU VERY MUCH!!
YOU SAVED ME!!

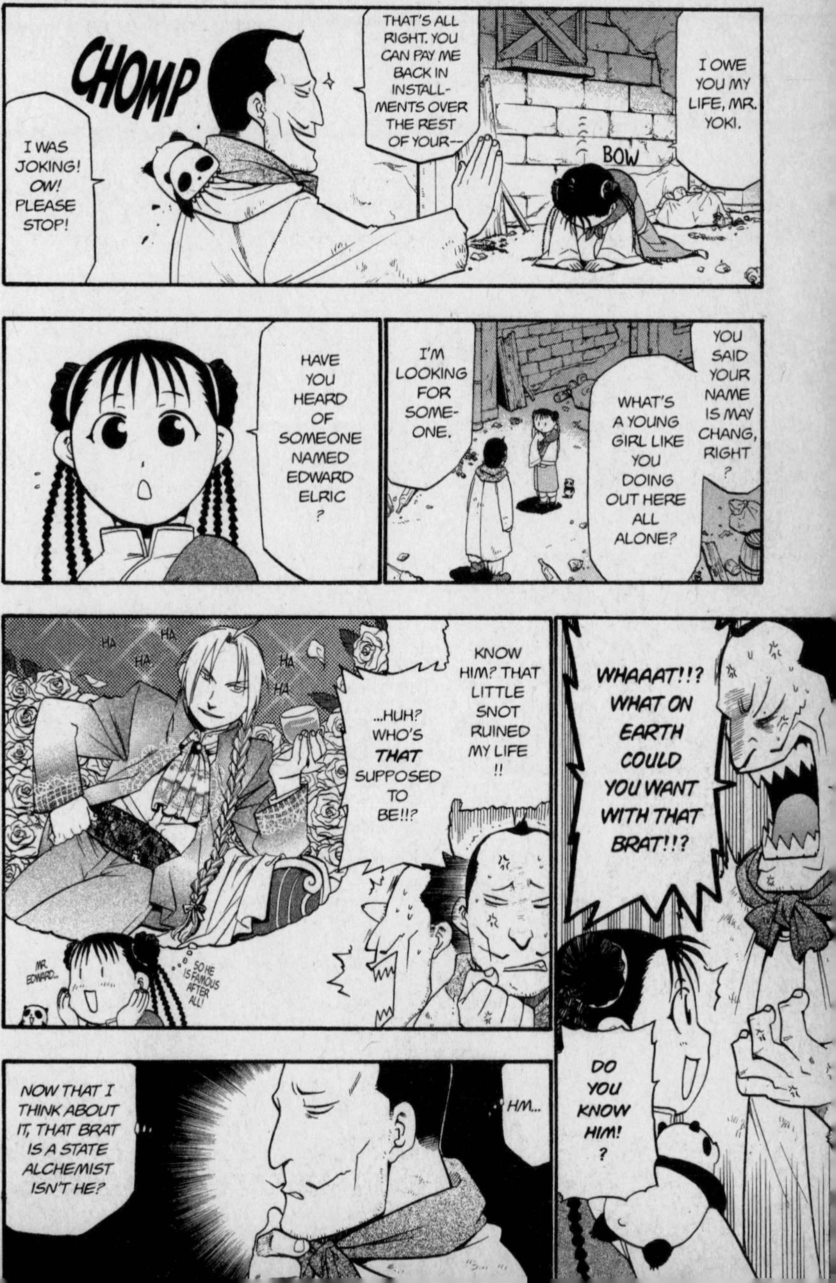
I OWE YOU MY LIFE, MR. YOKI.
BOW
THAT'S ALL RIGHT. YOU CAN PAY ME BACK IN INSTALL-MENTS OVER THE REST OF YOUR--
CHOMP
I WAS JOKING! OW! PLEASE STOP!
YOU SAID YOUR NAME IS MAY CHANG, RIGHT?
WHAT'S A YOUNG GIRL LIKE YOU DOING OUT HERE ALL ALONE?
I'M LOOKING FOR SOME-ONE.
HAVE YOU HEARD OF SOMEONE NAMED EDWARD ELRIC?
WHAAAT!!? WHAT ON EARTH COULD YOU WANT WITH THAT BRAT!!?
DO YOU KNOW HIM!?
KNOW HIM? THAT LITTLE SNOT RUINED MY LIFE!!
...HUH? WHO'S THAT SUPPOSED TO BE!!?
HA HA HA HA HA
SO HE IS FAMOUS AFTER ALL!
MR. EDWARD...
HM...
NOW THAT I THINK ABOUT IT, THAT BRAT IS A STATE ALCHEMIST ISN'T HE?

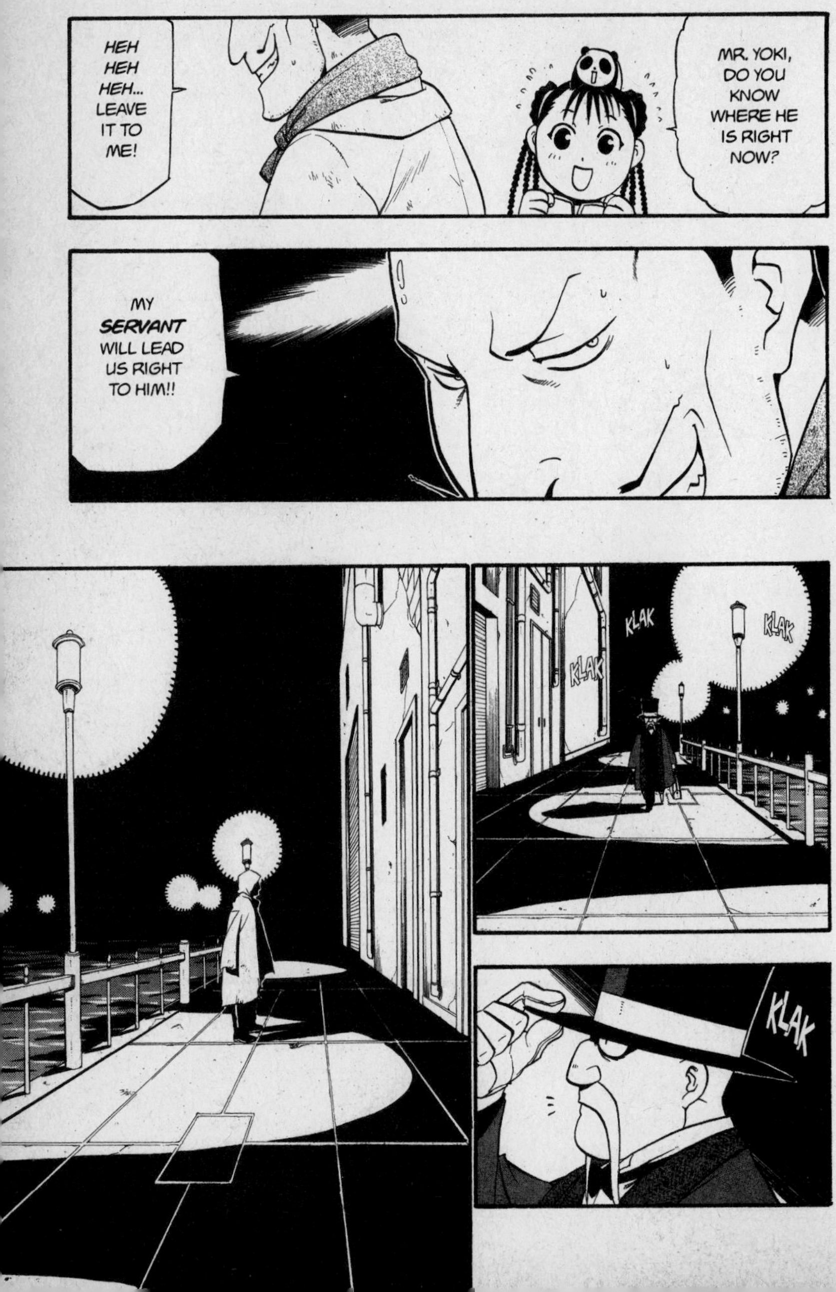
MR. YOKI, DO YOU KNOW WHERE HE IS RIGHT NOW?
HEH HEH HEH... LEAVE IT TO ME!
MY *SERVANT* WILL LEAD US RIGHT TO HIM!!
KLAK
KLAK
KLAK
KLAK

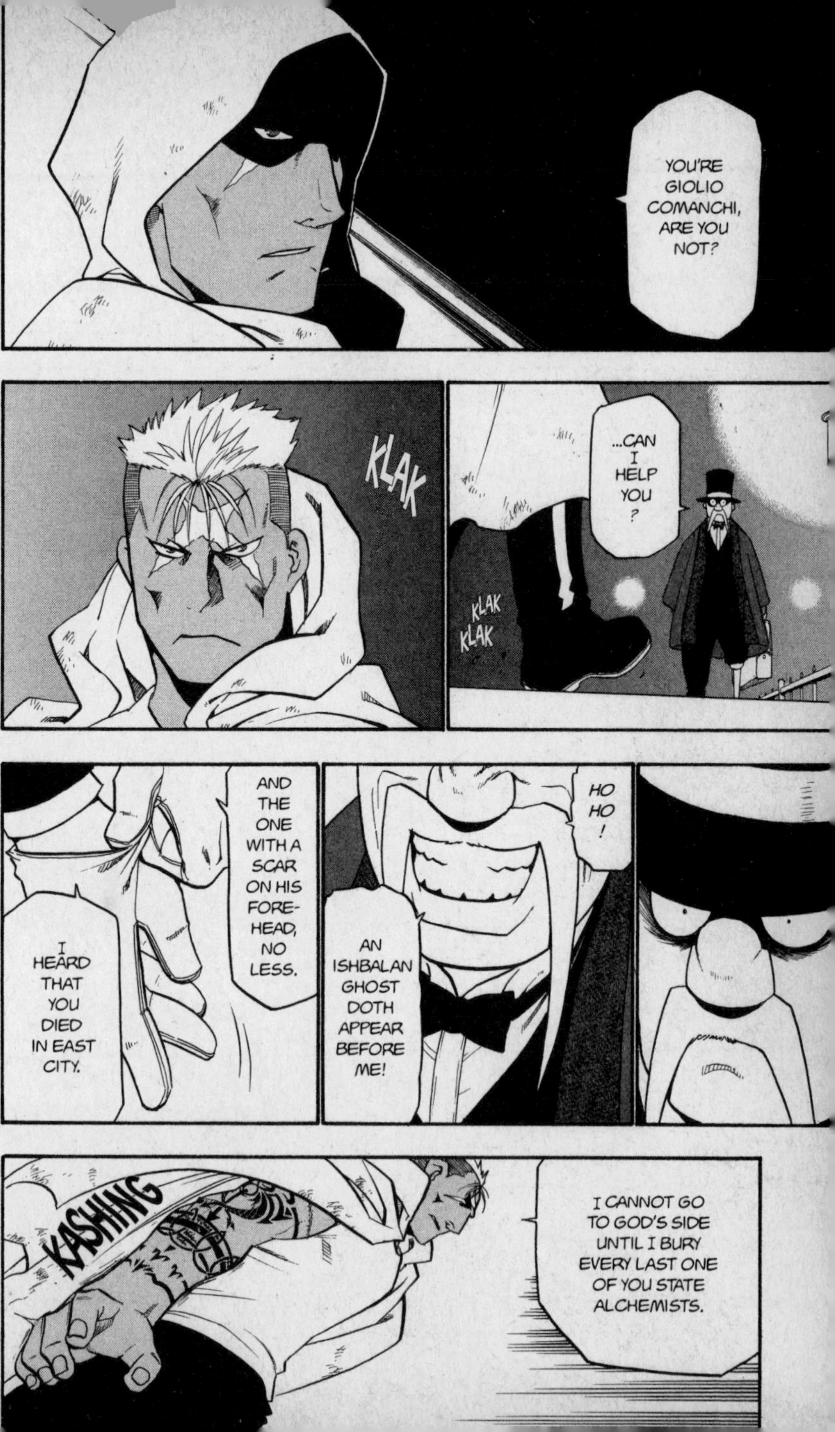
YOU'RE GIOLIO COMANCHI, ARE YOU NOT?
...CAN I HELP YOU ?
KLAK KLAK
KLAK
HO HO !
AN ISHBALAN GHOST DOTH APPEAR BEFORE ME!
AND THE ONE WITH A SCAR ON HIS FORE-HEAD, NO LESS.
I HEARD THAT YOU DIED IN EAST CITY.
I CANNOT GO TO GOD'S SIDE UNTIL I BURY EVERY LAST ONE OF YOU STATE ALCHEMISTS.
KASHING

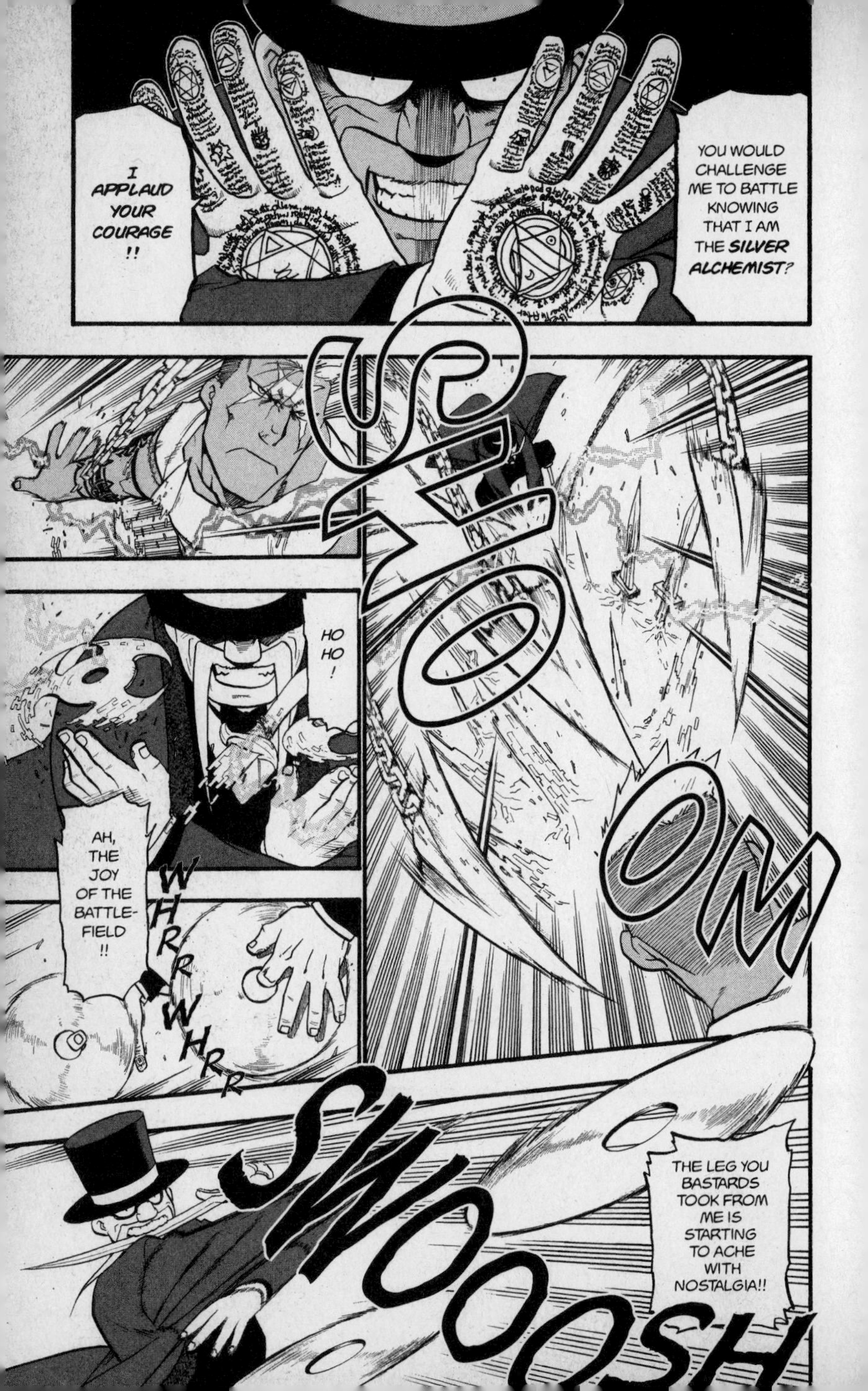
YOU WOULD CHALLENGE ME TO BATTLE KNOWING THAT I AM THE **SILVER ALCHEMIST**?
I APPLAUD YOUR COURAGE !!
SHOOOM
HO HO!
AH, THE JOY OF THE BATTLEFIELD !!
WHRR WHRR
THE LEG YOU BASTARDS TOOK FROM ME IS STARTING TO ACHE WITH NOSTALGIA!!
SWOOOSH

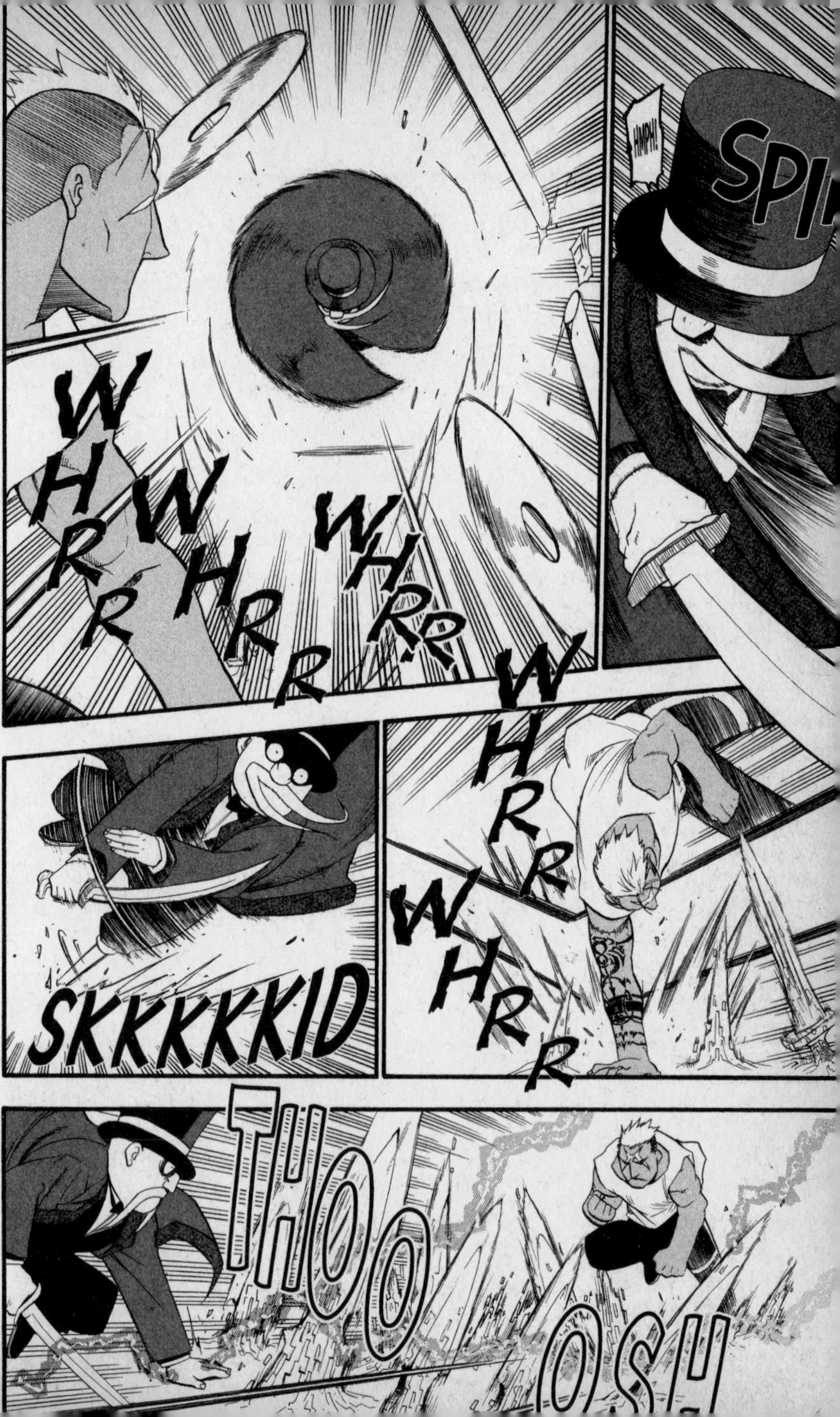
HMPH!
SPI
WHRR
WHRR
WHRR
WHRR
WHRR
SKKKKID
THOOOSH

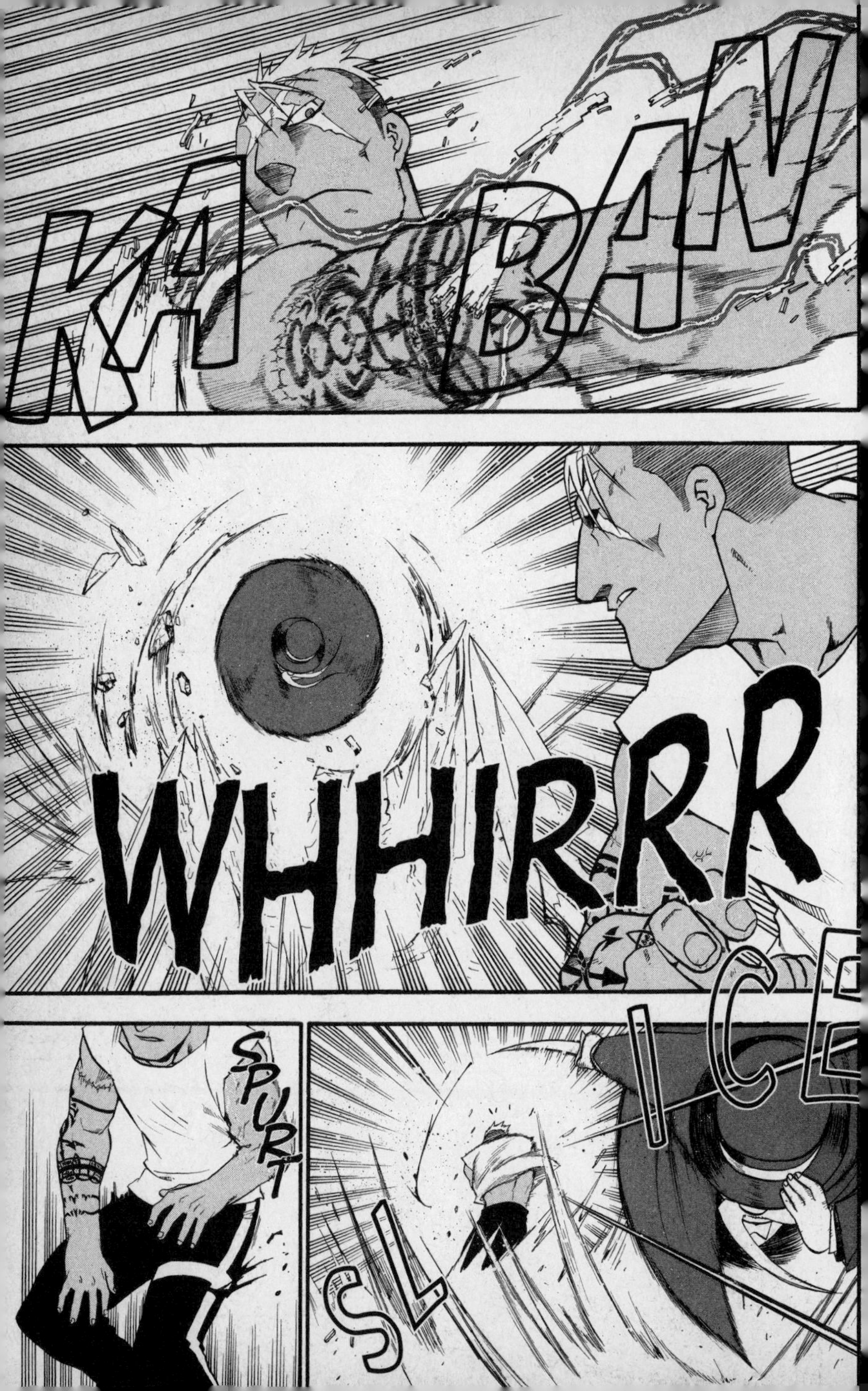
KABAN
WHHIRRR
SLICE
SPURT

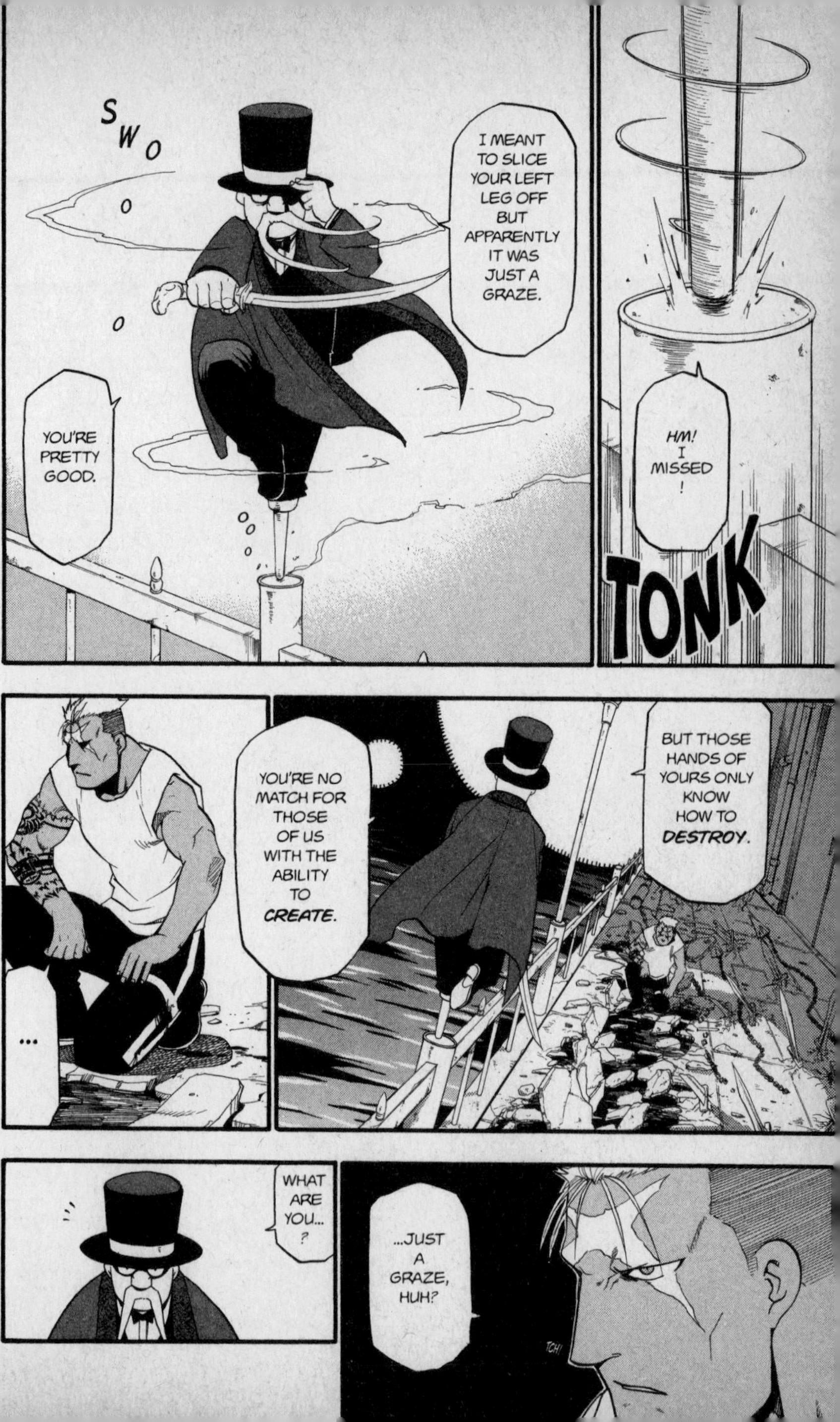
HM! I MISSED!
TONK
I MEANT TO SLICE YOUR LEFT LEG OFF BUT APPARENTLY IT WAS JUST A GRAZE.
SWOOOOO
YOU'RE PRETTY GOOD.
BUT THOSE HANDS OF YOURS ONLY KNOW HOW TO DESTROY.
YOU'RE NO MATCH FOR THOSE OF US WITH THE ABILITY TO CREATE.
...
...JUST A GRAZE, HUH?
TCH
WHAT ARE YOU...?

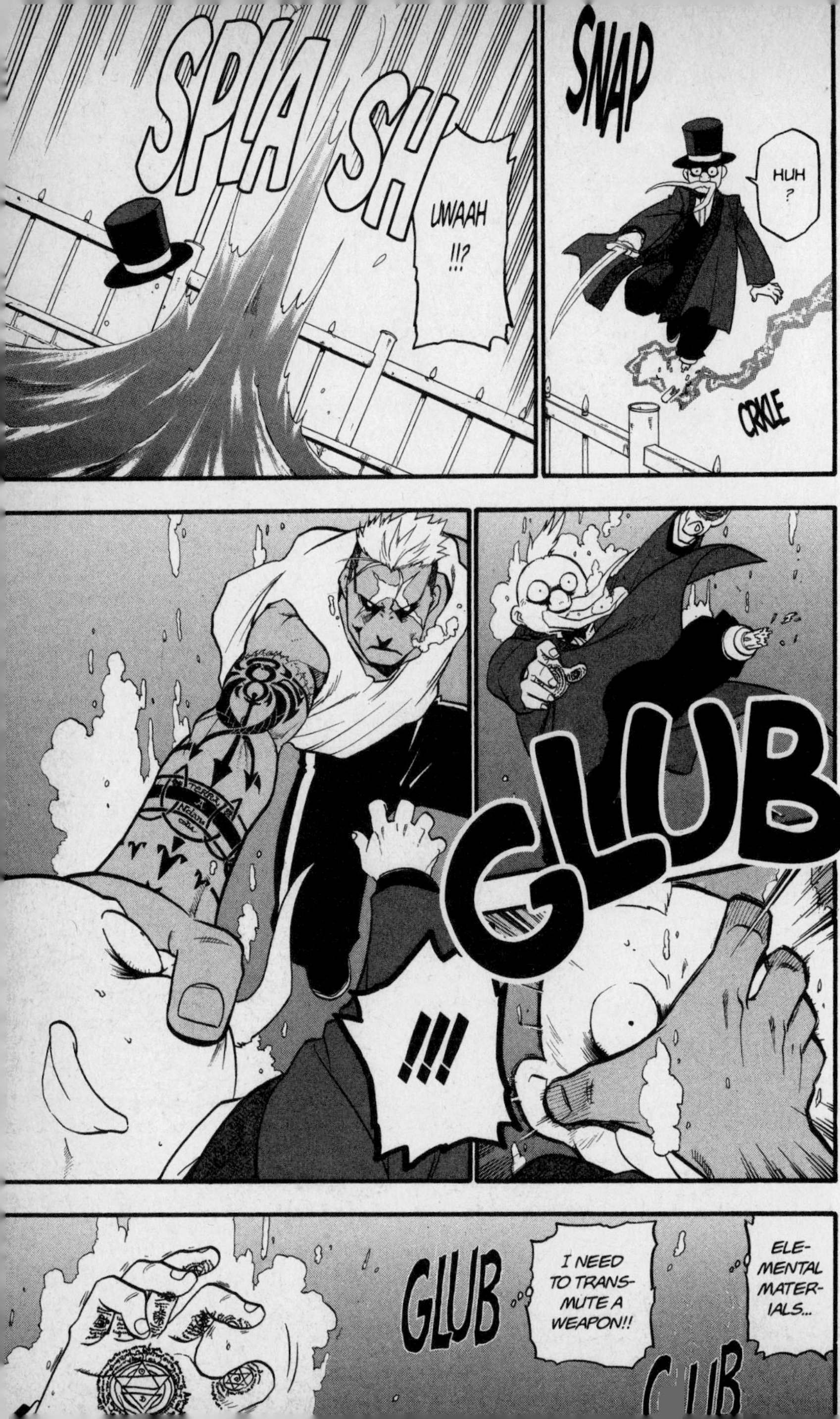

SNAP
HUH?
CRKLE
SPLASH
UWAAH!!?
GLUB
!!!
ELE-MENTAL MATER-IALS...
I NEED TO TRANS-MUTE A WEAPON!!
GLUB

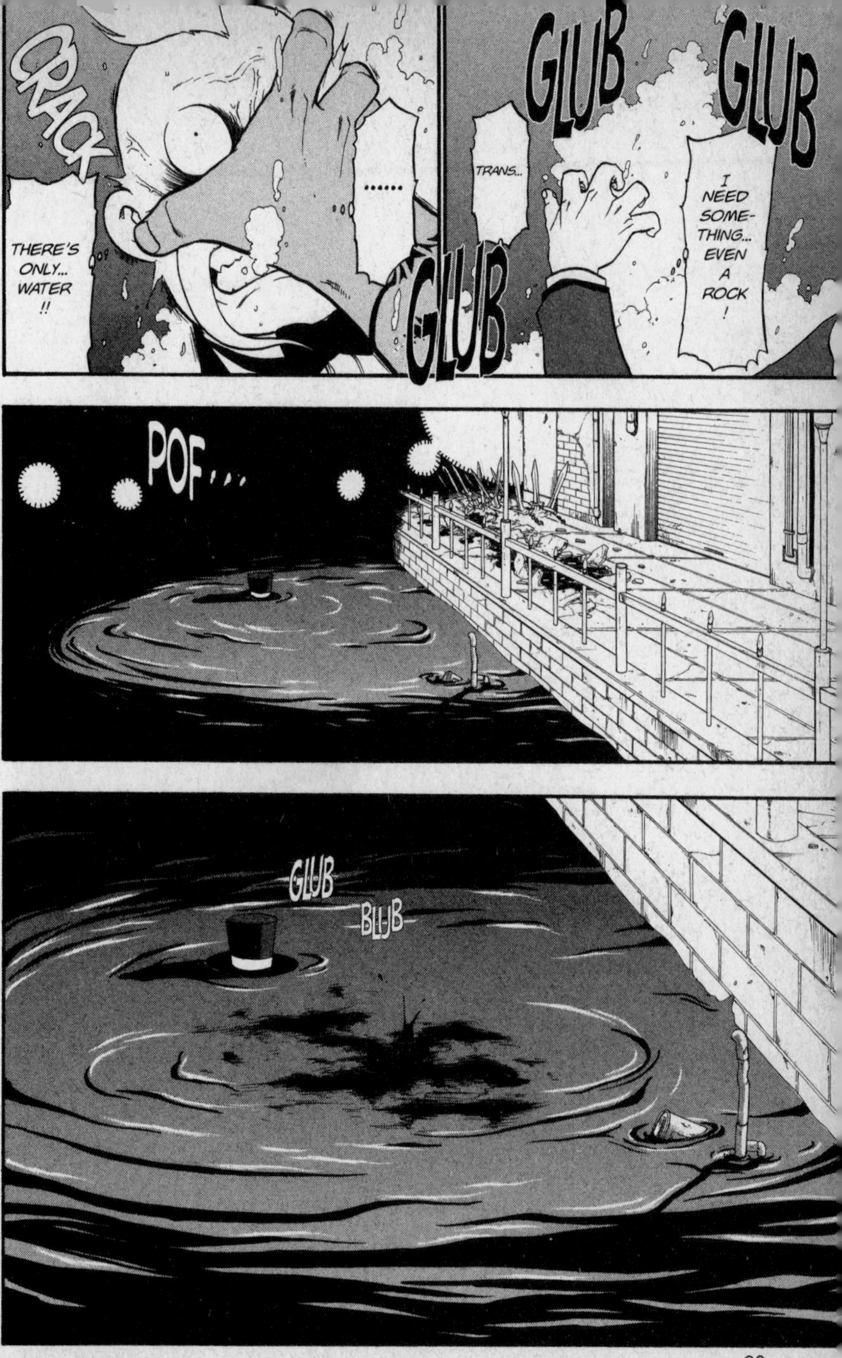
GLUB
I NEED SOMETHING... EVEN A ROCK!
GLUB
TRANS...
GLUB
......
CRACK
THERE'S ONLY... WATER!!
POF...
GLUB
BLUB

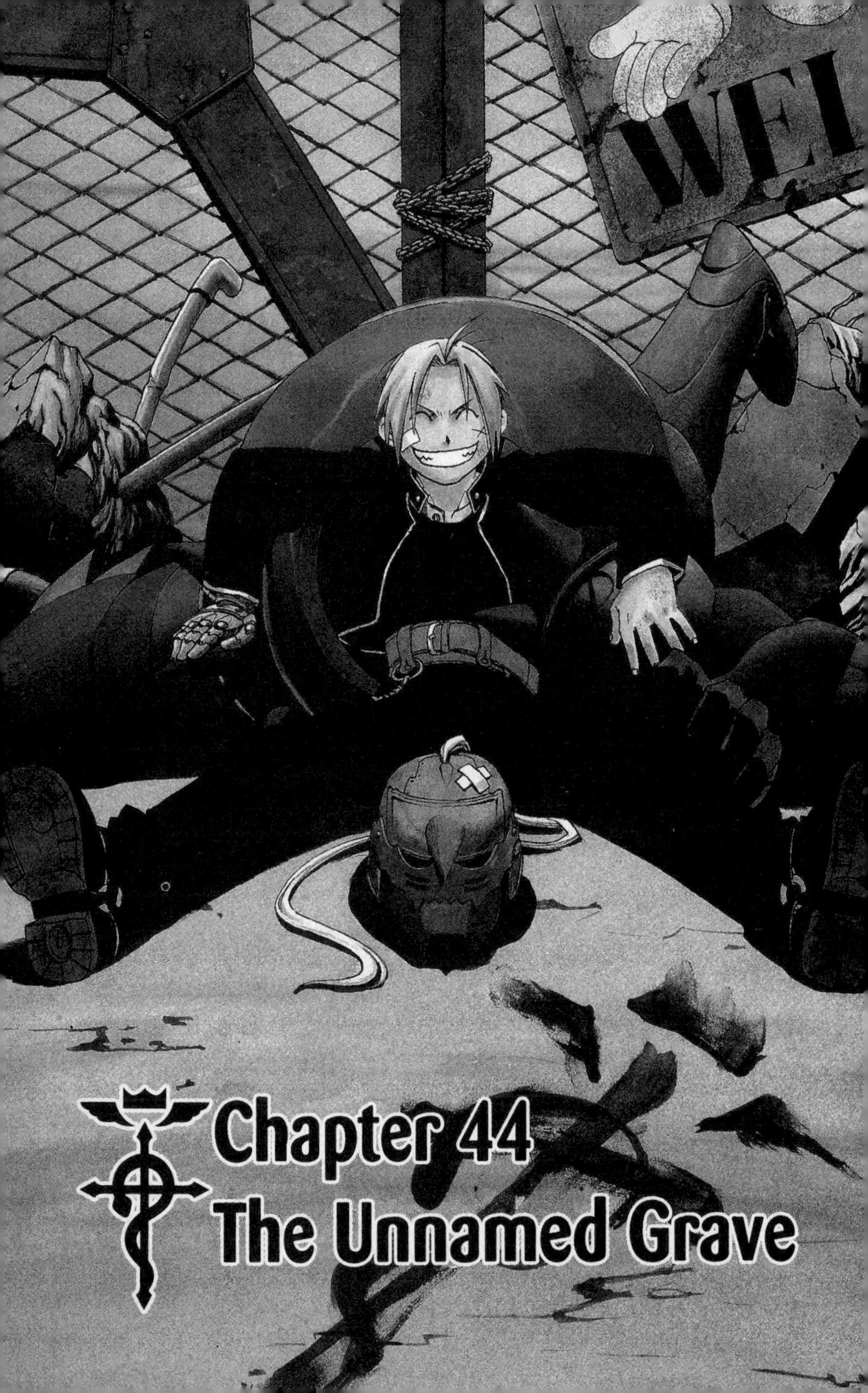
WEl
Chapter 44
The Unnamed Grave

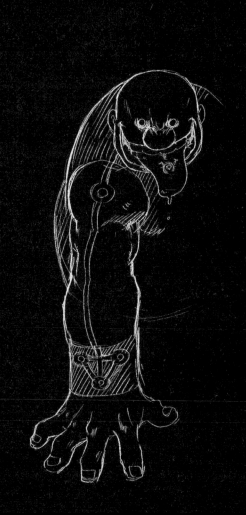

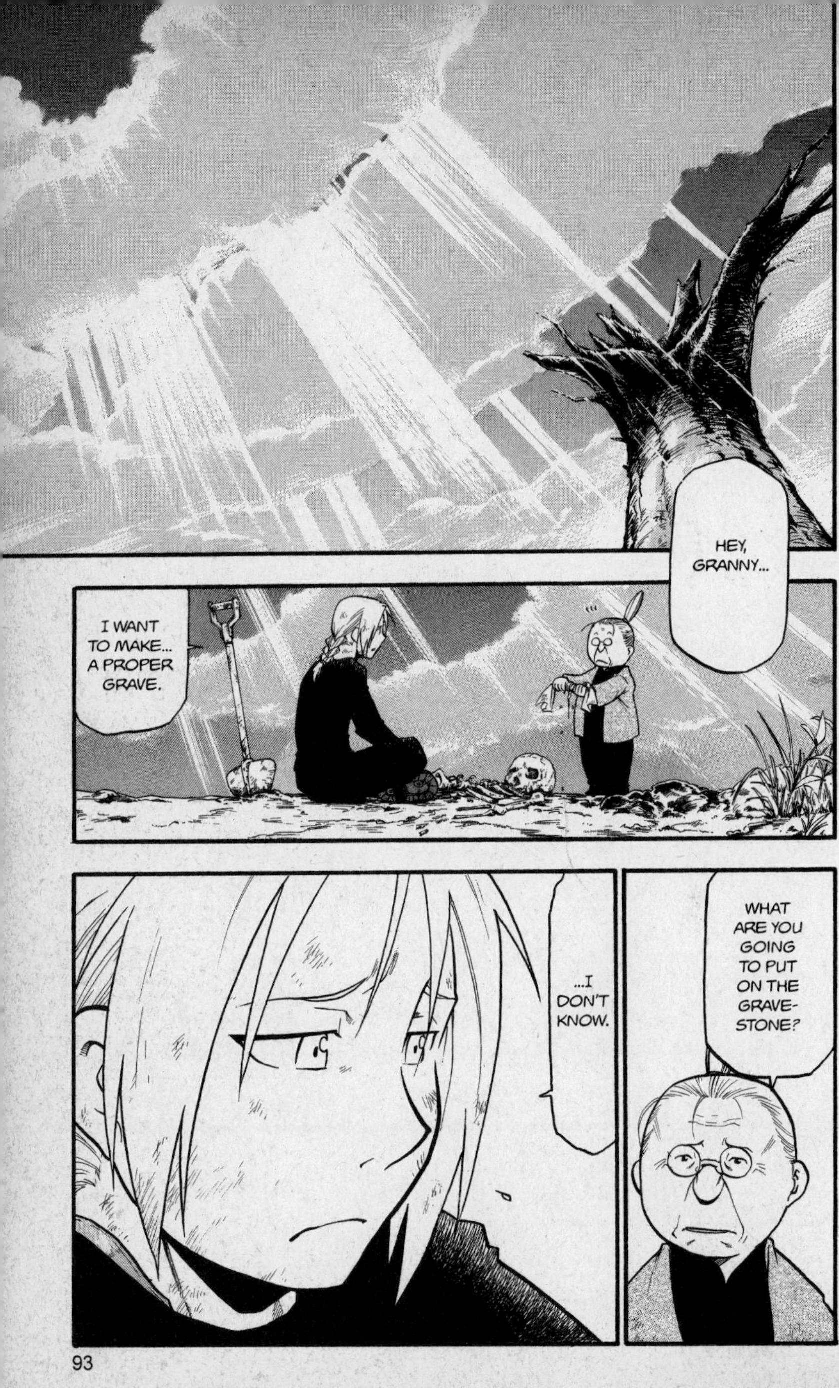

HEY, GRANNY...
I WANT TO MAKE... A PROPER GRAVE.
WHAT ARE YOU GOING TO PUT ON THE GRAVE-STONE?
...I DON'T KNOW.

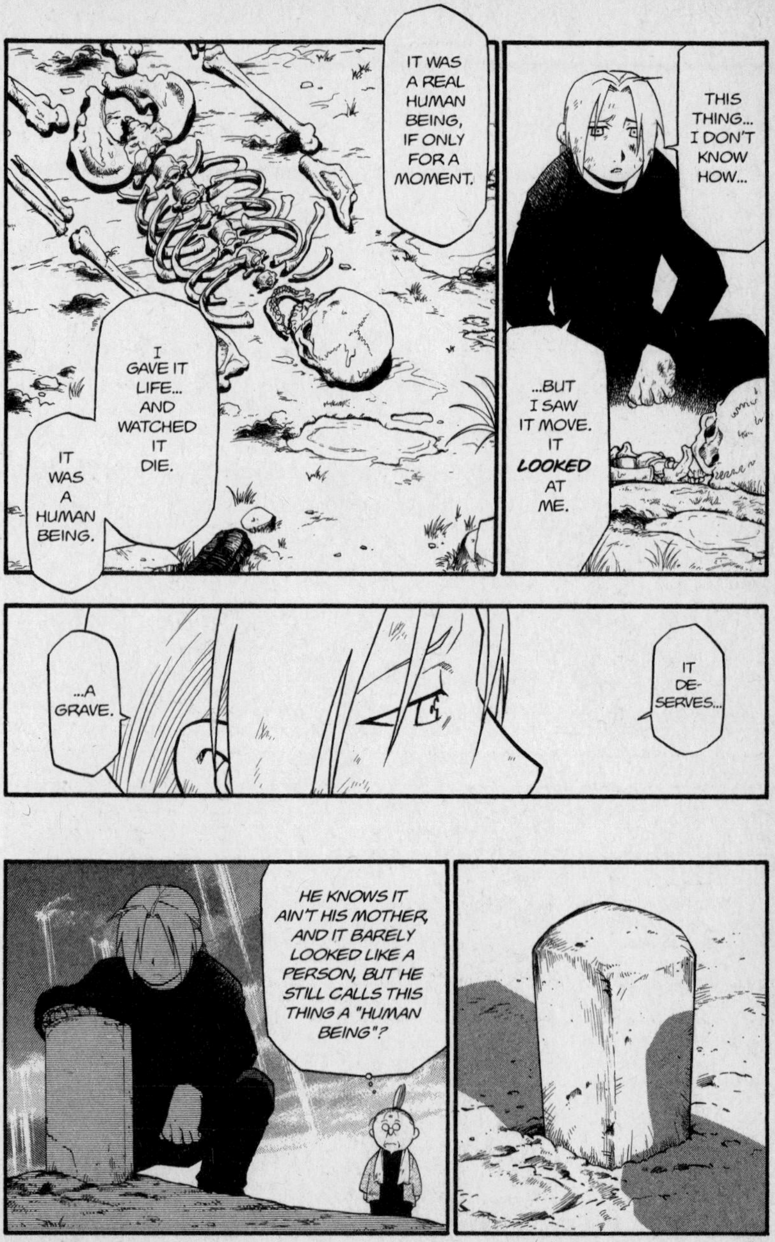
THIS THING... I DON'T KNOW HOW...
...BUT I SAW IT MOVE. IT LOOKED AT ME.
IT WAS A REAL HUMAN BEING, IF ONLY FOR A MOMENT.
I GAVE IT LIFE... AND WATCHED IT DIE.
IT WAS A HUMAN BEING.
IT DESERVES...
...A GRAVE.
HE KNOWS IT AIN'T HIS MOTHER, AND IT BARELY LOOKED LIKE A PERSON, BUT HE STILL CALLS THIS THING A "HUMAN BEING"?

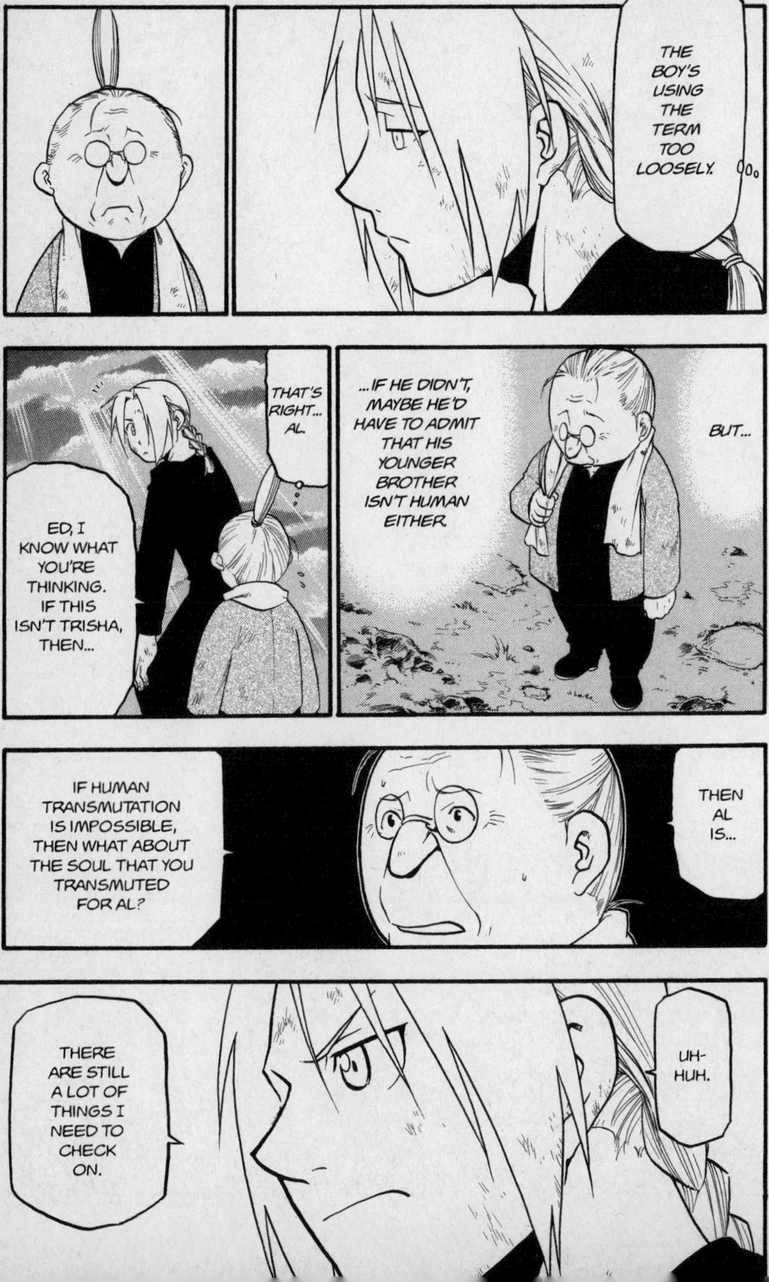
THE BOY'S USING THE TERM TOO LOOSELY.
BUT...
...IF HE DIDN'T, MAYBE HE'D HAVE TO ADMIT THAT HIS YOUNGER BROTHER ISN'T HUMAN EITHER.
THAT'S RIGHT... AL.
ED, I KNOW WHAT YOU'RE THINKING. IF THIS ISN'T TRISHA, THEN...
THEN AL IS...
IF HUMAN TRANSMUTATION IS IMPOSSIBLE, THEN WHAT ABOUT THE SOUL THAT YOU TRANSMUTED FOR AL?
UH-HUH.
THERE ARE STILL A LOT OF THINGS I NEED TO CHECK ON.

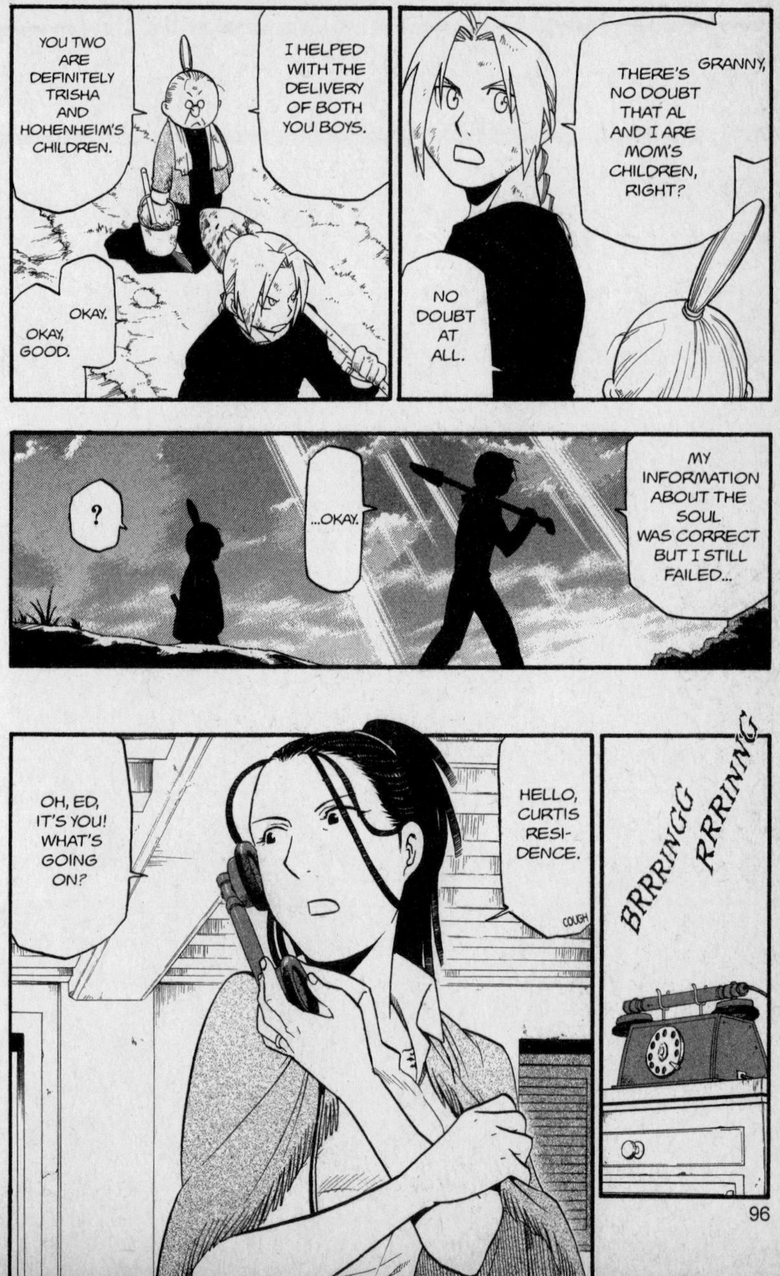
GRANNY, THERE'S NO DOUBT THAT AL AND I ARE MOM'S CHILDREN, RIGHT?
NO DOUBT AT ALL.
I HELPED WITH THE DELIVERY OF BOTH YOU BOYS.
YOU TWO ARE DEFINITELY TRISHA AND HOHENHEIM'S CHILDREN.
OKAY. OKAY, GOOD.
MY INFORMATION ABOUT THE SOUL WAS CORRECT BUT I STILL FAILED...
...OKAY.
?
RRRINNG
BRRRINGG
HELLO, CURTIS RESI-DENCE.
COUGH
OH, ED, IT'S YOU! WHAT'S GOING ON?

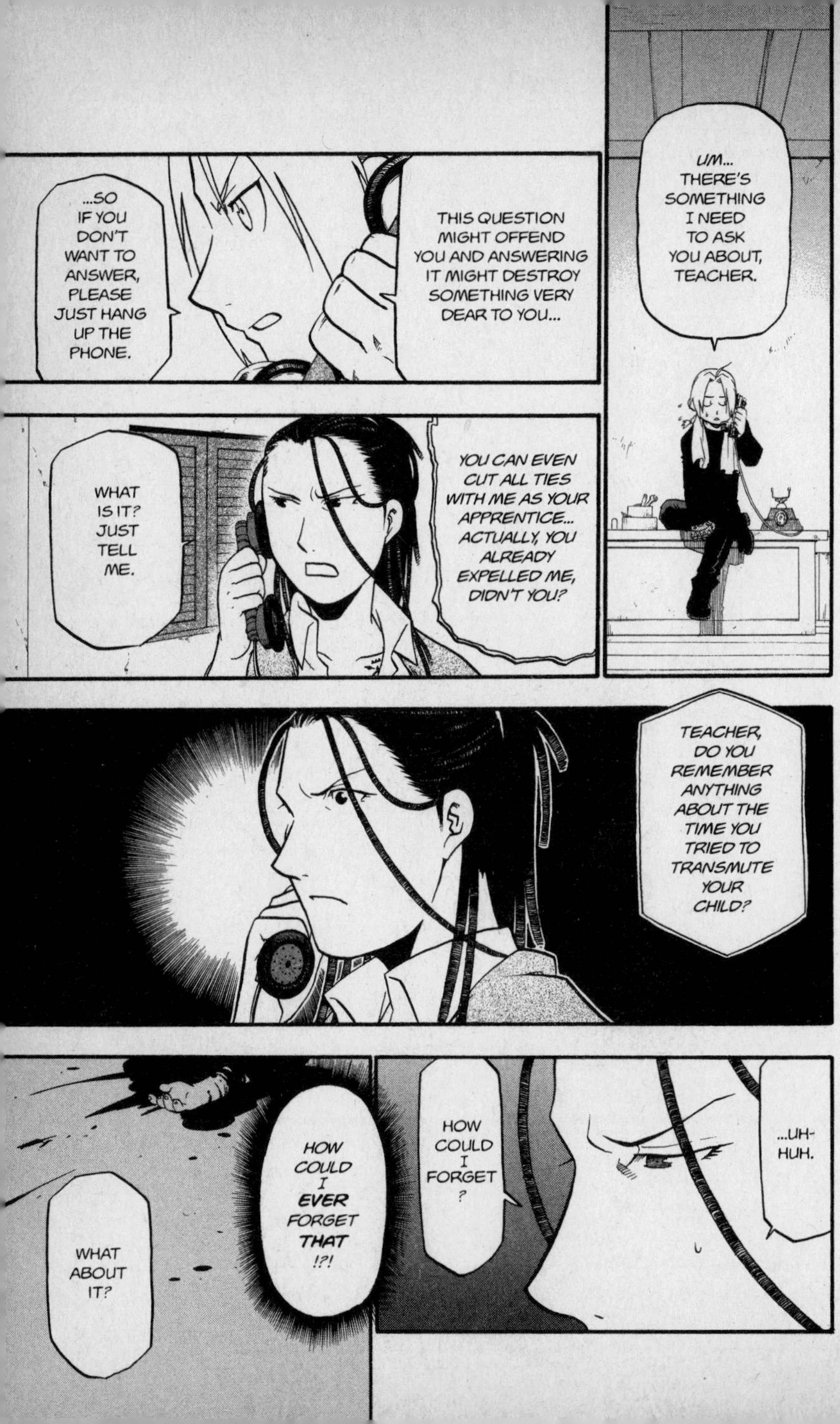
UM... THERE'S SOMETHING I NEED TO ASK YOU ABOUT, TEACHER.
THIS QUESTION MIGHT OFFEND YOU AND ANSWERING IT MIGHT DESTROY SOMETHING VERY DEAR TO YOU...
...SO IF YOU DON'T WANT TO ANSWER, PLEASE JUST HANG UP THE PHONE.
YOU CAN EVEN CUT ALL TIES WITH ME AS YOUR APPRENTICE... ACTUALLY, YOU ALREADY EXPELLED ME, DIDN'T YOU?
WHAT IS IT? JUST TELL ME.
TEACHER, DO YOU REMEMBER ANYTHING ABOUT THE TIME YOU TRIED TO TRANSMUTE YOUR CHILD?
...UH-HUH.
HOW COULD I FORGET?
HOW COULD I EVER FORGET THAT!?!
WHAT ABOUT IT?

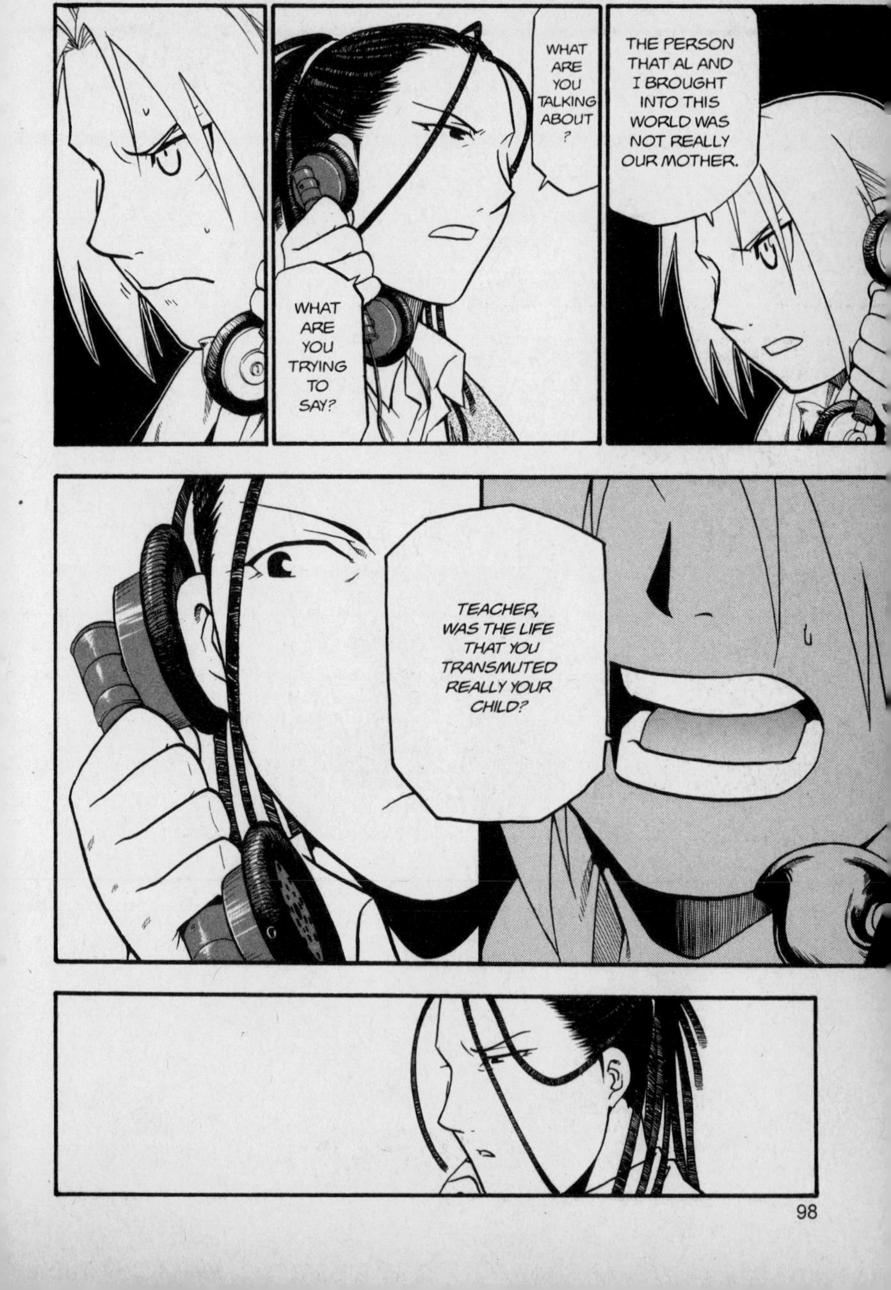
THE PERSON THAT AL AND I BROUGHT INTO THIS WORLD WAS NOT REALLY OUR MOTHER.
WHAT ARE YOU TALKING ABOUT?
WHAT ARE YOU TRYING TO SAY?
TEACHER, WAS THE LIFE THAT YOU TRANSMUTED REALLY YOUR CHILD?

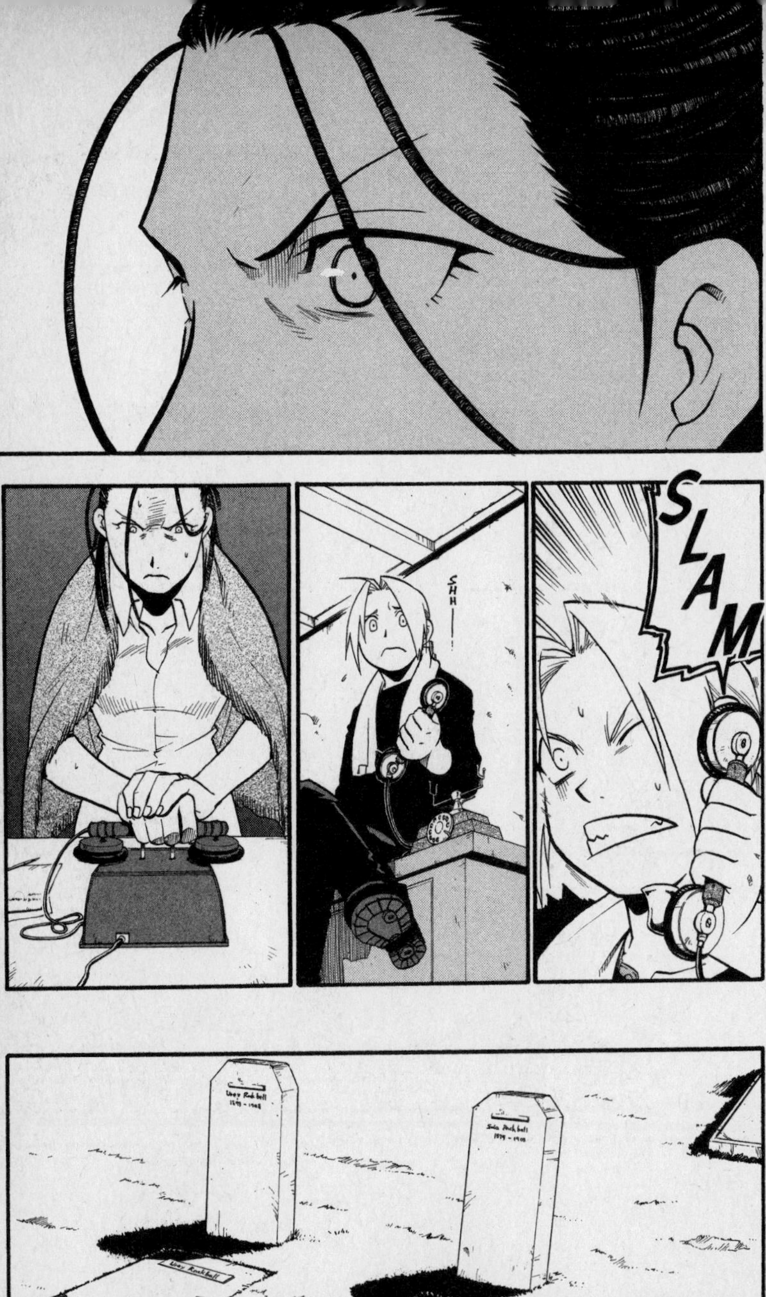
SLAM
SHH—!

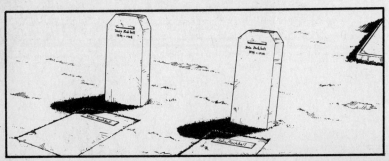

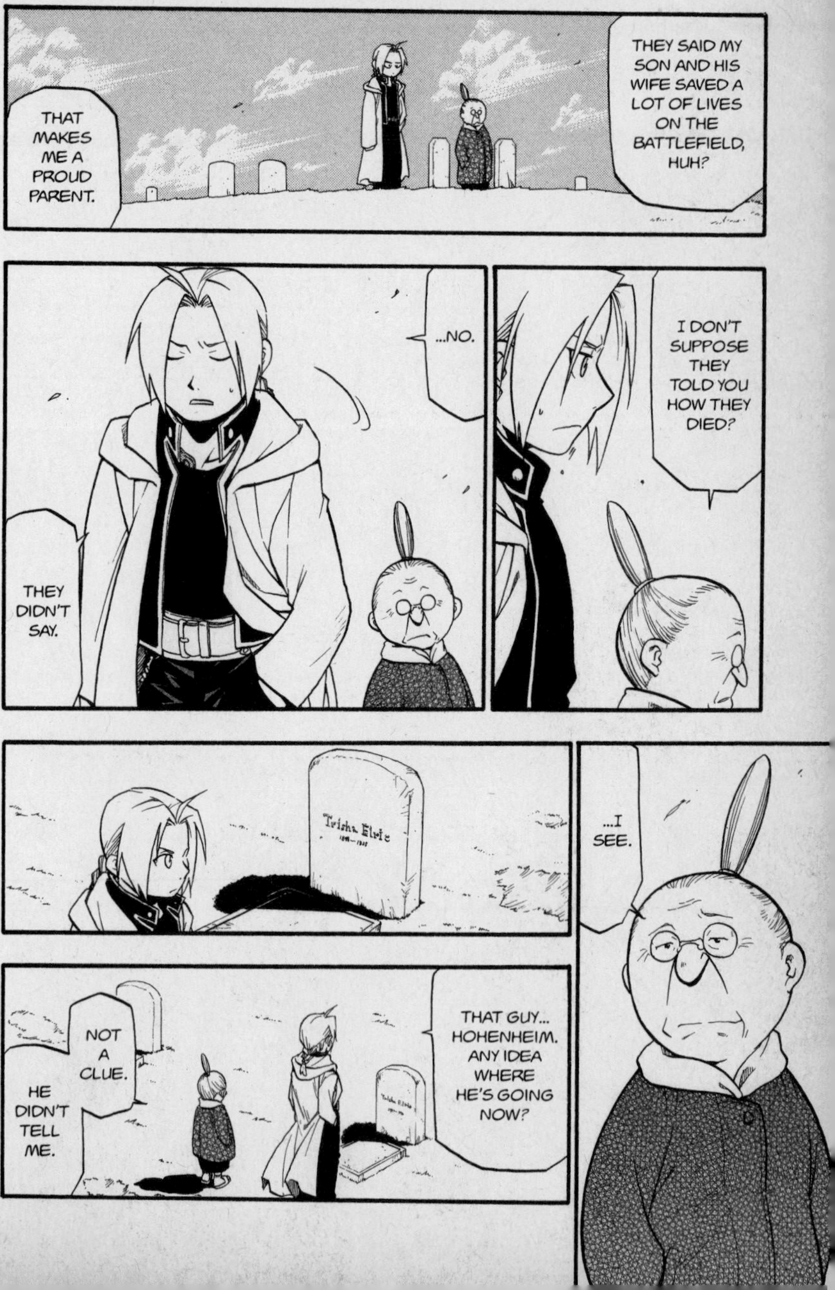
THEY SAID MY SON AND HIS WIFE SAVED A LOT OF LIVES ON THE BATTLEFIELD, HUH?
THAT MAKES ME A PROUD PARENT.
I DON'T SUPPOSE THEY TOLD YOU HOW THEY DIED?
...NO.
THEY DIDN'T SAY.
...I SEE.
Trisha Elric
THAT GUY... HOHENHEIM. ANY IDEA WHERE HE'S GOING NOW?
NOT A CLUE.
HE DIDN'T TELL ME.

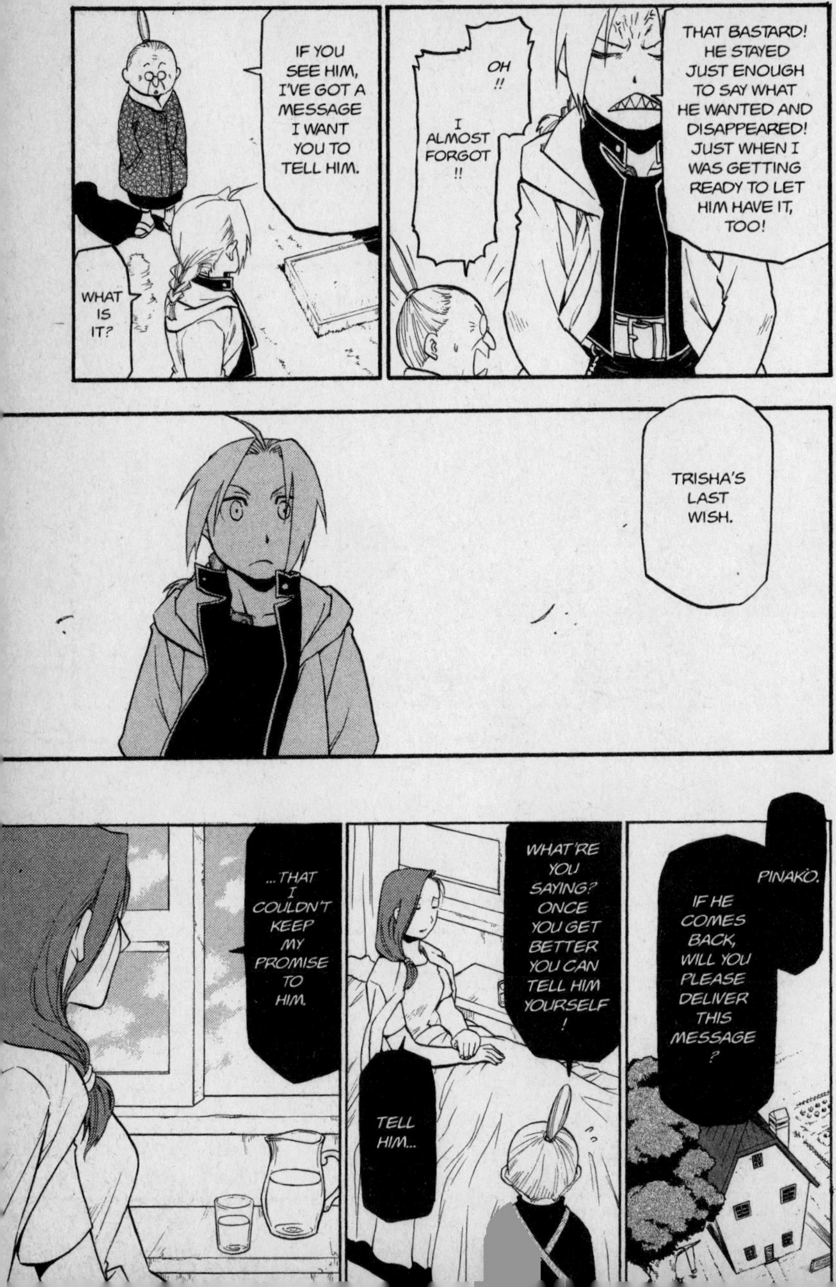
THAT BASTARD! HE STAYED JUST ENOUGH TO SAY WHAT HE WANTED AND DISAPPEARED! JUST WHEN I WAS GETTING READY TO LET HIM HAVE IT, TOO!
OH !! I ALMOST FORGOT !!
IF YOU SEE HIM, I'VE GOT A MESSAGE I WANT YOU TO TELL HIM.
WHAT IS IT?
TRISHA'S LAST WISH.
PINAKO.
IF HE COMES BACK, WILL YOU PLEASE DELIVER THIS MESSAGE ?
WHAT'RE YOU SAYING? ONCE YOU GET BETTER YOU CAN TELL HIM YOURSELF !
TELL HIM...
...THAT I COULDN'T KEEP MY PROMISE TO HIM.

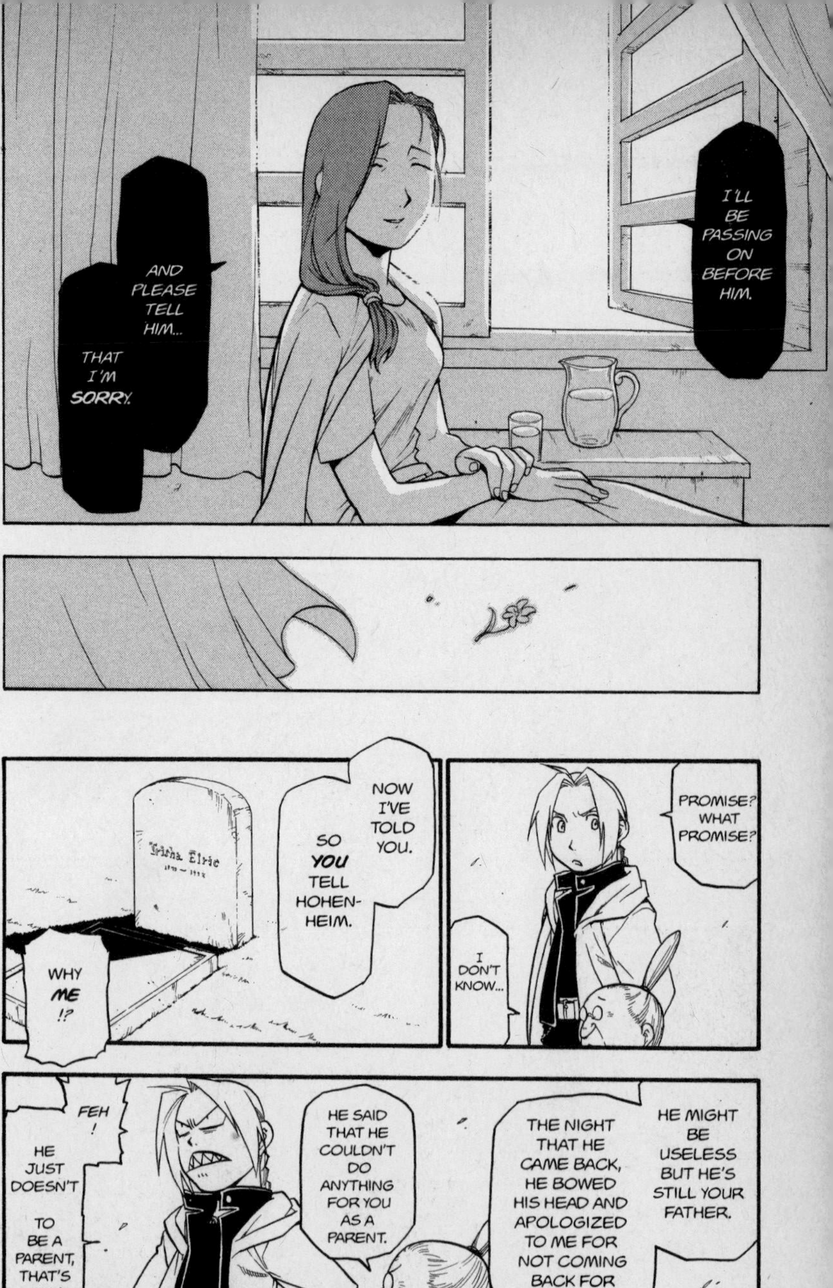
I'LL BE PASSING ON BEFORE HIM.
AND PLEASE TELL HIM...
THAT I'M **SORRY.**
PROMISE? WHAT PROMISE?
I DON'T KNOW...
NOW I'VE TOLD YOU.
SO **YOU** TELL HOHENHEIM.
Trisha Elric
WHY **ME** !?
HE MIGHT BE USELESS BUT HE'S STILL YOUR FATHER.
THE NIGHT THAT HE CAME BACK, HE BOWED HIS HEAD AND APOLOGIZED TO ME FOR NOT COMING BACK FOR YOU BOYS.
HE SAID THAT HE COULDN'T DO ANYTHING FOR YOU AS A PARENT.
FEH!
HE JUST DOESN'T TO BE A PARENT, THAT'S ALL!

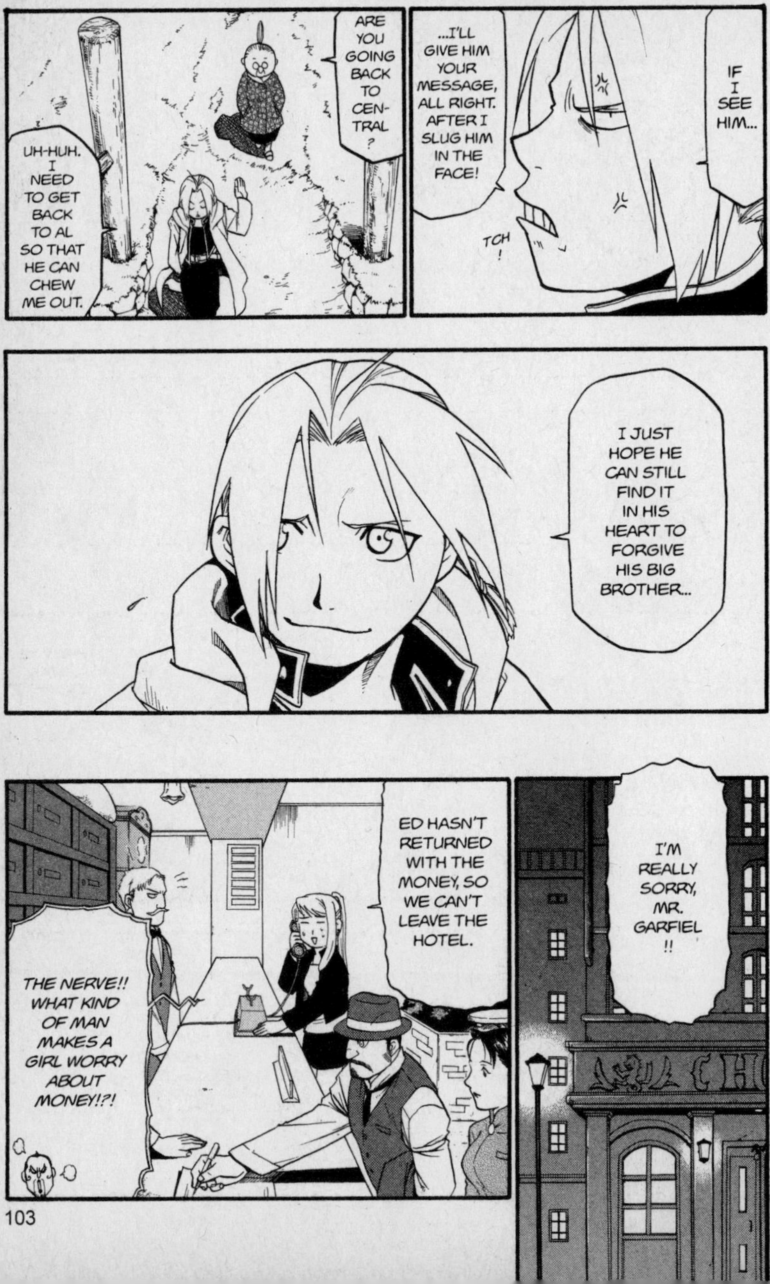
IF I SEE HIM...
...I'LL GIVE HIM YOUR MESSAGE, ALL RIGHT. AFTER I SLUG HIM IN THE FACE!
TCH!
ARE YOU GOING BACK TO CEN-TRAL?
UH-HUH. I NEED TO GET BACK TO AL SO THAT HE CAN CHEW ME OUT.
I JUST HOPE HE CAN STILL FIND IT IN HIS HEART TO FORGIVE HIS BIG BROTHER...
I'M REALLY SORRY, MR. GARFIEL!!
ED HASN'T RETURNED WITH THE MONEY, SO WE CAN'T LEAVE THE HOTEL.
THE NERVE!! WHAT KIND OF MAN MAKES A GIRL WORRY ABOUT MONEY!?!

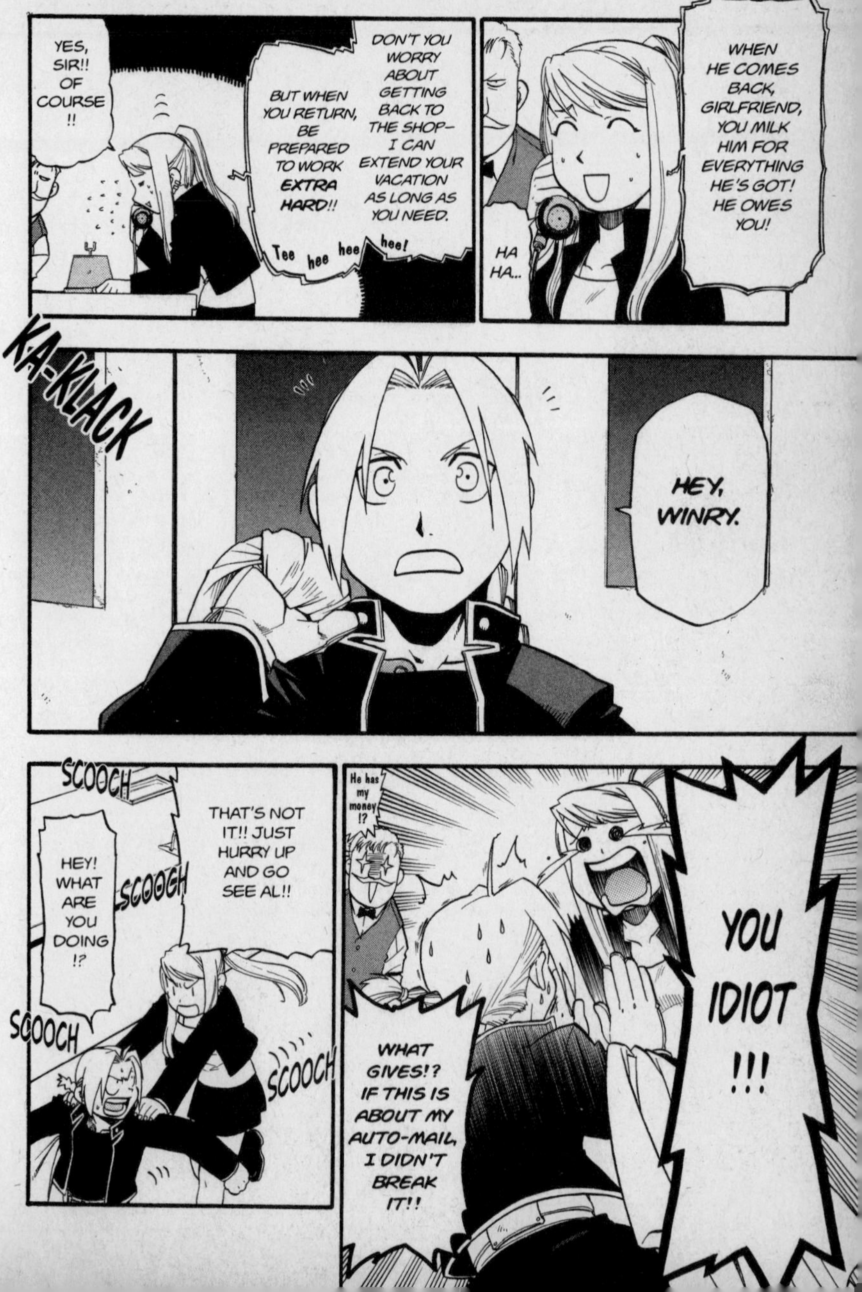
WHEN HE COMES BACK, GIRLFRIEND, YOU MILK HIM FOR EVERYTHING HE'S GOT! HE OWES YOU!
HA HA...
DON'T YOU WORRY ABOUT GETTING BACK TO THE SHOP– I CAN EXTEND YOUR VACATION AS LONG AS YOU NEED.
BUT WHEN YOU RETURN, BE PREPARED TO WORK EXTRA HARD!!
YES, SIR!! OF COURSE !!
Tee hee hee hee!
KA-KLACK
HEY, WINRY.
He has my money !?
YOU IDIOT !!!
WHAT GIVES!? IF THIS IS ABOUT MY AUTO-MAIL, I DIDN'T BREAK IT!!
SCOOCH
THAT'S NOT IT!! JUST HURRY UP AND GO SEE AL!!
HEY! WHAT ARE YOU DOING !?
SCOOGH
SCOOCH
SCOOCH

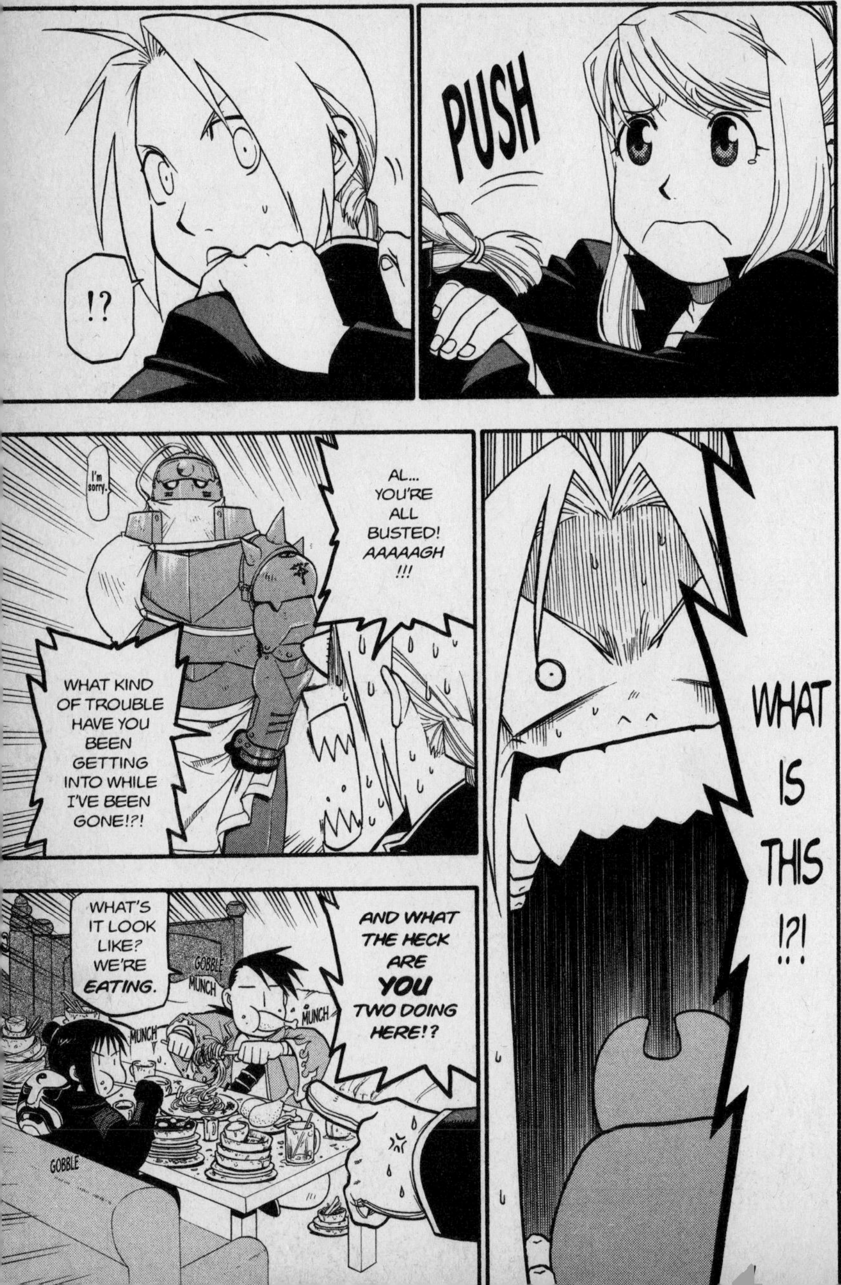
PUSH
!?
WHAT IS THIS !?!
AL... YOU'RE ALL BUSTED! AAAAAGH !!!
I'm sorry.
WHAT KIND OF TROUBLE HAVE YOU BEEN GETTING INTO WHILE I'VE BEEN GONE!?!
AND WHAT THE HECK ARE YOU TWO DOING HERE!?
WHAT'S IT LOOK LIKE? WE'RE EATING.
GOBBLE
MUNCH
MUNCH
MUNCH
GOBBLE

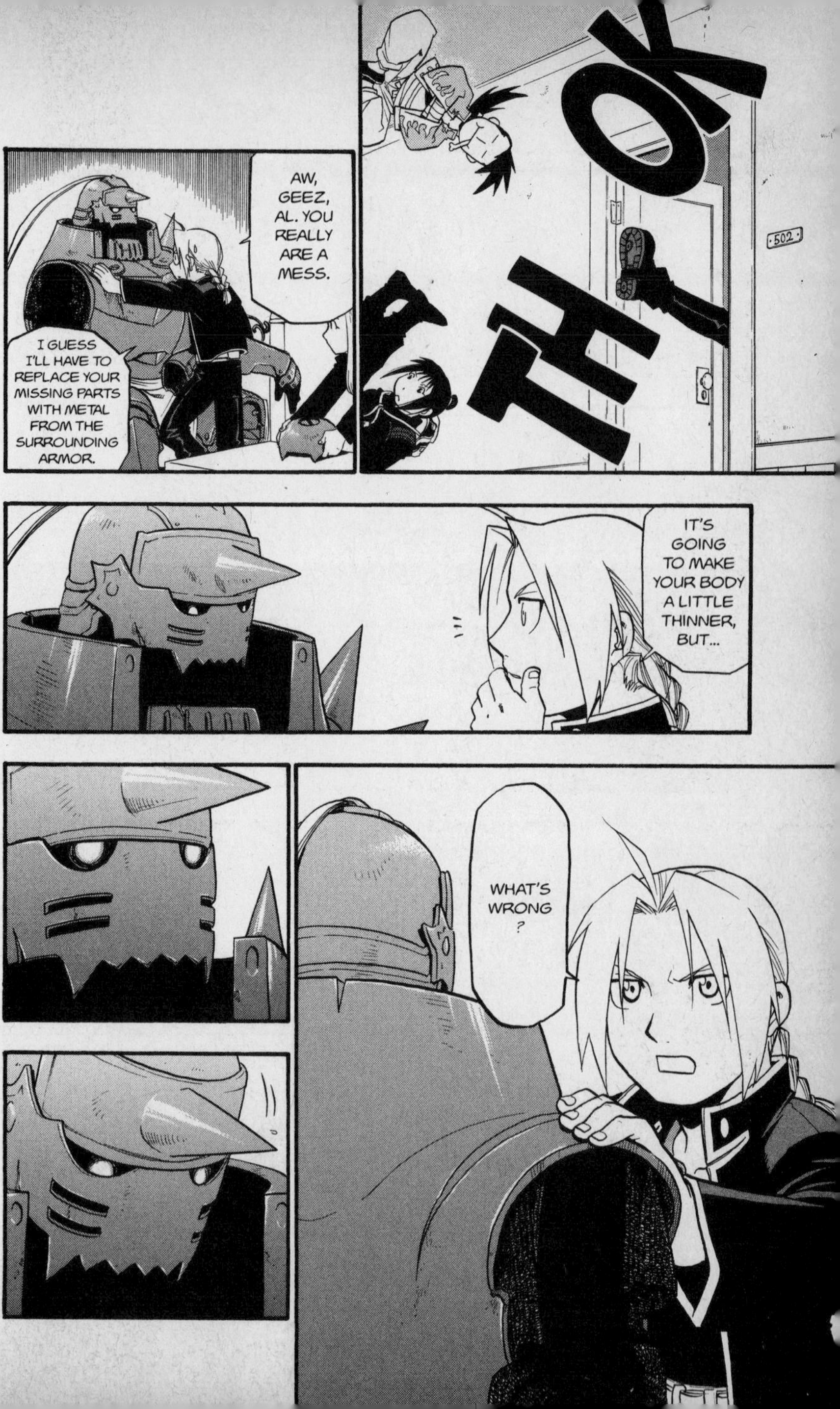
THOK
502
AW, GEEZ, AL. YOU REALLY ARE A MESS.
I GUESS I'LL HAVE TO REPLACE YOUR MISSING PARTS WITH METAL FROM THE SURROUNDING ARMOR.
IT'S GOING TO MAKE YOUR BODY A LITTLE THINNER, BUT...
WHAT'S WRONG?

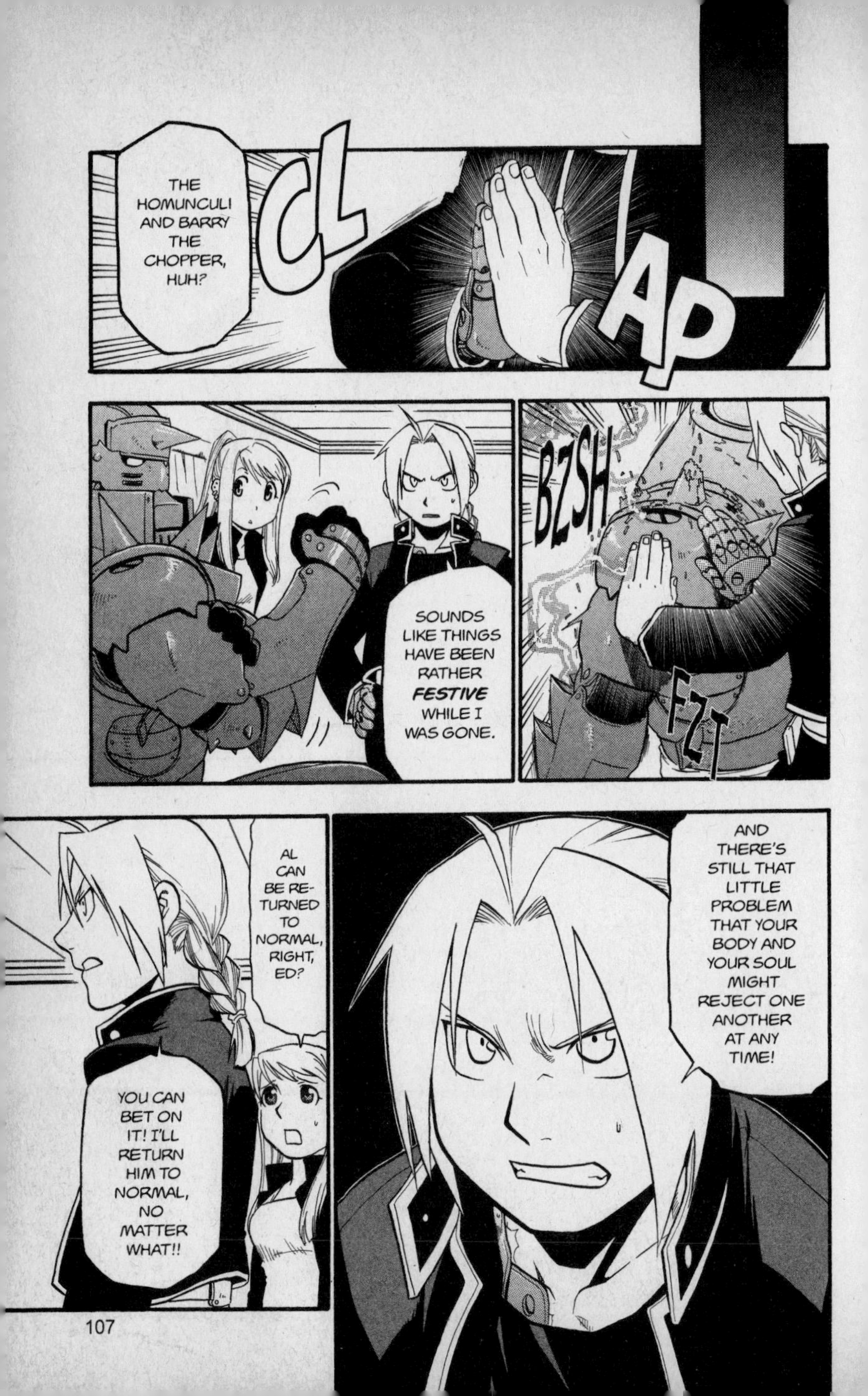
THE HOMUNCULI AND BARRY THE CHOPPER, HUH?
CLAP
SOUNDS LIKE THINGS HAVE BEEN RATHER *FESTIVE* WHILE I WAS GONE.
BZSH
FZT
AL CAN BE RE-TURNED TO NORMAL, RIGHT, ED?
YOU CAN BET ON IT! I'LL RETURN HIM TO NORMAL, NO MATTER WHAT!!
AND THERE'S STILL THAT LITTLE PROBLEM THAT YOUR BODY AND YOUR SOUL MIGHT REJECT ONE ANOTHER AT ANY TIME!

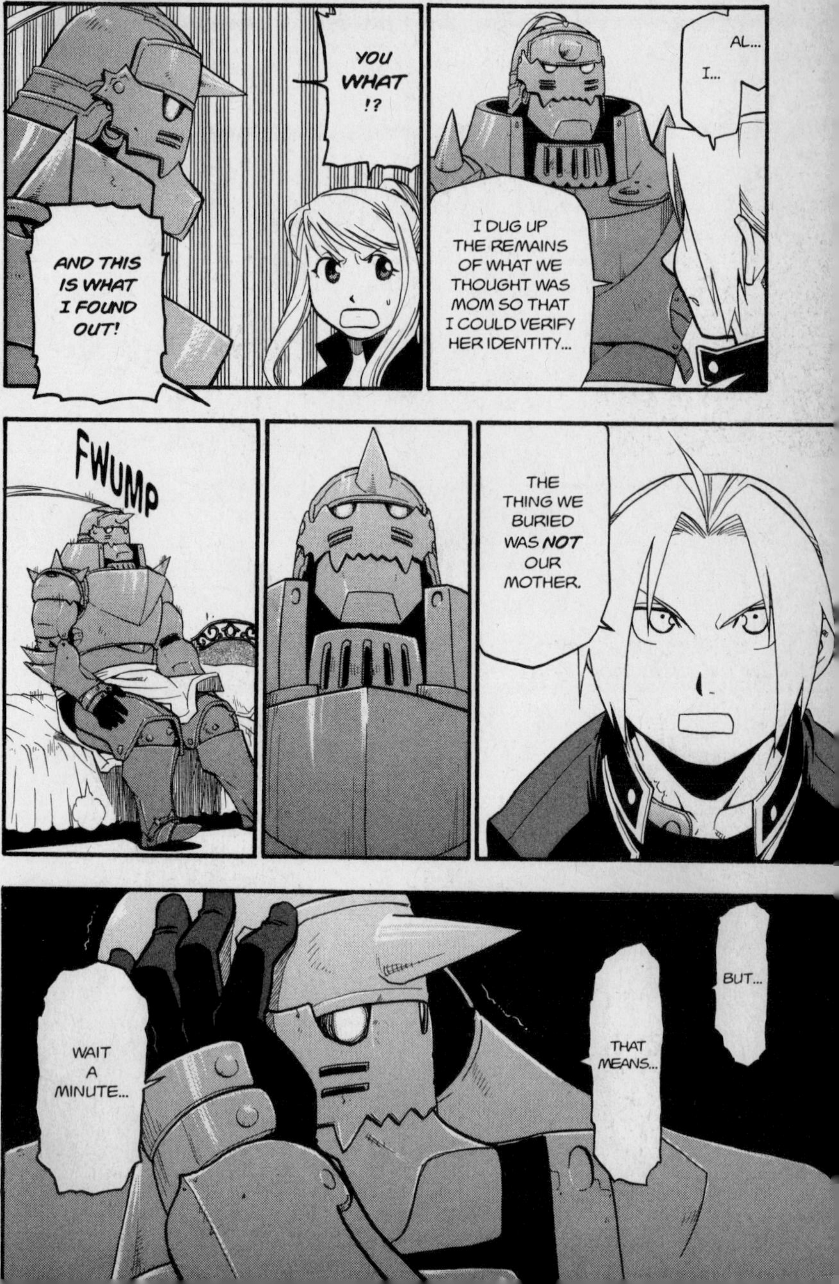
AL... I...
I DUG UP THE REMAINS OF WHAT WE THOUGHT WAS MOM SO THAT I COULD VERIFY HER IDENTITY...
YOU WHAT !?
AND THIS IS WHAT I FOUND OUT!
THE THING WE BURIED WAS **NOT** OUR MOTHER.
FWUMP
BUT...
THAT MEANS...
WAIT A MINUTE...

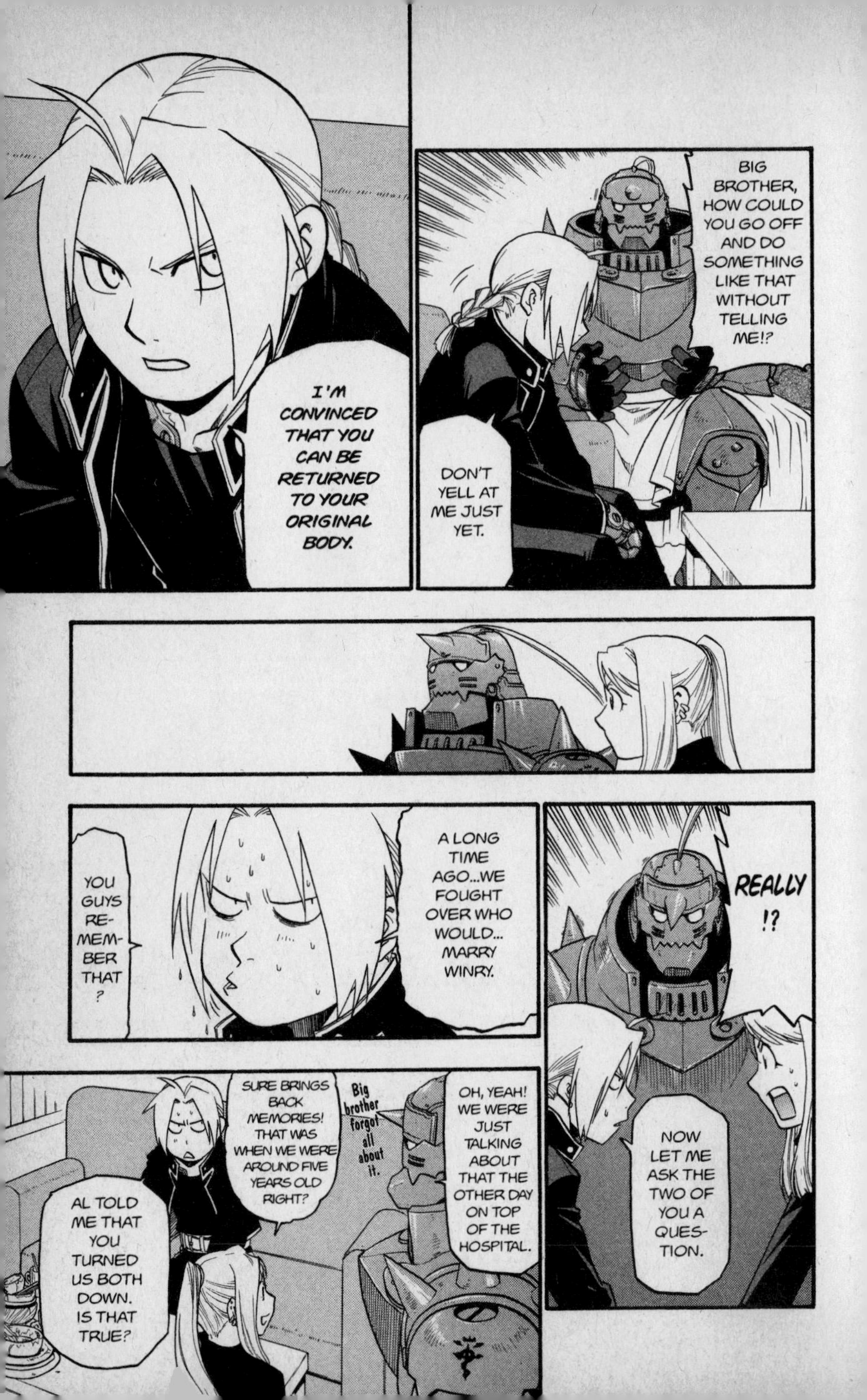
BIG BROTHER, HOW COULD YOU GO OFF AND DO SOMETHING LIKE THAT WITHOUT TELLING ME!?
DON'T YELL AT ME JUST YET.
I'M CONVINCED THAT YOU CAN BE RETURNED TO YOUR ORIGINAL BODY.
REALLY !?
NOW LET ME ASK THE TWO OF YOU A QUESTION.
A LONG TIME AGO...WE FOUGHT OVER WHO WOULD... MARRY WINRY.
YOU GUYS RE-MEM-BER THAT?
OH, YEAH! WE WERE JUST TALKING ABOUT THAT THE OTHER DAY ON TOP OF THE HOSPITAL.
Big brother forgot all about it.
SURE BRINGS BACK MEMORIES! THAT WAS WHEN WE WERE AROUND FIVE YEARS OLD RIGHT?
AL TOLD ME THAT YOU TURNED US BOTH DOWN. IS THAT TRUE?

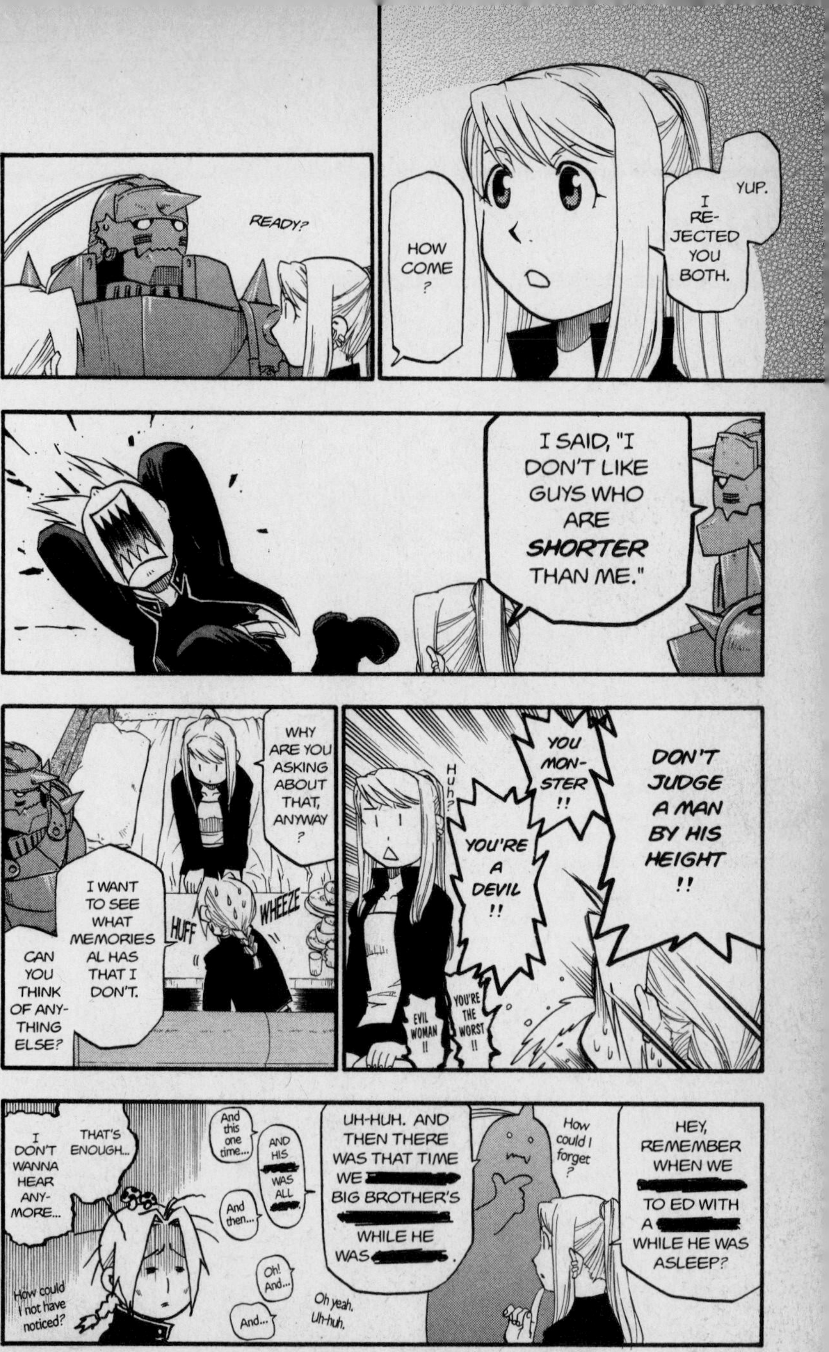
YUP. I REJECTED YOU BOTH.
HOW COME?
READY?
I SAID, "I DON'T LIKE GUYS WHO ARE **SHORTER** THAN ME."
DON'T JUDGE A MAN BY HIS HEIGHT!!
YOU MONSTER!!
Huh?
YOU'RE A DEVIL!!
YOU'RE THE WORST!!
EVIL WOMAN!!
WHY ARE YOU ASKING ABOUT THAT, ANYWAY?
I WANT TO SEE WHAT MEMORIES AL HAS THAT I DON'T.
WHEEZE
HUFF
CAN YOU THINK OF ANYTHING ELSE?
HEY, REMEMBER WHEN WE [redacted] TO ED WITH A [redacted] WHILE HE WAS ASLEEP?
How could I forget?
UH-HUH. AND THEN THERE WAS THAT TIME WE [redacted] BIG BROTHER'S [redacted] WHILE HE WAS [redacted].
Oh yeah. Uh-huh.
And this one time...
AND HIS [redacted] WAS ALL [redacted]
And then...
Oh! And...
And...
THAT'S ENOUGH...
I DON'T WANNA HEAR ANYMORE...
How could I not have noticed?

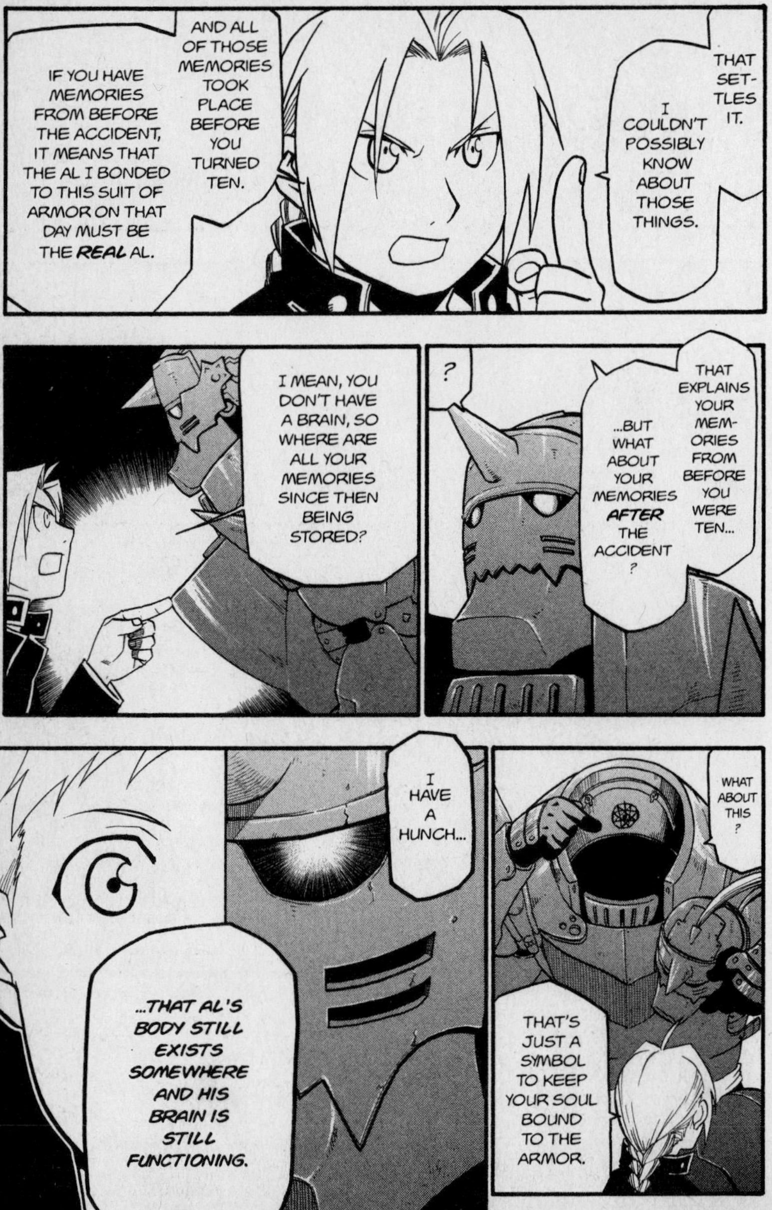
THAT SETTLES IT.
I COULDN'T POSSIBLY KNOW ABOUT THOSE THINGS.
AND ALL OF THOSE MEMORIES TOOK PLACE BEFORE YOU TURNED TEN.
IF YOU HAVE MEMORIES FROM BEFORE THE ACCIDENT, IT MEANS THAT THE AL I BONDED TO THIS SUIT OF ARMOR ON THAT DAY MUST BE THE ***REAL*** AL.
THAT EXPLAINS YOUR MEMORIES FROM BEFORE YOU WERE TEN...
...BUT WHAT ABOUT YOUR MEMORIES ***AFTER*** THE ACCIDENT?
?
I MEAN, YOU DON'T HAVE A BRAIN, SO WHERE ARE ALL YOUR MEMORIES SINCE THEN BEING STORED?
WHAT ABOUT THIS?
THAT'S JUST A SYMBOL TO KEEP YOUR SOUL BOUND TO THE ARMOR.
I HAVE A HUNCH...
...THAT AL'S BODY STILL EXISTS SOMEWHERE AND HIS BRAIN IS STILL FUNCTIONING.

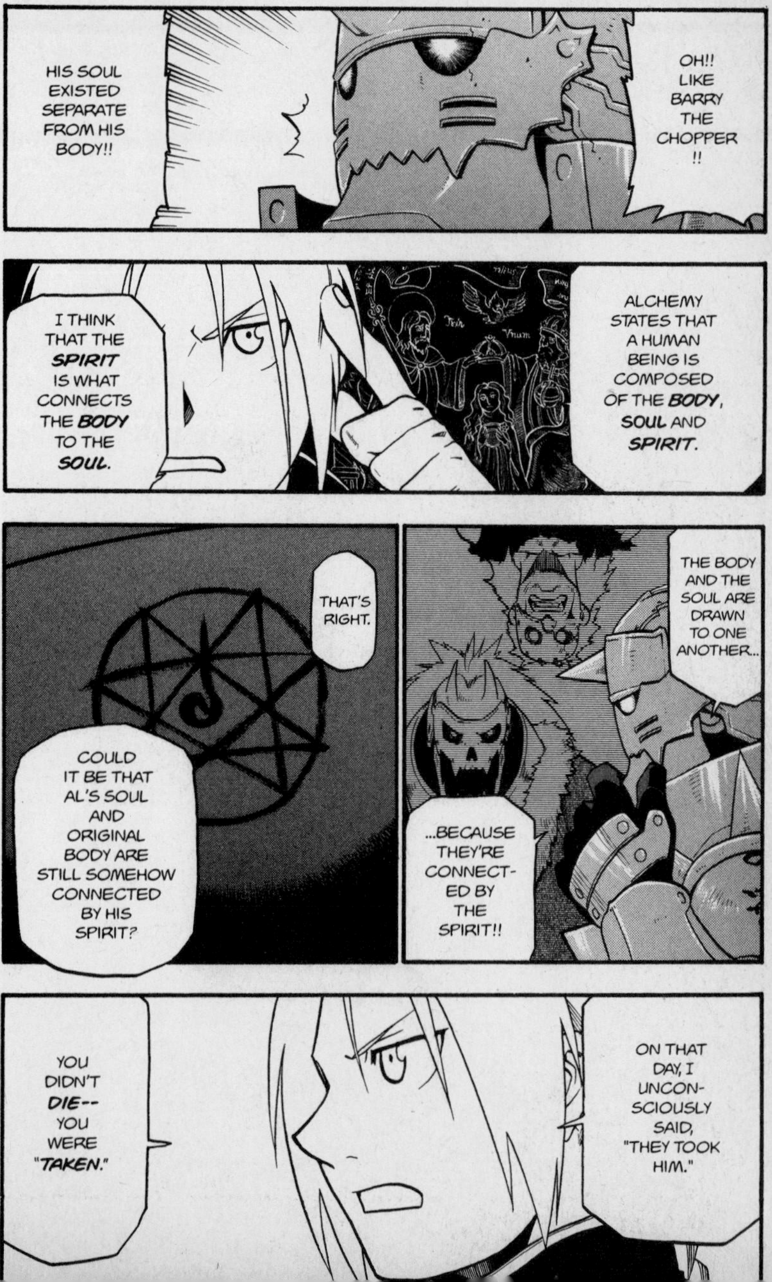
OH!! LIKE BARRY THE CHOPPER!!
HIS SOUL EXISTED SEPARATE FROM HIS BODY!!
ALCHEMY STATES THAT A HUMAN BEING IS COMPOSED OF THE BODY, SOUL AND SPIRIT.
I THINK THAT THE SPIRIT IS WHAT CONNECTS THE BODY TO THE SOUL.
THE BODY AND THE SOUL ARE DRAWN TO ONE ANOTHER...
...BECAUSE THEY'RE CONNECTED BY THE SPIRIT!!
THAT'S RIGHT.
COULD IT BE THAT AL'S SOUL AND ORIGINAL BODY ARE STILL SOMEHOW CONNECTED BY HIS SPIRIT?
ON THAT DAY, I UNCONSCIOUSLY SAID, "THEY TOOK HIM."
YOU DIDN'T DIE--YOU WERE "TAKEN."

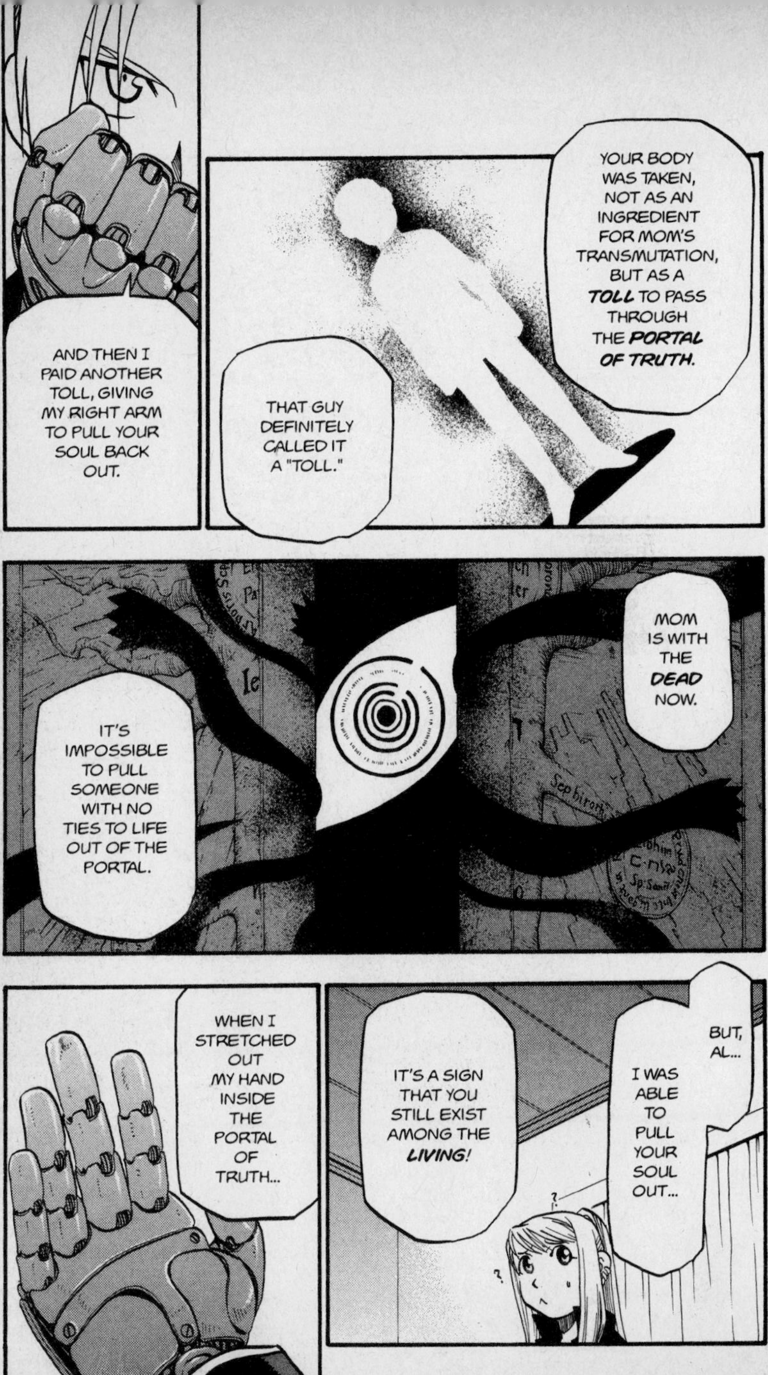
YOUR BODY WAS TAKEN, NOT AS AN INGREDIENT FOR MOM'S TRANSMUTATION, BUT AS A TOLL TO PASS THROUGH THE PORTAL OF TRUTH.
THAT GUY DEFINITELY CALLED IT A "TOLL."
AND THEN I PAID ANOTHER TOLL, GIVING MY RIGHT ARM TO PULL YOUR SOUL BACK OUT.
MOM IS WITH THE DEAD NOW.
IT'S IMPOSSIBLE TO PULL SOMEONE WITH NO TIES TO LIFE OUT OF THE PORTAL.
BUT, AL... I WAS ABLE TO PULL YOUR SOUL OUT...
IT'S A SIGN THAT YOU STILL EXIST AMONG THE LIVING!
WHEN I STRETCHED OUT MY HAND INSIDE THE PORTAL OF TRUTH...

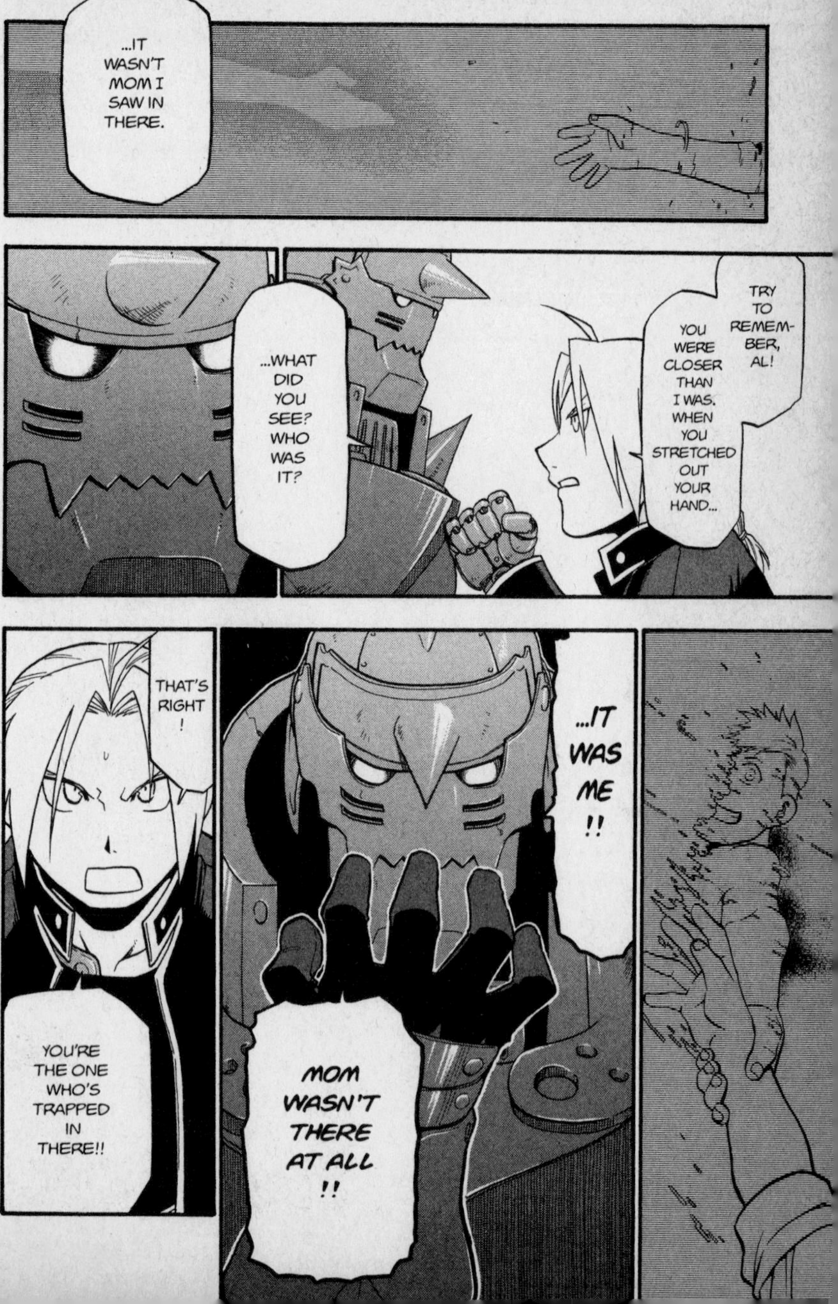
...IT WASN'T MOM I SAW IN THERE.
TRY TO REMEMBER, AL!
YOU WERE CLOSER THAN I WAS. WHEN YOU STRETCHED OUT YOUR HAND...
...WHAT DID YOU SEE? WHO WAS IT?
...IT WAS ME!!
MOM WASN'T THERE AT ALL!!
THAT'S RIGHT!
YOU'RE THE ONE WHO'S TRAPPED IN THERE!!

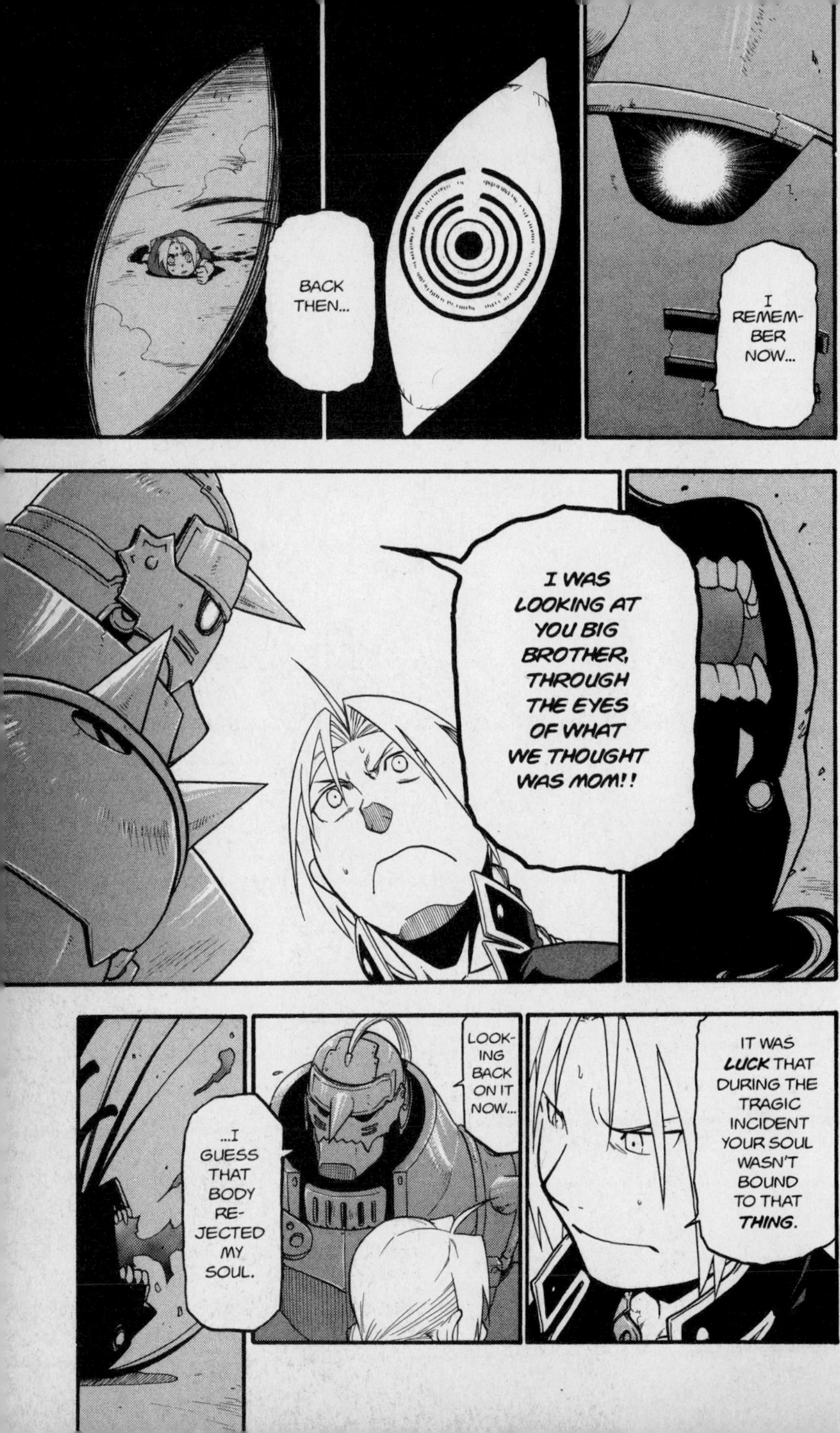
I REMEMBER NOW...
BACK THEN...
I WAS LOOKING AT YOU BIG BROTHER, THROUGH THE EYES OF WHAT WE THOUGHT WAS MOM!!
IT WAS *LUCK* THAT DURING THE TRAGIC INCIDENT YOUR SOUL WASN'T BOUND TO THAT *THING*.
LOOKING BACK ON IT NOW...
...I GUESS THAT BODY REJECTED MY SOUL.

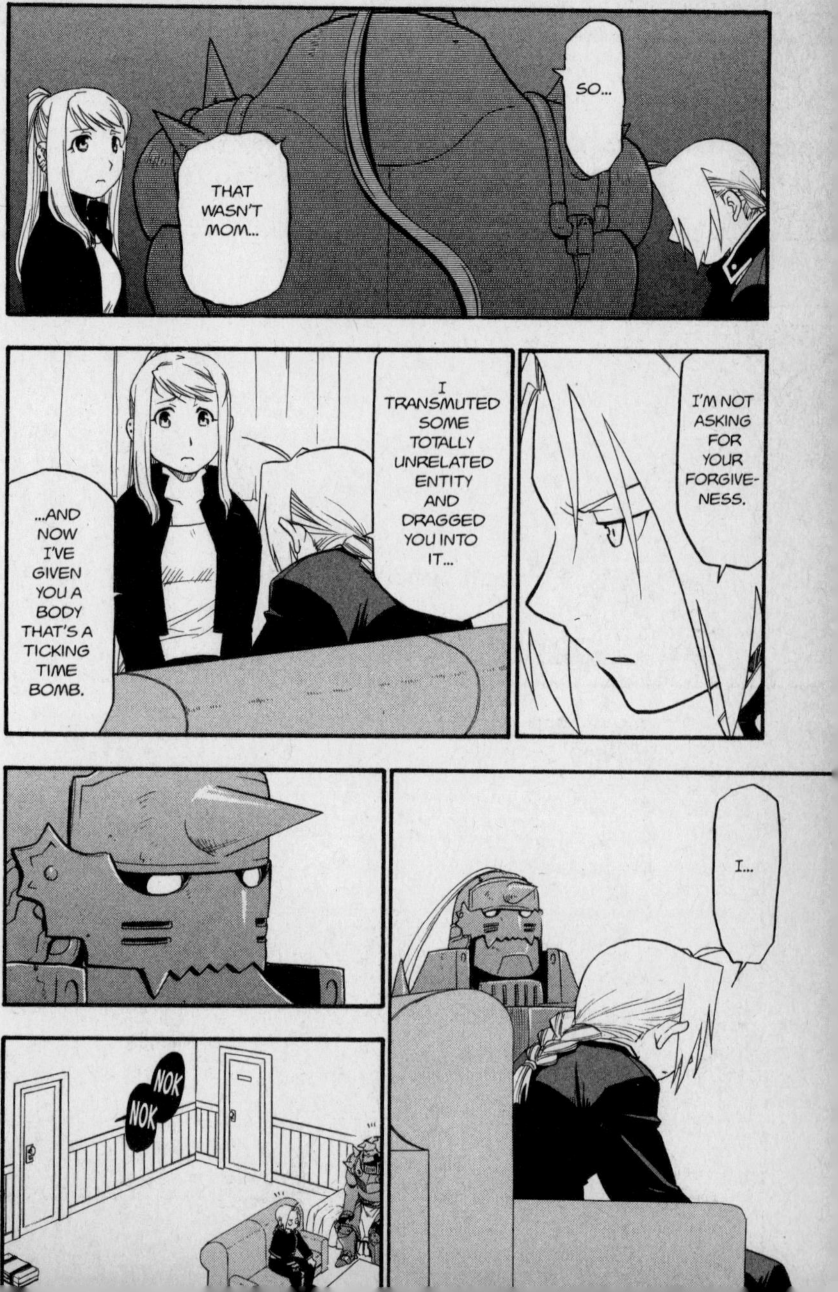
SO...
THAT WASN'T MOM...
I'M NOT ASKING FOR YOUR FORGIVE-NESS.
I TRANSMUTED SOME TOTALLY UNRELATED ENTITY AND DRAGGED YOU INTO IT...
...AND NOW I'VE GIVEN YOU A BODY THAT'S A TICKING TIME BOMB.
I...
NOK NOK

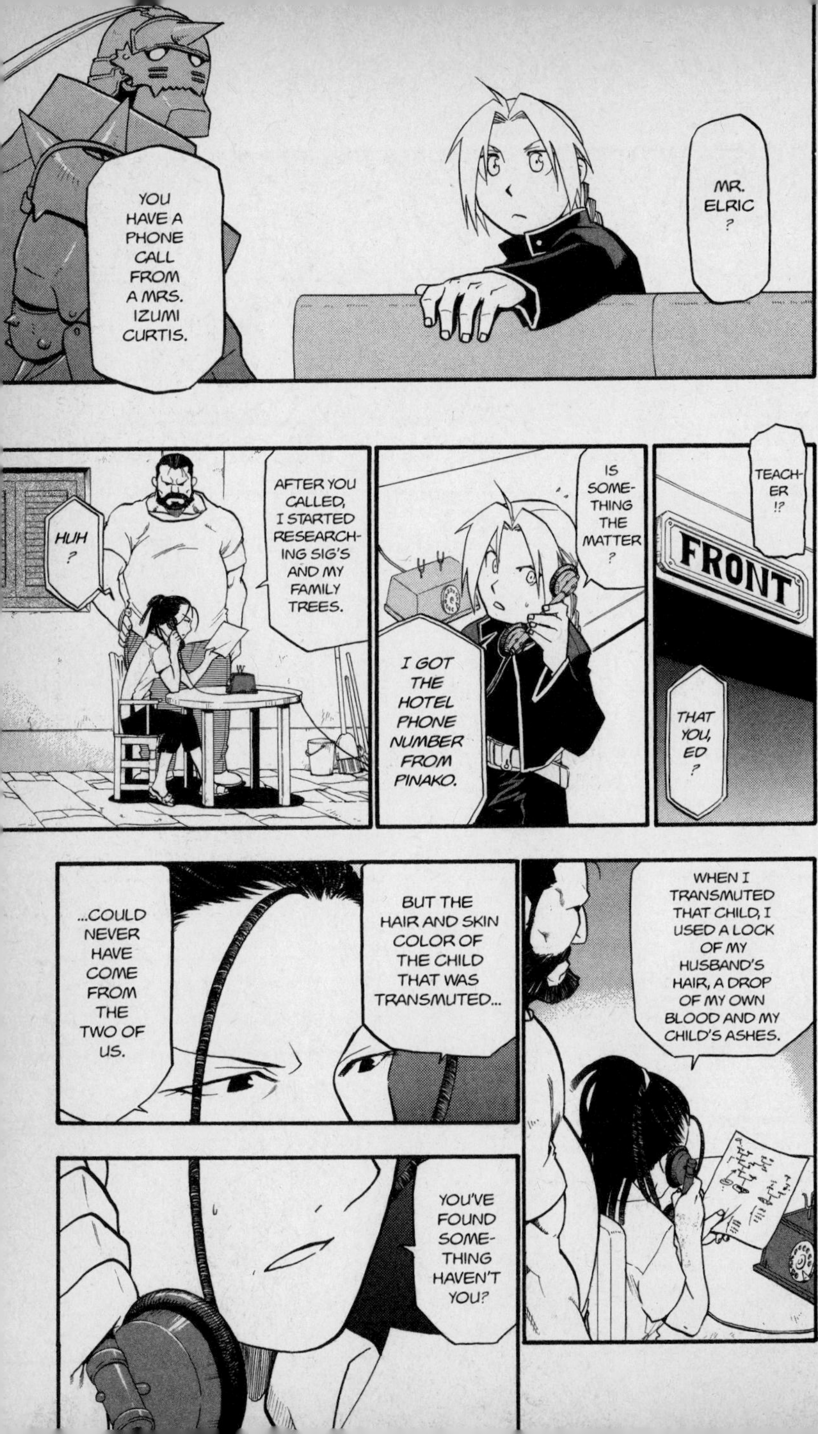
MR. ELRIC?
YOU HAVE A PHONE CALL FROM A MRS. IZUMI CURTIS.
TEACHER!?
FRONT
THAT YOU, ED?
IS SOMETHING THE MATTER?
I GOT THE HOTEL PHONE NUMBER FROM PINAKO.
AFTER YOU CALLED, I STARTED RESEARCHING SIG'S AND MY FAMILY TREES.
HUH?
WHEN I TRANSMUTED THAT CHILD, I USED A LOCK OF MY HUSBAND'S HAIR, A DROP OF MY OWN BLOOD AND MY CHILD'S ASHES.
BUT THE HAIR AND SKIN COLOR OF THE CHILD THAT WAS TRANSMUTED...
...COULD NEVER HAVE COME FROM THE TWO OF US.
YOU'VE FOUND SOMETHING HAVEN'T YOU?

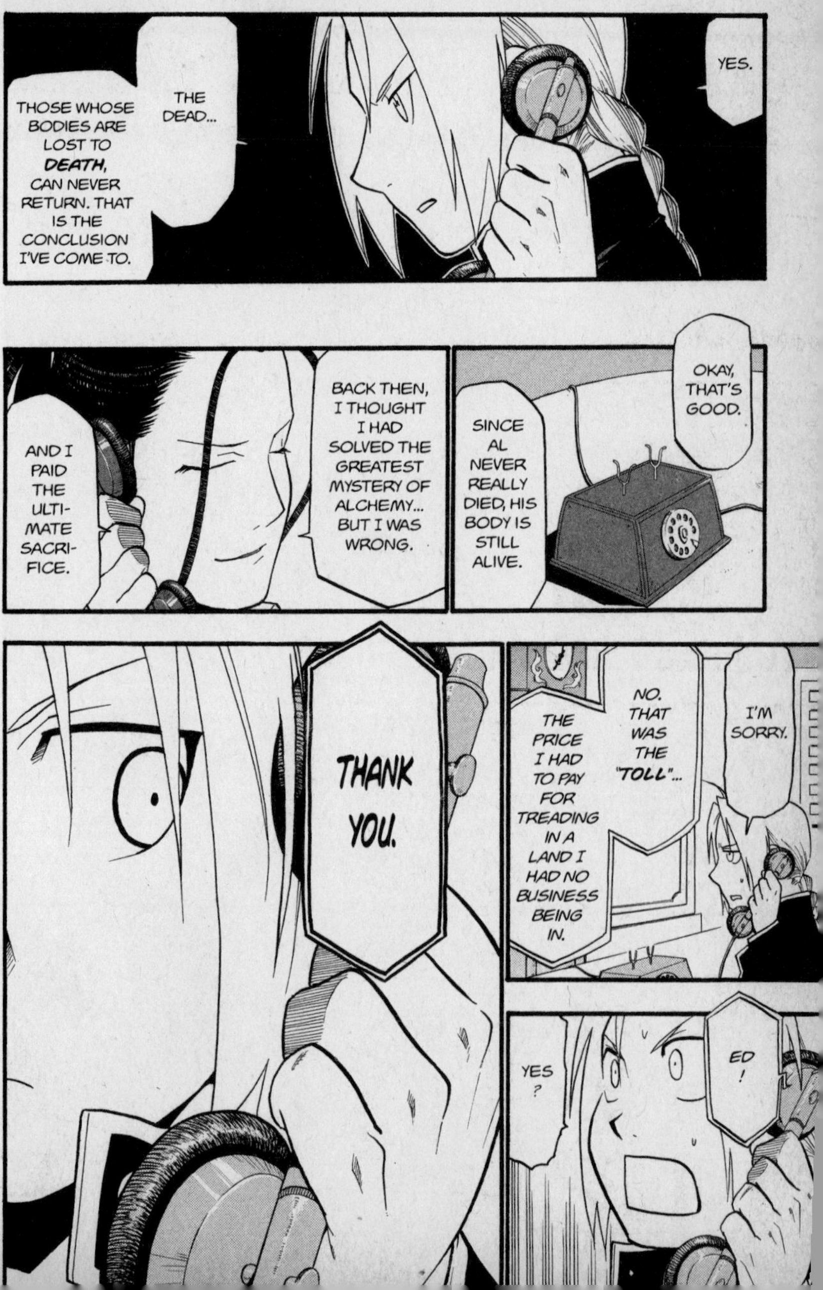
YES.
THE DEAD...
THOSE WHOSE BODIES ARE LOST TO **DEATH**, CAN NEVER RETURN. THAT IS THE CONCLUSION I'VE COME TO.
OKAY, THAT'S GOOD.
SINCE AL NEVER REALLY DIED, HIS BODY IS STILL ALIVE.
BACK THEN, I THOUGHT I HAD SOLVED THE GREATEST MYSTERY OF ALCHEMY... BUT I WAS WRONG.
AND I PAID THE ULTIMATE SACRIFICE.
I'M SORRY.
NO. THAT WAS THE "**TOLL**"...
THE PRICE I HAD TO PAY FOR TREADING IN A LAND I HAD NO BUSINESS BEING IN.
ED!
YES?
THANK YOU.

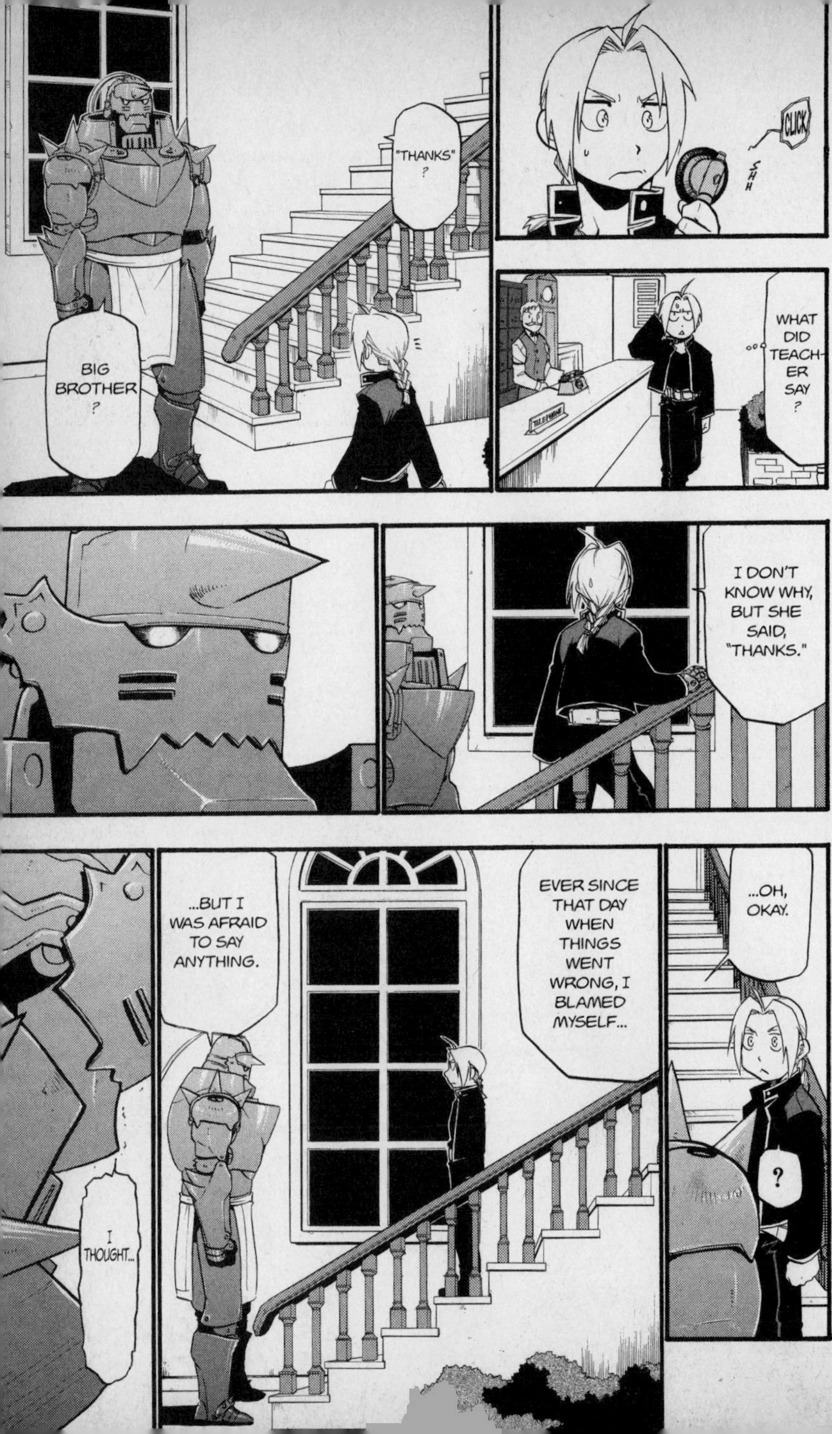
CLICK
SHH
WHAT DID TEACHER SAY?
"THANKS"?
BIG BROTHER?
I DON'T KNOW WHY, BUT SHE SAID, "THANKS."
...OH, OKAY.
?
EVER SINCE THAT DAY WHEN THINGS WENT WRONG, I BLAMED MYSELF...
...BUT I WAS AFRAID TO SAY ANYTHING.
I THOUGHT...

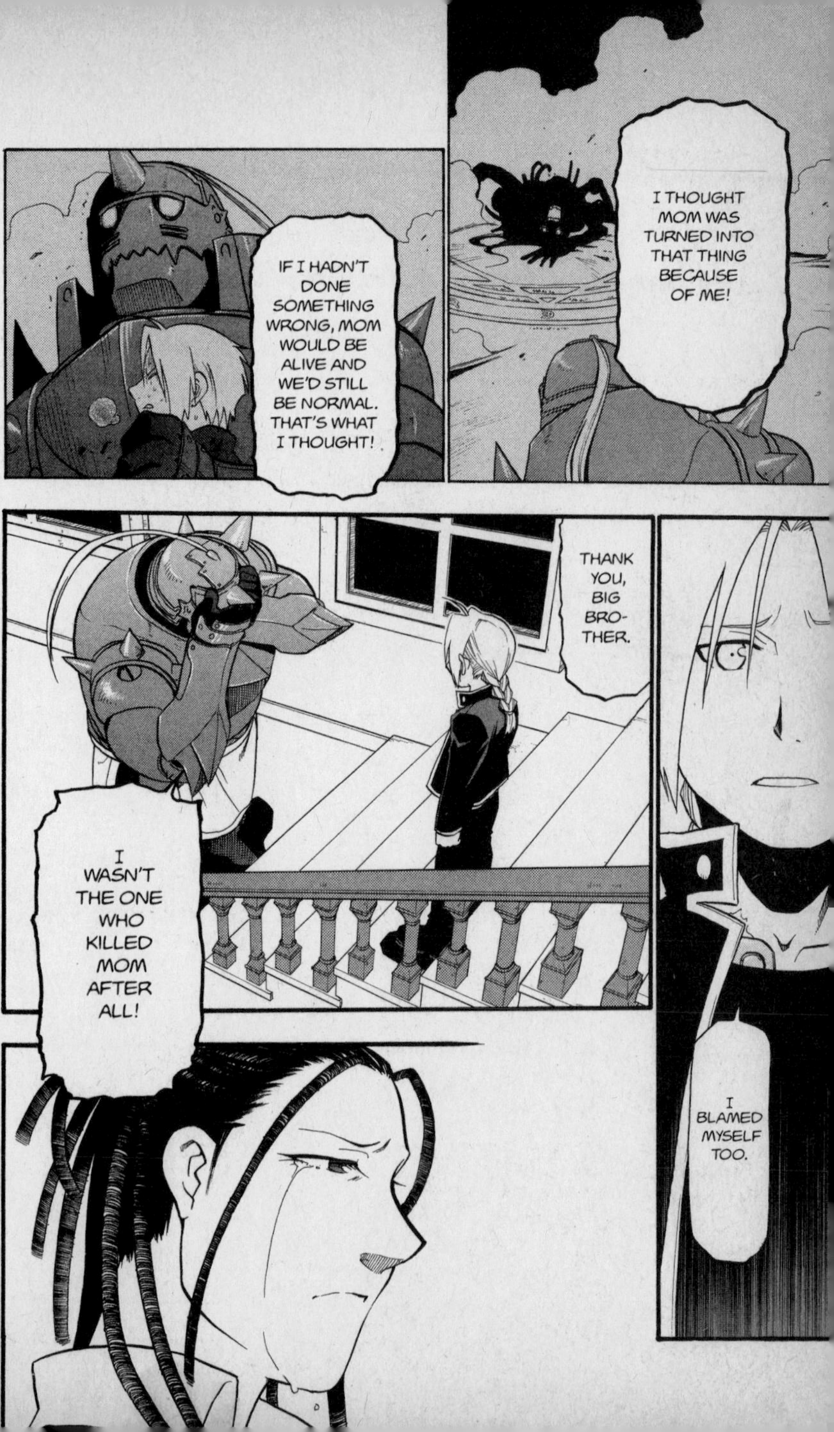
I THOUGHT MOM WAS TURNED INTO THAT THING BECAUSE OF ME!
IF I HADN'T DONE SOMETHING WRONG, MOM WOULD BE ALIVE AND WE'D STILL BE NORMAL. THAT'S WHAT I THOUGHT!
I BLAMED MYSELF TOO.
THANK YOU, BIG BRO-THER.
I WASN'T THE ONE WHO KILLED MOM AFTER ALL!

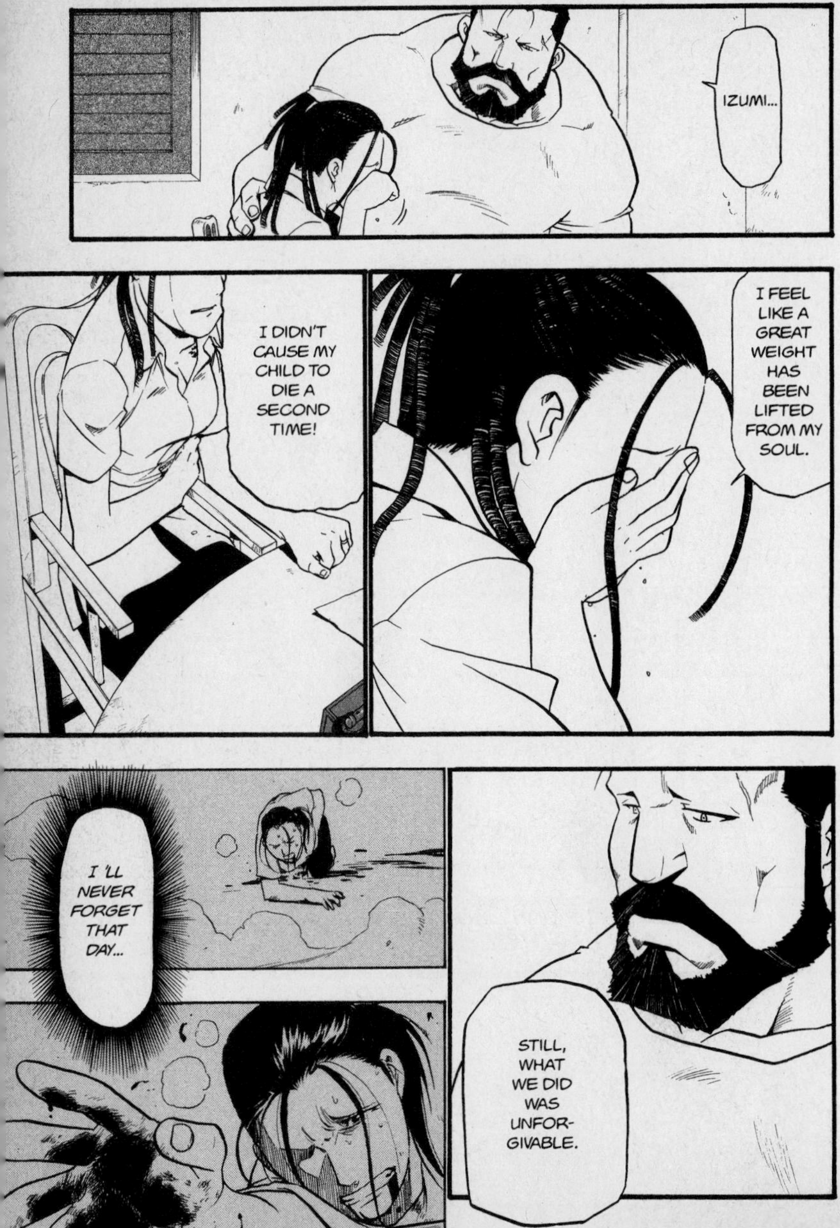
IZUMI...
I FEEL LIKE A GREAT WEIGHT HAS BEEN LIFTED FROM MY SOUL.
I DIDN'T CAUSE MY CHILD TO DIE A SECOND TIME!
STILL, WHAT WE DID WAS UNFORGIVABLE.
I'LL NEVER FORGET THAT DAY...

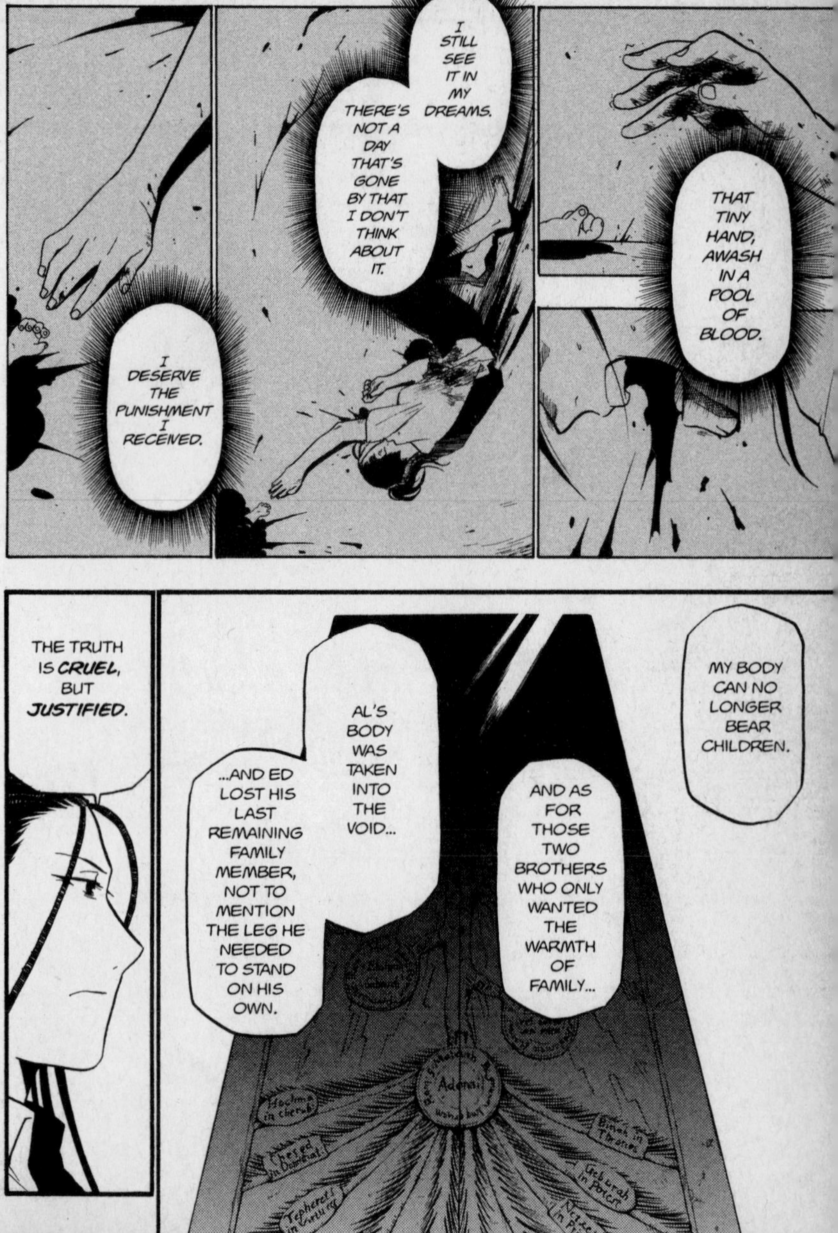
THAT TINY HAND, AWASH IN A POOL OF BLOOD.
I STILL SEE IT IN MY DREAMS.
THERE'S NOT A DAY THAT'S GONE BY THAT I DON'T THINK ABOUT IT.
I DESERVE THE PUNISHMENT I RECEIVED.
MY BODY CAN NO LONGER BEAR CHILDREN.
AND AS FOR THOSE TWO BROTHERS WHO ONLY WANTED THE WARMTH OF FAMILY...
AL'S BODY WAS TAKEN INTO THE VOID...
...AND ED LOST HIS LAST REMAINING FAMILY MEMBER, NOT TO MENTION THE LEG HE NEEDED TO STAND ON HIS OWN.
THE TRUTH IS CRUEL, BUT JUSTIFIED.

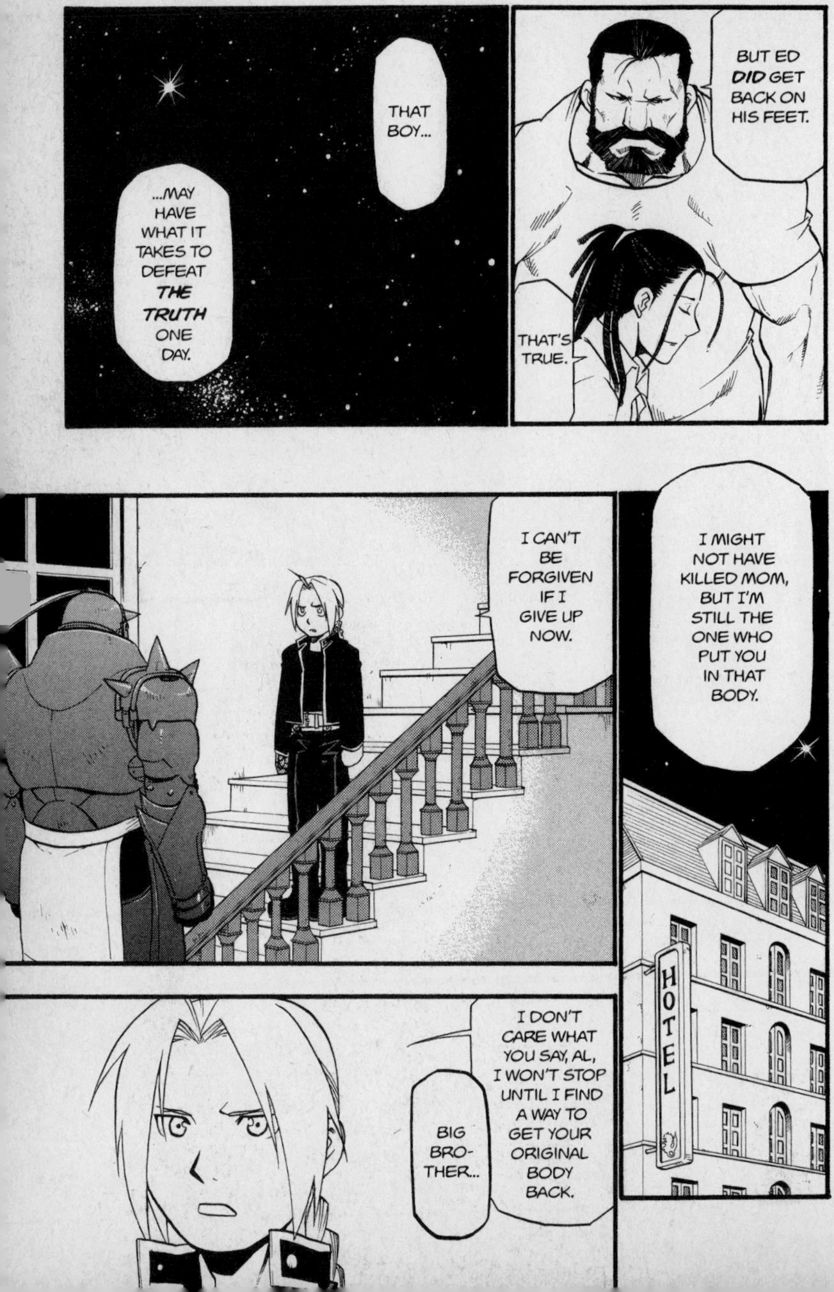
BUT ED DID GET BACK ON HIS FEET.
THAT'S TRUE.
THAT BOY...
...MAY HAVE WHAT IT TAKES TO DEFEAT THE TRUTH ONE DAY.
I MIGHT NOT HAVE KILLED MOM, BUT I'M STILL THE ONE WHO PUT YOU IN THAT BODY.
I CAN'T BE FORGIVEN IF I GIVE UP NOW.
HOTEL
I DON'T CARE WHAT YOU SAY, AL, I WON'T STOP UNTIL I FIND A WAY TO GET YOUR ORIGINAL BODY BACK.
BIG BROTHER...

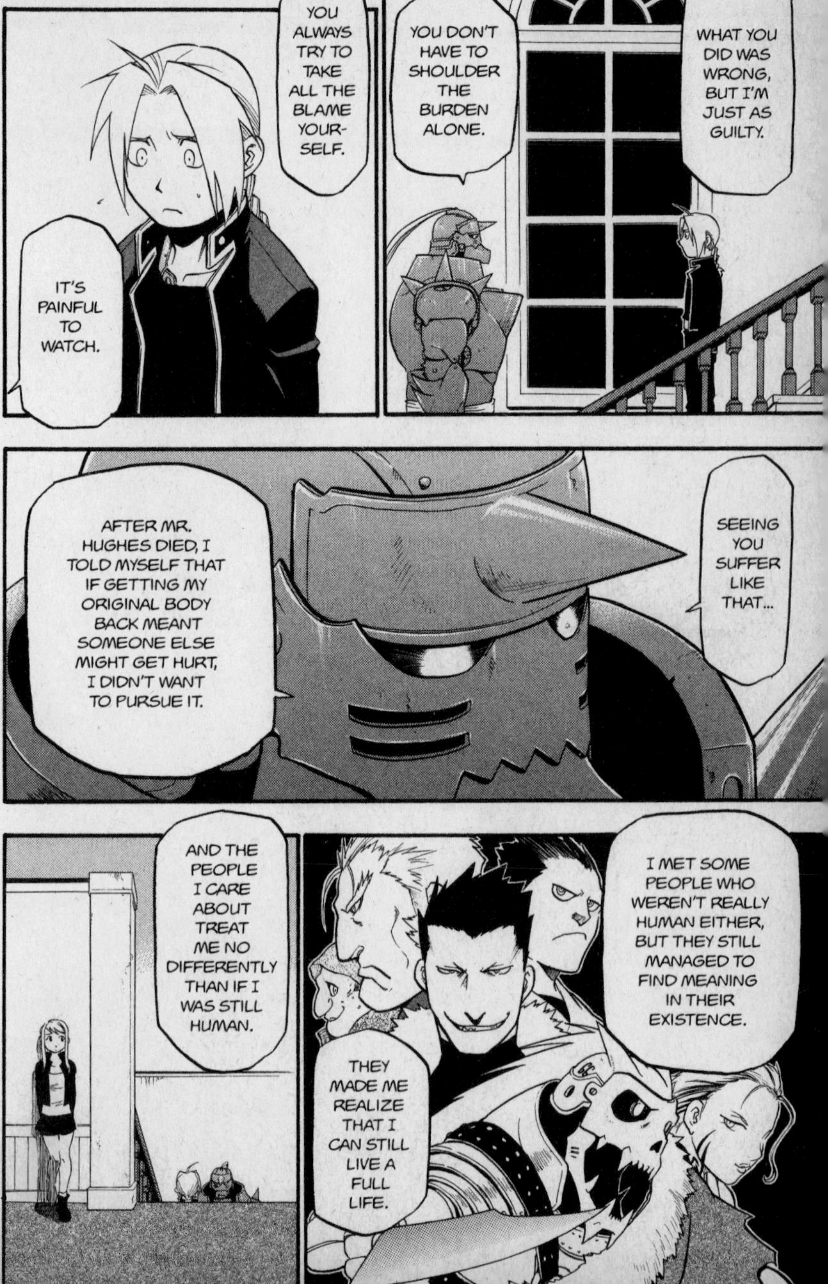
WHAT YOU DID WAS WRONG, BUT I'M JUST AS GUILTY.
YOU DON'T HAVE TO SHOULDER THE BURDEN ALONE.
YOU ALWAYS TRY TO TAKE ALL THE BLAME YOUR-SELF.
IT'S PAINFUL TO WATCH.
SEEING YOU SUFFER LIKE THAT...
AFTER MR. HUGHES DIED, I TOLD MYSELF THAT IF GETTING MY ORIGINAL BODY BACK MEANT SOMEONE ELSE MIGHT GET HURT, I DIDN'T WANT TO PURSUE IT.
I MET SOME PEOPLE WHO WEREN'T REALLY HUMAN EITHER, BUT THEY STILL MANAGED TO FIND MEANING IN THEIR EXISTENCE.
THEY MADE ME REALIZE THAT I CAN STILL LIVE A FULL LIFE.
AND THE PEOPLE I CARE ABOUT TREAT ME NO DIFFERENTLY THAN IF I WAS STILL HUMAN.

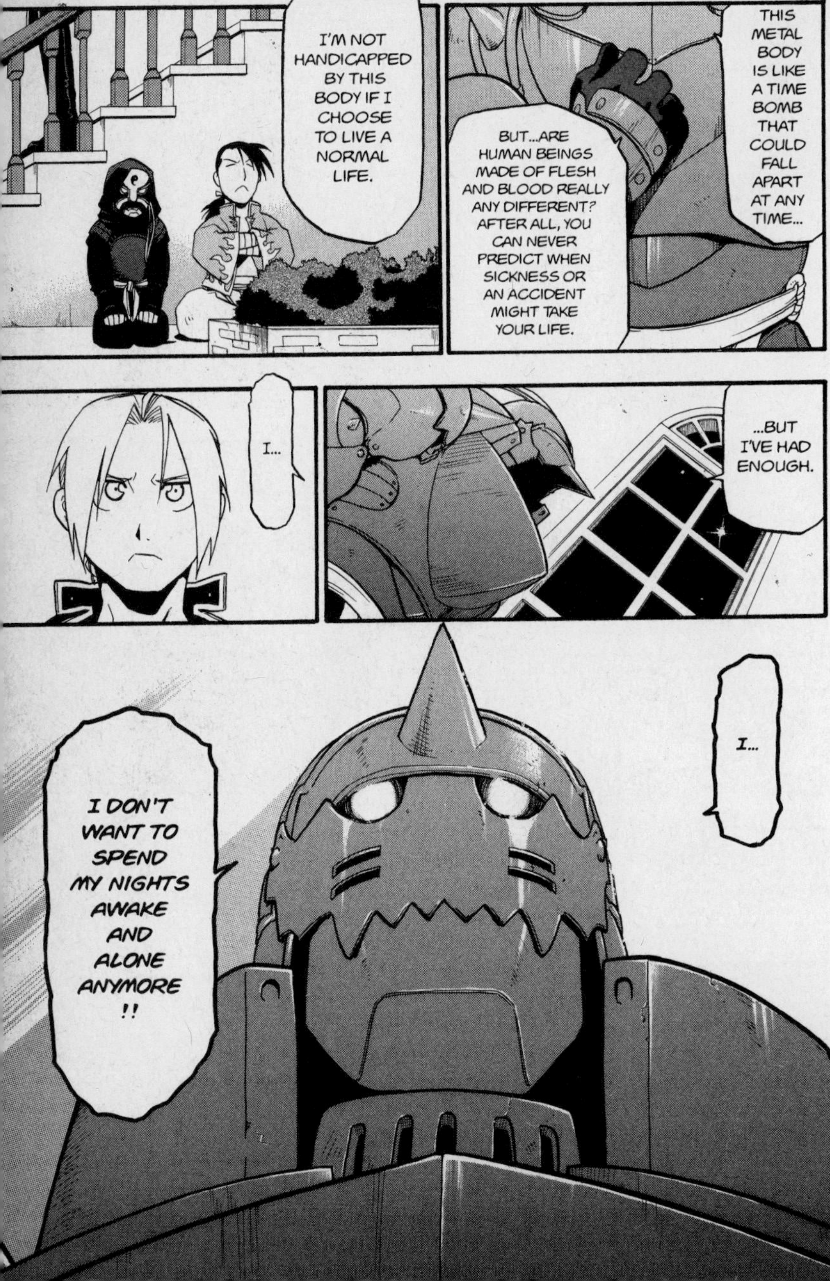
THIS METAL BODY IS LIKE A TIME BOMB THAT COULD FALL APART AT ANY TIME...
BUT...ARE HUMAN BEINGS MADE OF FLESH AND BLOOD REALLY ANY DIFFERENT? AFTER ALL, YOU CAN NEVER PREDICT WHEN SICKNESS OR AN ACCIDENT MIGHT TAKE YOUR LIFE.
I'M NOT HANDICAPPED BY THIS BODY IF I CHOOSE TO LIVE A NORMAL LIFE.
...BUT I'VE HAD ENOUGH.
I...
I...
I DON'T WANT TO SPEND MY NIGHTS AWAKE AND ALONE ANYMORE!!

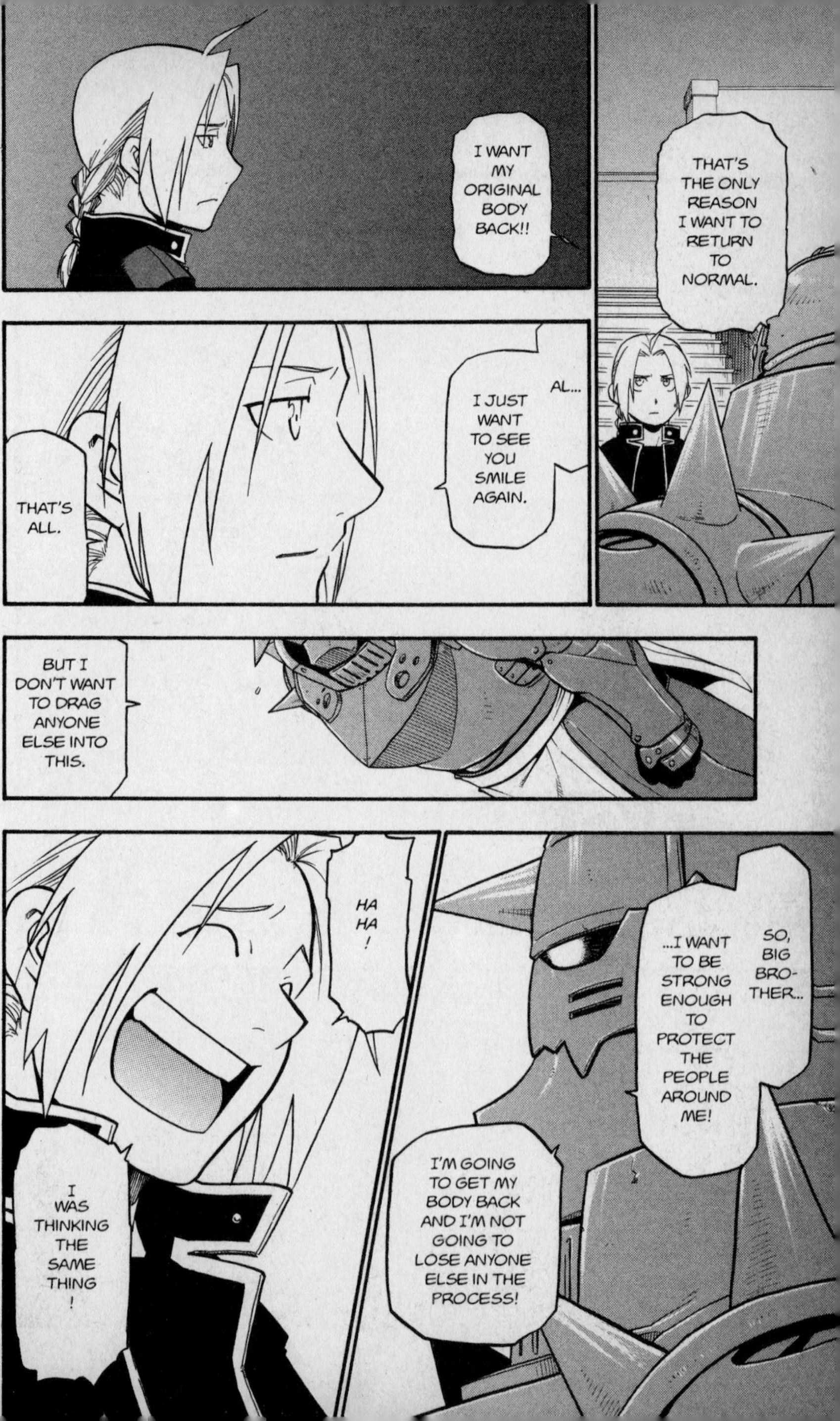
THAT'S THE ONLY REASON I WANT TO RETURN TO NORMAL.
I WANT MY ORIGINAL BODY BACK!!
AL...
I JUST WANT TO SEE YOU SMILE AGAIN.
THAT'S ALL.
BUT I DON'T WANT TO DRAG ANYONE ELSE INTO THIS.
SO, BIG BRO-THER...
...I WANT TO BE STRONG ENOUGH TO PROTECT THE PEOPLE AROUND ME!
I'M GOING TO GET MY BODY BACK AND I'M NOT GOING TO LOSE ANYONE ELSE IN THE PROCESS!
HA HA!
I WAS THINKING THE SAME THING!

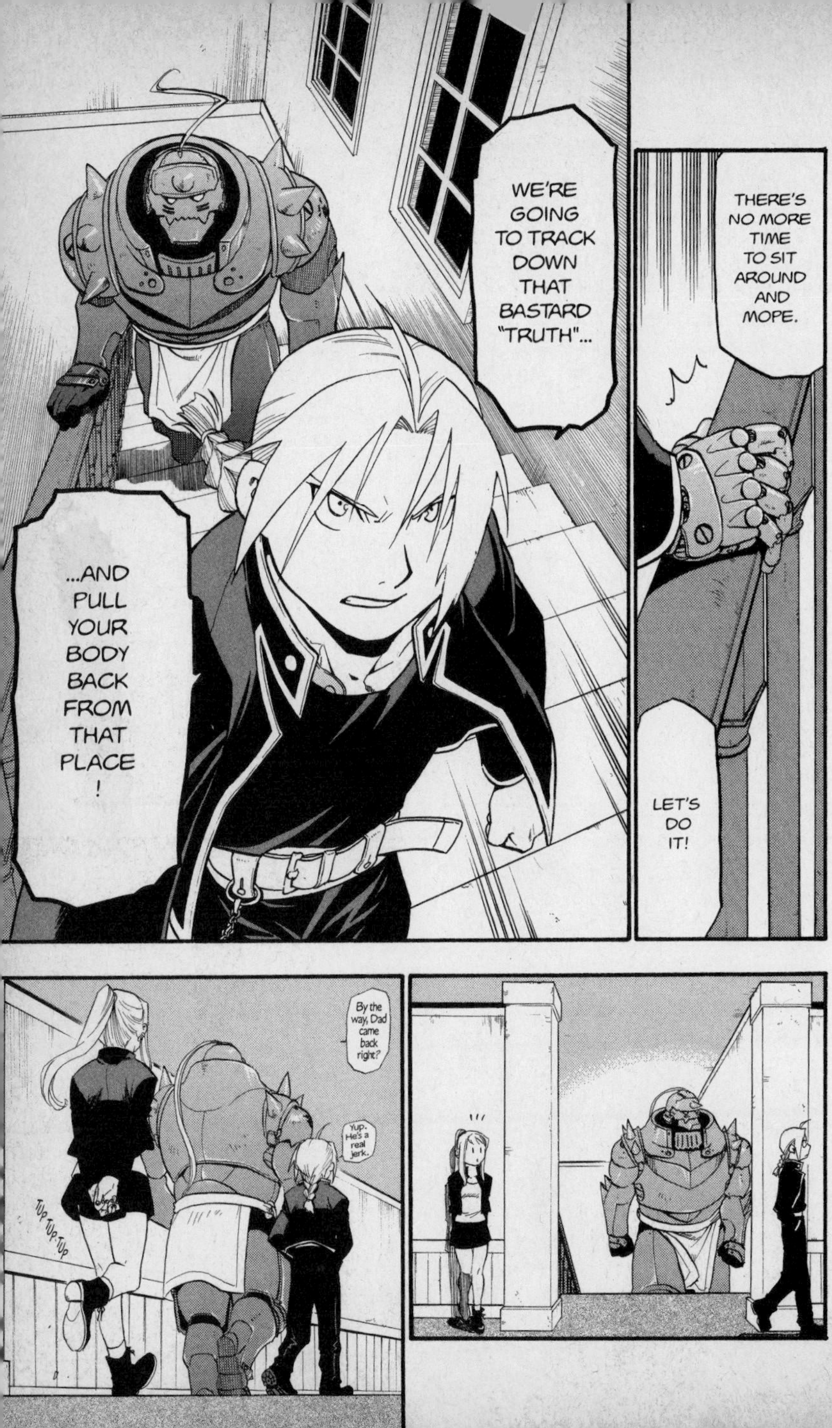
THERE'S NO MORE TIME TO SIT AROUND AND MOPE.
LET'S DO IT!
WE'RE GOING TO TRACK DOWN THAT BASTARD "TRUTH"...
...AND PULL YOUR BODY BACK FROM THAT PLACE!
By the way, Dad came back right?
Yup. He's a real jerk.
TUP TUP TUP

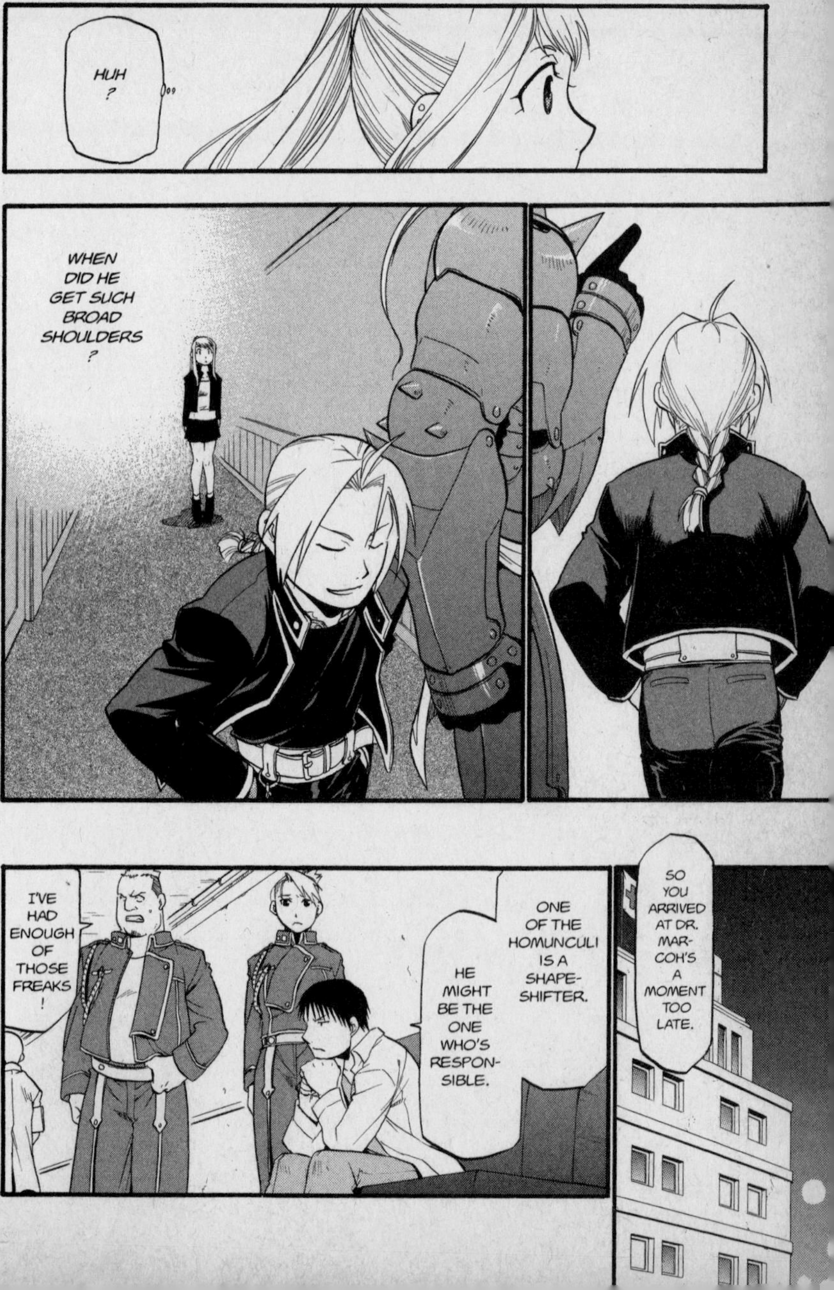
HUH?
WHEN DID HE GET SUCH BROAD SHOULDERS?
SO YOU ARRIVED AT DR. MARCOH'S A MOMENT TOO LATE.
ONE OF THE HOMUNCULI IS A SHAPE-SHIFTER.
HE MIGHT BE THE ONE WHO'S RESPONSIBLE.
I'VE HAD ENOUGH OF THOSE FREAKS!

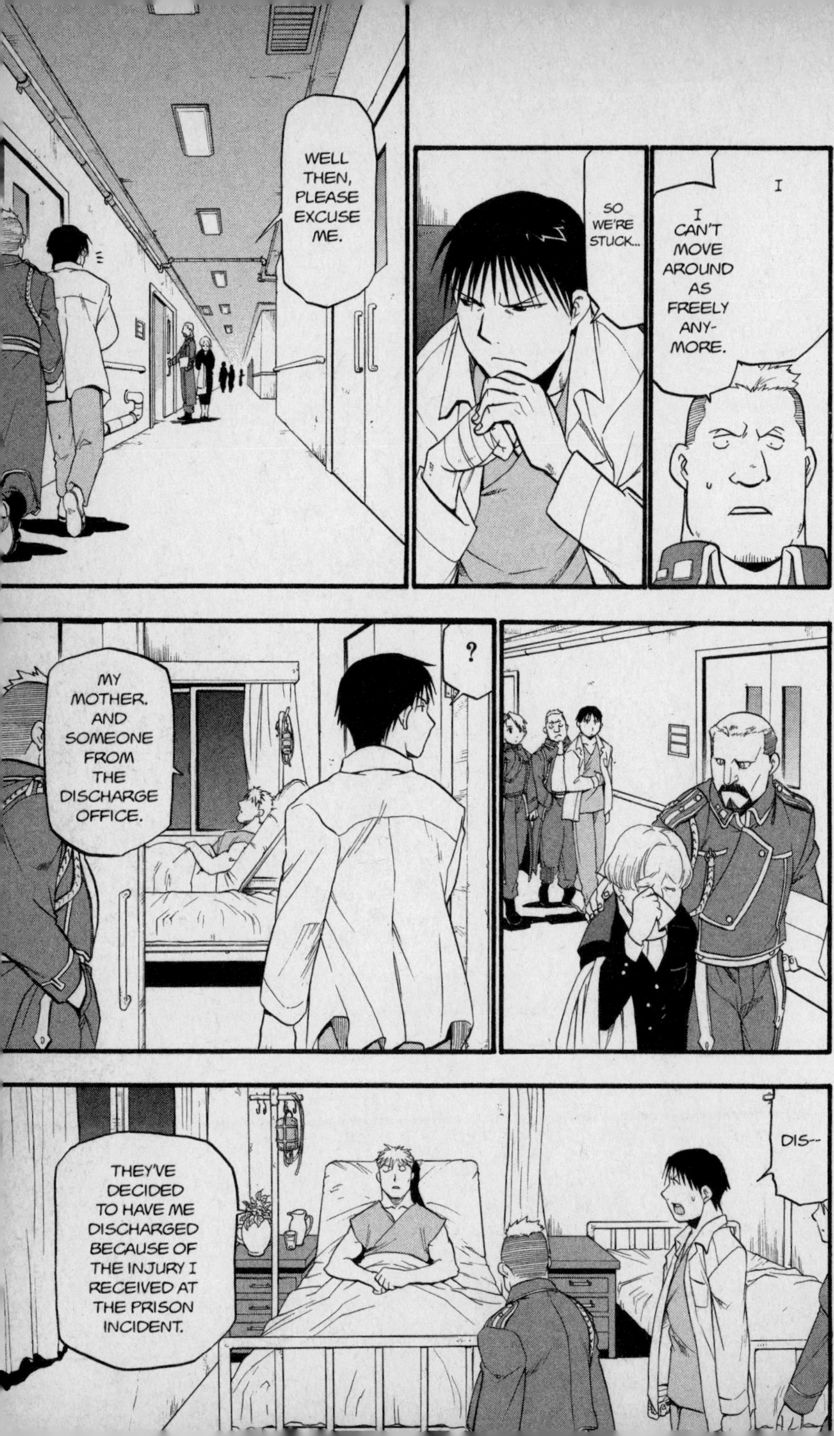
I
I CAN'T MOVE AROUND AS FREELY ANYMORE.
SO WE'RE STUCK...
WELL THEN, PLEASE EXCUSE ME.
?
MY MOTHER. AND SOMEONE FROM THE DISCHARGE OFFICE.
DIS--
THEY'VE DECIDED TO HAVE ME DISCHARGED BECAUSE OF THE INJURY I RECEIVED AT THE PRISON INCIDENT.

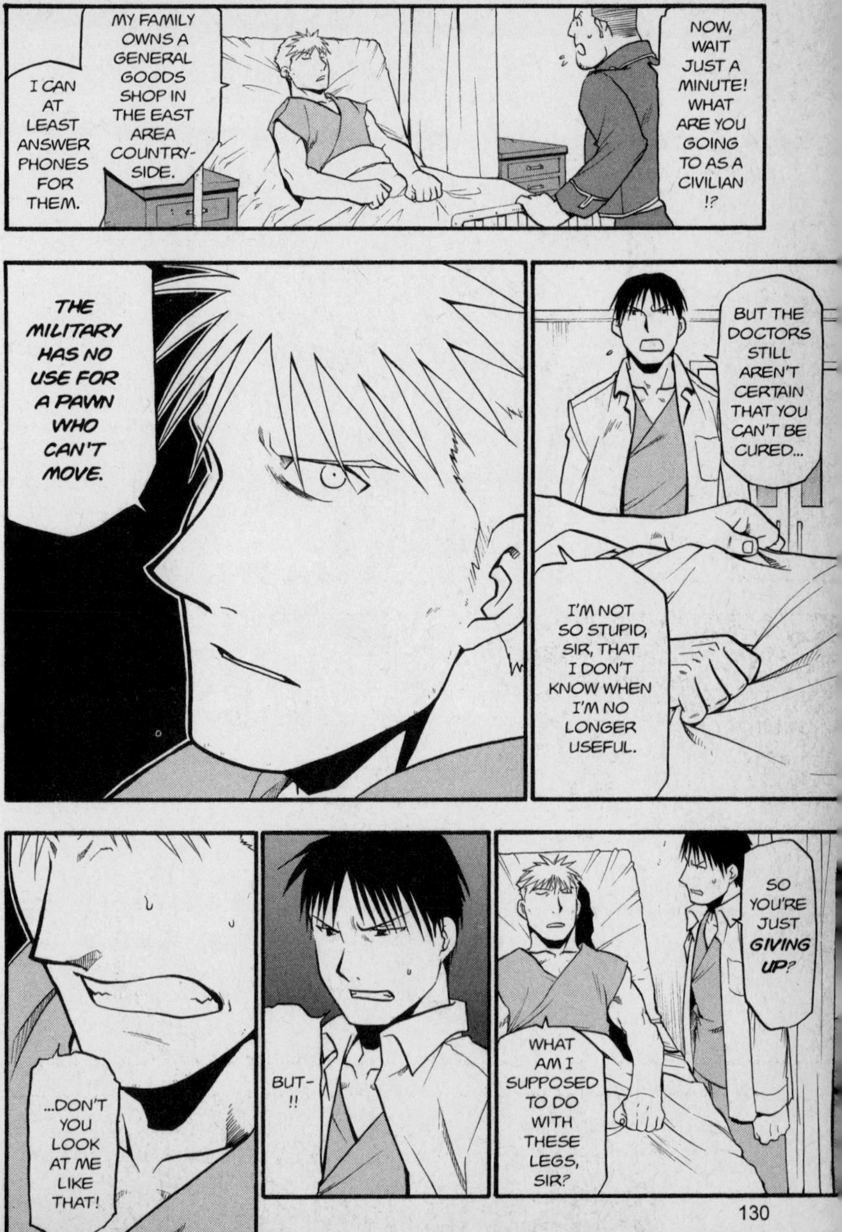
NOW, WAIT JUST A MINUTE! WHAT ARE YOU GOING TO AS A CIVILIAN !?
MY FAMILY OWNS A GENERAL GOODS SHOP IN THE EAST AREA COUNTRY-SIDE.
I CAN AT LEAST ANSWER PHONES FOR THEM.
BUT THE DOCTORS STILL AREN'T CERTAIN THAT YOU CAN'T BE CURED...
I'M NOT SO STUPID, SIR, THAT I DON'T KNOW WHEN I'M NO LONGER USEFUL.
THE MILITARY HAS NO USE FOR A PAWN WHO CAN'T MOVE.
SO YOU'RE JUST ***GIVING UP?***
WHAT AM I SUPPOSED TO DO WITH THESE LEGS, SIR?
BUT-!!
...DON'T YOU LOOK AT ME LIKE THAT!

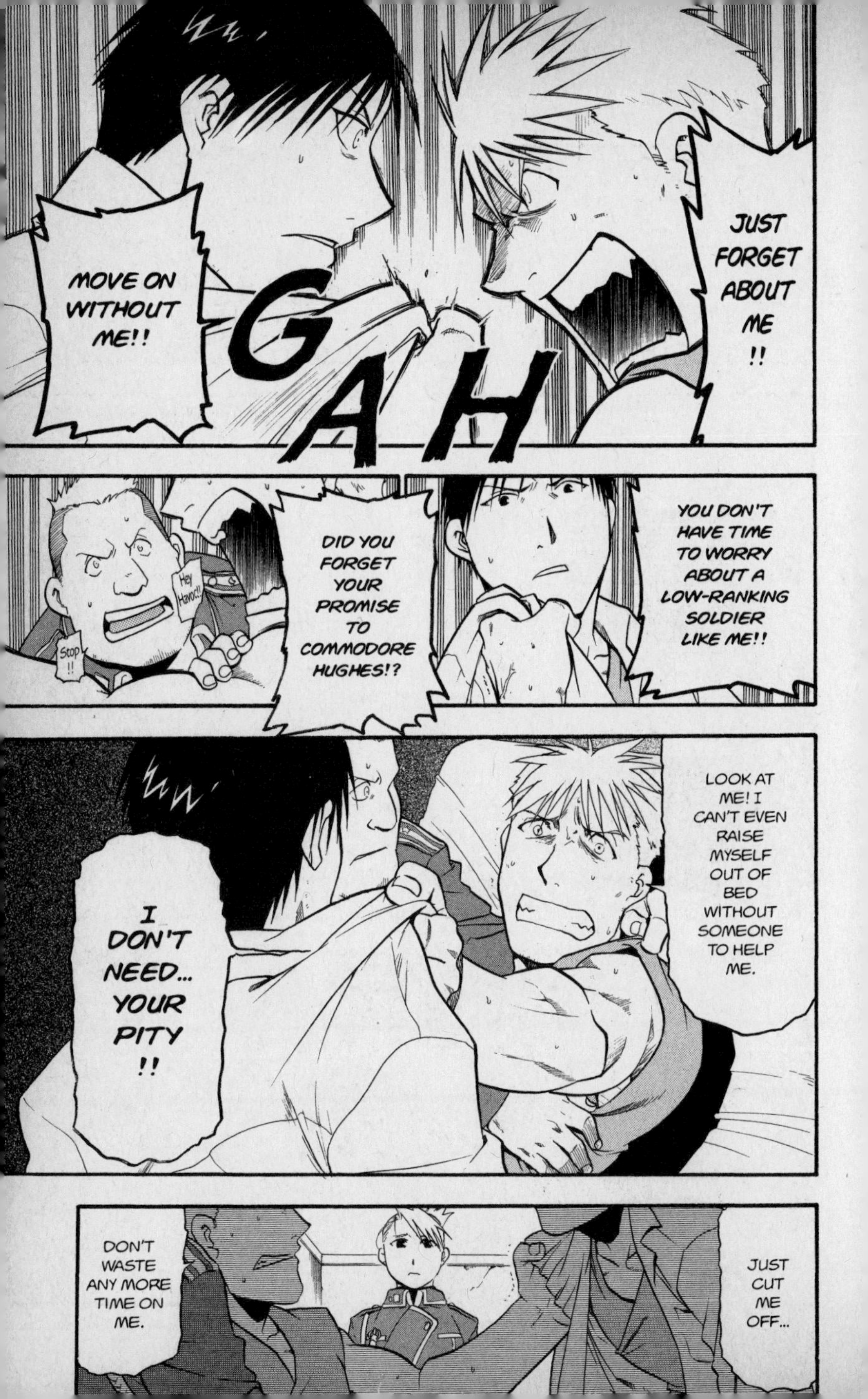
JUST FORGET ABOUT ME !!
GAH
MOVE ON WITHOUT ME!!
YOU DON'T HAVE TIME TO WORRY ABOUT A LOW-RANKING SOLDIER LIKE ME!!
DID YOU FORGET YOUR PROMISE TO COMMODORE HUGHES!?
Hey Havoc!!
Stop !!
LOOK AT ME! I CAN'T EVEN RAISE MYSELF OUT OF BED WITHOUT SOMEONE TO HELP ME.
I DON'T NEED... YOUR PITY !!
JUST CUT ME OFF...
DON'T WASTE ANY MORE TIME ON ME.

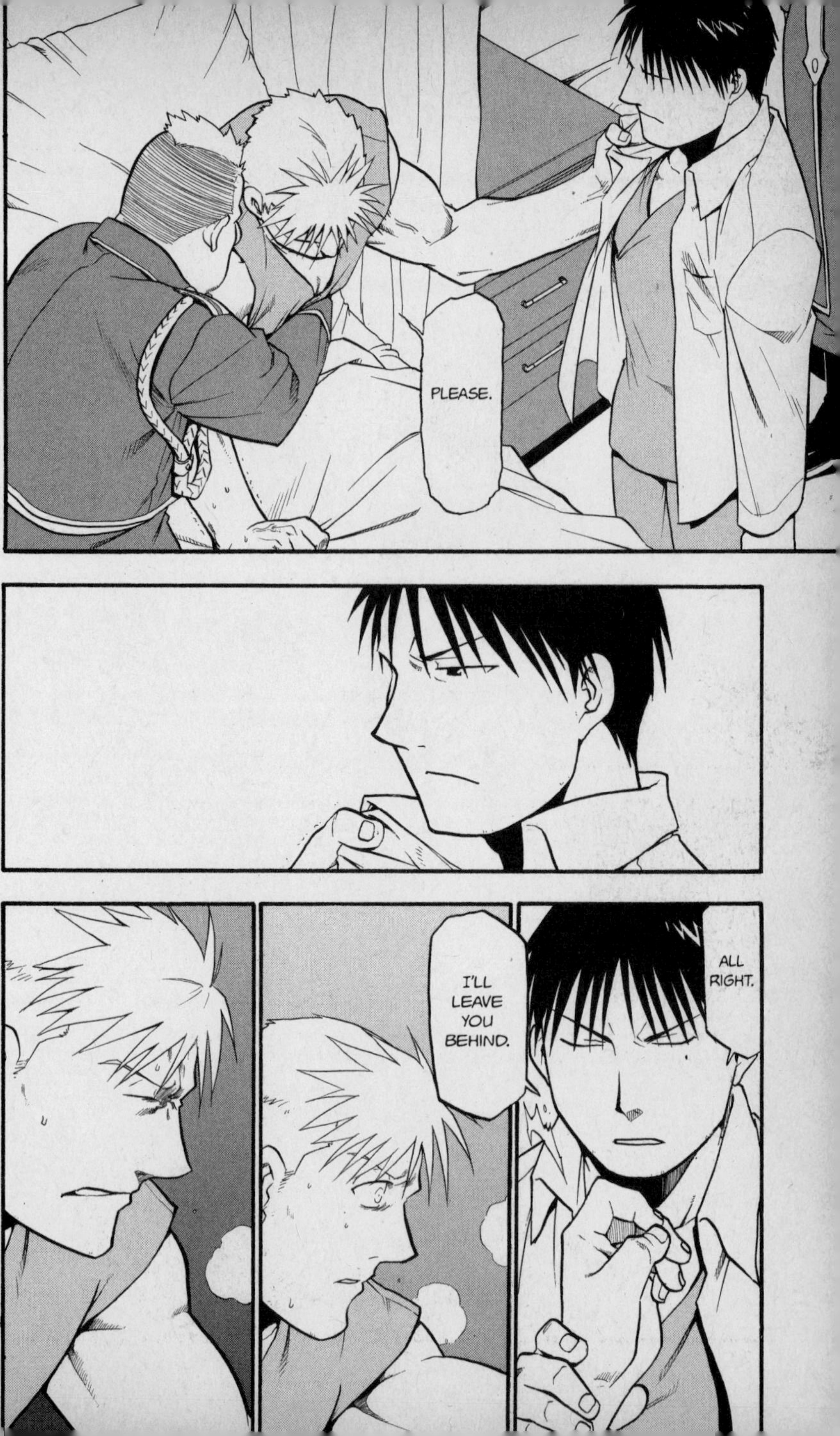
PLEASE.
ALL RIGHT.
I'LL LEAVE YOU BEHIND.

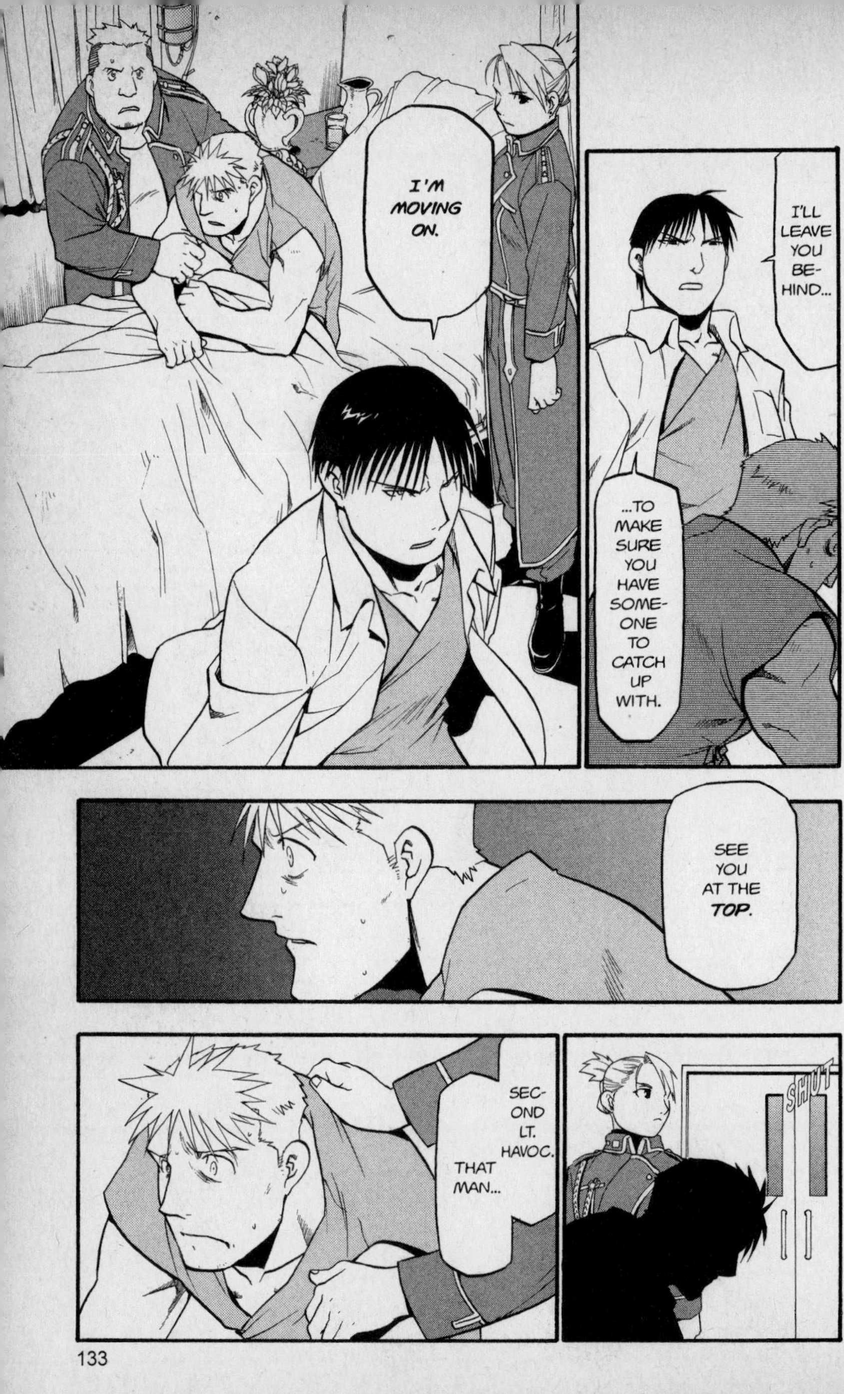
I'LL LEAVE YOU BE-HIND...
...TO MAKE SURE YOU HAVE SOME-ONE TO CATCH UP WITH.
I'M MOVING ON.
SEE YOU AT THE ***TOP***.
SHUT
SEC-OND LT. HAVOC.
THAT MAN...

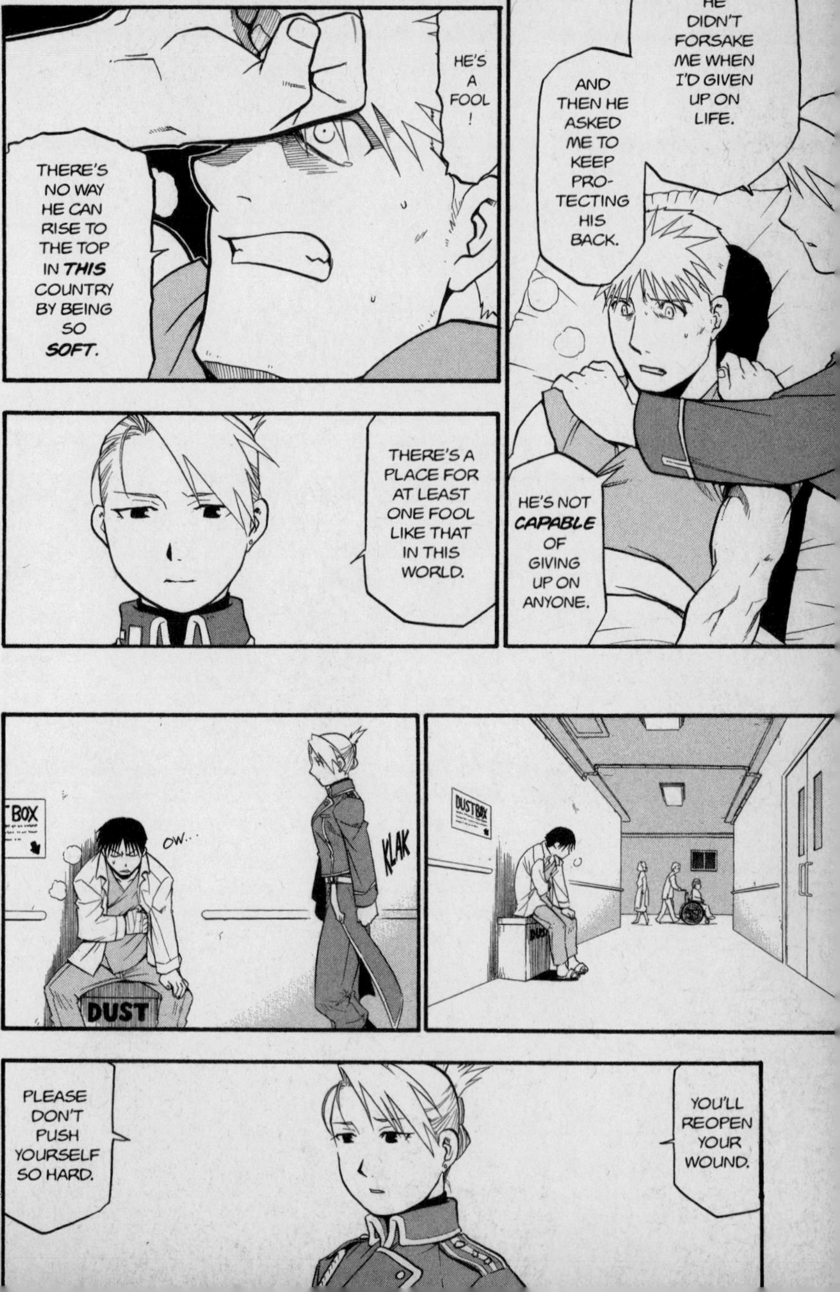
HE DIDN'T FORSAKE ME WHEN I'D GIVEN UP ON LIFE.
AND THEN HE ASKED ME TO KEEP PROTECTING HIS BACK.
HE'S NOT **CAPABLE** OF GIVING UP ON ANYONE.
HE'S A FOOL!
THERE'S NO WAY HE CAN RISE TO THE TOP IN **THIS** COUNTRY BY BEING SO **SOFT**.
THERE'S A PLACE FOR AT LEAST ONE FOOL LIKE THAT IN THIS WORLD.
OW...
KLAK
DUST
YOU'LL REOPEN YOUR WOUND.
PLEASE DON'T PUSH YOURSELF SO HARD.

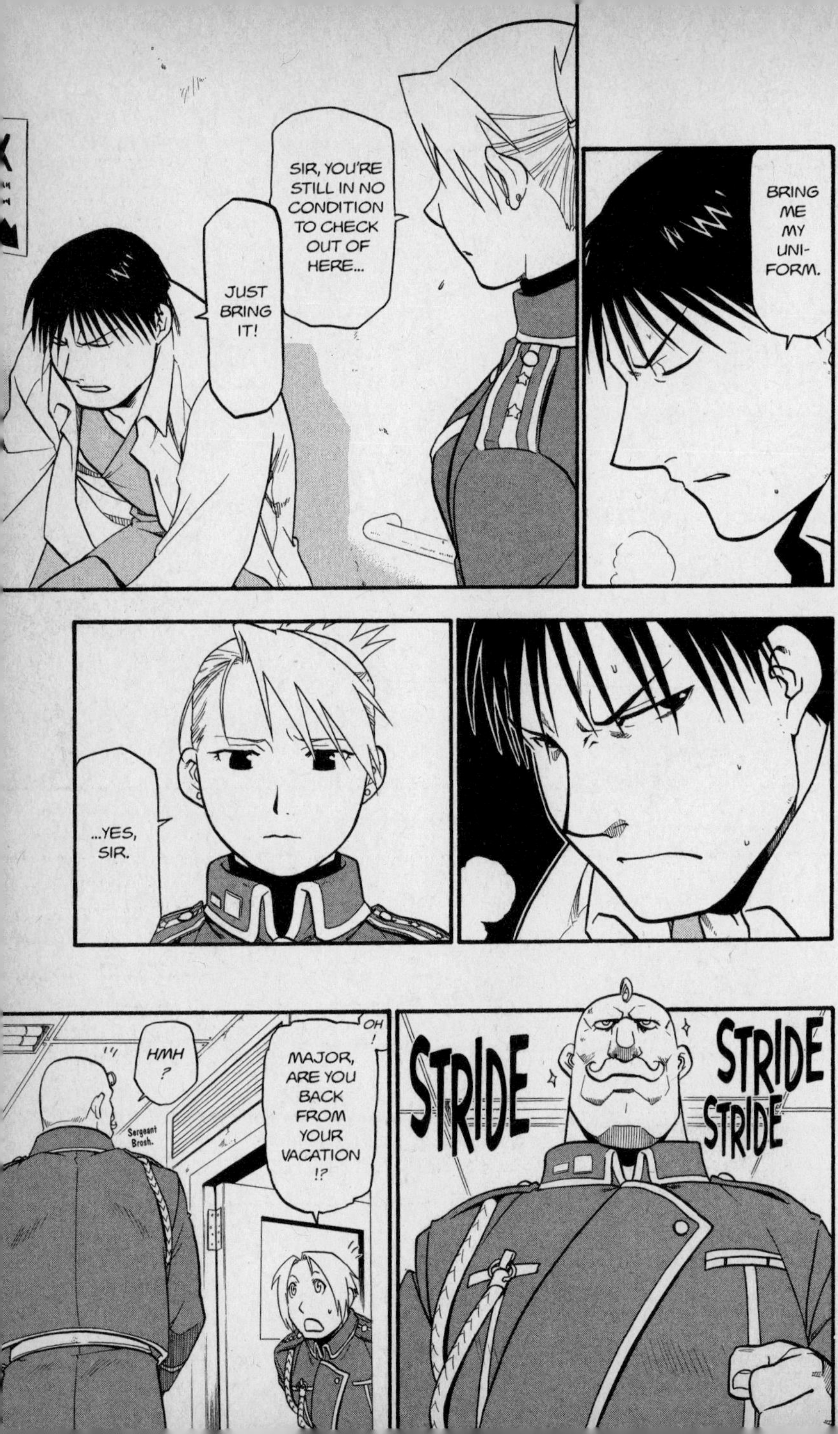
BRING ME MY UNI-FORM.
SIR, YOU'RE STILL IN NO CONDITION TO CHECK OUT OF HERE...
JUST BRING IT!
...YES, SIR.
STRIDE
STRIDE
STRIDE
OH!
MAJOR, ARE YOU BACK FROM YOUR VACATION!?
HMH?
Sergeant Brosh.

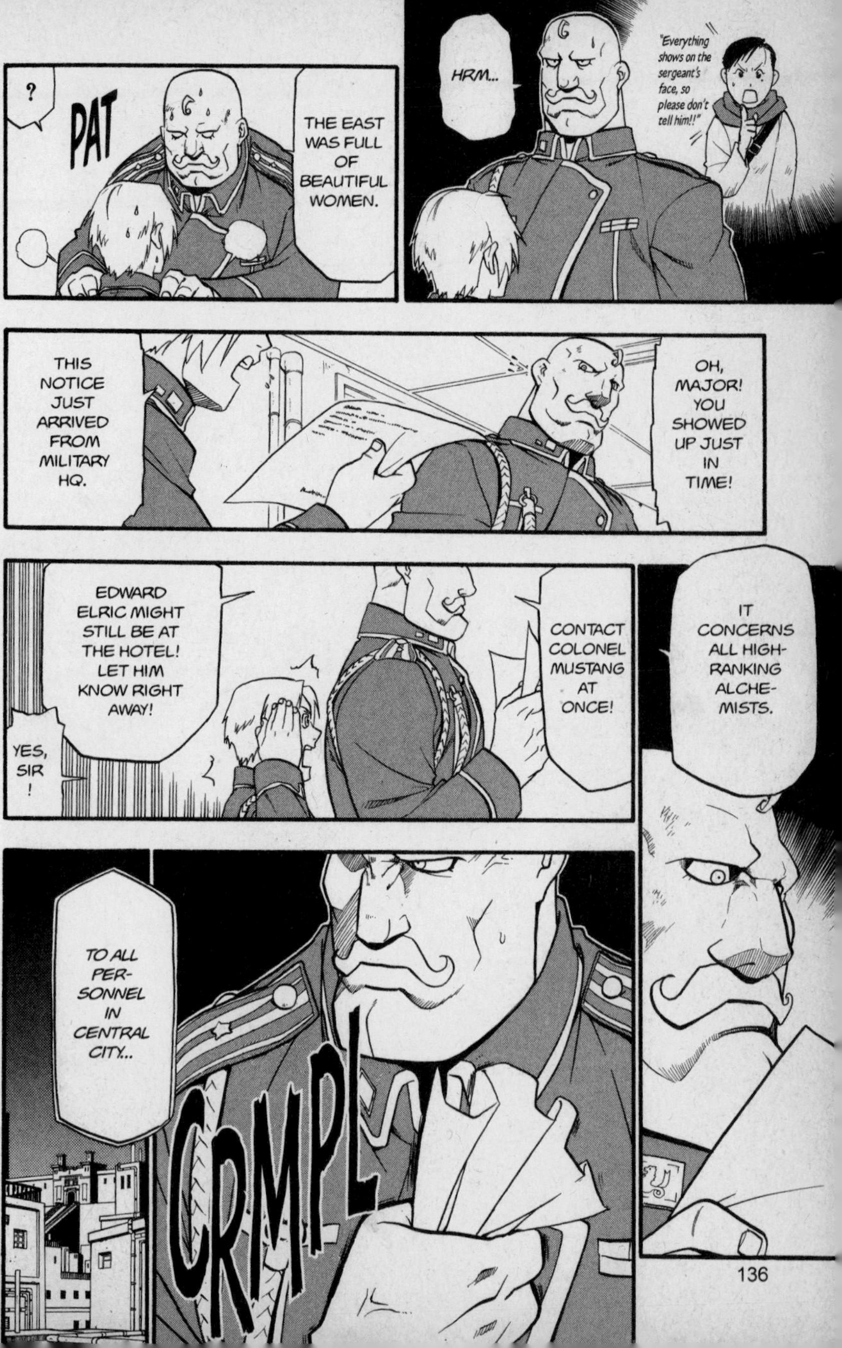
HRM...
"Everything shows on the sergeant's face, so please don't tell him!!"
THE EAST WAS FULL OF BEAUTIFUL WOMEN.
PAT
?
OH, MAJOR! YOU SHOWED UP JUST IN TIME!
THIS NOTICE JUST ARRIVED FROM MILITARY HQ.
IT CONCERNS ALL HIGH-RANKING ALCHEMISTS.
CONTACT COLONEL MUSTANG AT ONCE!
EDWARD ELRIC MIGHT STILL BE AT THE HOTEL! LET HIM KNOW RIGHT AWAY!
YES, SIR!
TO ALL PERSONNEL IN CENTRAL CITY...
CRMPL

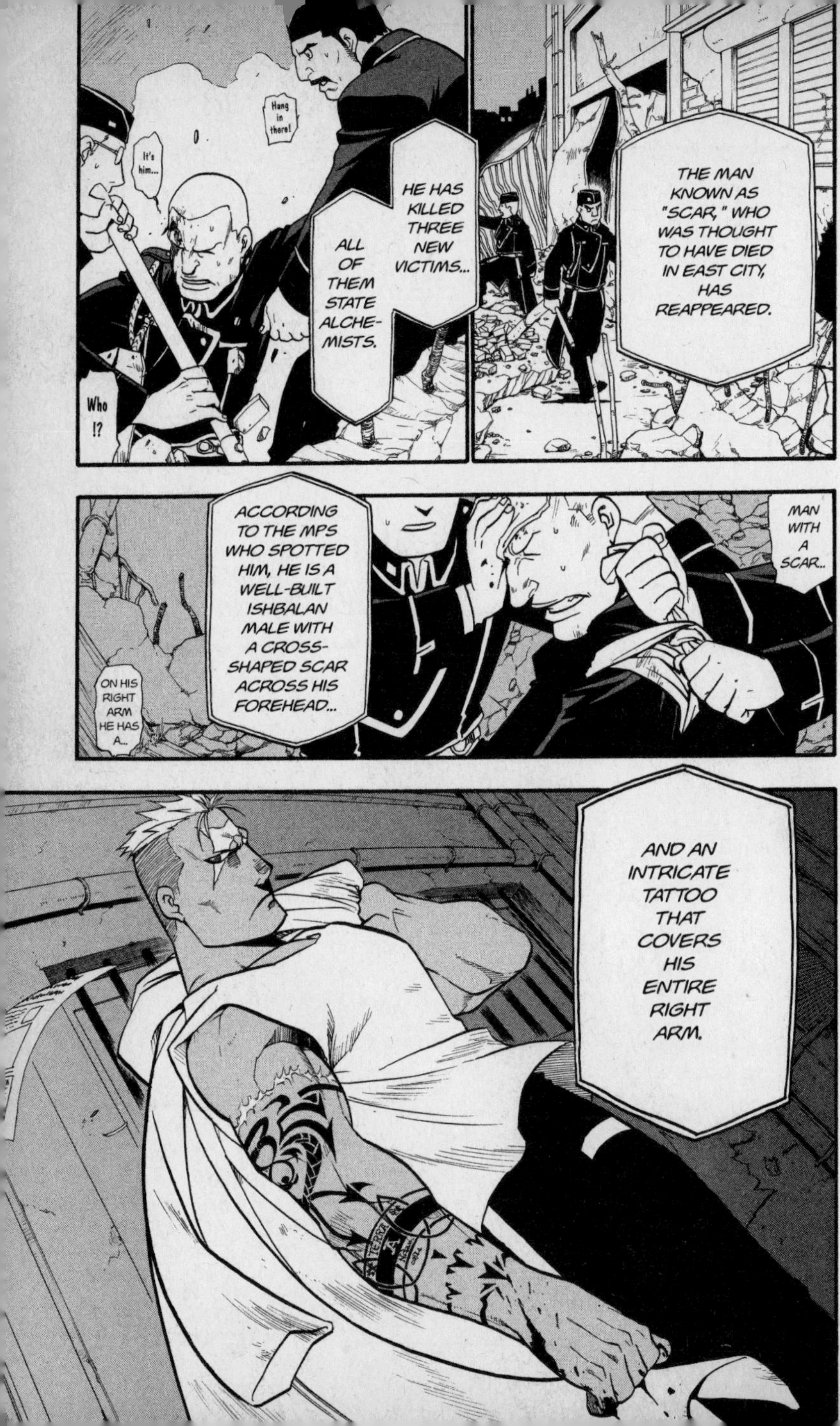

THE MAN KNOWN AS "SCAR," WHO WAS THOUGHT TO HAVE DIED IN EAST CITY, HAS REAPPEARED.
HE HAS KILLED THREE NEW VICTIMS...
Hang in there!
ALL OF THEM STATE ALCHEMISTS.
It's him...
Who !?
MAN WITH A SCAR...
ACCORDING TO THE MPS WHO SPOTTED HIM, HE IS A WELL-BUILT ISHBALAN MALE WITH A CROSS-SHAPED SCAR ACROSS HIS FOREHEAD...
ON HIS RIGHT ARM HE HAS A...
AND AN INTRICATE TATTOO THAT COVERS HIS ENTIRE RIGHT ARM.

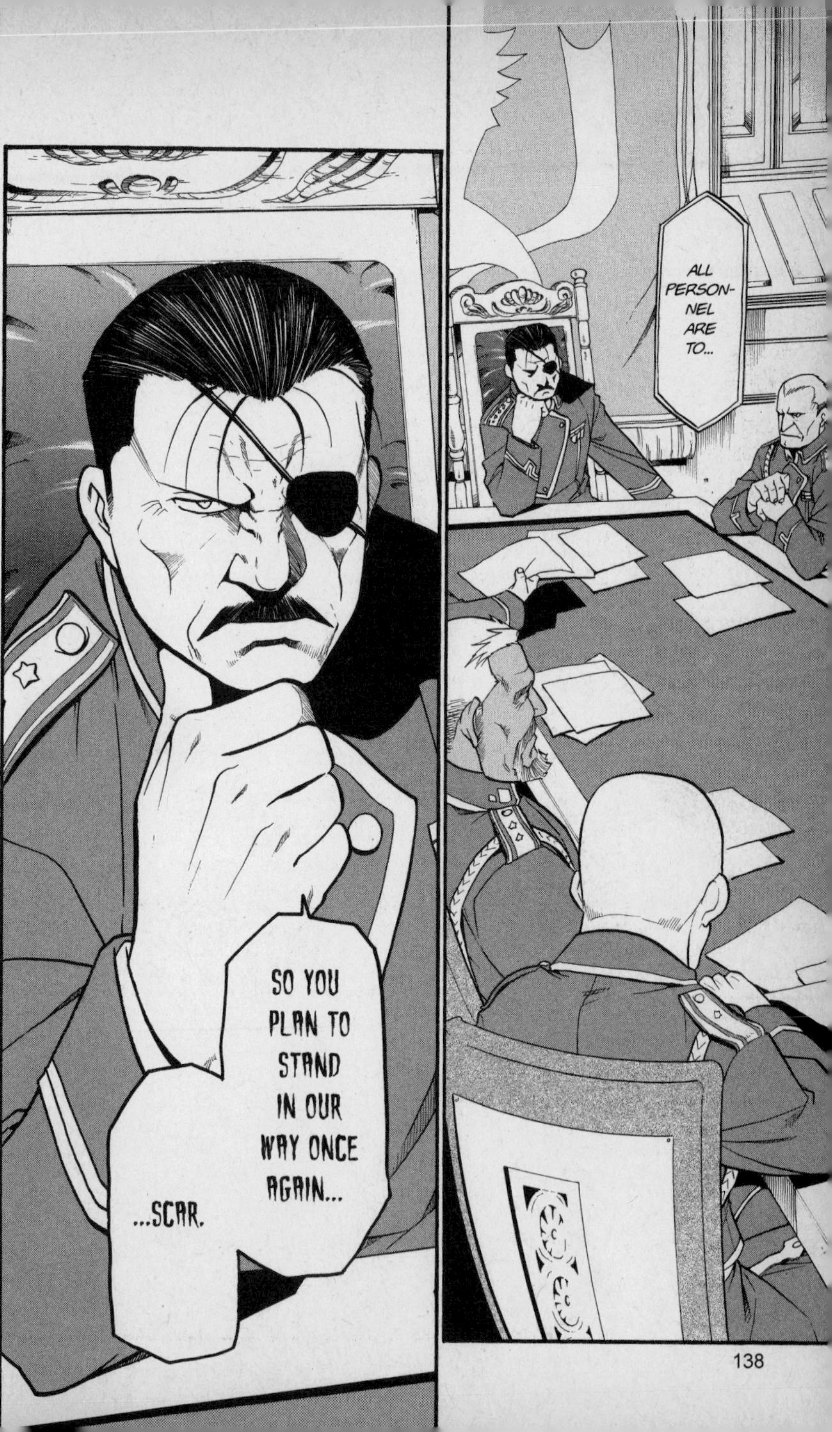
ALL PERSON-NEL ARE TO...
SO YOU PLAN TO STAND IN OUR WAY ONCE AGAIN...
...SCAR.

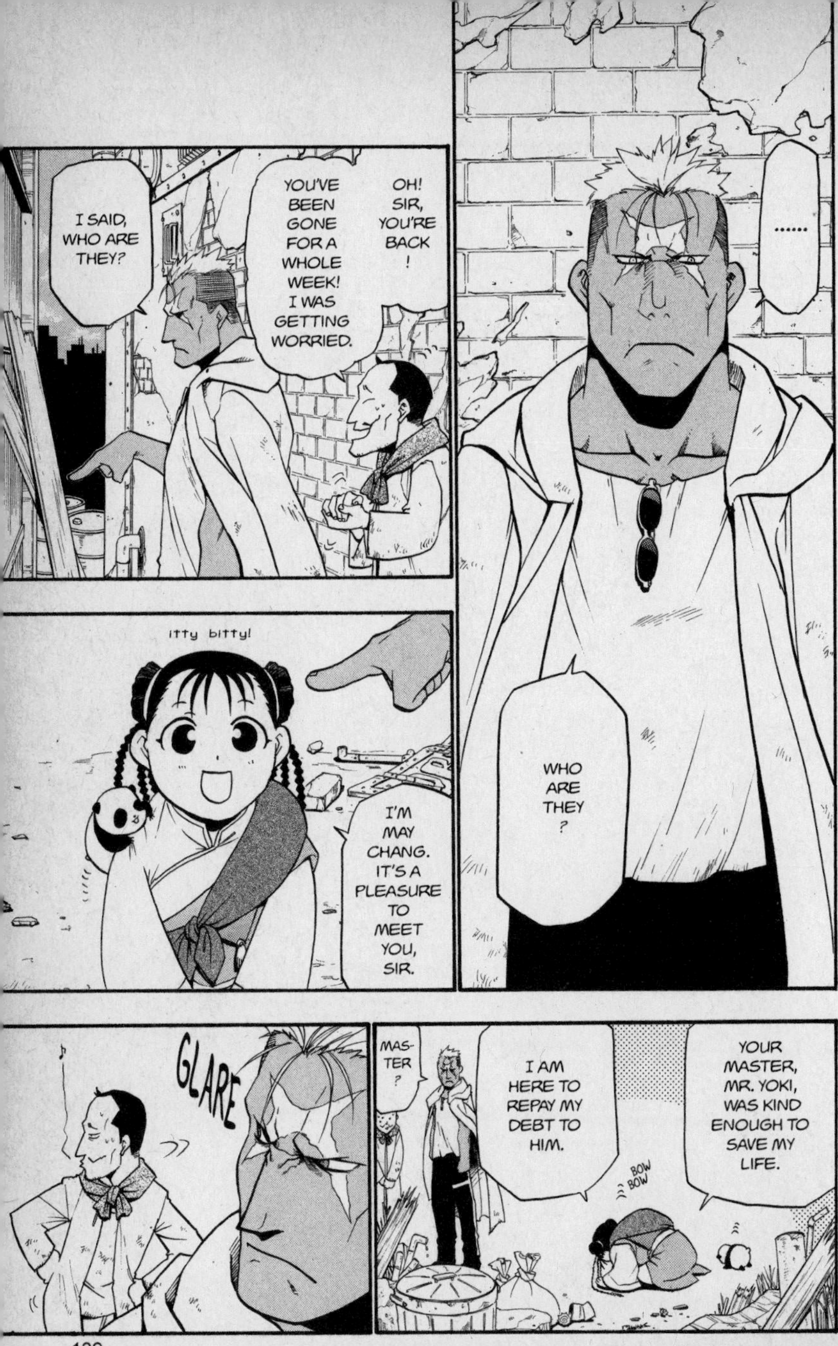
......
WHO ARE THEY?
OH! SIR, YOU'RE BACK!
YOU'VE BEEN GONE FOR A WHOLE WEEK! I WAS GETTING WORRIED.
I SAID, WHO ARE THEY?
itty bitty!
I'M MAY CHANG. IT'S A PLEASURE TO MEET YOU, SIR.
YOUR MASTER, MR. YOKI, WAS KIND ENOUGH TO SAVE MY LIFE.
BOW BOW
I AM HERE TO REPAY MY DEBT TO HIM.
MASTER?
GLARE

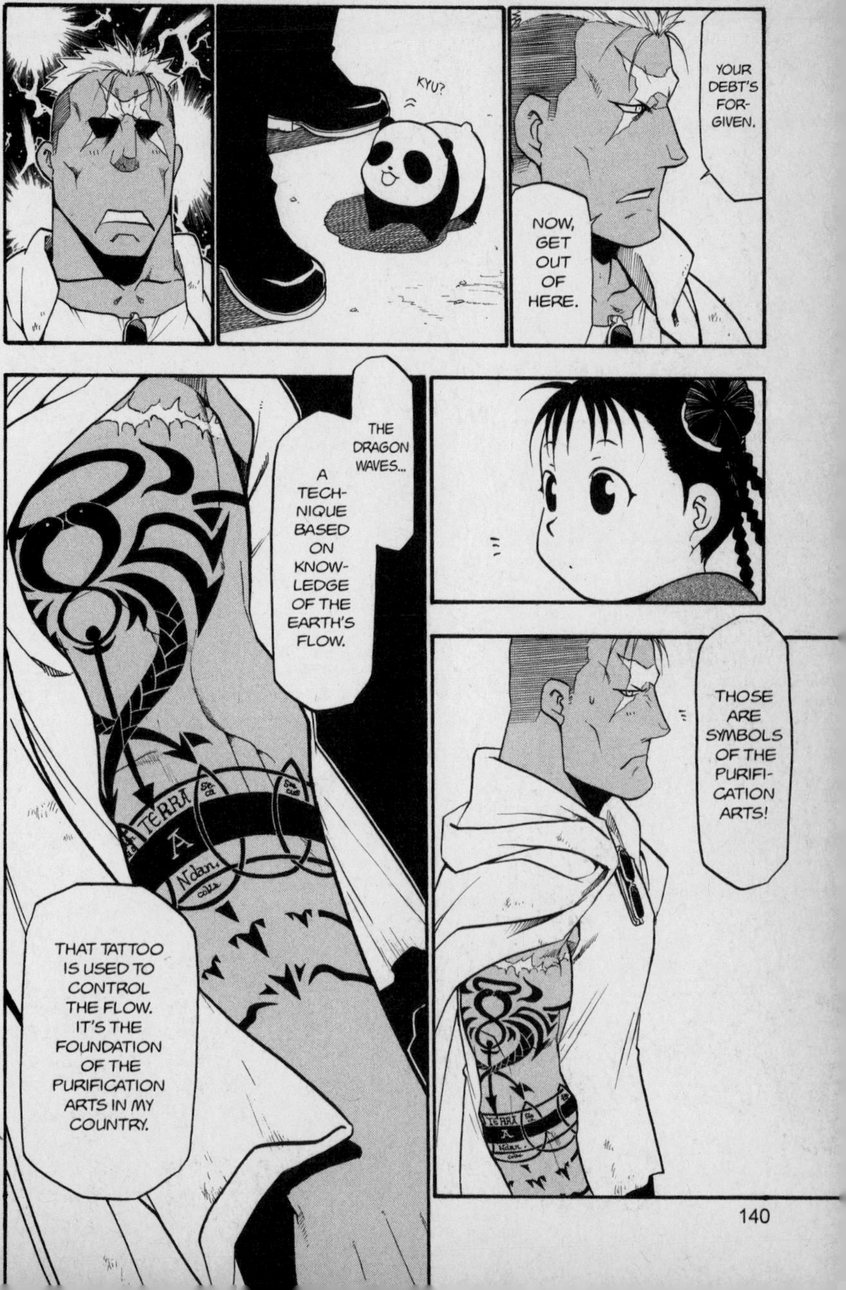
YOUR DEBT'S FORGIVEN.
NOW, GET OUT OF HERE.
KYU?
THOSE ARE SYMBOLS OF THE PURIFICATION ARTS!
THE DRAGON WAVES...
A TECHNIQUE BASED ON KNOWLEDGE OF THE EARTH'S FLOW.
THAT TATTOO IS USED TO CONTROL THE FLOW. IT'S THE FOUNDATION OF THE PURIFICATION ARTS IN MY COUNTRY.

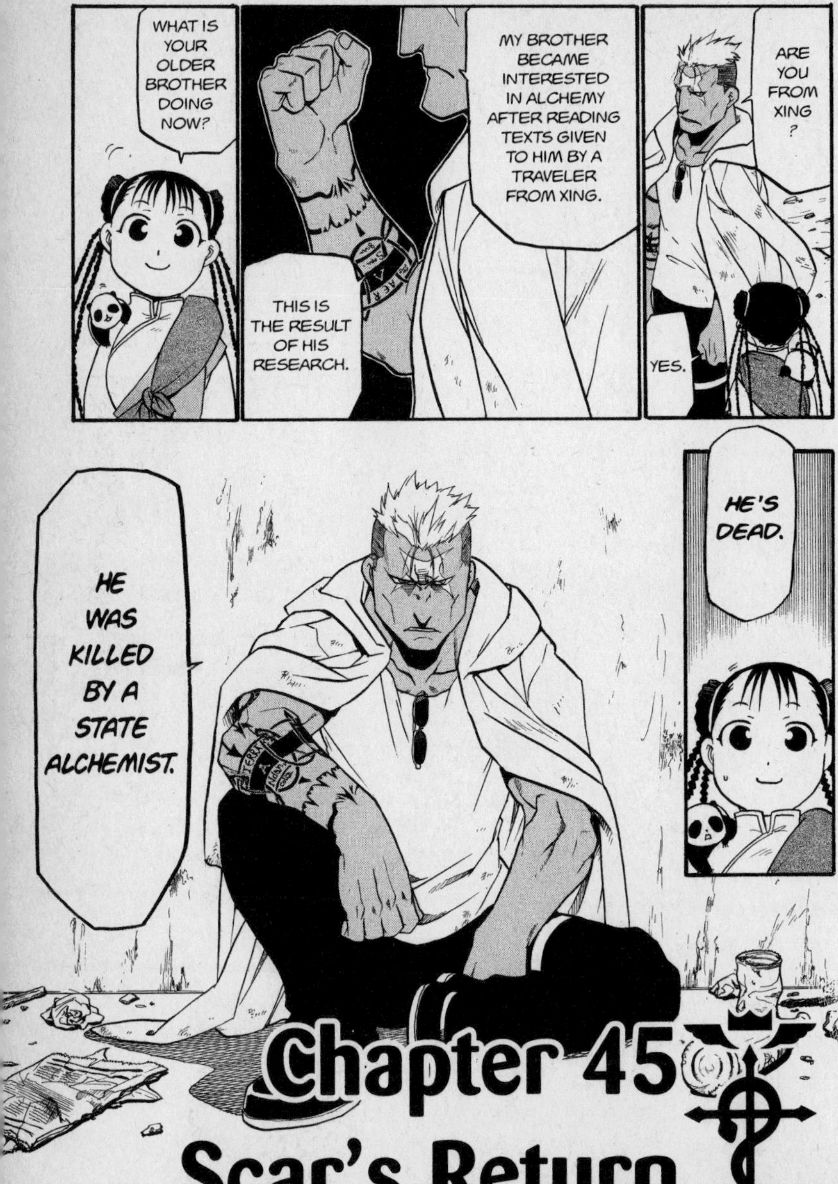
ARE YOU FROM XING?
YES.
MY BROTHER BECAME INTERESTED IN ALCHEMY AFTER READING TEXTS GIVEN TO HIM BY A TRAVELER FROM XING.
THIS IS THE RESULT OF HIS RESEARCH.
WHAT IS YOUR OLDER BROTHER DOING NOW?
HE'S DEAD.
HE WAS KILLED BY A STATE ALCHEMIST.

Chapter 45 Scar's Return

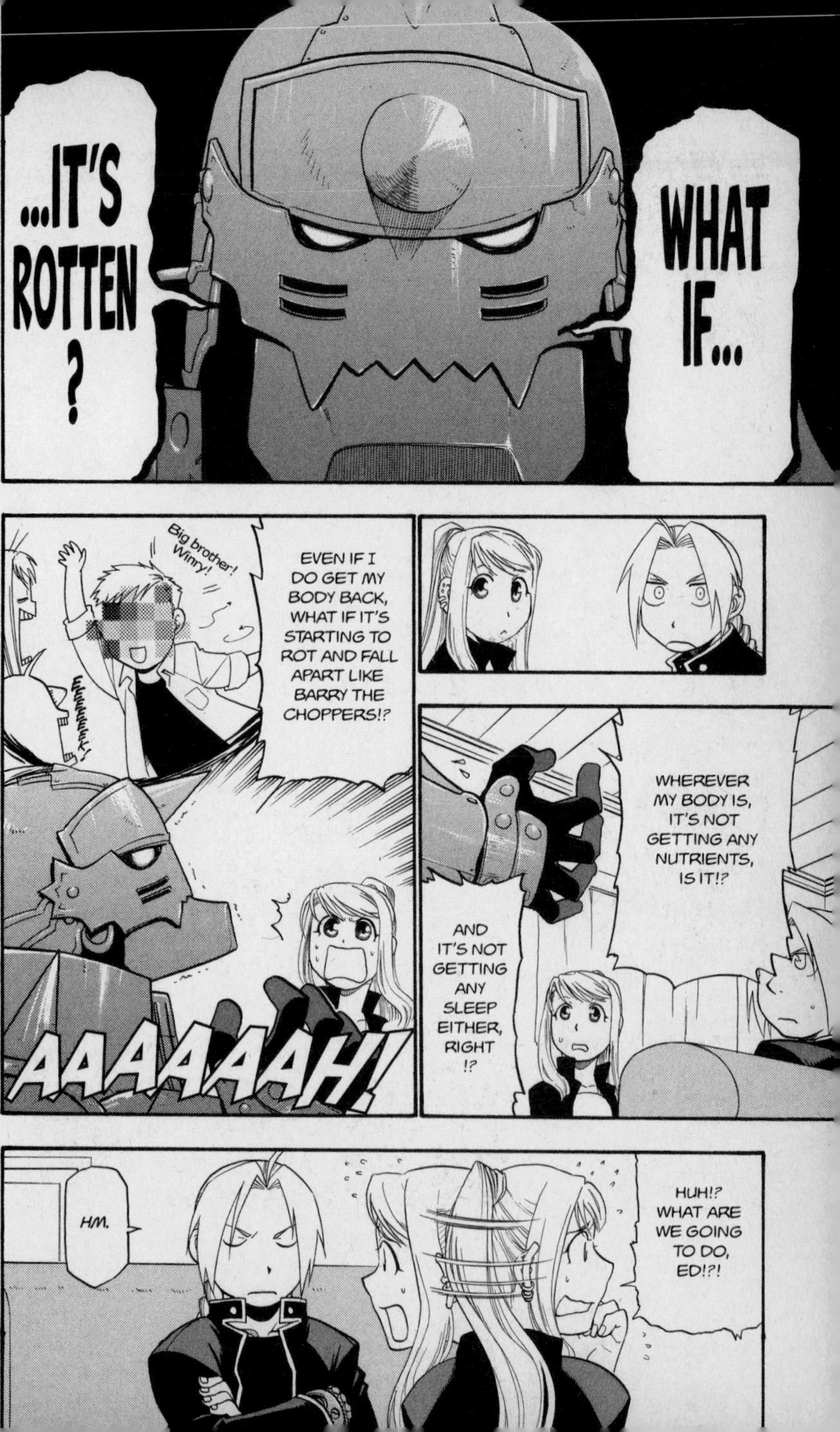
WHAT IF...
...IT'S ROTTEN?
WHEREVER MY BODY IS, IT'S NOT GETTING ANY NUTRIENTS, IS IT!?
AND IT'S NOT GETTING ANY SLEEP EITHER, RIGHT!?
EVEN IF I DO GET MY BODY BACK, WHAT IF IT'S STARTING TO ROT AND FALL APART LIKE BARRY THE CHOPPERS!?
Big brother! Winry!
AAAAAAH!
HUH!? WHAT ARE WE GOING TO DO, ED!?!
HM.

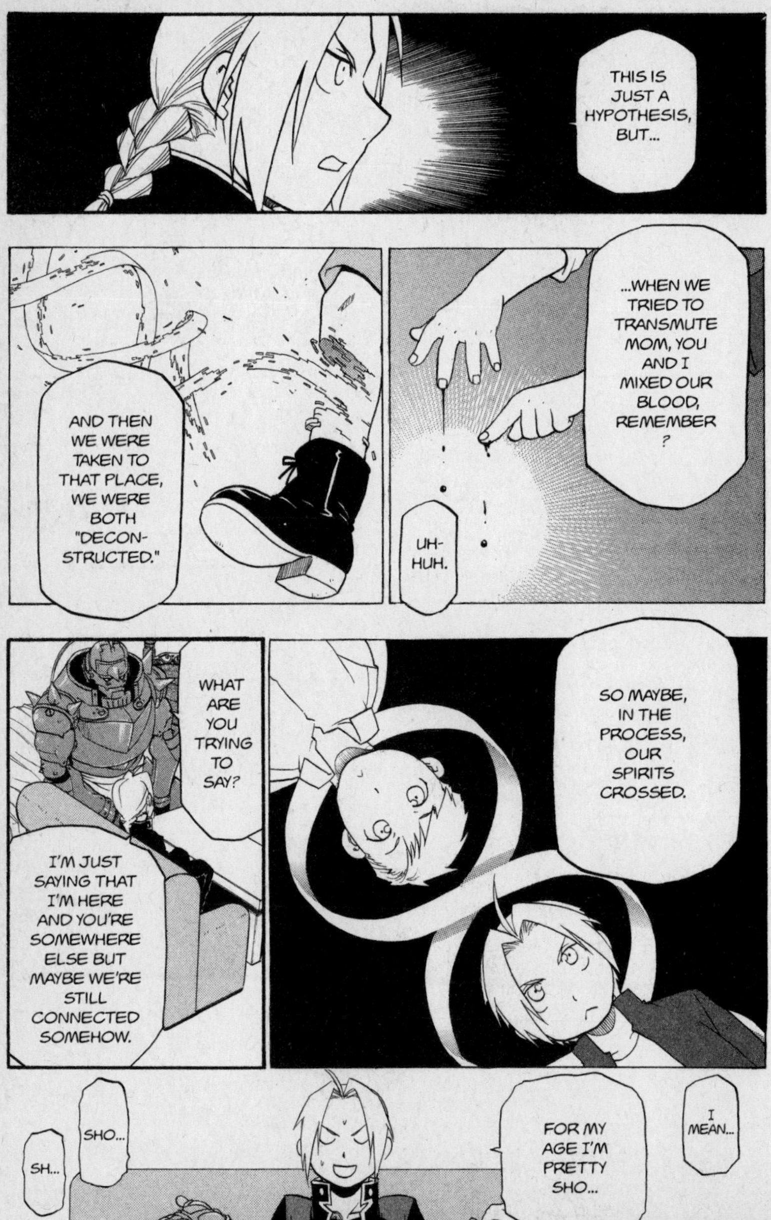
THIS IS JUST A HYPOTHESIS, BUT...
...WHEN WE TRIED TO TRANSMUTE MOM, YOU AND I MIXED OUR BLOOD, REMEMBER?
UH-HUH.
AND THEN WE WERE TAKEN TO THAT PLACE, WE WERE BOTH "DECON-STRUCTED."
SO MAYBE, IN THE PROCESS, OUR SPIRITS CROSSED.
WHAT ARE YOU TRYING TO SAY?
I'M JUST SAYING THAT I'M HERE AND YOU'RE SOMEWHERE ELSE BUT MAYBE WE'RE STILL CONNECTED SOMEHOW.
I MEAN...
FOR MY AGE I'M PRETTY SHO...
SHO...
SH...

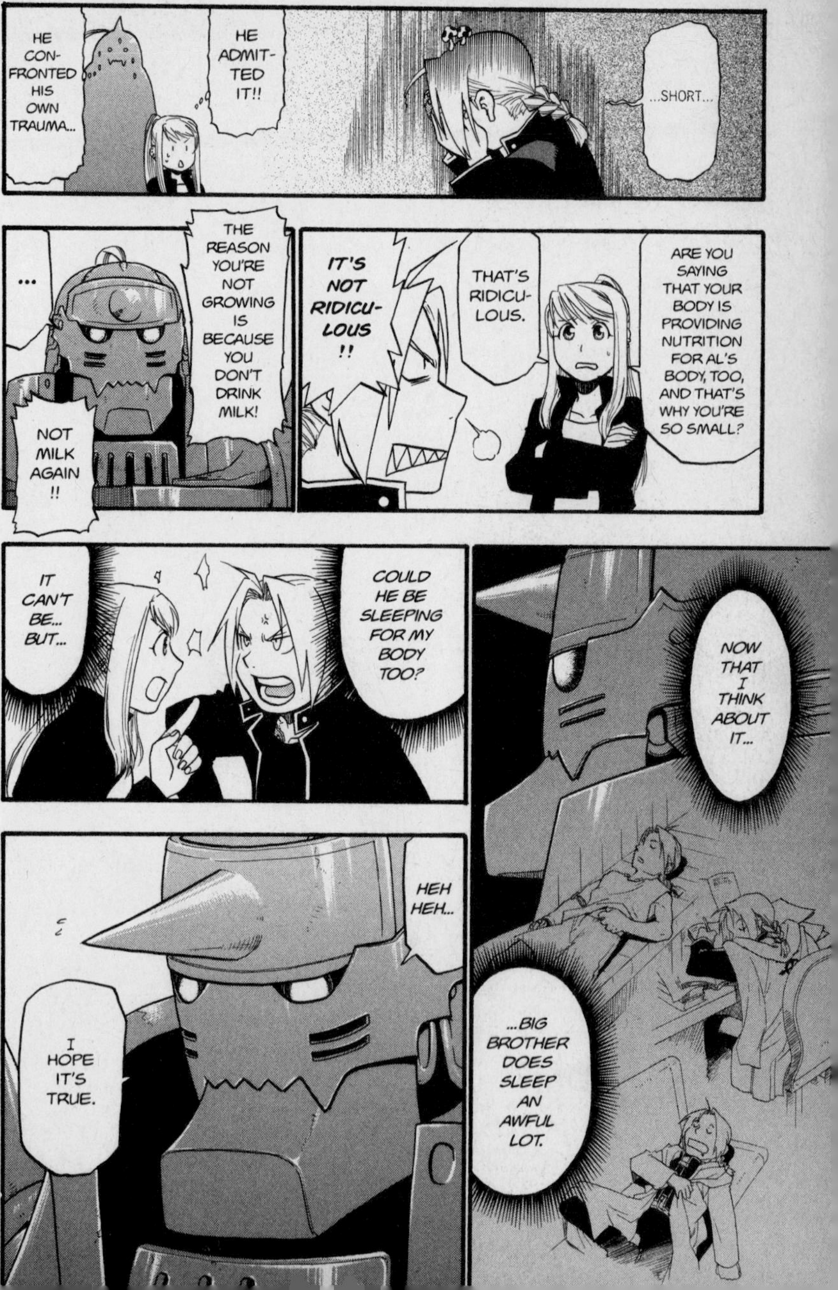
...SHORT...
HE ADMITTED IT!!
HE CONFRONTED HIS OWN TRAUMA...
ARE YOU SAYING THAT YOUR BODY IS PROVIDING NUTRITION FOR AL'S BODY, TOO, AND THAT'S WHY YOU'RE SO SMALL?
THAT'S RIDICULOUS.
IT'S NOT RIDICULOUS!!
THE REASON YOU'RE NOT GROWING IS BECAUSE YOU DON'T DRINK MILK!
...
NOT MILK AGAIN!!
NOW THAT I THINK ABOUT IT...
...BIG BROTHER DOES SLEEP AN AWFUL LOT.
COULD HE BE SLEEPING FOR MY BODY TOO?
IT CAN'T BE... BUT...
HEH HEH...
I HOPE IT'S TRUE.

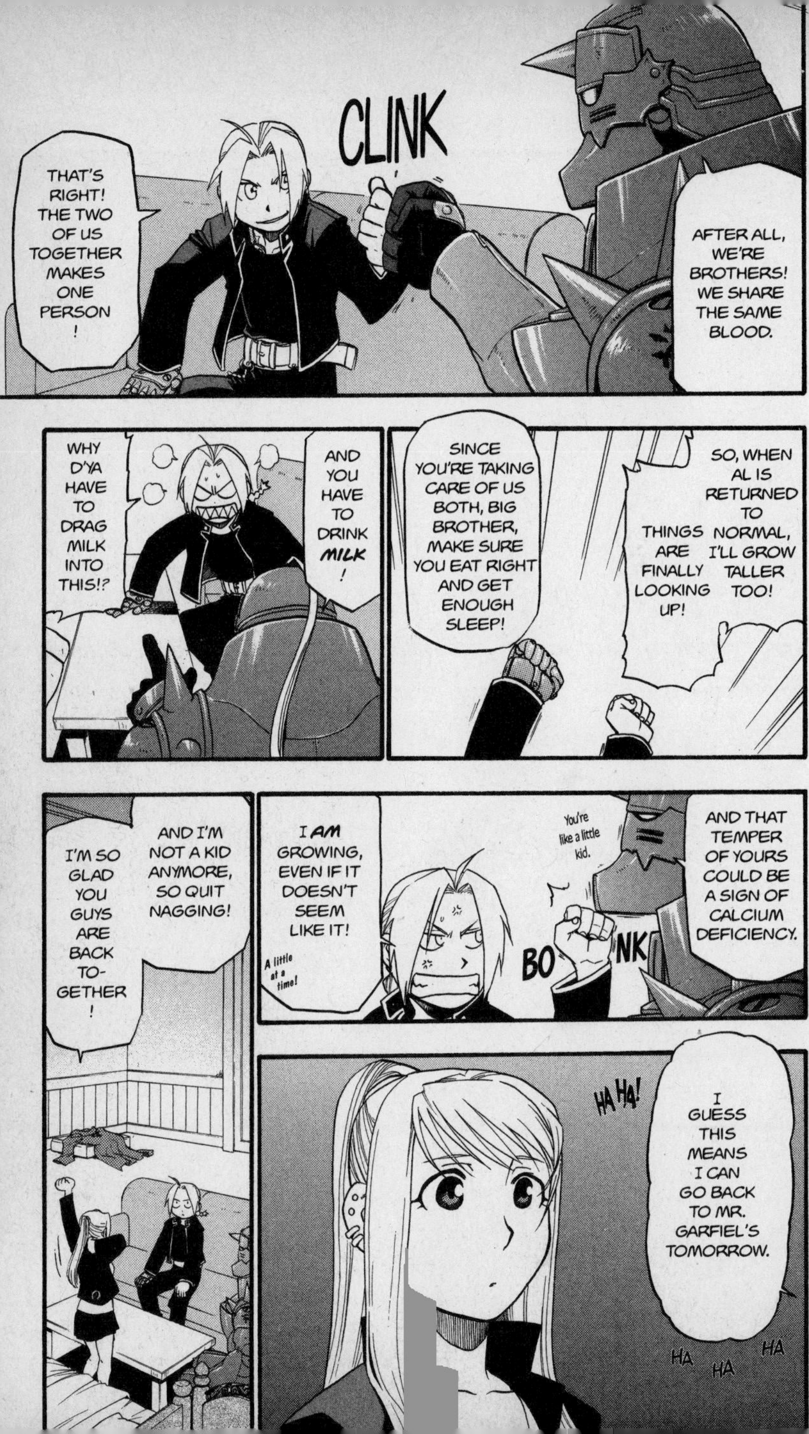
AFTER ALL, WE'RE BROTHERS! WE SHARE THE SAME BLOOD.
CLINK
THAT'S RIGHT! THE TWO OF US TOGETHER MAKES ONE PERSON!
SO, WHEN AL IS RETURNED TO NORMAL, I'LL GROW TALLER TOO!
THINGS ARE FINALLY LOOKING UP!
SINCE YOU'RE TAKING CARE OF US BOTH, BIG BROTHER, MAKE SURE YOU EAT RIGHT AND GET ENOUGH SLEEP!
AND YOU HAVE TO DRINK MILK!
WHY D'YA HAVE TO DRAG MILK INTO THIS!?
AND THAT TEMPER OF YOURS COULD BE A SIGN OF CALCIUM DEFICIENCY.
You're like a little kid.
BONK
I AM GROWING, EVEN IF IT DOESN'T SEEM LIKE IT!
A little at a time!
HA HA!
I GUESS THIS MEANS I CAN GO BACK TO MR. GARFIEL'S TOMORROW.
HA HA HA
AND I'M NOT A KID ANYMORE, SO QUIT NAGGING!
I'M SO GLAD YOU GUYS ARE BACK TOGETHER!

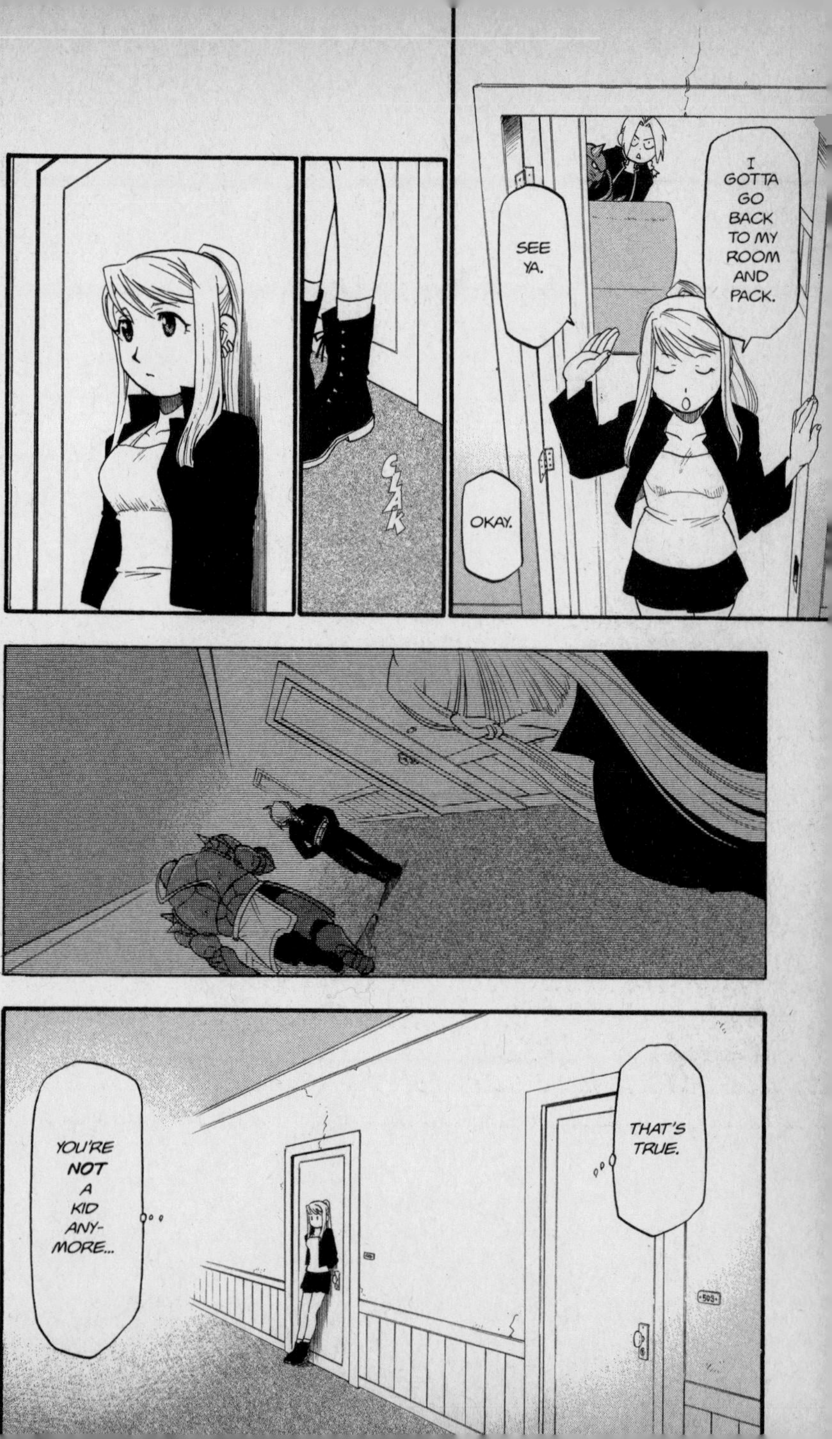
I GOTTA GO BACK TO MY ROOM AND PACK.
SEE YA.
OKAY.
CLAK
THAT'S TRUE.
YOU'RE NOT A KID ANYMORE...

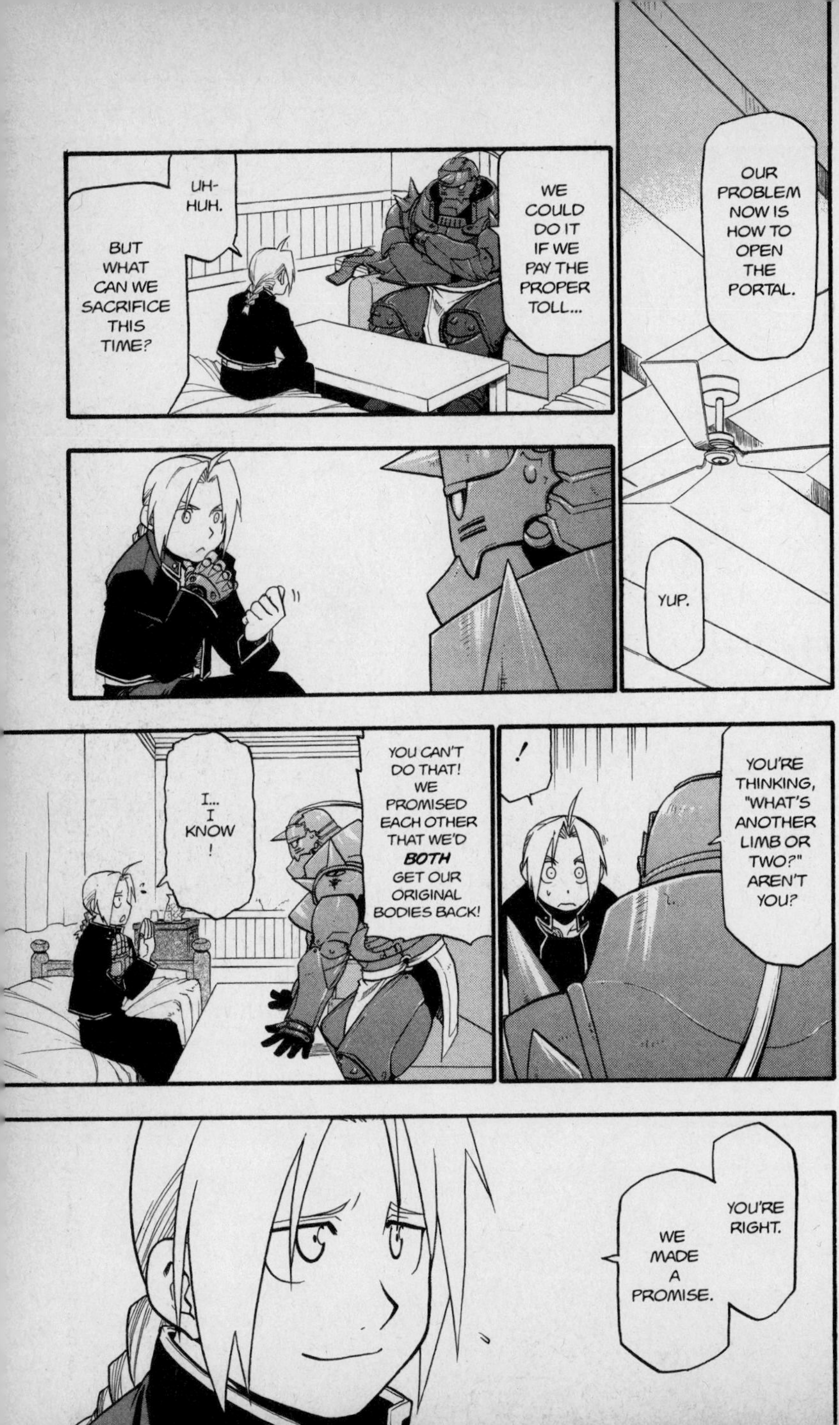
OUR PROBLEM NOW IS HOW TO OPEN THE PORTAL.
YUP.
WE COULD DO IT IF WE PAY THE PROPER TOLL...
UH-HUH.
BUT WHAT CAN WE SACRIFICE THIS TIME?
YOU'RE THINKING, "WHAT'S ANOTHER LIMB OR TWO?" AREN'T YOU?
!
YOU CAN'T DO THAT! WE PROMISED EACH OTHER THAT WE'D **BOTH** GET OUR ORIGINAL BODIES BACK!
I... I KNOW!
YOU'RE RIGHT.
WE MADE A PROMISE.

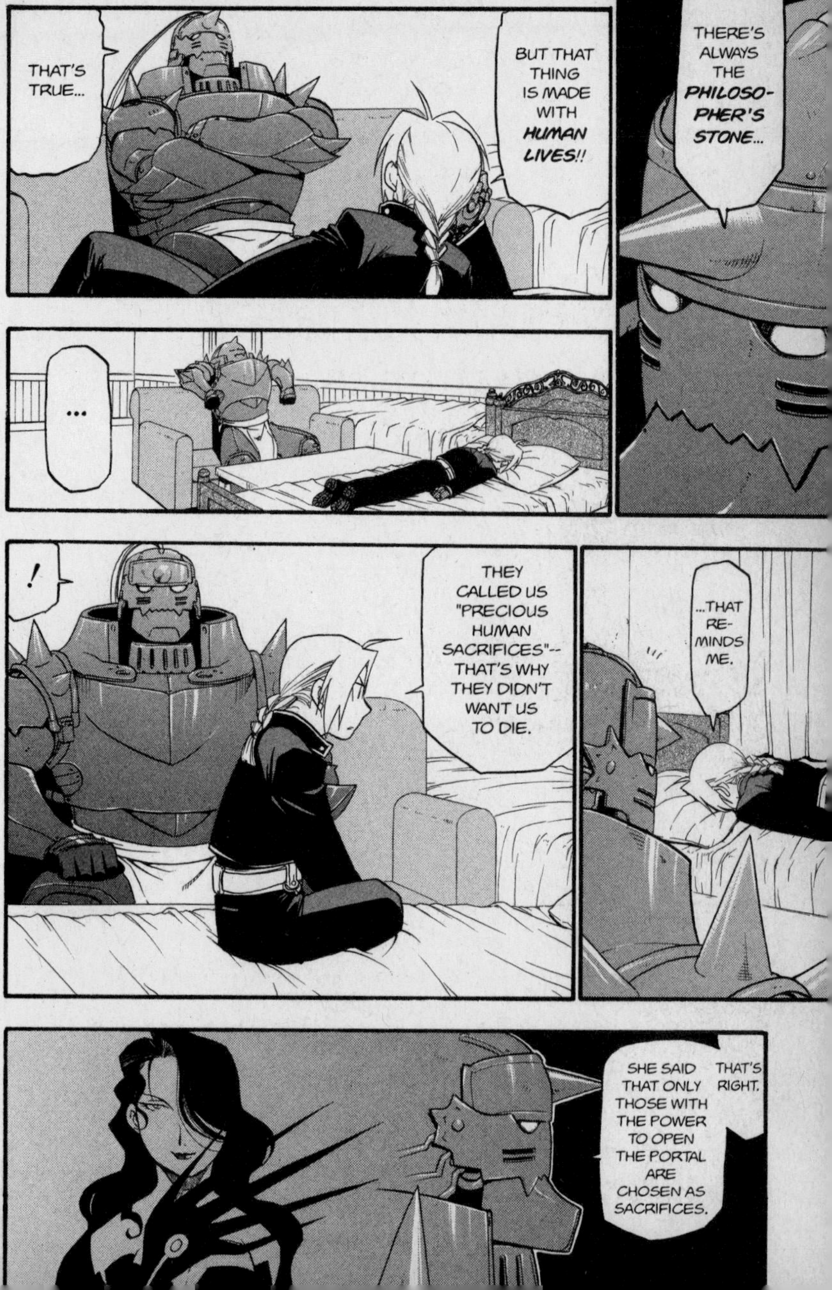
THERE'S ALWAYS THE PHILOSOPHER'S STONE...
BUT THAT THING IS MADE WITH HUMAN LIVES!!
THAT'S TRUE...
...
...THAT REMINDS ME.
THEY CALLED US "PRECIOUS HUMAN SACRIFICES"-- THAT'S WHY THEY DIDN'T WANT US TO DIE.
!
THAT'S RIGHT.
SHE SAID THAT ONLY THOSE WITH THE POWER TO OPEN THE PORTAL ARE CHOSEN AS SACRIFICES.

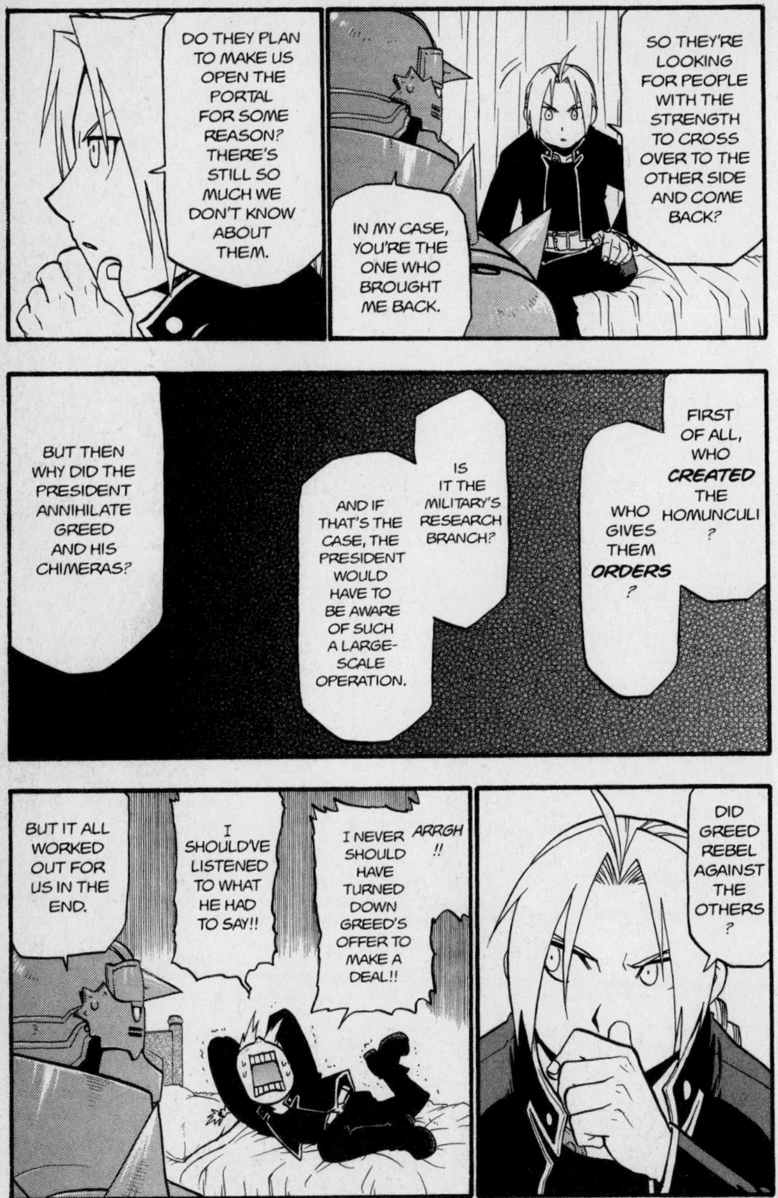
SO THEY'RE LOOKING FOR PEOPLE WITH THE STRENGTH TO CROSS OVER TO THE OTHER SIDE AND COME BACK?
IN MY CASE, YOU'RE THE ONE WHO BROUGHT ME BACK.
DO THEY PLAN TO MAKE US OPEN THE PORTAL FOR SOME REASON? THERE'S STILL SO MUCH WE DON'T KNOW ABOUT THEM.
FIRST OF ALL, WHO **CREATED** THE HOMUNCULI?
WHO GIVES THEM **ORDERS**?
IS IT THE MILITARY'S RESEARCH BRANCH?
AND IF THAT'S THE CASE, THE PRESIDENT WOULD HAVE TO BE AWARE OF SUCH A LARGE-SCALE OPERATION.
BUT THEN WHY DID THE PRESIDENT ANNIHILATE GREED AND HIS CHIMERAS?
DID GREED REBEL AGAINST THE OTHERS?
ARRGH!!
I NEVER SHOULD HAVE TURNED DOWN GREED'S OFFER TO MAKE A DEAL!!
I SHOULD'VE LISTENED TO WHAT HE HAD TO SAY!!
BUT IT ALL WORKED OUT FOR US IN THE END.

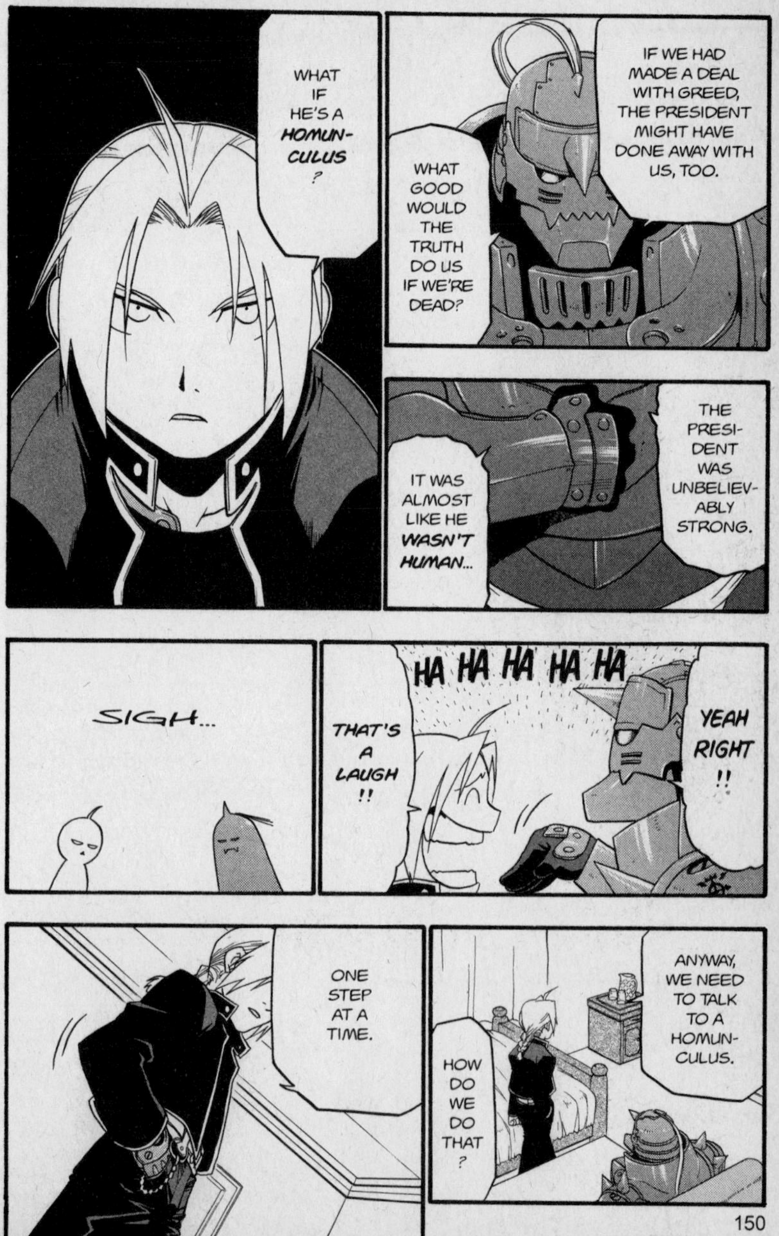
IF WE HAD MADE A DEAL WITH GREED, THE PRESIDENT MIGHT HAVE DONE AWAY WITH US, TOO.
WHAT GOOD WOULD THE TRUTH DO US IF WE'RE DEAD?
THE PRESIDENT WAS UNBELIEVABLY STRONG.
IT WAS ALMOST LIKE HE ***WASN'T HUMAN***...
WHAT IF HE'S A ***HOMUNCULUS***?
HA HA HA HA HA
YEAH RIGHT!!
THAT'S A LAUGH!!
SIGH...
ANYWAY, WE NEED TO TALK TO A HOMUNCULUS.
HOW DO WE DO THAT?
ONE STEP AT A TIME.

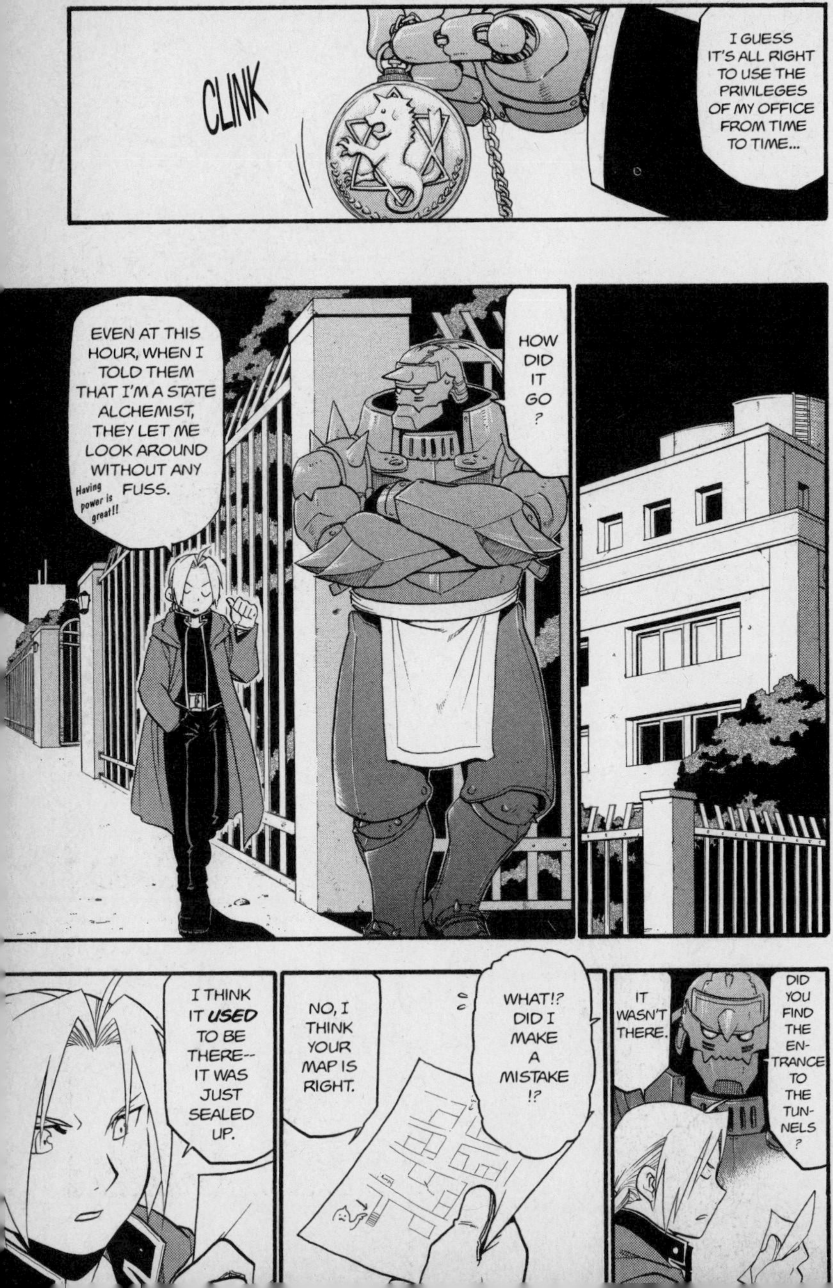
I GUESS IT'S ALL RIGHT TO USE THE PRIVILEGES OF MY OFFICE FROM TIME TO TIME...
CLINK
HOW DID IT GO?
EVEN AT THIS HOUR, WHEN I TOLD THEM THAT I'M A STATE ALCHEMIST, THEY LET ME LOOK AROUND WITHOUT ANY FUSS.
Having power is great!!
DID YOU FIND THE ENTRANCE TO THE TUNNELS?
IT WASN'T THERE.
WHAT!? DID I MAKE A MISTAKE!?
NO, I THINK YOUR MAP IS RIGHT.
I THINK IT *USED* TO BE THERE-- IT WAS JUST SEALED UP.

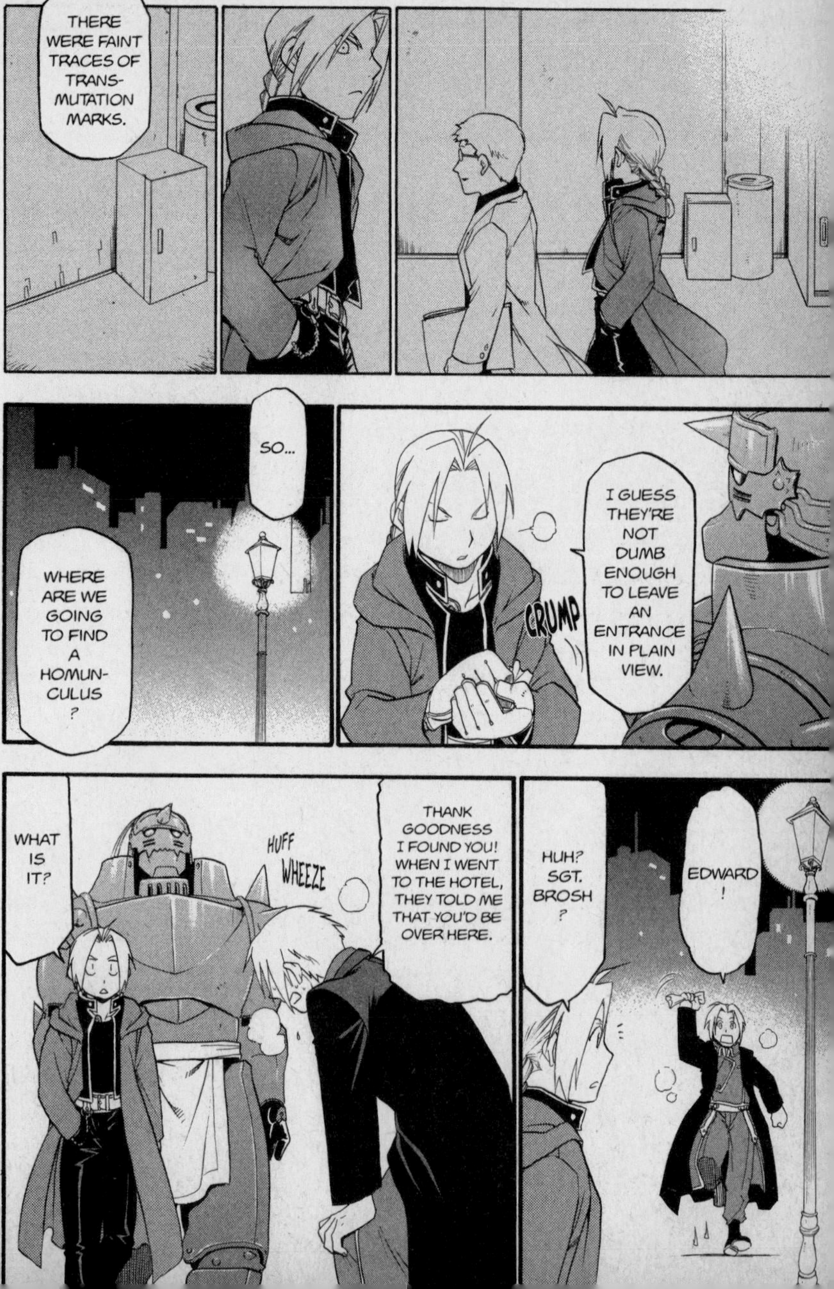
THERE WERE FAINT TRACES OF TRANS-MUTATION MARKS.
I GUESS THEY'RE NOT DUMB ENOUGH TO LEAVE AN ENTRANCE IN PLAIN VIEW.
CRUMP
SO...
WHERE ARE WE GOING TO FIND A HOMUN-CULUS?
EDWARD!
HUH? SGT. BROSH?
THANK GOODNESS I FOUND YOU! WHEN I WENT TO THE HOTEL, THEY TOLD ME THAT YOU'D BE OVER HERE.
HUFF
WHEEZE
WHAT IS IT?

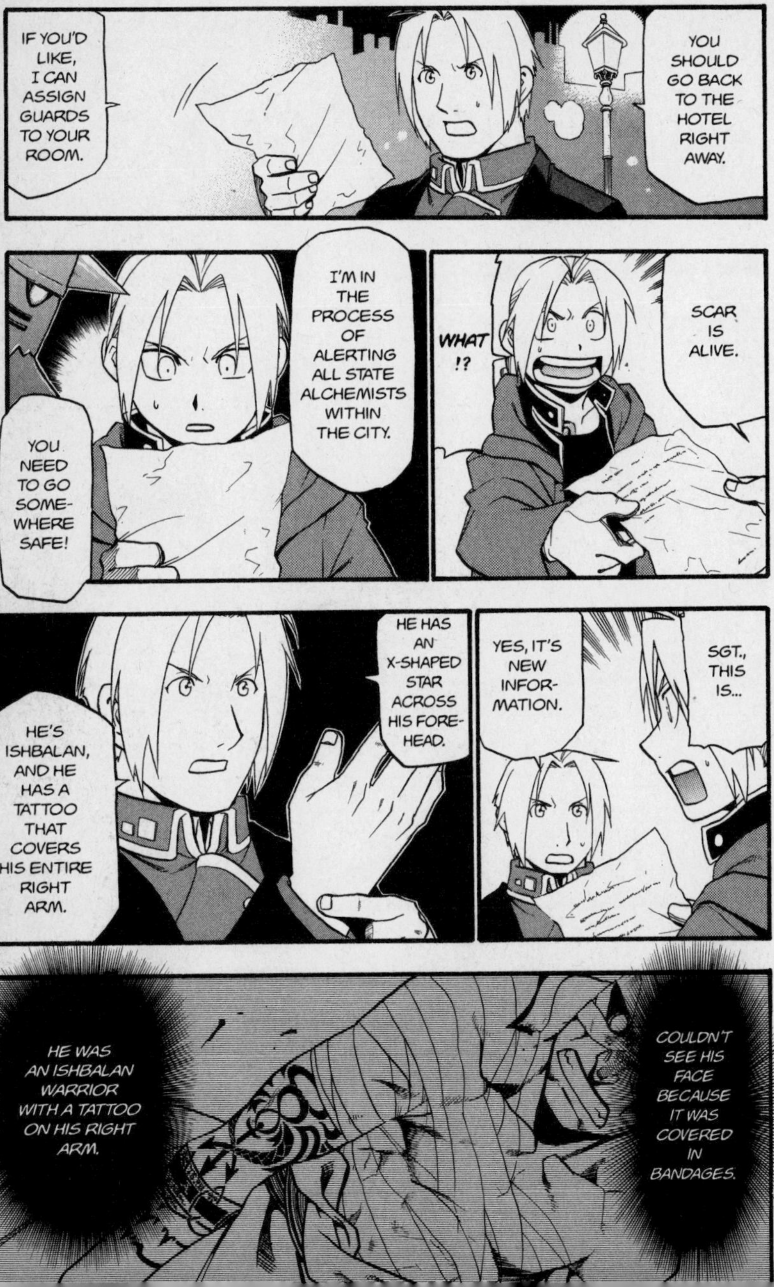
YOU SHOULD GO BACK TO THE HOTEL RIGHT AWAY.
IF YOU'D LIKE, I CAN ASSIGN GUARDS TO YOUR ROOM.
SCAR IS ALIVE.
WHAT !?
I'M IN THE PROCESS OF ALERTING ALL STATE ALCHEMISTS WITHIN THE CITY.
YOU NEED TO GO SOMEWHERE SAFE!
SGT., THIS IS...
YES, IT'S NEW INFORMATION.
HE HAS AN X-SHAPED STAR ACROSS HIS FOREHEAD.
HE'S ISHBALAN, AND HE HAS A TATTOO THAT COVERS HIS ENTIRE RIGHT ARM.
COULDN'T SEE HIS FACE BECAUSE IT WAS COVERED IN BANDAGES.
HE WAS AN ISHBALAN WARRIOR WITH A TATTOO ON HIS RIGHT ARM.

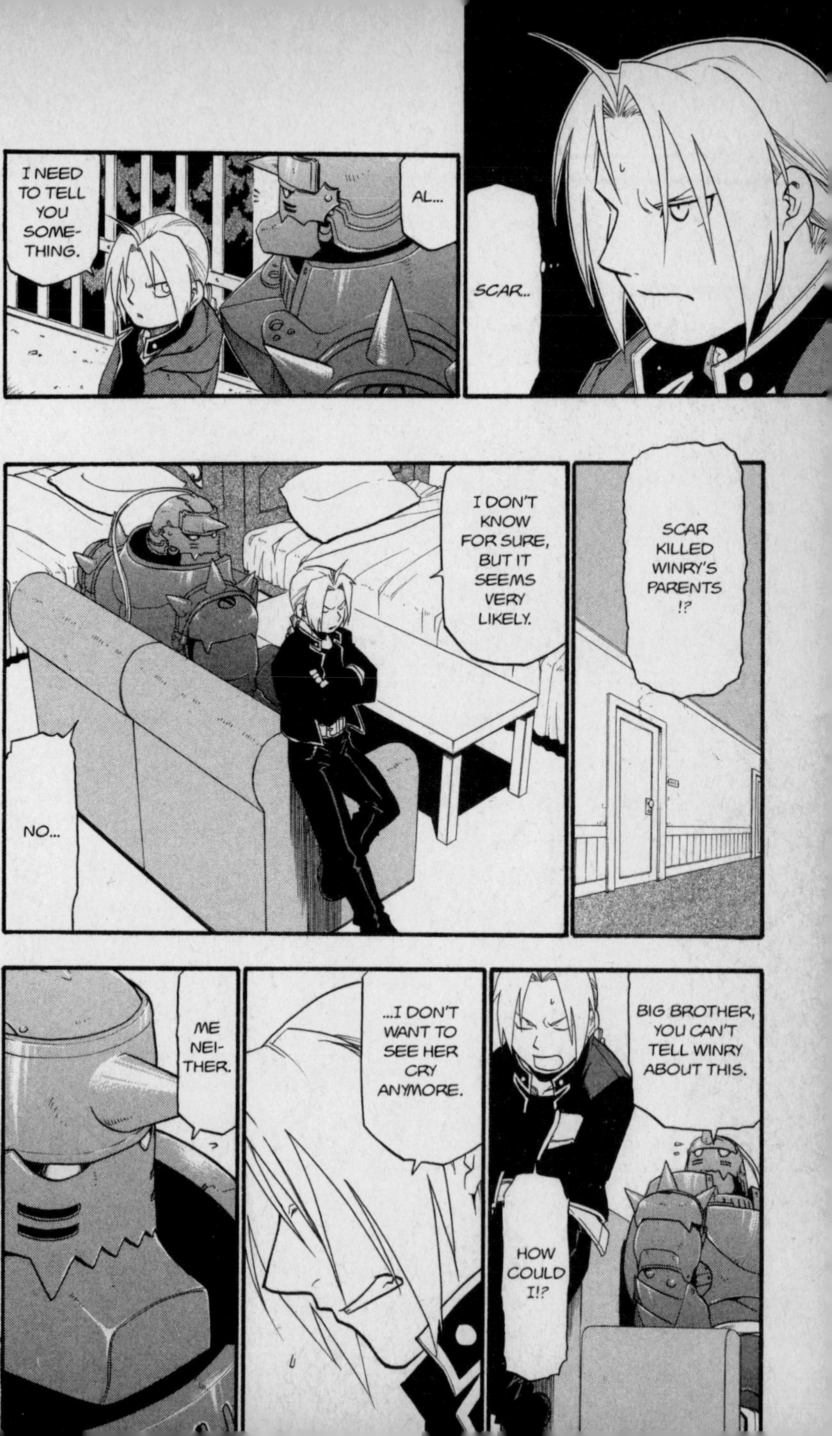
SCAR...
AL...
I NEED TO TELL YOU SOME-THING.
SCAR KILLED WINRY'S PARENTS !?
I DON'T KNOW FOR SURE, BUT IT SEEMS VERY LIKELY.
NO...
BIG BROTHER, YOU CAN'T TELL WINRY ABOUT THIS.
HOW COULD I!?
...I DON'T WANT TO SEE HER CRY ANYMORE.
ME NEI-THER.

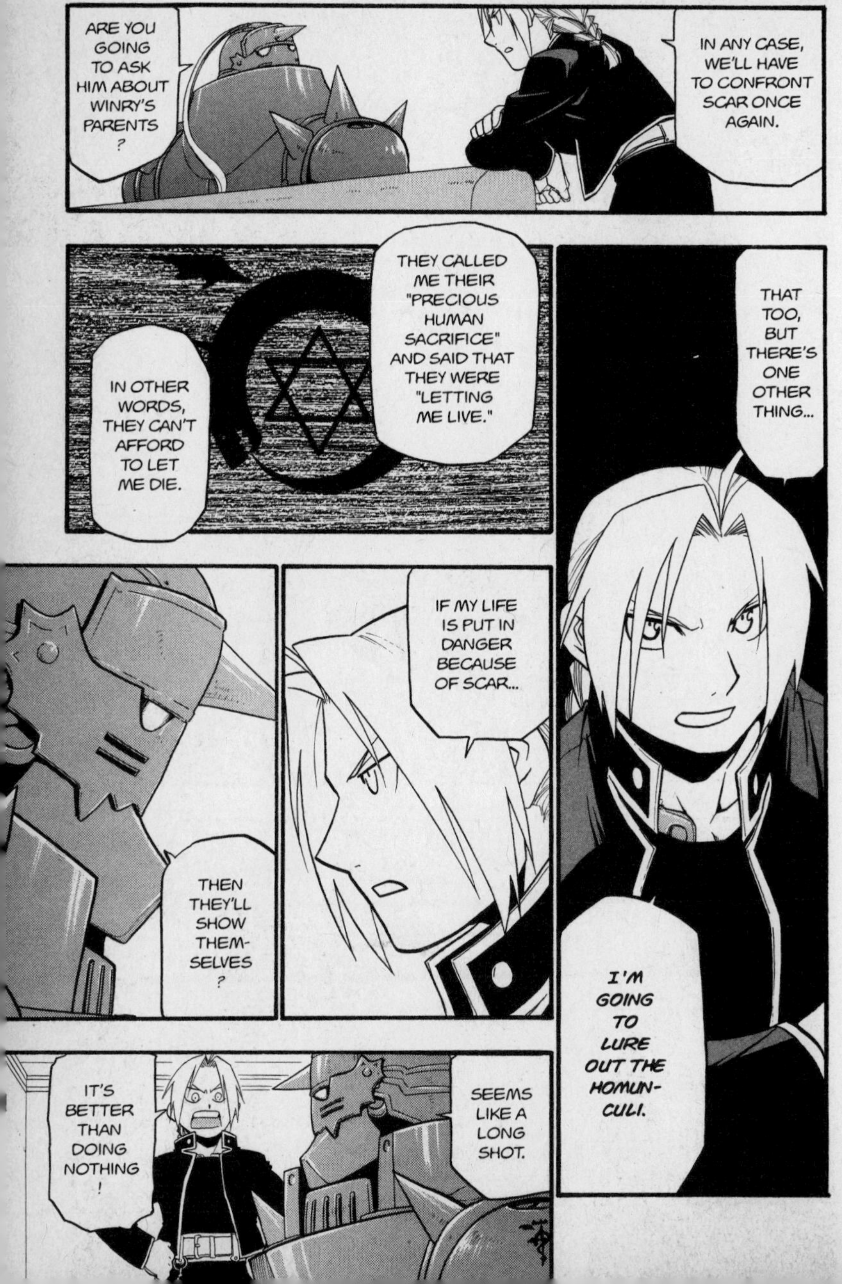

IN ANY CASE, WE'LL HAVE TO CONFRONT SCAR ONCE AGAIN.
ARE YOU GOING TO ASK HIM ABOUT WINRY'S PARENTS?
THAT TOO, BUT THERE'S ONE OTHER THING...
I'M GOING TO LURE OUT THE HOMUNCULI.
THEY CALLED ME THEIR "PRECIOUS HUMAN SACRIFICE" AND SAID THAT THEY WERE "LETTING ME LIVE."
IN OTHER WORDS, THEY CAN'T AFFORD TO LET ME DIE.
IF MY LIFE IS PUT IN DANGER BECAUSE OF SCAR...
THEN THEY'LL SHOW THEMSELVES?
SEEMS LIKE A LONG SHOT.
IT'S BETTER THAN DOING NOTHING!

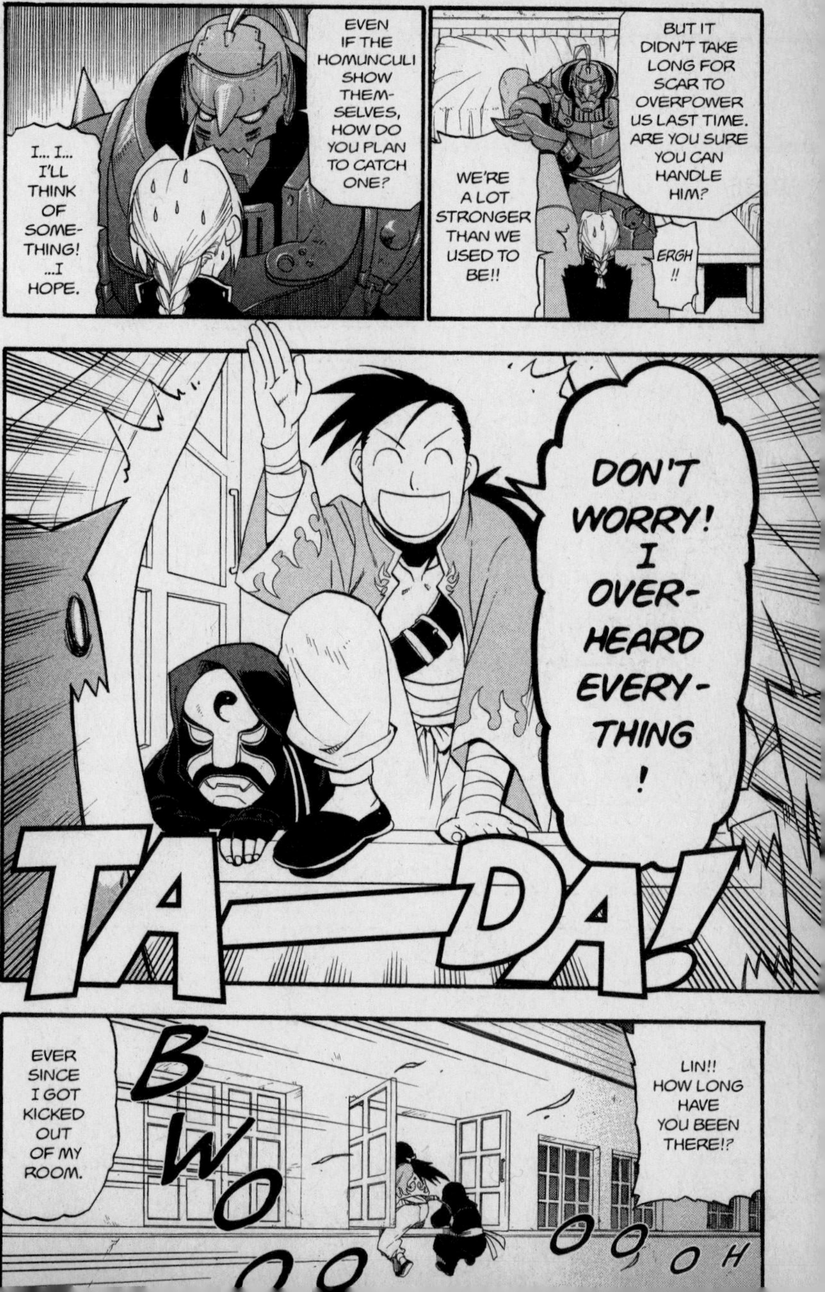
BUT IT DIDN'T TAKE LONG FOR SCAR TO OVERPOWER US LAST TIME. ARE YOU SURE YOU CAN HANDLE HIM?
WE'RE A LOT STRONGER THAN WE USED TO BE!!
ERGH!!
EVEN IF THE HOMUNCULI SHOW THEM-SELVES, HOW DO YOU PLAN TO CATCH ONE?
I... I... I'LL THINK OF SOME-THING! ...I HOPE.
DON'T WORRY! I OVER-HEARD EVERY-THING!
TA—DA!
LIN!! HOW LONG HAVE YOU BEEN THERE!?
EVER SINCE I GOT KICKED OUT OF MY ROOM.
BWOOOOOOOH

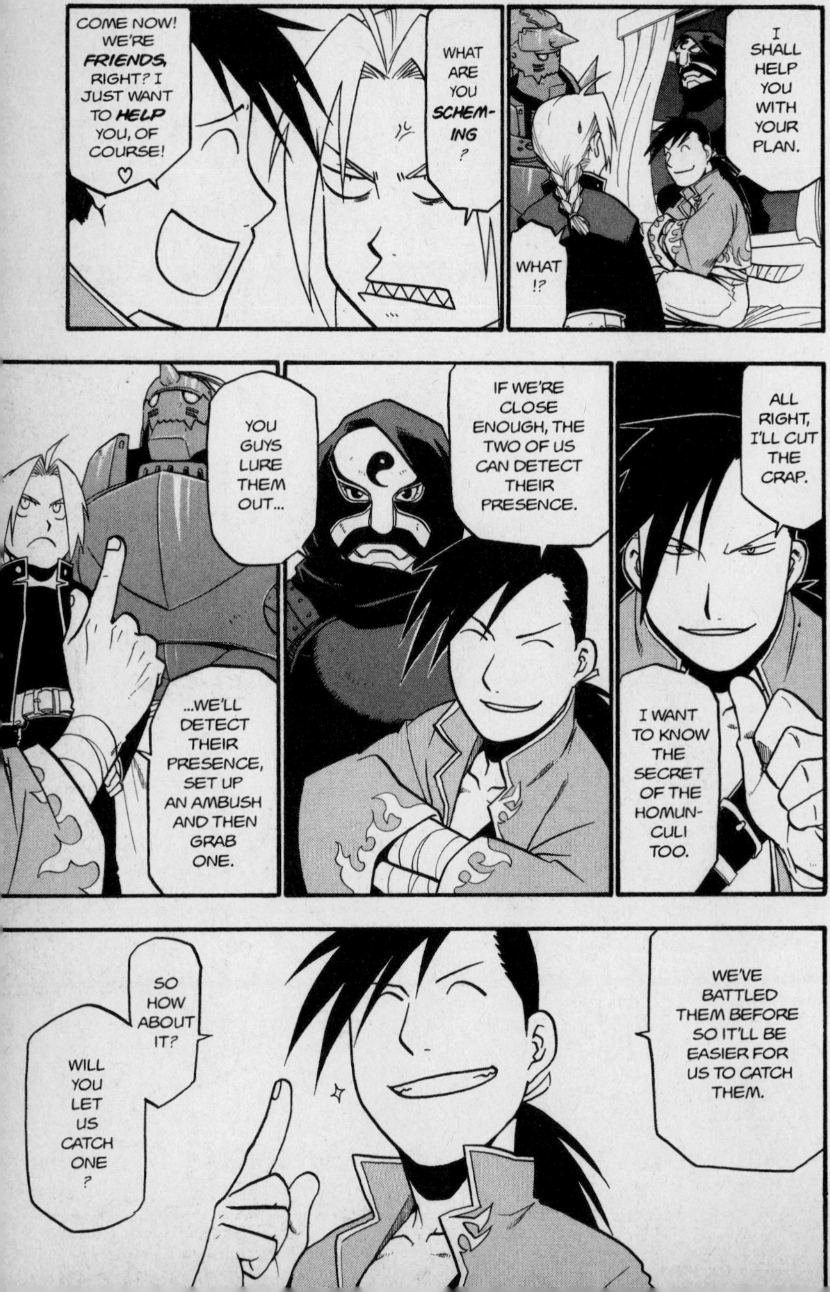
I SHALL HELP YOU WITH YOUR PLAN.
WHAT!?
WHAT ARE YOU SCHEMING?
COME NOW! WE'RE FRIENDS, RIGHT? I JUST WANT TO HELP YOU, OF COURSE! ♡
ALL RIGHT, I'LL CUT THE CRAP.
I WANT TO KNOW THE SECRET OF THE HOMUNCULI TOO.
IF WE'RE CLOSE ENOUGH, THE TWO OF US CAN DETECT THEIR PRESENCE.
YOU GUYS LURE THEM OUT...
...WE'LL DETECT THEIR PRESENCE, SET UP AN AMBUSH AND THEN GRAB ONE.
WE'VE BATTLED THEM BEFORE SO IT'LL BE EASIER FOR US TO CATCH THEM.
SO HOW ABOUT IT?
WILL YOU LET US CATCH ONE?

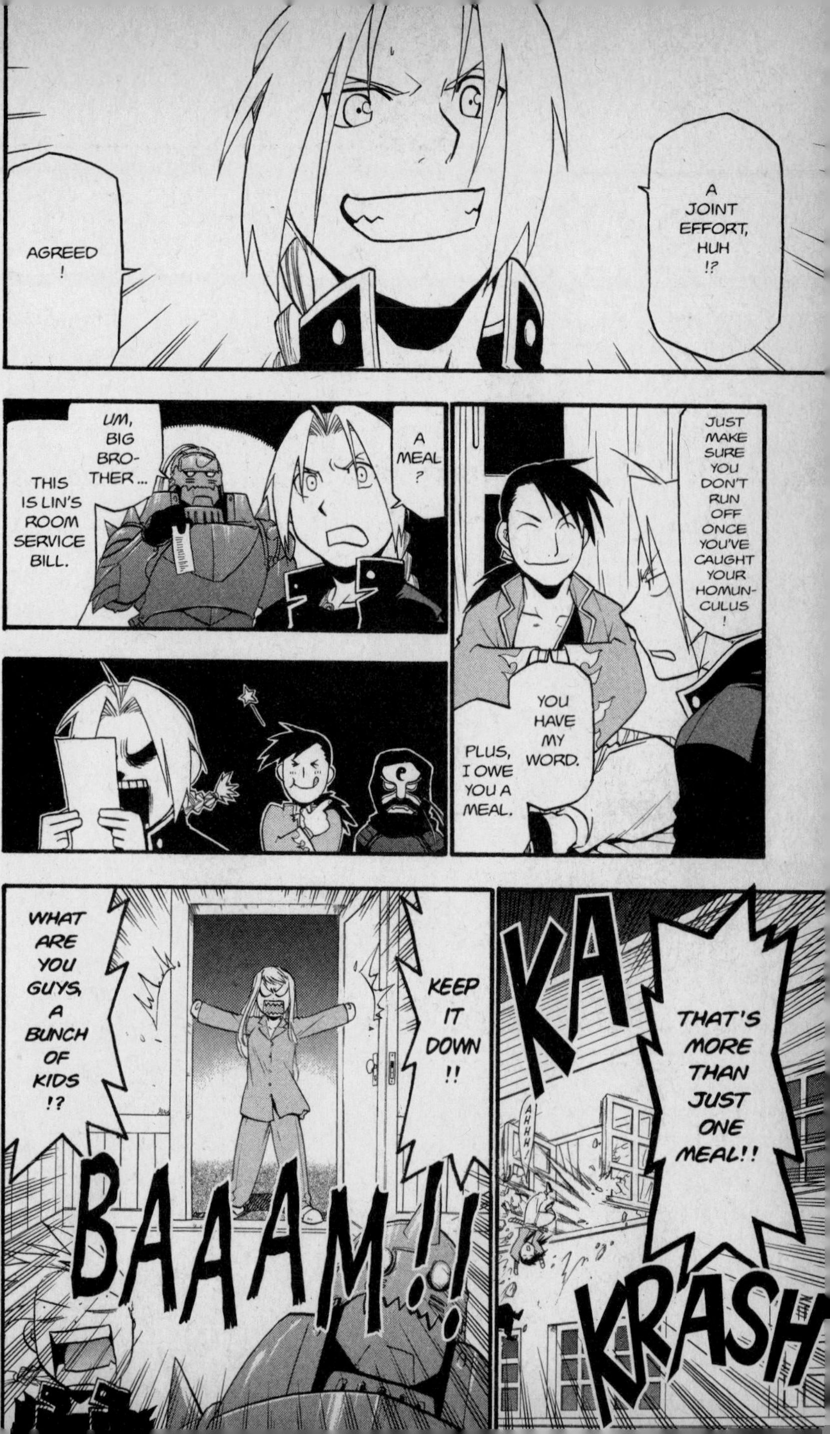
A JOINT EFFORT, HUH !?
AGREED !
JUST MAKE SURE YOU DON'T RUN OFF ONCE YOU'VE CAUGHT YOUR HOMUNCULUS !
YOU HAVE MY WORD.
PLUS, I OWE YOU A MEAL.
A MEAL ?
UM, BIG BRO- THER ...
THIS IS LIN'S ROOM SERVICE BILL.
KA
THAT'S MORE THAN JUST ONE MEAL!!
KRASH
KEEP IT DOWN !!
WHAT ARE YOU GUYS, A BUNCH OF KIDS !?
BAAAM!!

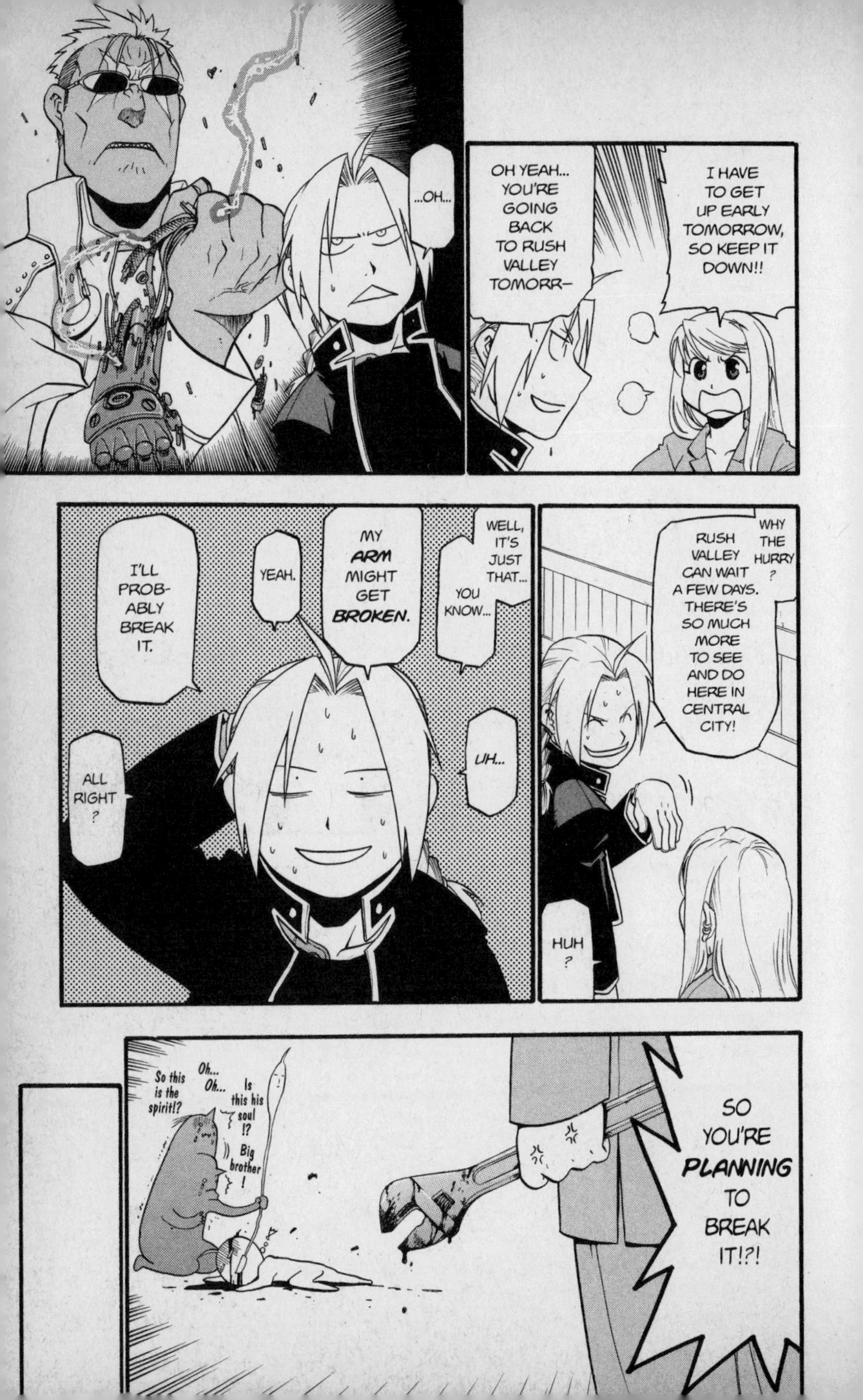
I HAVE TO GET UP EARLY TOMORROW, SO KEEP IT DOWN!!
OH YEAH... YOU'RE GOING BACK TO RUSH VALLEY TOMORR—
...OH...
WHY THE HURRY?
RUSH VALLEY CAN WAIT A FEW DAYS. THERE'S SO MUCH MORE TO SEE AND DO HERE IN CENTRAL CITY!
HUH?
WELL, IT'S JUST THAT...
YOU KNOW...
MY ARM MIGHT GET BROKEN.
YEAH.
I'LL PROBABLY BREAK IT.
UH...
ALL RIGHT?
SO YOU'RE PLANNING TO BREAK IT!?!
Is this his soul!?
Big brother!
Oh... Oh...
So this is the spirit!?

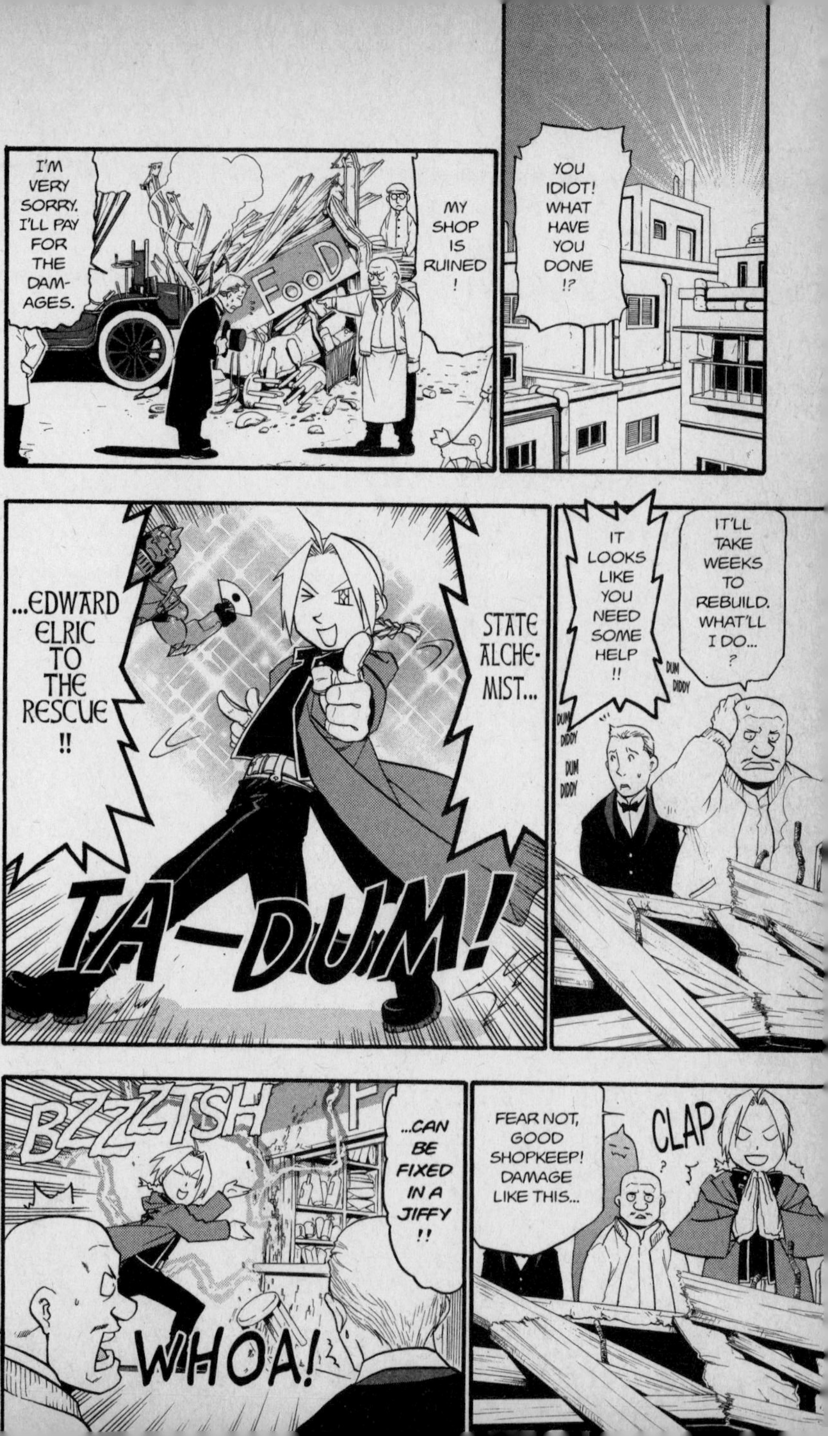
YOU IDIOT! WHAT HAVE YOU DONE!?
MY SHOP IS RUINED!
I'M VERY SORRY. I'LL PAY FOR THE DAMAGES.
IT'LL TAKE WEEKS TO REBUILD. WHAT'LL I DO...?
IT LOOKS LIKE YOU NEED SOME HELP!!
DUM DIDDY
DUM DIDDY
DUM DIDDY
STATE ALCHEMIST...
...EDWARD ELRIC TO THE RESCUE!!
TA-DUM!
CLAP
FEAR NOT, GOOD SHOPKEEP! DAMAGE LIKE THIS...
...CAN BE FIXED IN A JIFFY!!
BZZZTSH
WHOA!

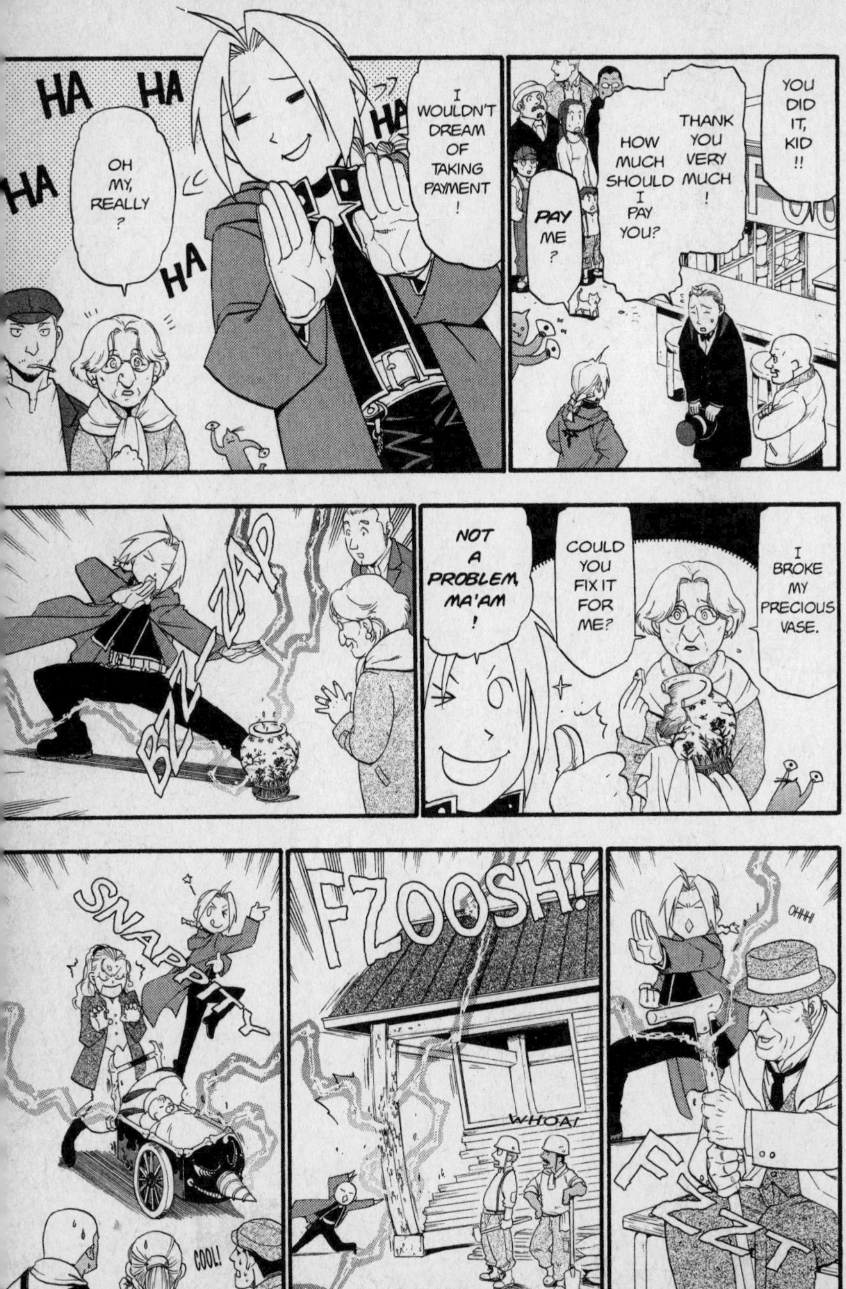
YOU DID IT, KID !!
THANK YOU VERY MUCH !
HOW MUCH SHOULD I PAY YOU?
PAY ME ?
I WOULDN'T DREAM OF TAKING PAYMENT !
HA HA HA HA HA
OH MY, REALLY ?
I BROKE MY PRECIOUS VASE.
COULD YOU FIX IT FOR ME?
NOT A PROBLEM, MA'AM !
ZAP
BZZ
OHHH
FZZZT
FZOOSH!
WHOA!
SNAPPIT
COOL!

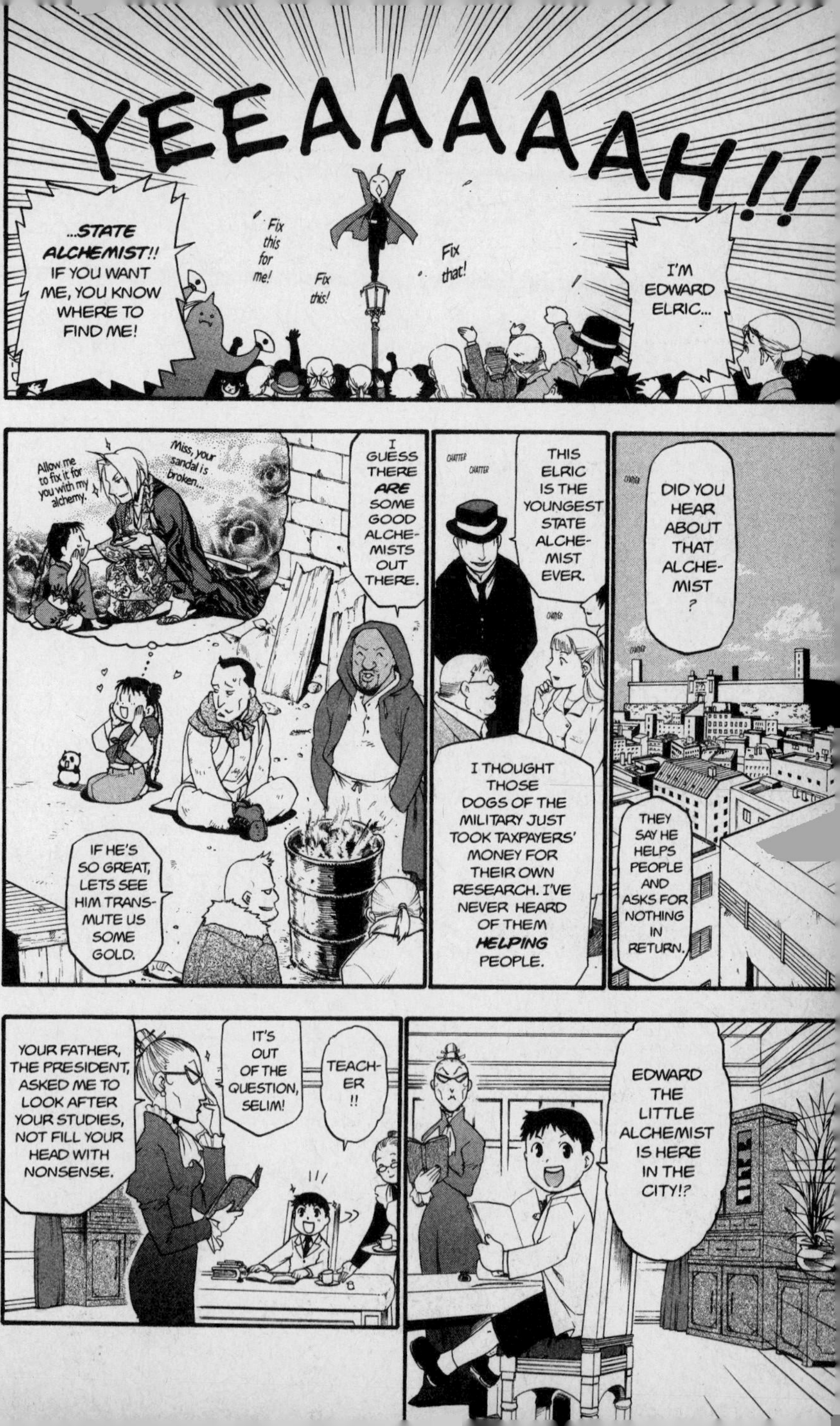
YEEAAAAAAH!!
I'M EDWARD ELRIC...
Fix that!
Fix this!
Fix this for me!
...STATE ALCHEMIST!! IF YOU WANT ME, YOU KNOW WHERE TO FIND ME!
DID YOU HEAR ABOUT THAT ALCHEMIST?
THEY SAY HE HELPS PEOPLE AND ASKS FOR NOTHING IN RETURN.
CHATTER
CHATTER
THIS ELRIC IS THE YOUNGEST STATE ALCHEMIST EVER.
I THOUGHT THOSE DOGS OF THE MILITARY JUST TOOK TAXPAYERS' MONEY FOR THEIR OWN RESEARCH. I'VE NEVER HEARD OF THEM HELPING PEOPLE.
I GUESS THERE ARE SOME GOOD ALCHEMISTS OUT THERE.
Miss, your sandal is broken...
Allow me to fix it for you with my alchemy.
IF HE'S SO GREAT, LETS SEE HIM TRANSMUTE US SOME GOLD.
EDWARD THE LITTLE ALCHEMIST IS HERE IN THE CITY!?
TEACHER!!
IT'S OUT OF THE QUESTION, SELIM!
YOUR FATHER, THE PRESIDENT, ASKED ME TO LOOK AFTER YOUR STUDIES, NOT FILL YOUR HEAD WITH NONSENSE.

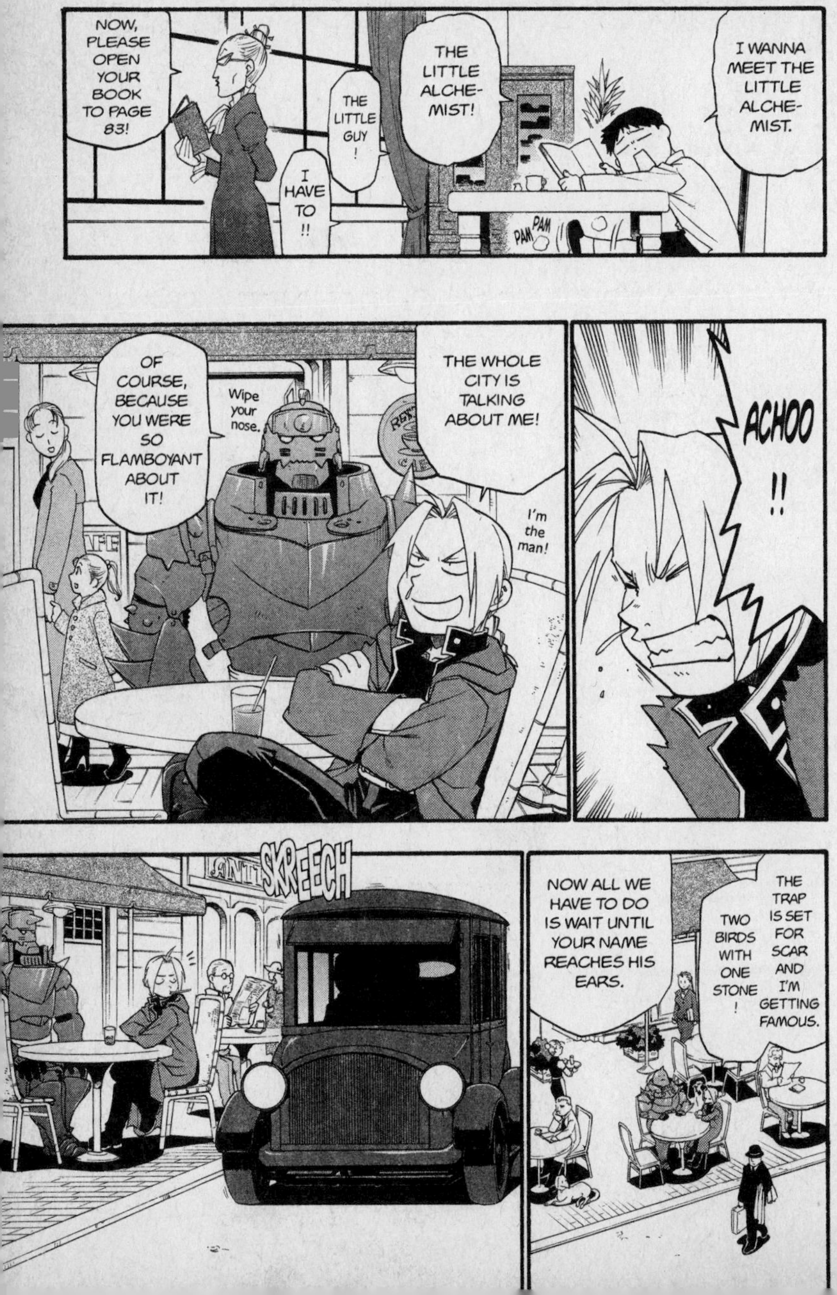
I WANNA MEET THE LITTLE ALCHEMIST.
PAM PAM
THE LITTLE ALCHEMIST!
THE LITTLE GUY!
I HAVE TO!!
NOW, PLEASE OPEN YOUR BOOK TO PAGE 83!
ACHOO!!
THE WHOLE CITY IS TALKING ABOUT ME!
I'm the man!
OF COURSE, BECAUSE YOU WERE SO FLAMBOYANT ABOUT IT!
Wipe your nose.
THE TRAP IS SET FOR SCAR AND I'M GETTING FAMOUS.
TWO BIRDS WITH ONE STONE!
NOW ALL WE HAVE TO DO IS WAIT UNTIL YOUR NAME REACHES HIS EARS.
SKREECH

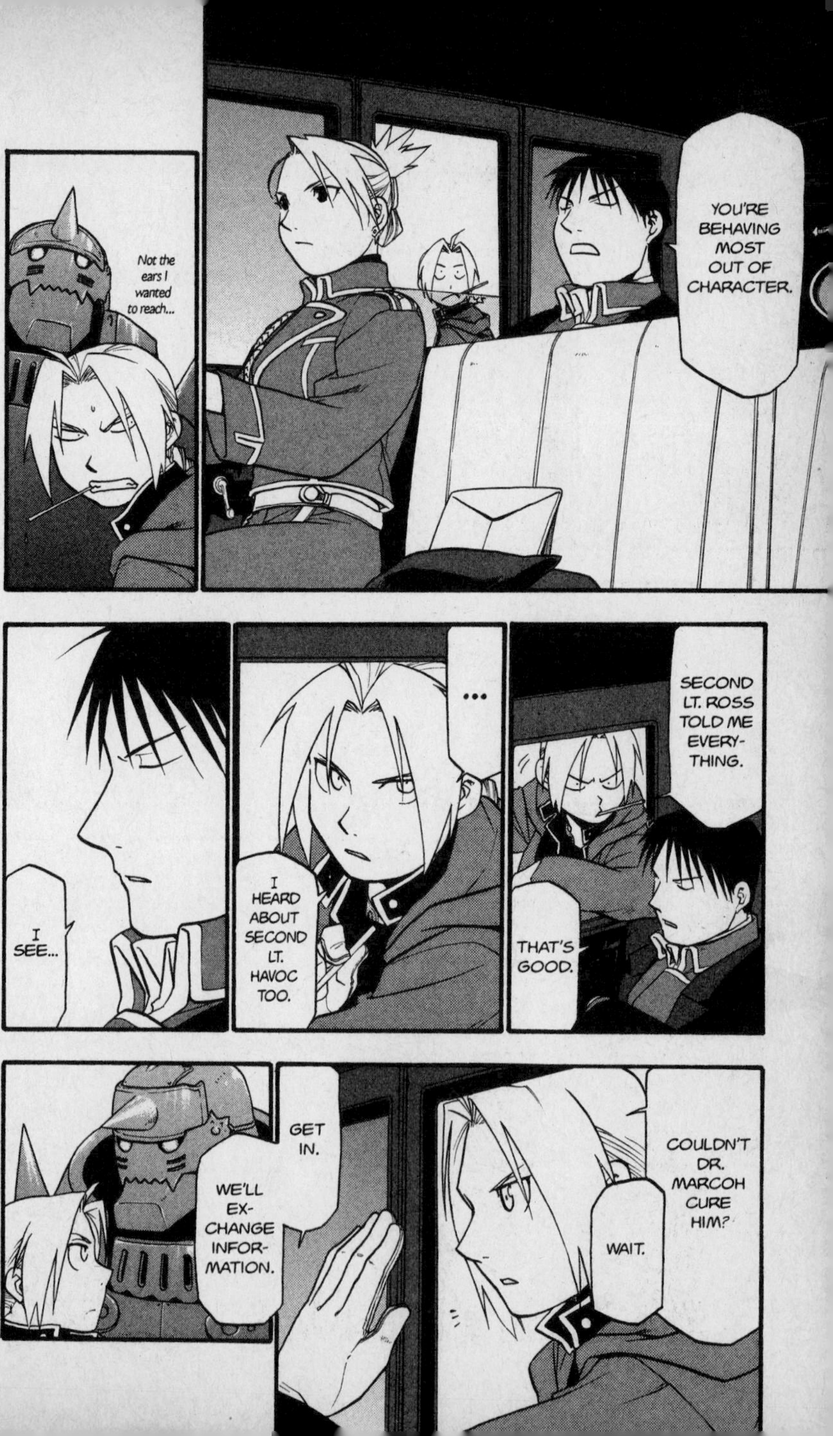
YOU'RE BEHAVING MOST OUT OF CHARACTER.
Not the ears I wanted to reach...
SECOND LT. ROSS TOLD ME EVERYTHING.
THAT'S GOOD.
...
I HEARD ABOUT SECOND LT. HAVOC TOO.
I SEE...
COULDN'T DR. MARCOH CURE HIM?
WAIT.
GET IN.
WE'LL EXCHANGE INFORMATION.

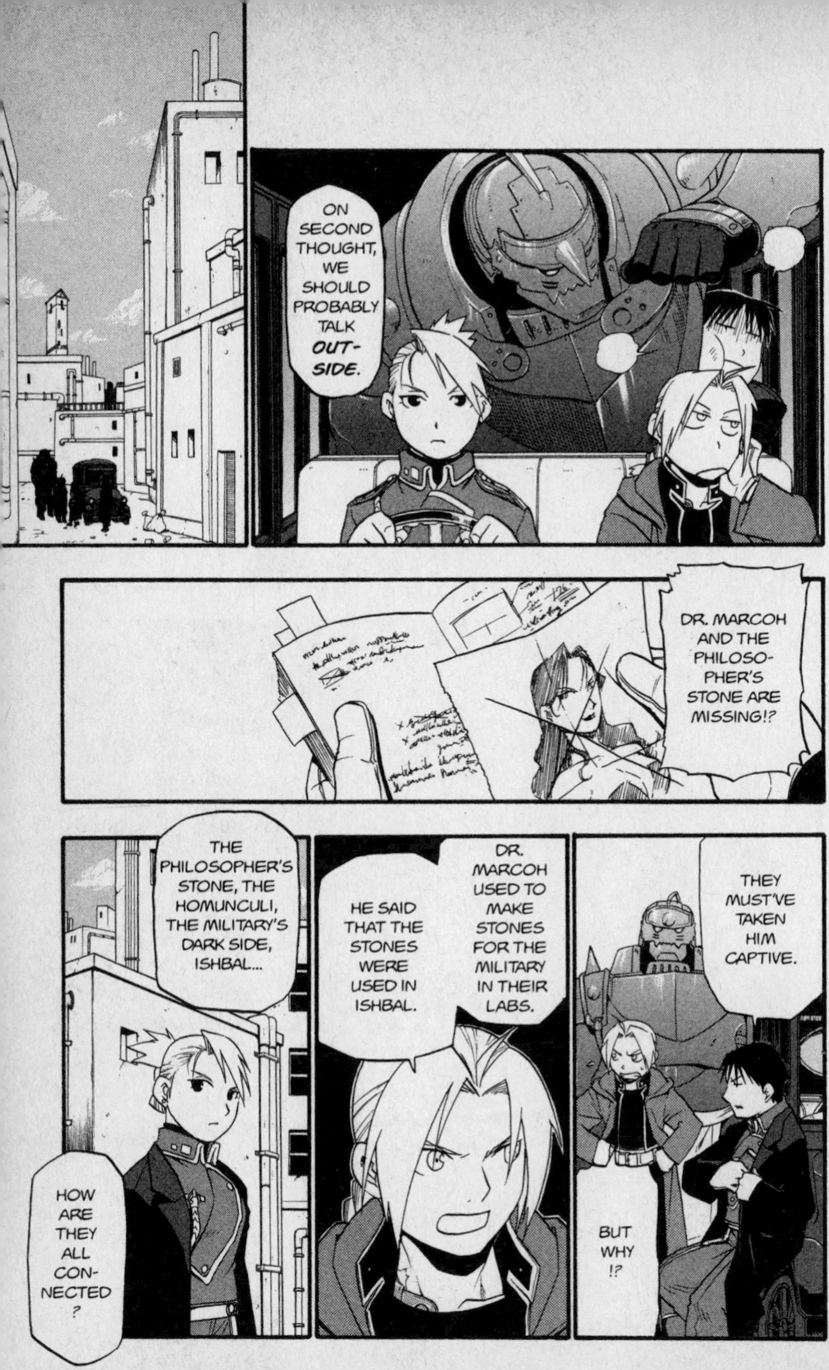
ON SECOND THOUGHT, WE SHOULD PROBABLY TALK *OUTSIDE*.
DR. MARCOH AND THE PHILOSOPHER'S STONE ARE MISSING!?
THEY MUST'VE TAKEN HIM CAPTIVE.
BUT WHY!?
DR. MARCOH USED TO MAKE STONES FOR THE MILITARY IN THEIR LABS.
HE SAID THAT THE STONES WERE USED IN ISHBAL.
THE PHILOSOPHER'S STONE, THE HOMUNCULI, THE MILITARY'S DARK SIDE, ISHBAL...
HOW ARE THEY ALL CONNECTED?

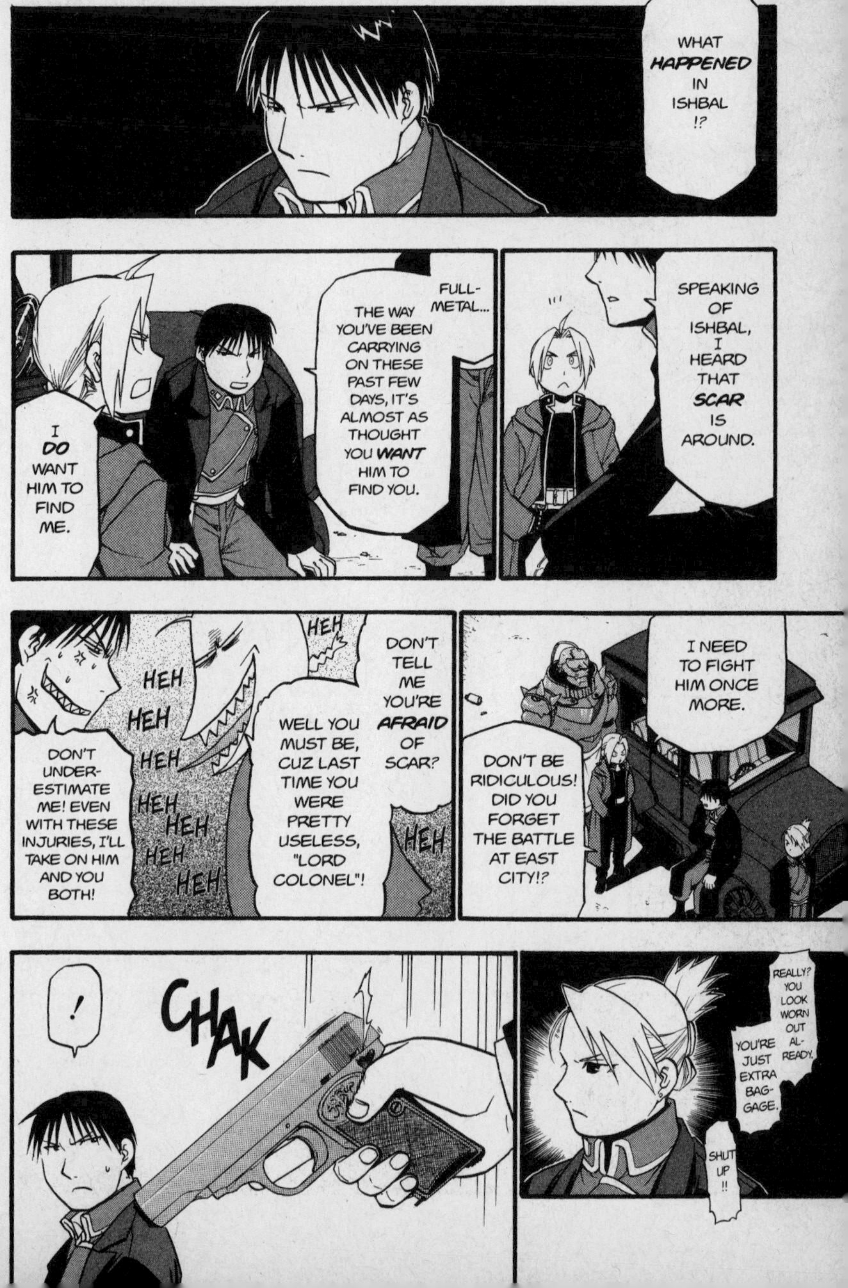
WHAT HAPPENED IN ISHBAL !?
SPEAKING OF ISHBAL, I HEARD THAT SCAR IS AROUND.
FULL-METAL...
THE WAY YOU'VE BEEN CARRYING ON THESE PAST FEW DAYS, IT'S ALMOST AS THOUGHT YOU WANT HIM TO FIND YOU.
I DO WANT HIM TO FIND ME.
I NEED TO FIGHT HIM ONCE MORE.
DON'T BE RIDICULOUS! DID YOU FORGET THE BATTLE AT EAST CITY!?
HEH
DON'T TELL ME YOU'RE AFRAID OF SCAR?
WELL YOU MUST BE, CUZ LAST TIME YOU WERE PRETTY USELESS, "LORD COLONEL"!
HEH
HEH HEH HEH HEH HEH HEH HEH
DON'T UNDER-ESTIMATE ME! EVEN WITH THESE INJURIES, I'LL TAKE ON HIM AND YOU BOTH!
REALLY? YOU LOOK WORN OUT AL-READY.
YOU'RE JUST EXTRA BAG-GAGE.
SHUT UP !!
CHAK
!

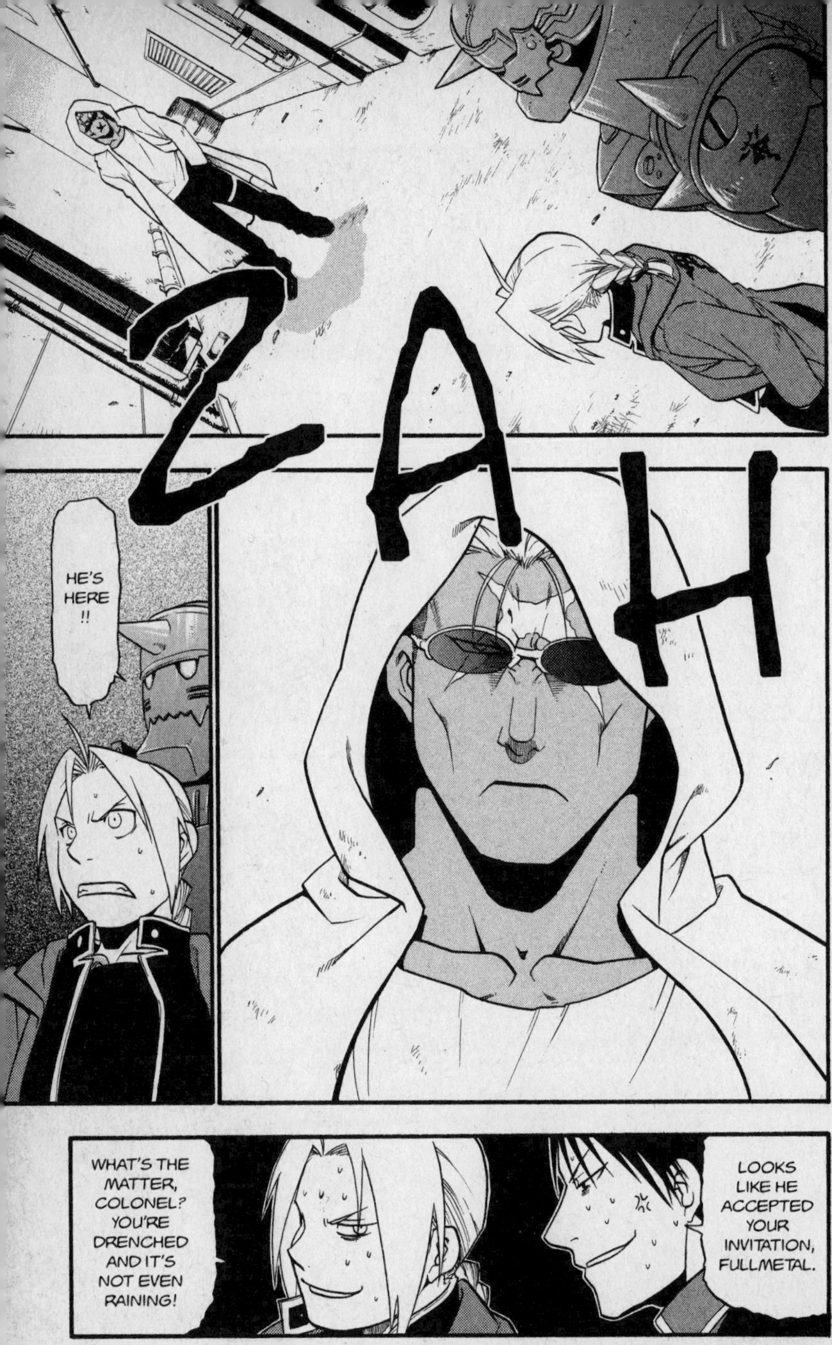
ZAH
HE'S HERE !!
LOOKS LIKE HE ACCEPTED YOUR INVITATION, FULLMETAL.
WHAT'S THE MATTER, COLONEL? YOU'RE DRENCHED AND IT'S NOT EVEN RAINING!

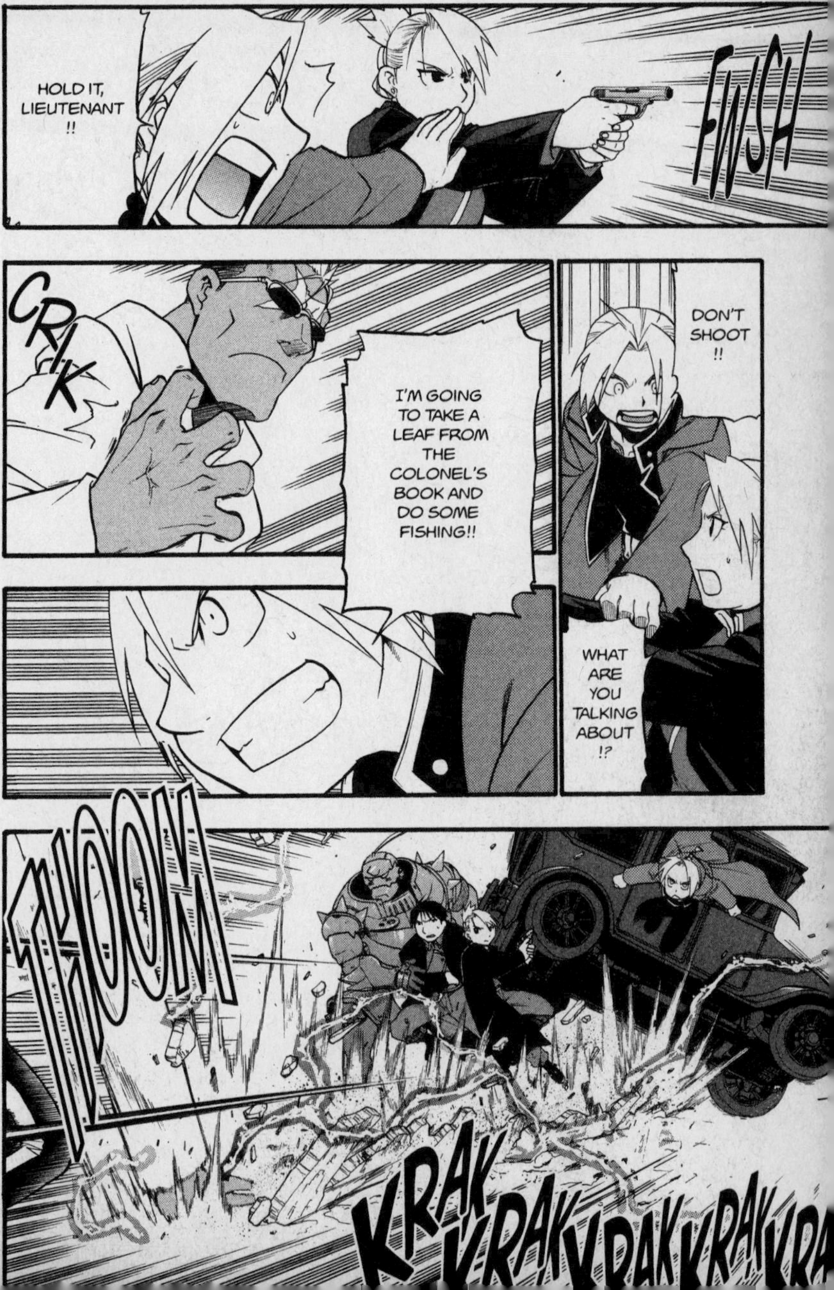
FWSH
HOLD IT, LIEUTENANT!!
DON'T SHOOT!!
WHAT ARE YOU TALKING ABOUT!?
CRIK
I'M GOING TO TAKE A LEAF FROM THE COLONEL'S BOOK AND DO SOME FISHING!!
THOOM
KRAK KRAK KRAK KRAK KRA

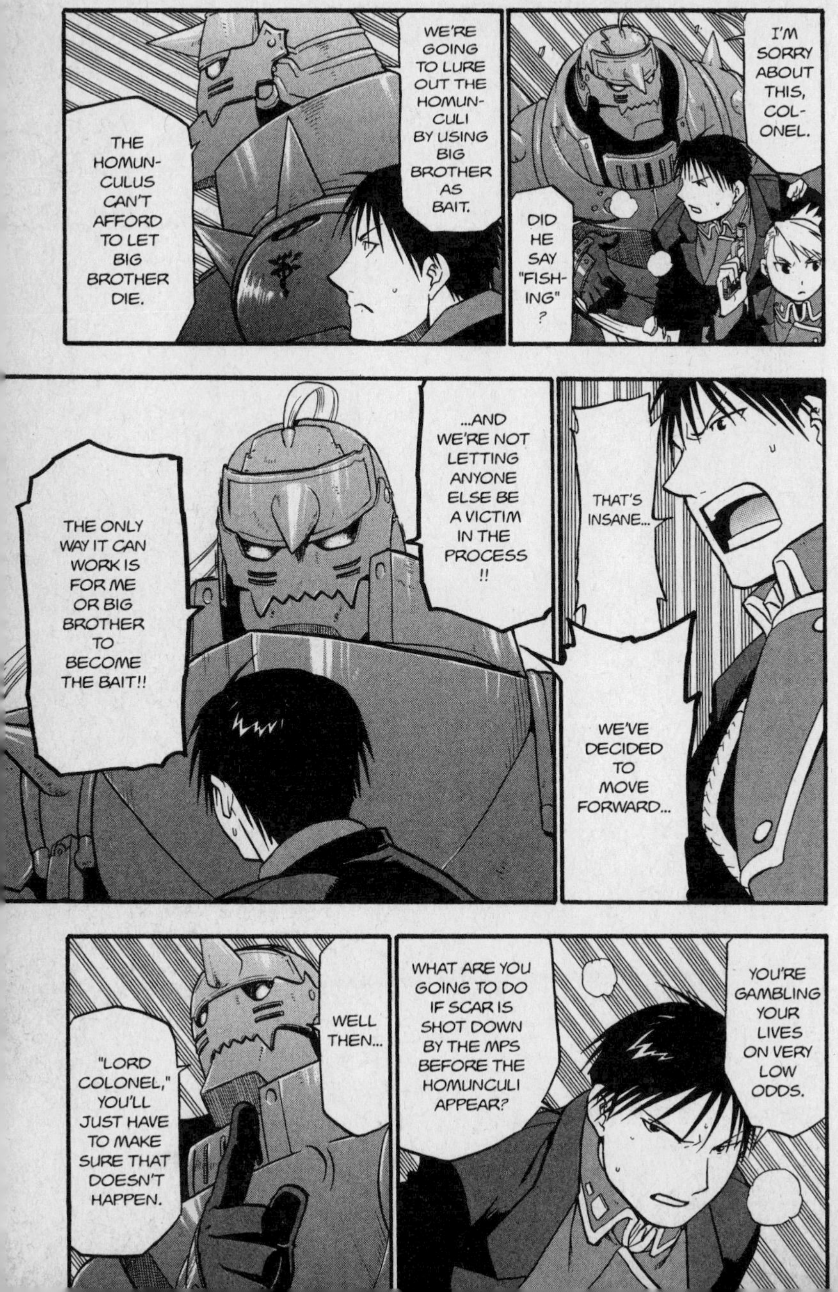
I'M SORRY ABOUT THIS, COLONEL.
DID HE SAY "FISHING"?
WE'RE GOING TO LURE OUT THE HOMUNCULI BY USING BIG BROTHER AS BAIT.
THE HOMUNCULUS CAN'T AFFORD TO LET BIG BROTHER DIE.
THAT'S INSANE...
WE'VE DECIDED TO MOVE FORWARD...
...AND WE'RE NOT LETTING ANYONE ELSE BE A VICTIM IN THE PROCESS!!
THE ONLY WAY IT CAN WORK IS FOR ME OR BIG BROTHER TO BECOME THE BAIT!!
YOU'RE GAMBLING YOUR LIVES ON VERY LOW ODDS.
WHAT ARE YOU GOING TO DO IF SCAR IS SHOT DOWN BY THE MPS BEFORE THE HOMUNCULI APPEAR?
WELL THEN...
"LORD COLONEL," YOU'LL JUST HAVE TO MAKE SURE THAT DOESN'T HAPPEN.

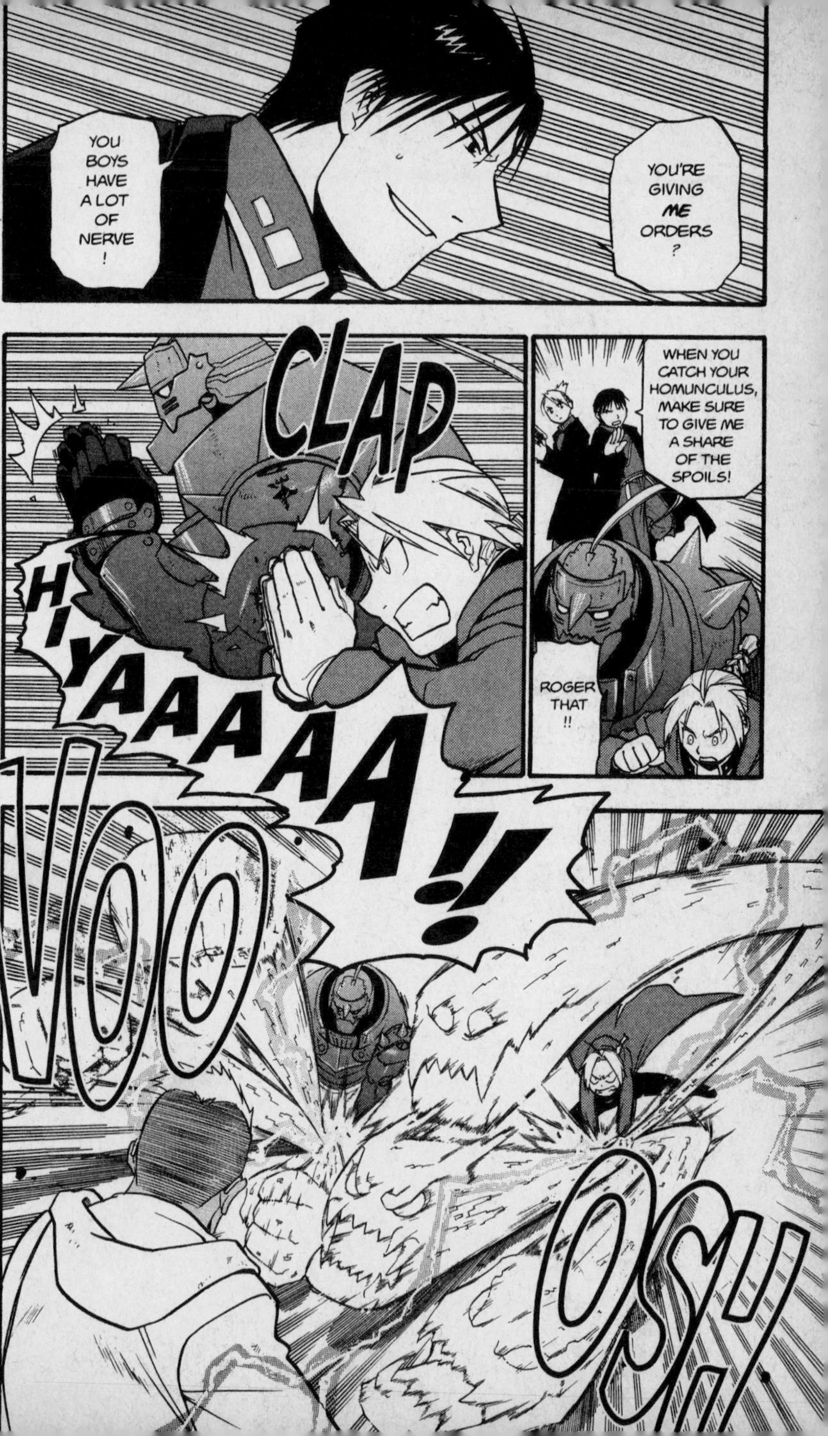
YOU'RE GIVING *ME* ORDERS?
YOU BOYS HAVE A LOT OF NERVE!
WHEN YOU CATCH YOUR HOMUNCULUS, MAKE SURE TO GIVE ME A SHARE OF THE SPOILS!
ROGER THAT!!
CLAP
HIYAAAAAA!!
VOOOSH

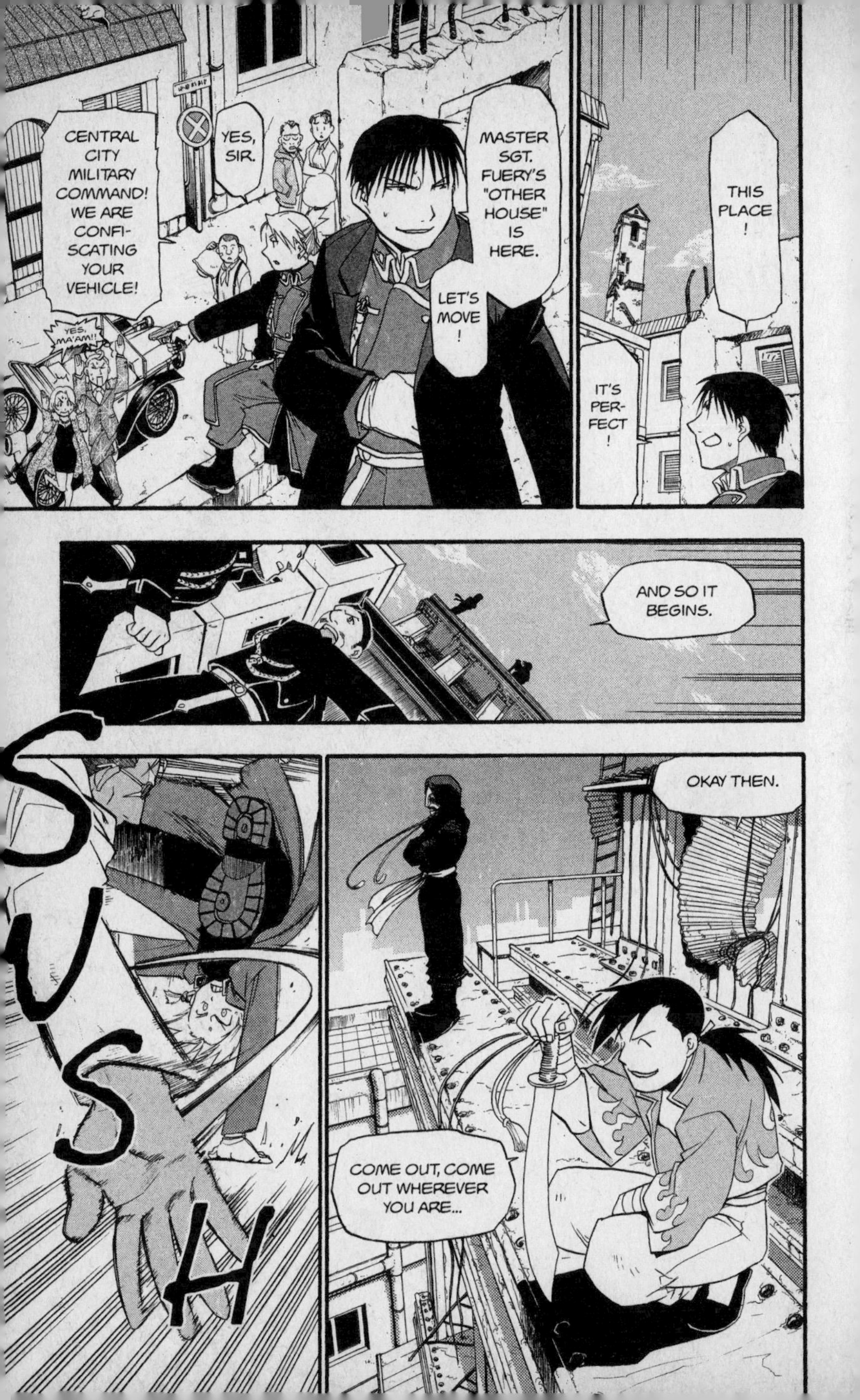
THIS PLACE!
IT'S PERFECT!
MASTER SGT. FUERY'S "OTHER HOUSE" IS HERE.
LET'S MOVE!
YES, SIR.
CENTRAL CITY MILITARY COMMAND! WE ARE CONFISCATING YOUR VEHICLE!
YES, MA'AM!!
AND SO IT BEGINS.
OKAY THEN.
COME OUT, COME OUT WHEREVER YOU ARE...
SWISH

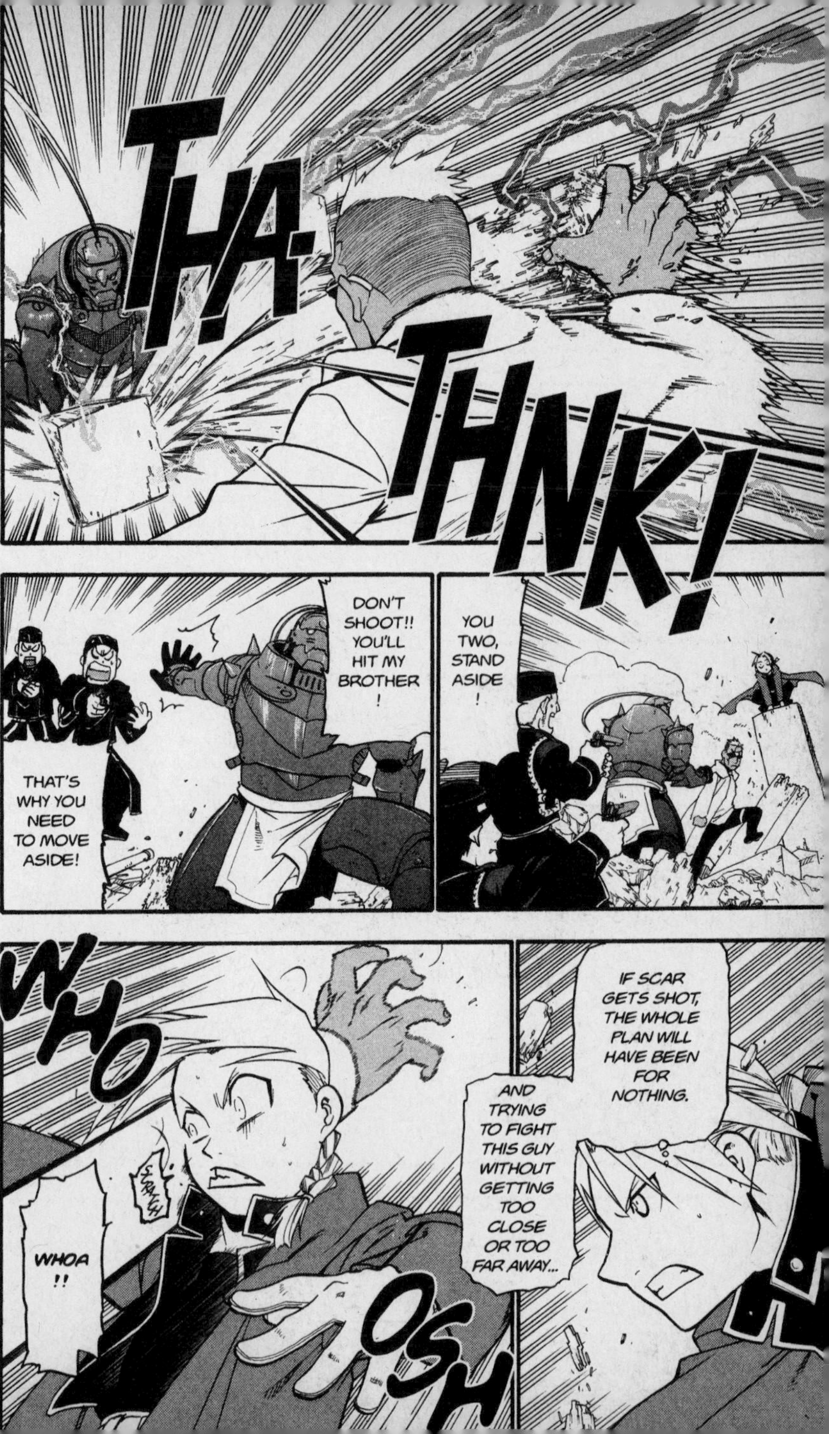
THA-THNK!
YOU TWO, STAND ASIDE !
DON'T SHOOT!! YOU'LL HIT MY BROTHER !
THAT'S WHY YOU NEED TO MOVE ASIDE!
IF SCAR GETS SHOT, THE WHOLE PLAN WILL HAVE BEEN FOR NOTHING.
AND TRYING TO FIGHT THIS GUY WITHOUT GETTING TOO CLOSE OR TOO FAR AWAY...
WHOOSH
WHOA !!

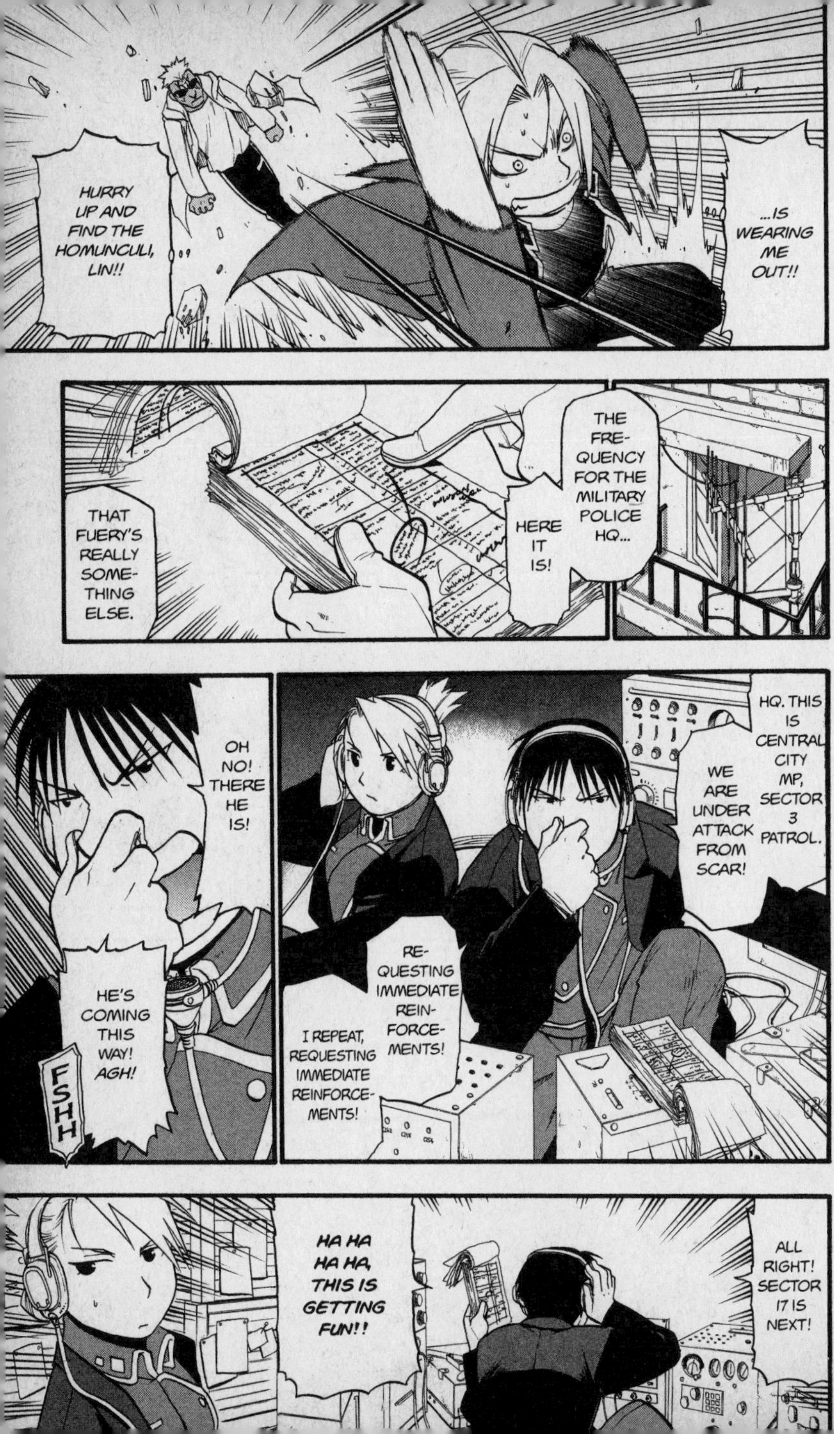
...IS WEARING ME OUT!!
HURRY UP AND FIND THE HOMUNCULI, LIN!!
THE FREQUENCY FOR THE MILITARY POLICE HQ...
HERE IT IS!
THAT FUERY'S REALLY SOMETHING ELSE.
HQ. THIS IS CENTRAL CITY MP, SECTOR 3 PATROL.
WE ARE UNDER ATTACK FROM SCAR!
REQUESTING IMMEDIATE REINFORCEMENTS!
I REPEAT, REQUESTING IMMEDIATE REINFORCEMENTS!
OH NO! THERE HE IS!
HE'S COMING THIS WAY! AGH!
FSHH
ALL RIGHT! SECTOR 17 IS NEXT!
HA HA HA HA, THIS IS GETTING FUN!!

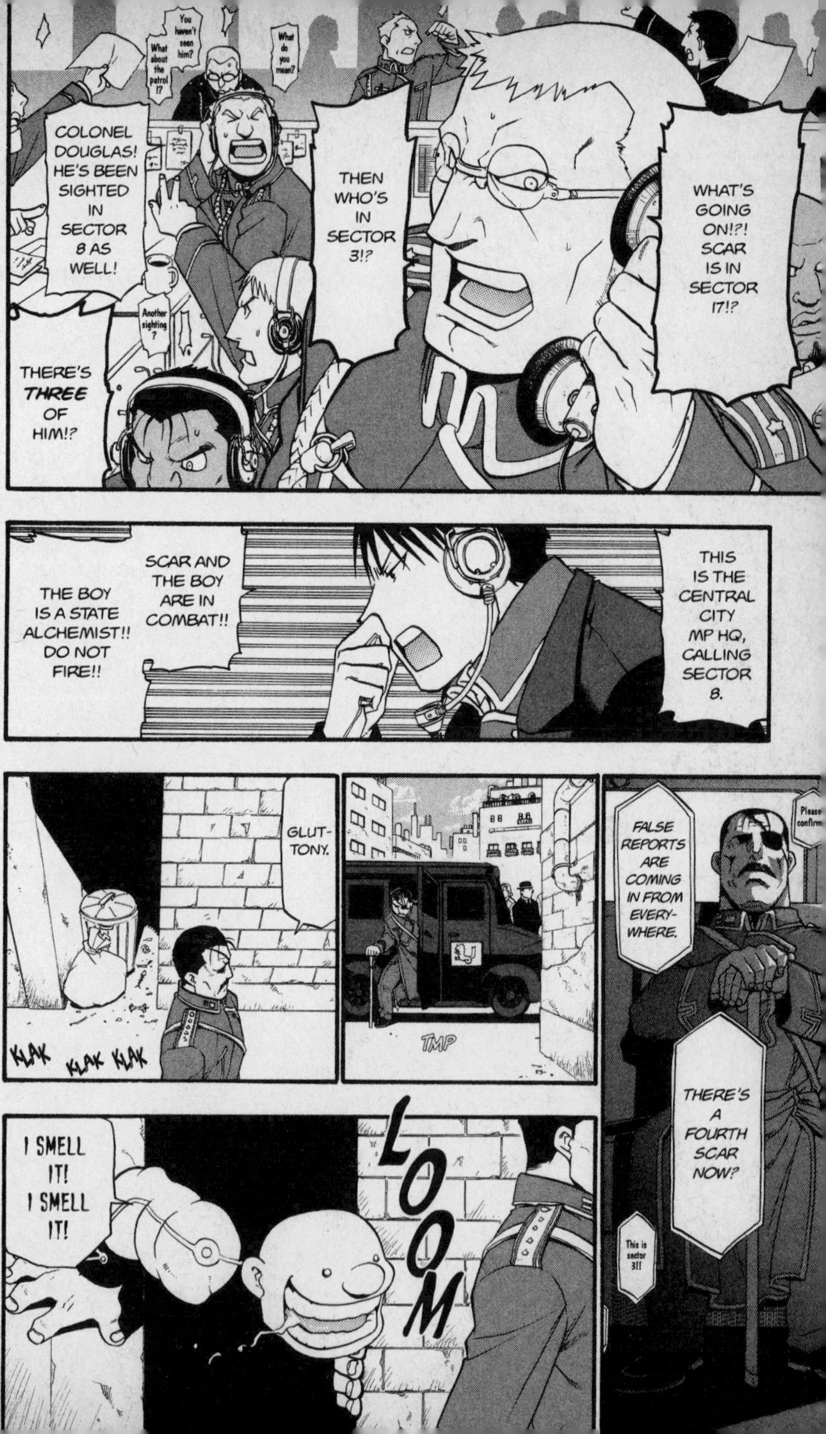
WHAT'S GOING ON!?! SCAR IS IN SECTOR 17!?
What do you mean?
THEN WHO'S IN SECTOR 3!?
You haven't seen him?
What about the patrol!?
COLONEL DOUGLAS! HE'S BEEN SIGHTED IN SECTOR 8 AS WELL!
Another sighting?
THERE'S THREE OF HIM!?
THIS IS THE CENTRAL CITY MP HQ, CALLING SECTOR 8.
SCAR AND THE BOY ARE IN COMBAT!!
THE BOY IS A STATE ALCHEMIST!! DO NOT FIRE!!
Please confirm
FALSE REPORTS ARE COMING IN FROM EVERYWHERE.
THERE'S A FOURTH SCAR NOW?
This is sector 3!!
TMP
GLUTTONY.
KLAK KLAK KLAK
LOOM
I SMELL IT! I SMELL IT!

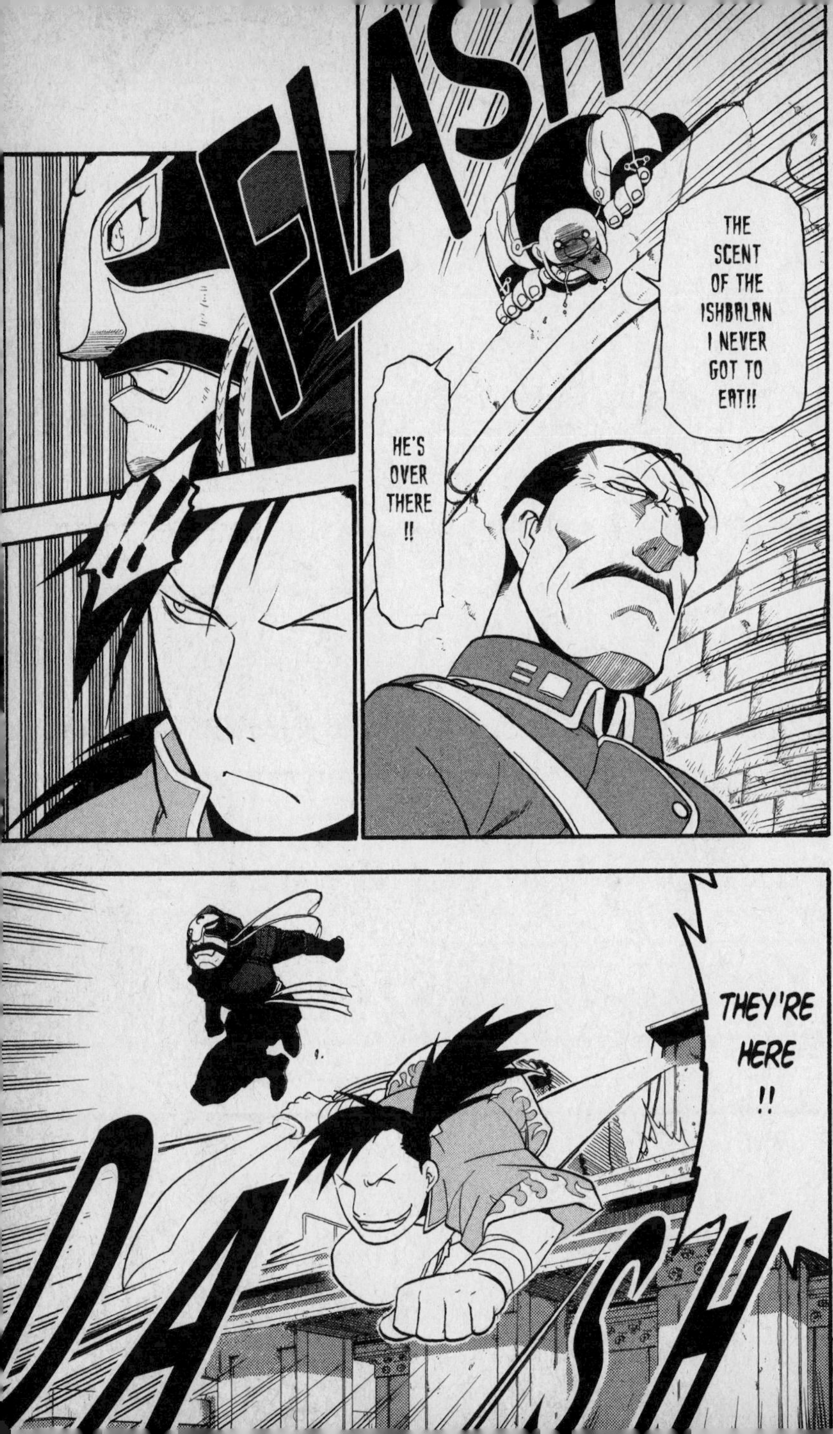
FLASH
THE SCENT OF THE ISHBALAN I NEVER GOT TO EAT!!
HE'S OVER THERE !!
THEY'RE HERE !!
DASH

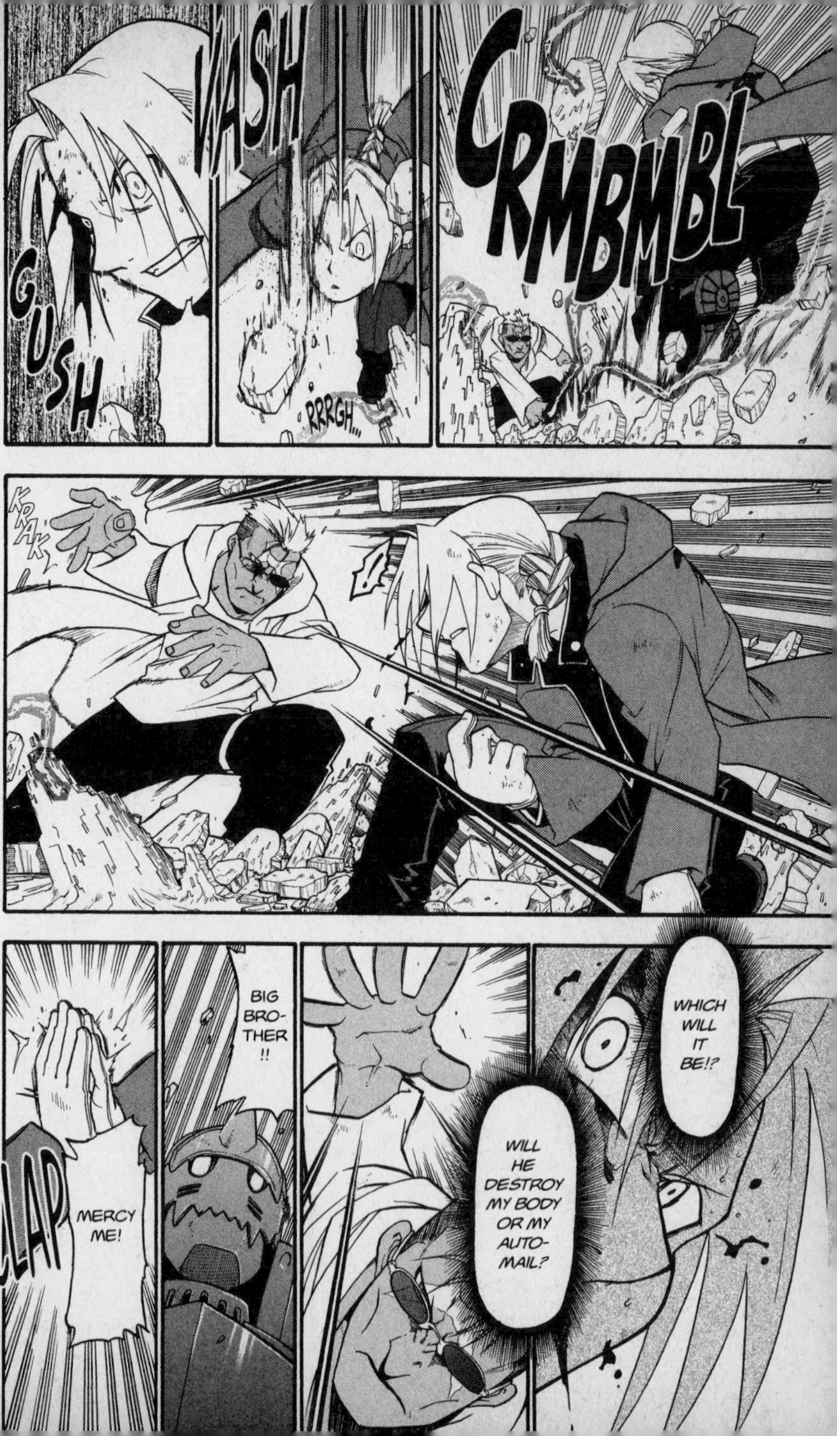
CRMBMBL
VASH
RRRGH...
GUSH
KRAK
!
WHICH WILL IT BE!?
WILL HE DESTROY MY BODY OR MY AUTO-MAIL?
BIG BRO-THER !!
CLAP
MERCY ME!

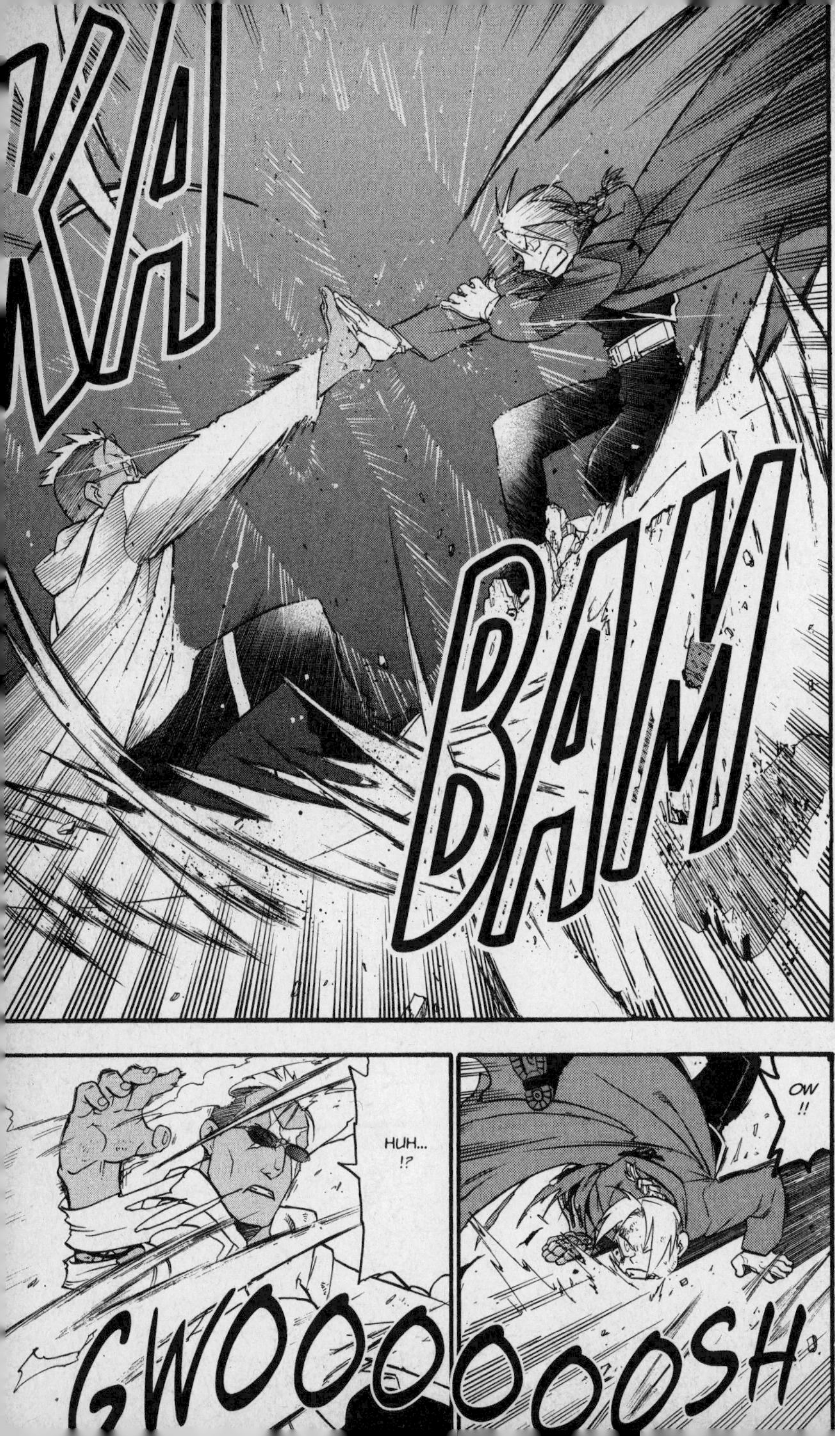
KA
BAM
OW !!
HUH... !?
GWOOOOOOSH

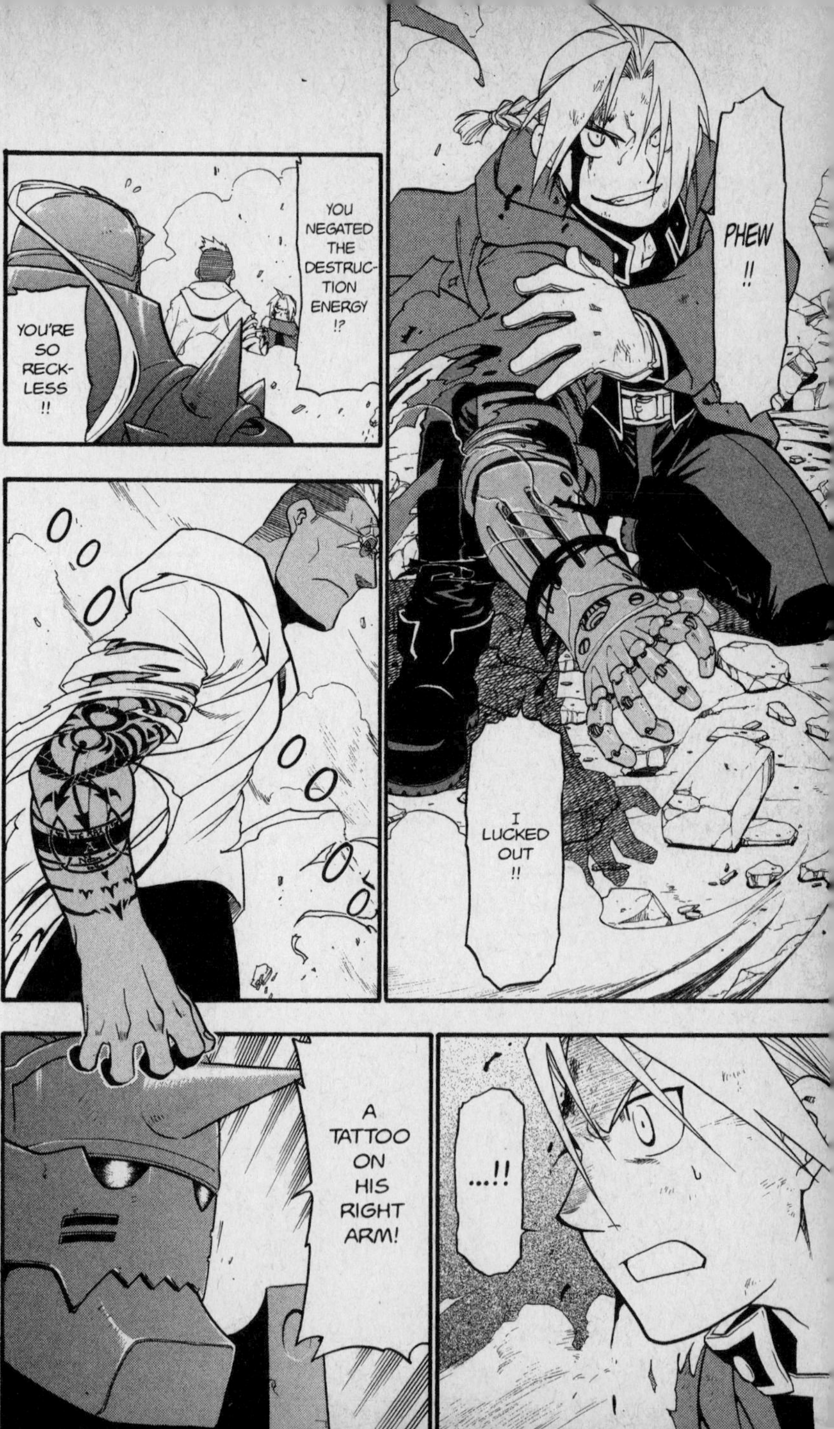
PHEW!!
I LUCKED OUT!!
YOU NEGATED THE DESTRUCTION ENERGY!?
YOU'RE SO RECKLESS!!
...!!
A TATTOO ON HIS RIGHT ARM!

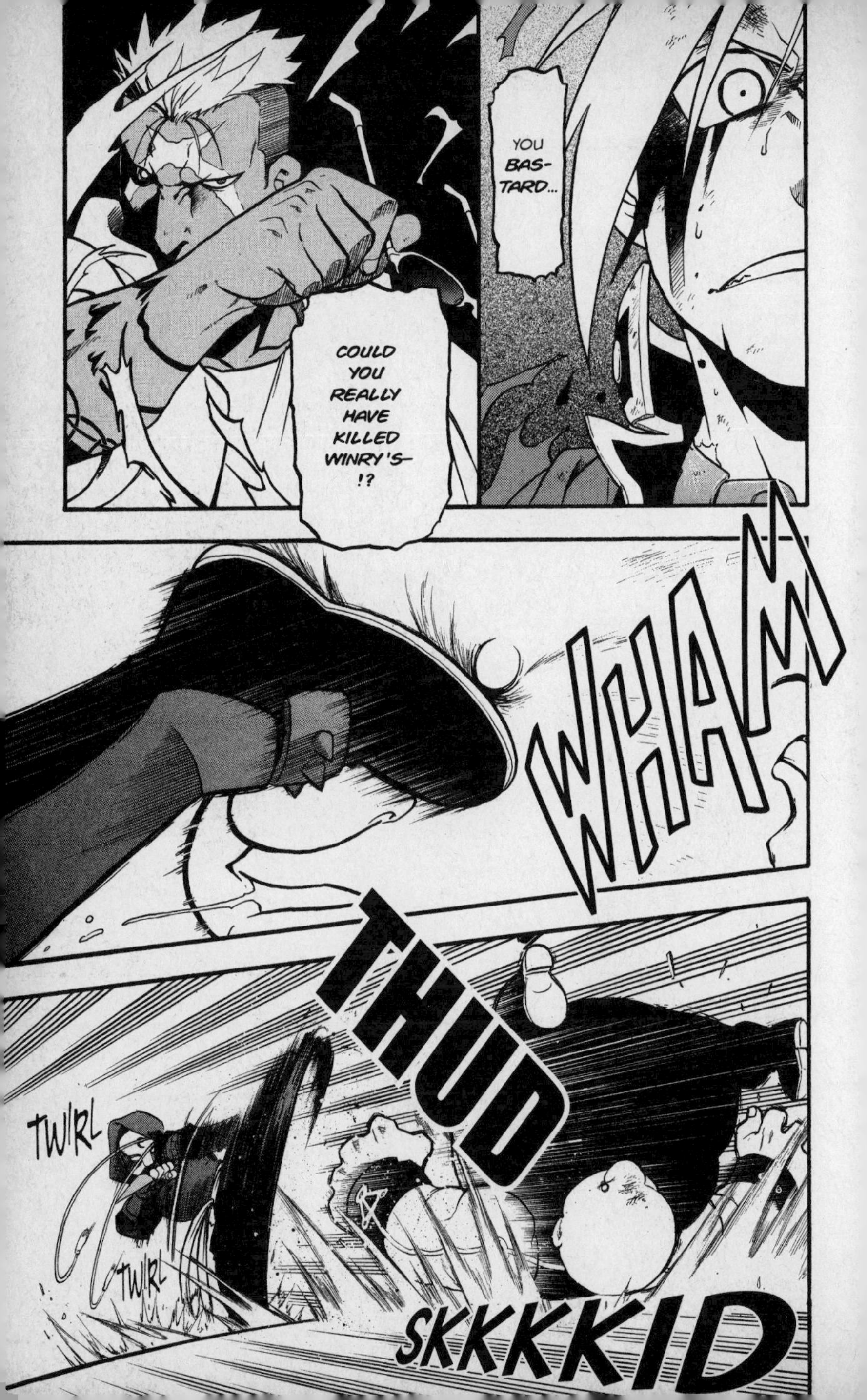

YOU BASTARD...
COULD YOU REALLY HAVE KILLED WINRY'S—!?
WHAM
THUD
TWIRL
TWIRL
SKKKID

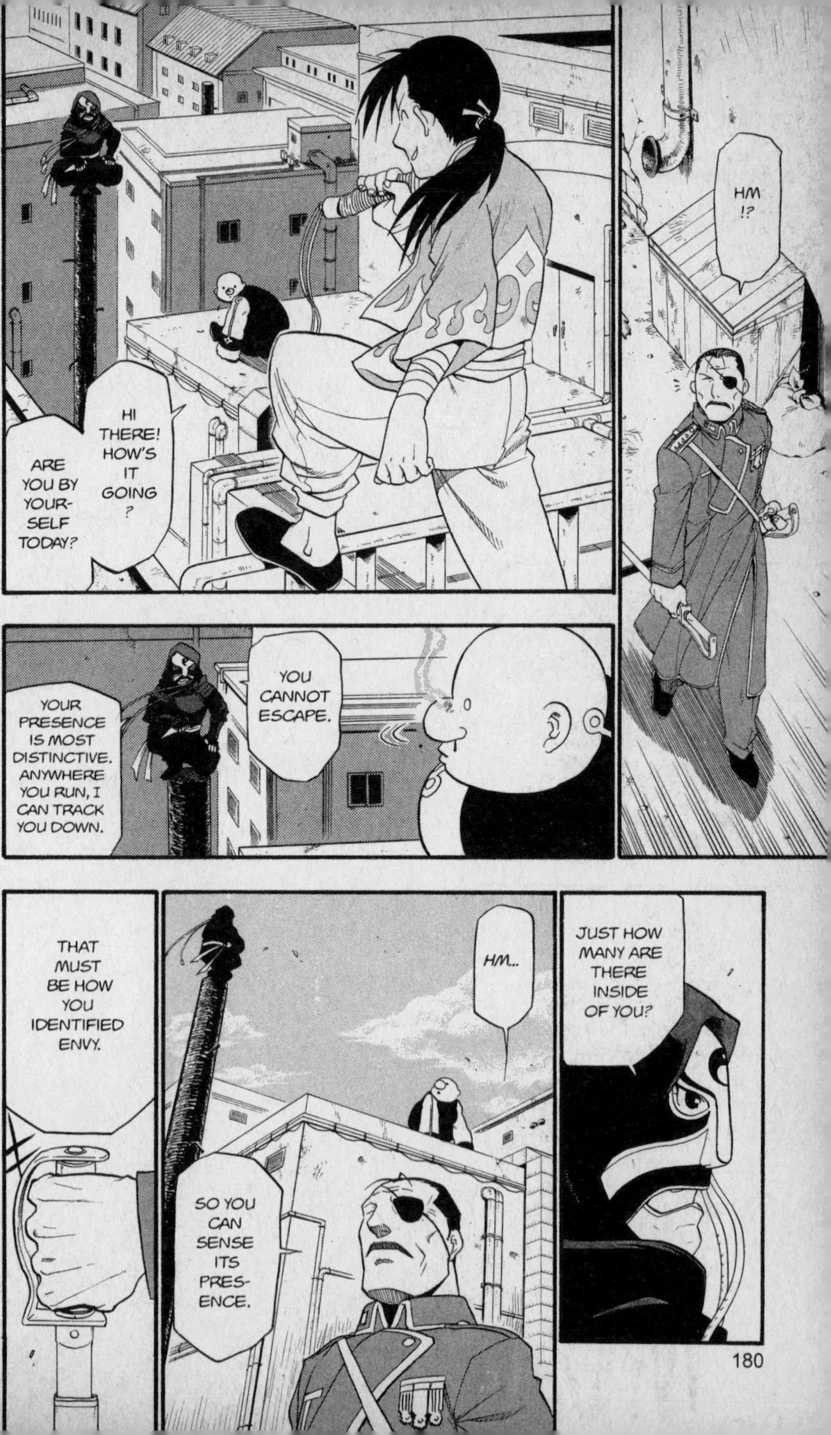
HM !?
HI THERE! HOW'S IT GOING?
ARE YOU BY YOURSELF TODAY?
YOU CANNOT ESCAPE.
YOUR PRESENCE IS MOST DISTINCTIVE. ANYWHERE YOU RUN, I CAN TRACK YOU DOWN.
JUST HOW MANY ARE THERE INSIDE OF YOU?
HM...
SO YOU CAN SENSE ITS PRESENCE.
THAT MUST BE HOW YOU IDENTIFIED ENVY.

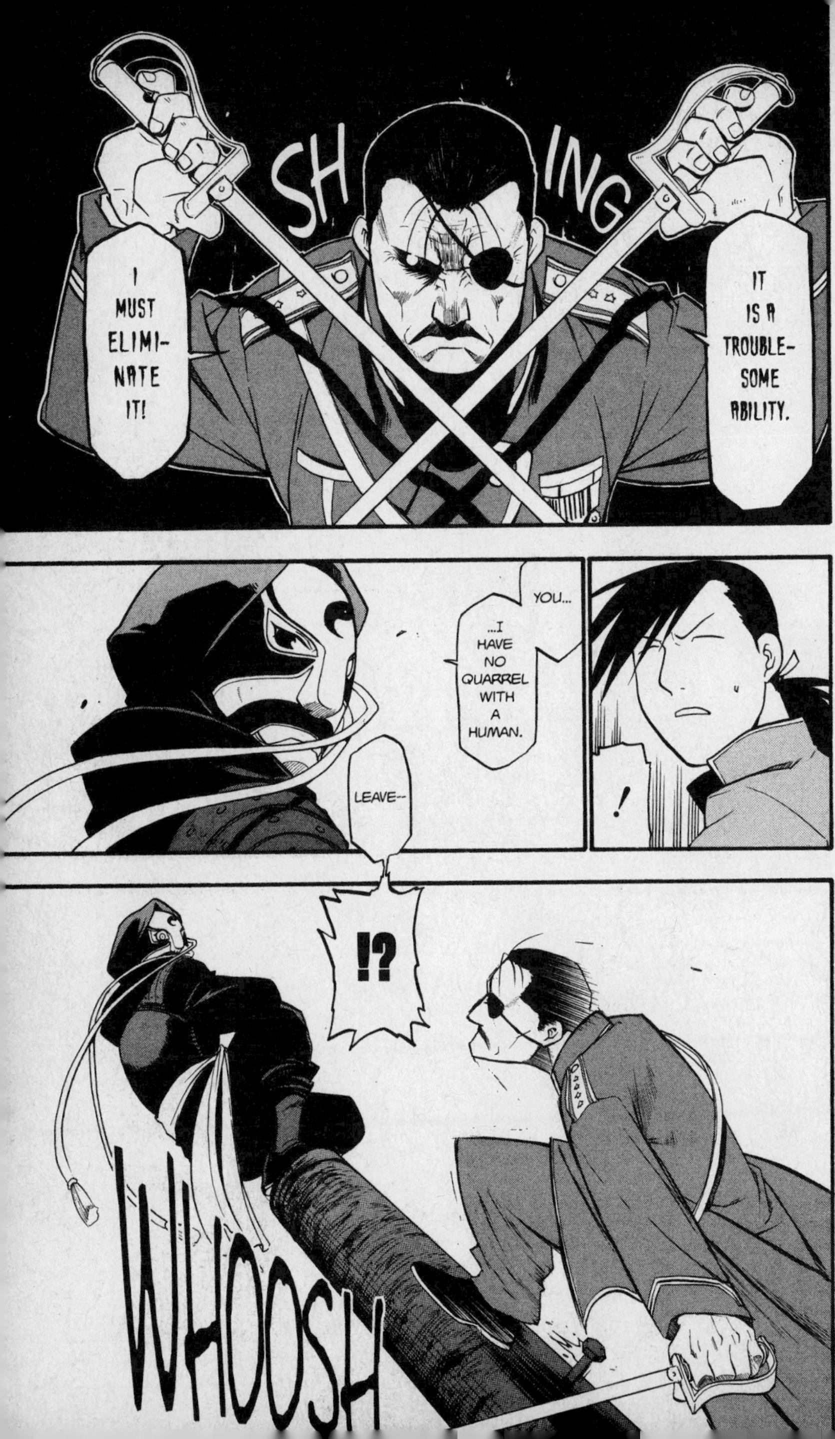
IT IS A TROUBLE-SOME ABILITY.
SH ING
I MUST ELIMI-NATE IT!
!
YOU...
...I HAVE NO QUARREL WITH A HUMAN.
LEAVE--
!?
WHOOSH

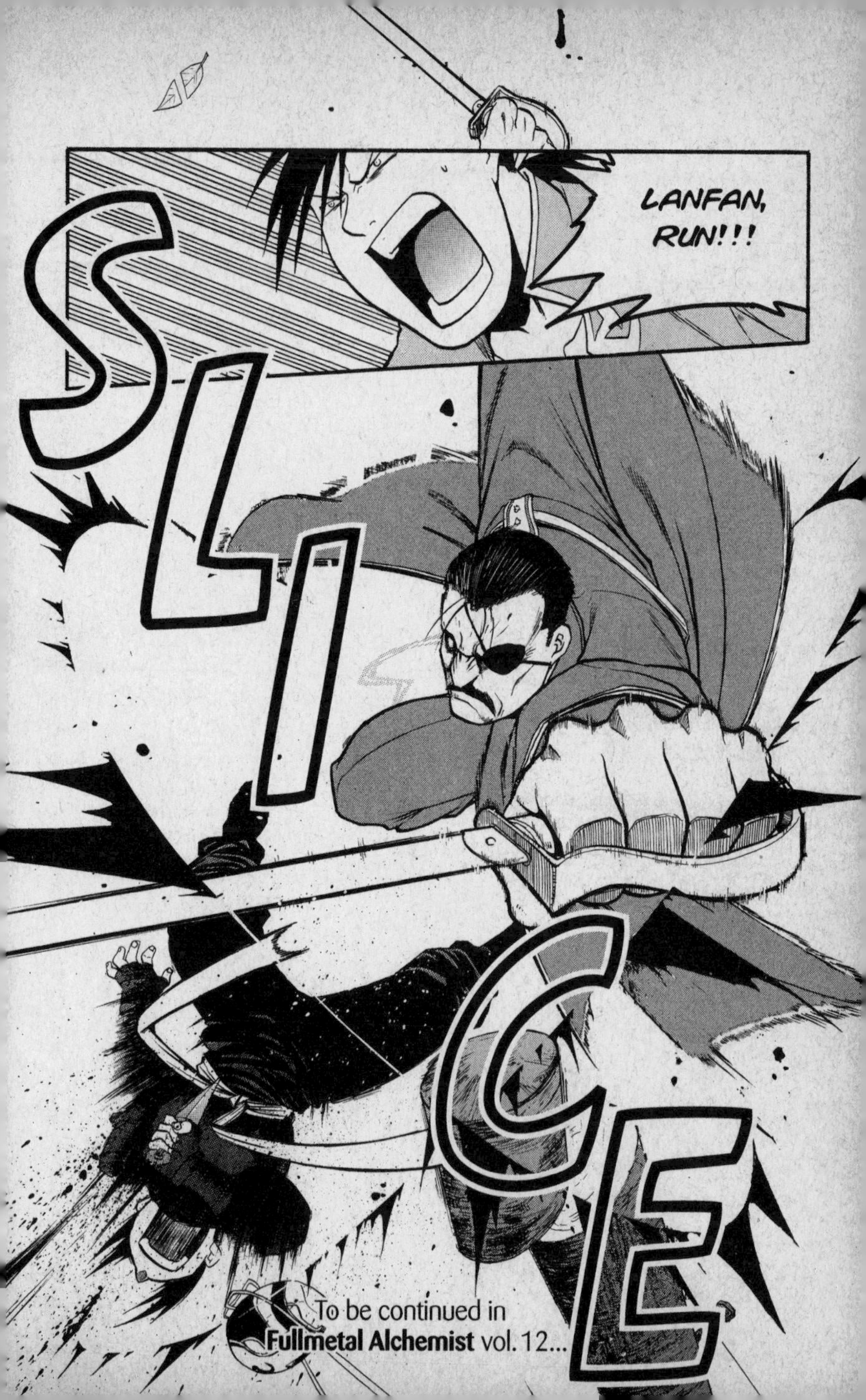
LANFAN, RUN!!!
SLICE
To be continued in Fullmetal Alchemist vol. 12...

FULLMETAL
ALCHEMIST

Return Of The Bastard.
(Gift Included)

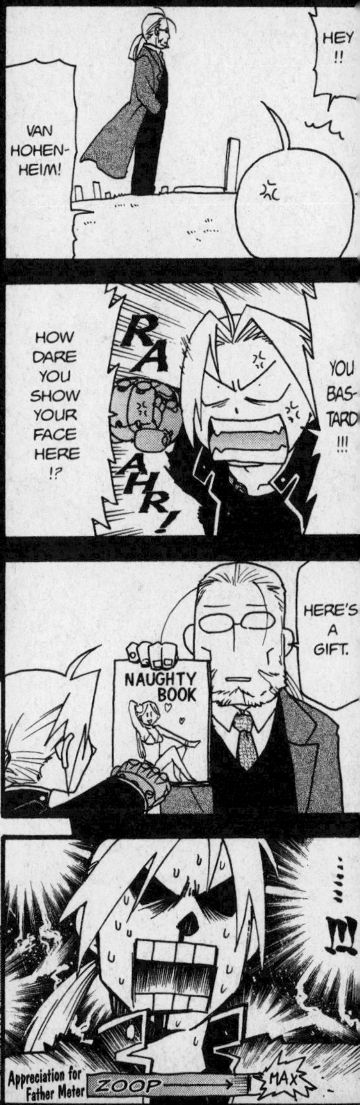
HEY !!
VAN HOHENHEIM!
YOU BASTARD !!!
RAAAHR!
HOW DARE YOU SHOW YOUR FACE HERE !?
HERE'S A GIFT.
NAUGHTY BOOK
......!!!
Appreciation for Father Meter
ZOOP
MAX

FULLMETAL ALCHEMIST 11

SPECIAL THANKS

KEISUI TAKAEDA
SANKICHI HINODEYA
JUN TOKO
AIYABALL
NONO
YOICHI KAMITONO
EDITOR YOICHI SHIMOMURA

AND YOU!!

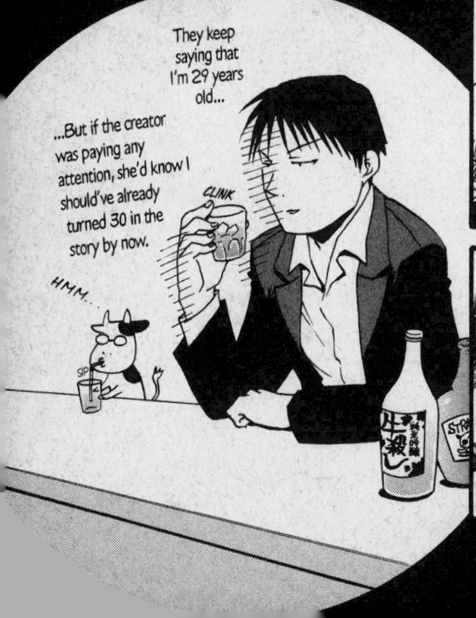
They keep saying that I'm 29 years old...
...But if the creator was paying any attention, she'd know I should've already turned 30 in the story by now.
CLINK
HMM...
SIP

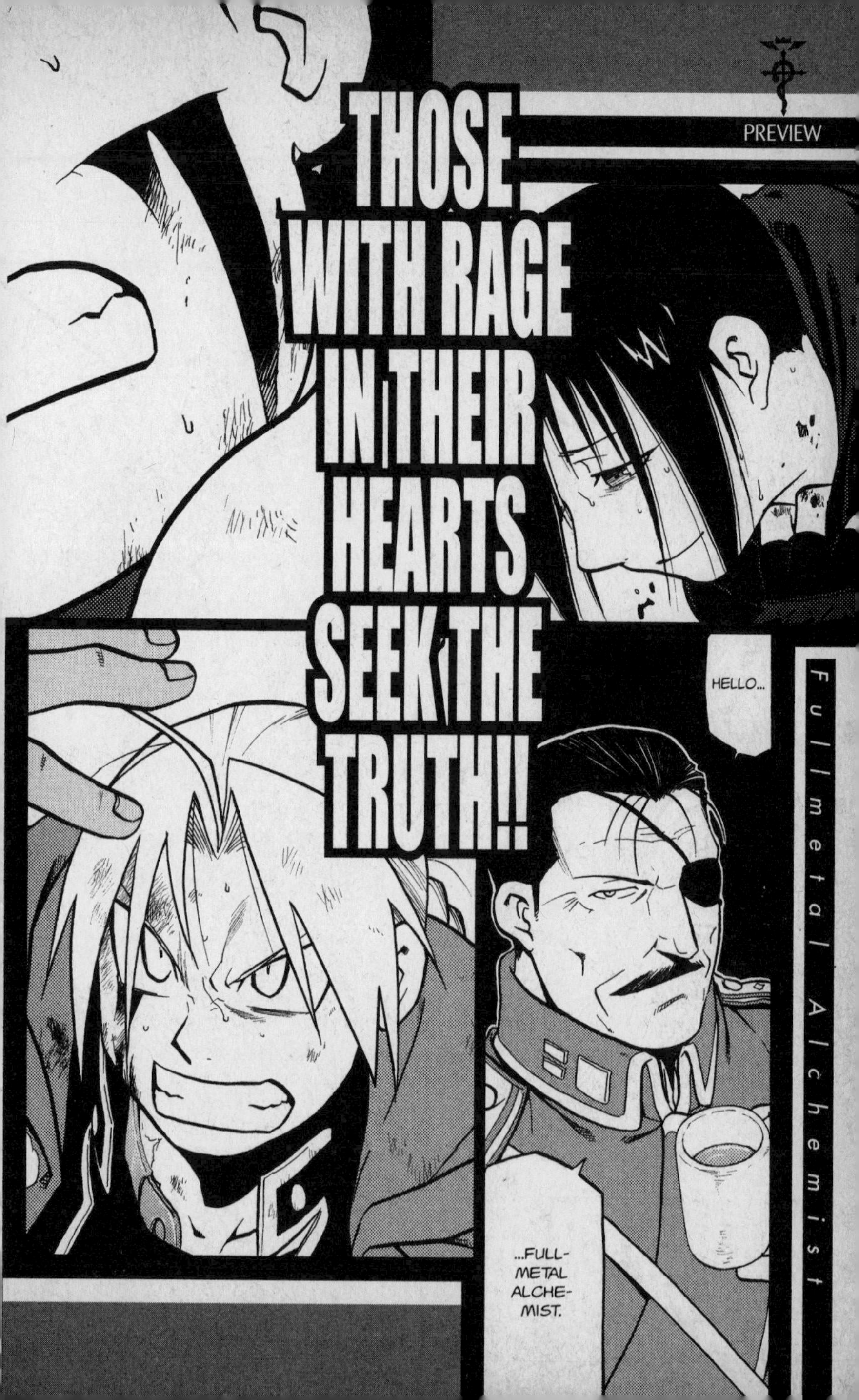
PREVIEW
THOSE WITH RAGE IN THEIR HEARTS SEEK THE TRUTH!!
Fullmetal Alchemist
HELLO...
...FULL-METAL ALCHE-MIST.

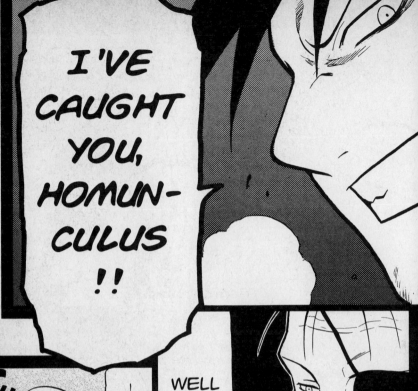

I'VE CAUGHT YOU, HOMUNCULUS!!

WELL DONE!!

I FOUND THE ISHBALAN!!

SH

LURP

The Elric brothers, the military and the Great Xing Empire! Three powers team up to trap the ultimate prey! But the homunculi have overpowering abilities! What sacrifice will Ed and the others need to make in order to unlock the secrets of the homunculi!?

FULLMETAL ALCHEMIST VOL. 12
DON'T MISS IT!

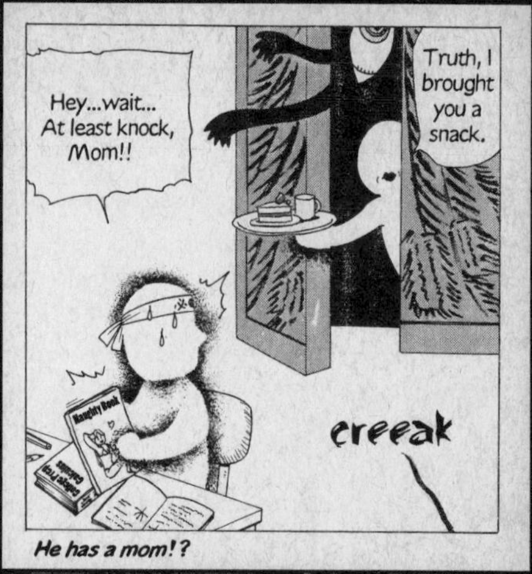
Truth, I brought you a snack.
Hey...wait... At least knock, Mom!!
Naughty Book
creeak
He has a mom!?

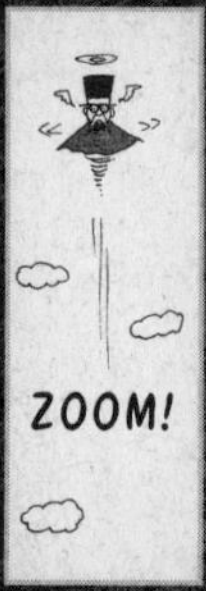
ZOOM!
In Memoriam

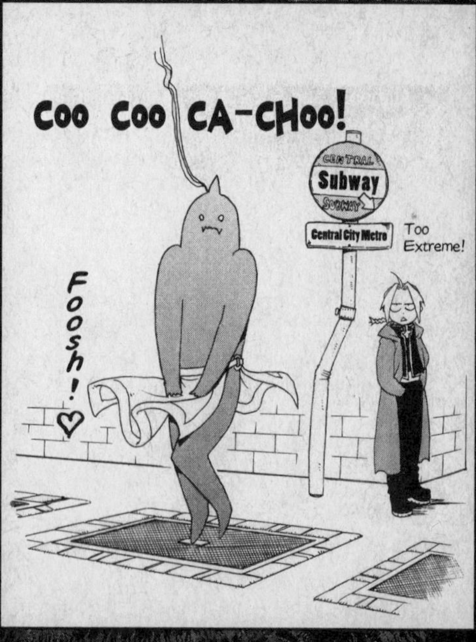
COO COO CA-CHOO!
CENTRAL
Subway
SUBWAY
Central City Metro
Too Extreme!
Foosh!♡

Fullmetal Alchemist Profiles

Get the background story and world history of the manga, plus:

- Character bios
- New, original artwork
- Interview with creator Hiromu Arakawa
- Bonus manga episode only available in this book

Fullmetal Alchemist Anime Profiles

Stay on top of your favorite episodes and characters with:

- Actual cel artwork from the TV series
- Summaries of all 51 TV episodes
- Definitive cast biographies
- Exclusive poster for your wall